A Roof Cutter's Secrets

To Framing the Custom Home

Fourth Edition

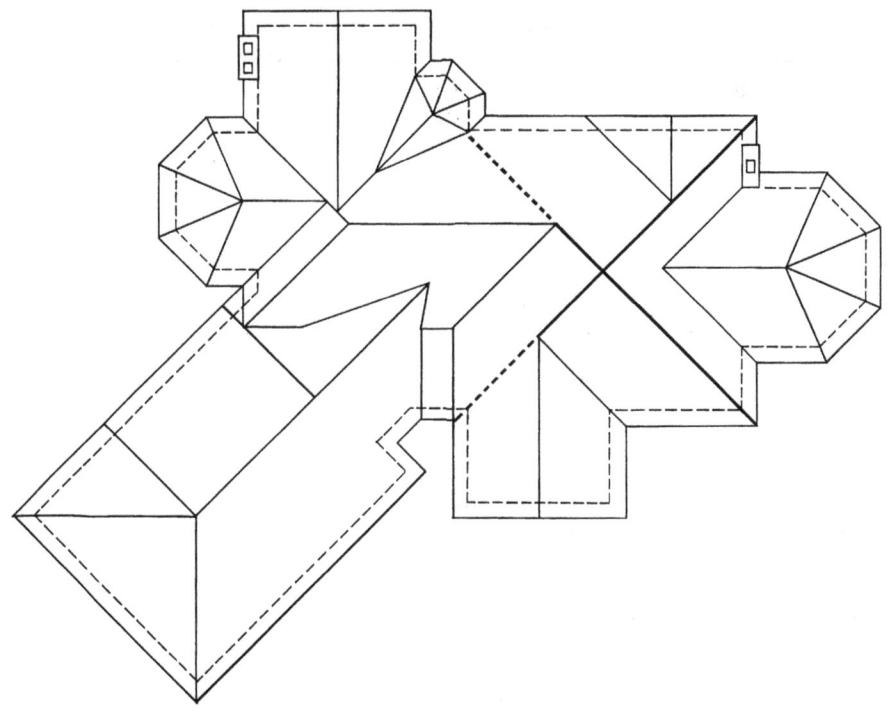

by Will Holladay

DISCLAIMER OF LIABILITY

Roof framing is inherently dangerous work and should be undertaken only by trained building professionals. This book is intended for expert building professionals who are competent to evaluate the information provided and who will accept full responsibility for the application of this information. The techniques, practices, and tools described herein may or may not meet current safety requirements in your jurisdiction. The author and publisher do not approve of the violation of any safety regulations and urge readers to follow all current codes and regulations as well as commonsense safety practices.

The author and publisher hereby fully disclaim liability to any and all parties for any loss, and do not assume any liability whatsoever for any loss or alleged damages caused by the reader's use or interpretation of the information found in this book, whether such errors or omissions result from negligence, accident, or any other cause that may be attributed to the author or publisher.

Copyright ©2002 by Will Holladay
All rights reserved

First Edition: W&H Publishers, 1989
Second Edition: Journal of Light Construction Books, 2002
Third Edition: W&H Publishers, 2014
Forth Edition: W&H Publishers, 2023

ISBN: 978-0-945186-20-5 (HC)
Library of Congress Control Number: 2002110344

Printed in the United States of America

whframingconsultant@gmail.com

W&H Publishers
Minersville, PA

The Author at Work
This roof, in all its intricacy, was precut on the ground using techniques shown in this book.

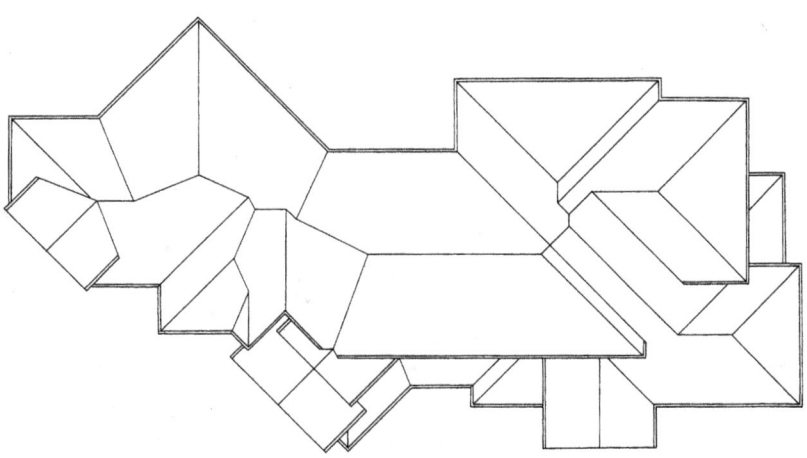

Building Design: *Glush Design Associates*
Framing Contractor: *SR Freeman Construction*
Roof Cutter: *Will Holladay*
Photo by: *Hawkeye Aerial Photography*

Acknowledgements

I had a lot of help this time around. First I would like to thank Dominic Ridge and professional illustrator James Goold for their help with the illustrations. Their comments, ideas, and time made a big difference in this book. Nick, by the way, is not only an excellent draftsman and master of trigonometry, but his passion in life is cutting and stacking roofs.

Secondly, I would like to thank Clayton DeKorne, a former editor of *The Journal of Light Construction*, for his help in reorganizing this book. He spent several long weeks of his own time in the trenches with me because he had the dream of making *A Roof Cutter's Secrets* into a really good book. His friendship also afforded me the opportunity to teach roof-cutting workshops around the United States and thereby meet some of you.

I am very impressed by the many sharp-minded and skilled people out there framing. It is clear by your interest and knowledge that the art of roof cutting is not dying at all. Many of you have tackled roofs that would have easily stumped me. To those who have written me with questions, comments, tips, or suggestions: I salute you. I have tried to show my gratitude by incorporating many of your ideas into this new edition. Think of it as our book. There is always more to learn, so keep your ideas coming.

I am much indebted to the following technical readers for their suggestions and review: veteran roof cutters Shone Freeman and Eric Kralonovich, master carpenter and author Larry Haun, building-inspection expert David Utterback, and newspaper editor David Lesher. Along this same line, thanks to Mike Diamond of Calculated Industries, who worked with me to create the section entitled, "Applying the Construction Master® Calculator," located in Appendix B. As with any book encompassing such large amounts of technical detail, there are bound to be small errors that have slipped by unnoticed. We certainly did our best to limit them. If you spot an error please let us know.

It is imperative that I acknowledge, as I did in the original edition, the special motivational role my former framing partner Chuck Cline played in driving me to put this book together in the first place. He, in addition to Dave Sylvester, Dan Daley, Dave Saunders, Ken Nichols and both Shone and Nick, have continued to encourage me to keep on framing long past the point my body would so desire.

It should also be noted that while it was many years ago and early on in my development as a framer, I am still very grateful for the two years of excellent background training I received from the Orange Coast College Construction Technology Department. They got me heading in the right direction.

And not to be forgotten while I'm doling out gratitude is the book production staff at *The Journal of Light Construction*. Specifically, much thanks to Ursula Jones, Steven Bliss, Tim Healey, Theresa Emerson, and Annie Clark. They had the daunting task of amassing this material into what you have in your hands — in spite of me.

Lastly and most importantly, I thank the Lord Jesus for directing my life though all its stages; first, providing me the situations to gain framing knowledge and experience; and second, allowing me the opportunity to pass it on to you.

PREFACE

In 1987, when I first put all my notes together as *A Roof Cutter's Secrets*, I never dreamed the book would become as popular as it has.

Since then, many things have changed. Not only has there been an overproliferation of building codes and framing metals invading the home construction field, but also I am getting old. I can't move nearly as fast as I once could, and there seems to be a lot more gray hair on my head. Hopefully I've gained a little wisdom to help balance my body's decline (although many might disagree). Since writing the first edition, I've learned many new things, I've learned better ways of doing old things, and I've discovered where I just plain screwed up. So it was high time to put together a revised edition.

This book is not for the beginner. It deals with many advanced subjects where prior knowledge is essential. The reader is expected to be familiar with carpentry skills, terminology, methods, and tools. A good math background including geometry and trigonometry is helpful, though not essential. If you're not a math wizard, join the club — neither am I. I've read many other roof framing books that are so technical they thoroughly confuse me. I try to keep things quick and easy. I believe many people make roof cutting much more difficult than it needs to be. For those of you just starting out in the roof framing profession, I recommend *Simplified Roof Framing*, by Wilson and Werner (McGraw-Hill; ISBN 07-070959-9). Try to get a copy of this out-of-print text; it is, in my estimation, the best book written on roof framing basics.

Throughout this book, various models of the Construction Master® calculator (Calculated Industries Inc., Carson City, Nev.) can be used instead of the LL/RR ratios and snapped floor drawings to quickly find rafter lengths, cheek-cut angles, etc. Samples of its usage for many of the specific situations included in this book are shown in Appendix B. Those who are really sharp with trigonometry can also easily solve all the non-standard roof situations with only a regular calculator and the trig tables found in Chart 5, Appendix A (or without the trig tables by using a trig calculator). The rest of us may feel more comfortable working from a full-size snapped-out plan view with a minimal amount of math. In my world, a picture is worth a thousand calculations.

I originally wrote this book because there seemed to be a need for an advanced practical book that explains how to do some of the unusual framing one encounters in the custom home. I hope it helps to fill that gap. I don't claim to have all the answers, but I'm glad to share what I have learned over the years. I have tried to deal with general problem areas rather than specifics since that would take volumes, and I am a carpenter, not a writer. It is my hope that you can adapt some of the ideas and principles in this book to your own situation. Keep this book around on the job to use as a reference when you are stumped (as I do), and please share it with others.

God bless you,
Will

About the Author

Like many in the trades, Will Holladay began his framing career as a job-site laborer with a shovel in his hands. Blessed with a knack for driving nails (he still uses his old 28-oz. hammer) coupled with a love of roofs and the desire to be a roof cutter, he worked his way through the ranks. Will eventually realized his dream when he learned production roof cutting/stacking in the Southern California housing tracts in the mid 1970s. When trusses gained prominence in the late 1970s, he moved north into the custom home market along the central California coast. There he specialized in framing large custom homes for various general contractors. Will eventually moved on to work up and down the West Coast and in New England. The custom home market greatly refined his knowledge as he was exposed to a variety of difficult roof situations. The notes he kept throughout the years have become the basis for this book.

For more than a decade, Will has shared his expertise as an occasional contributor to *The Journal of Light Construction* and other leading trade magazines. He has also taught roof cutting courses at *JLC* Live.

This book is dedicated to my Lord and Savior,
Jesus Christ.

Table of Contents

Abbreviation Legend x

Introduction: Laying the Groundwork 1
    Rafter parts 1
    Horizontal standards 1
    LL/RR method 3

Chapter 1: Figuring and Framing Walls 7
    Snap 7
    Plate 10
    Scratch 11
    Figuring tall walls 14
    Framing straight walls 15
    Figuring rake walls 19
    Framing rake walls 23
    Raising walls 25
    Underpinning for hillside lots 28

Chapter 2: Plumb, Line, and Joist 31
    Plumb and line 31
    Ceiling joists 35
    Floor joists 41

Chapter 3: Gable Roofs/Production Roof Cutting 47
    Racks for gang-cutting rafters 47
    Common rafters to a ridge board 49
    The history and tools of production roof cutting 54
    Common rafters lapping over a center ridge beam .. 59
    Gable studs 59

Chapter 4: Regular Hip Roofs 63
    Hip roof ridge lengths 63
    The hip rafter 63
    Backing a hip 67
    Hip jacks 68
    Hip-valley jacks 73
    Hip (or valley) head-cuts for rafters that sit on a ridge beam 75
    Broken hips 79
    Snub-nose hips 81
    Dutch hips 82
    Hips from a 45° corner wall 84

Chapter 5: Regular Valley Intersections 87
    The valley rafter.. 87
    Regular valley jacks 89
    California valley sleepers 93
    California valley jacks 97
    Over/under intersections 98
    Offset valleys 100
    Supported valley situations 100

Chapter 6: Roof Stacking 109
    Stacking a gable roof 109
    Collar ties... 116
    Purlins 118
    Tailless rafters...................................... 119
    Ridge height.. 120
    Stacking a simple hip roof 120
    Stacking a valley..................................... 122
    Stacking a complex hip roof........................... 124

Chapter 7: Eaves and Plywood 129
    Fascia methods.. 129
    Outriggers and barge fascia 133
    Fake valley tails 134
    Miscellaneous fascia techniques....................... 134
    Roof sheathing.. 137
    Rigid insulation 142
    Beam tails 143
    Swaled tails around a corner 144

Chapter 8: Bastard Hips and Valleys 149
    Dog-leg bastard hips/valleys.......................... 151
    Dog-leg bastard broken hips........................... 154
    Dovetail hips 158
    A diamond hip roof.................................... 162
    Diamond roof hip jacks 167
    The unequal-pitch relationship 170
    An unequal-pitch hip roof with equal-length overhangs 172
    Unequal-pitch valleys................................. 177
    Off-angle California jacks............................ 183
    Backing bastard rafters............................... 183

Chapter 9: Dormers 189
    Gable and hip dormers. 189
    Shed dormers. 193
    Shed dormer California-cuts. 194
    Eyebrow dormers 194

Chapter 10: Towers and Polygons. 205
    Hexagons. 205
    Octagons 208
    Other polygons 211
    Conical tower construction 216
    California valley at a tower 227

Chapter 11: Bay Roofs. 231
    Common bay roofs 231
    Bay window roofs against a wall 237

Chapter 12: Other Miscellaneous Roofs 241
    Equal-pitch roofs from varying plate heights 241
    Matching ridge heights 241
    Parallel-roof California-cuts 242
    Unequal-pitch gables 246
    Cantilever eaves. 247
    Common rafters across an angled wall. 248
    Swiss chalet-style roofs. 251
    Gambrel roofs 253
    Site-made trusses 255

Chapter 13: Beam Work 257
    Miscellaneous beam work 257
    Exposed trusses 265

Chapter 14: Stairs. 269
    Cut stringers. 269
    Exposed stringers 273
    Pyramid stairs. 273
    90° winders 274
    Circular stairs. 277
    Circular-stair handrail cap 278
    Contoured stairs. 281

Chapter 15: Pick Up 283
    Miscellaneous pick up 283
    Arches and curves 285
    Chandelier domes 287
    Skylights 291
    Coffer ceilings 291
    Pop-out bays 295

Appendix A: Reference Charts 297
    Chart 1: Decimal Equivalents 298
    Chart 2: Rafter Line-Length (LL) Ratios 298
    Chart 3: Roof-Pitch/Degrees 299
    Chart 4: Roof-Rise (RR) Ratios 299
    Chart 5: Trigonometric Values 300
    Chart 6: Regular Hip/Valley Backing Angles 302
    Chart 7: Side- and Bevel-Cuts on the Hip/Valley
            Rafter Tail with Square-Hung Fascia 303
    Chart 8: Regular California Valley Sleeper Head/Tail-Cuts 304

Appendix B: Applying the Construction Master® Calculator ... 305

Appendix C: Tool Resources 325

List of Figures and Photos 327

Index 331

ABBREVIATION LEGEND

CV	California valley
COM LL ratio	common rafter line-length ratio
H/V LL ratio	hip/valley line-length ratio
LL	line length
LP	long point
o.c.	on-center
OH	overhang
RO	rough opening
RR ratio	roof-rise ratio
SP	short point
T&G	tongue-and-groove
Trig	trigonometry
$1/2$ thk.	one half the thickness
$1/2$ 45° thk.	one half the 45° thickness

Introduction

Laying the Groundwork

Before you dive into this book, we need to discuss a few definitions and general roof framing principles. Throughout the world, different names may be given to various parts of a rafter, so I'll quickly review the ones I use.

Rafter parts. There are three main parts of a rafter that concern us: the head-cut, the birdsmouth notch, and the tail *(Figure 0-1)*. For regular roofs the head-cut can be a plumb-line cut square, as in the case of a common rafter or a valley jack that butt to the ridge (often referred to as a ridge-cut); it can be a single 45° cheek-cut, as in the case of a regular hip jack; or it can be a double 45° cheek-cut as in the case of a hip or valley.

The birdsmouth notch consists of two cuts: one in the vertical plane called the heel-cut; the other in the horizontal plane called the seat-cut. The plumb distance above the plate at the outside wall line is called the heel-stand. The heel-stand measurement is needed when setting the height of any ridge boards or beams so they will flush with the top of the rafters.

The tail is — simply put — the part of the rafter that sticks out of the building.

Horizontal standards. In *Figure 0-2*, the roof **span**

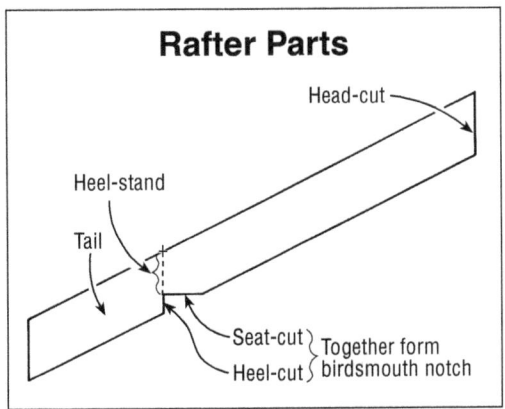

Figure 0-1. The three main parts of the rafter are the head-cut, the birdsmouth notch, and the tail.

LAYING THE GROUNDWORK   **1**

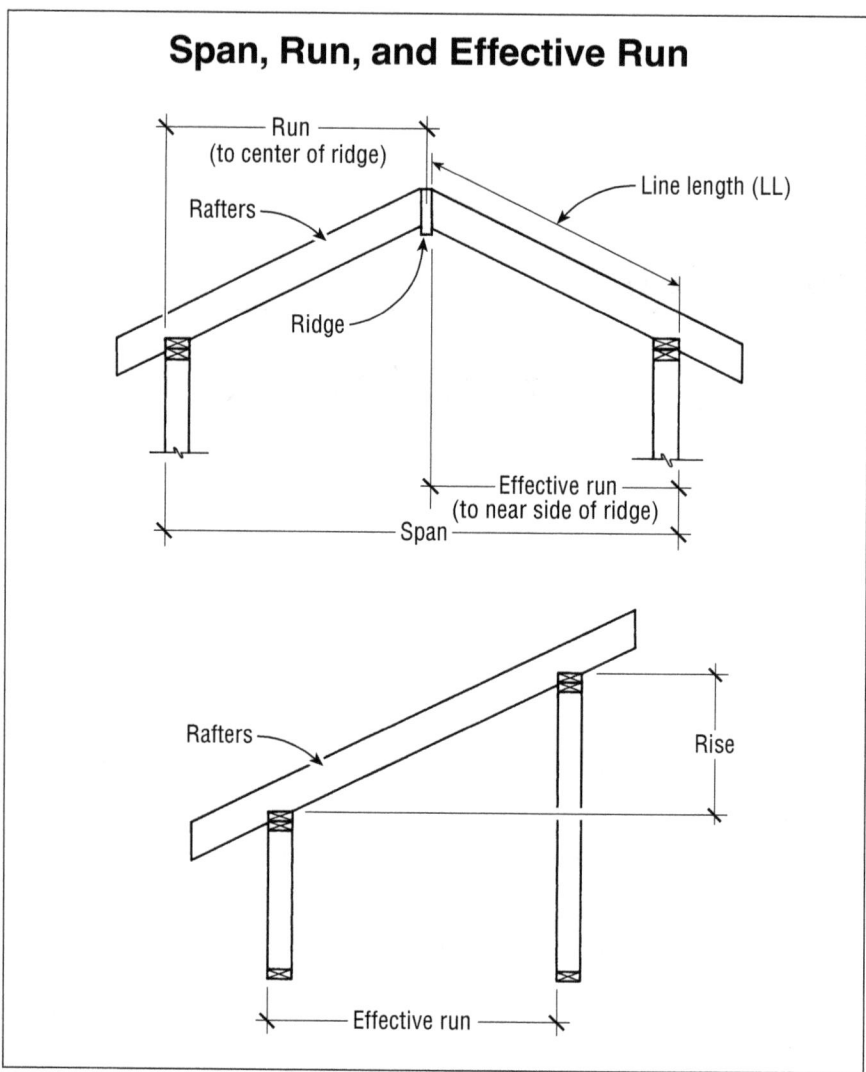

Figure 0-2. The span is the total building width. The run is half the building width, and the effective run is the run less half the thickness of the ridge.

is the total building width from outside wall to outside wall; the **run** (or theoretical run) is half the span; and the **effective run** is the run less half the thickness of the ridge.

I use the effective run when calculating most rafter lengths, as this eliminates having to shorten for the ridge thickness later. Sometimes when there is no ridge involved, the run and the effective run are the same and can be used interchangeably. Think of the effective run as an actual distance a rafter travels. Only on irregular roofs radiating from a centerpoint (bay roofs, polygons, etc.) is it more practical to calculate some rafters to the theoretical roof center and then shorten for a top connection.

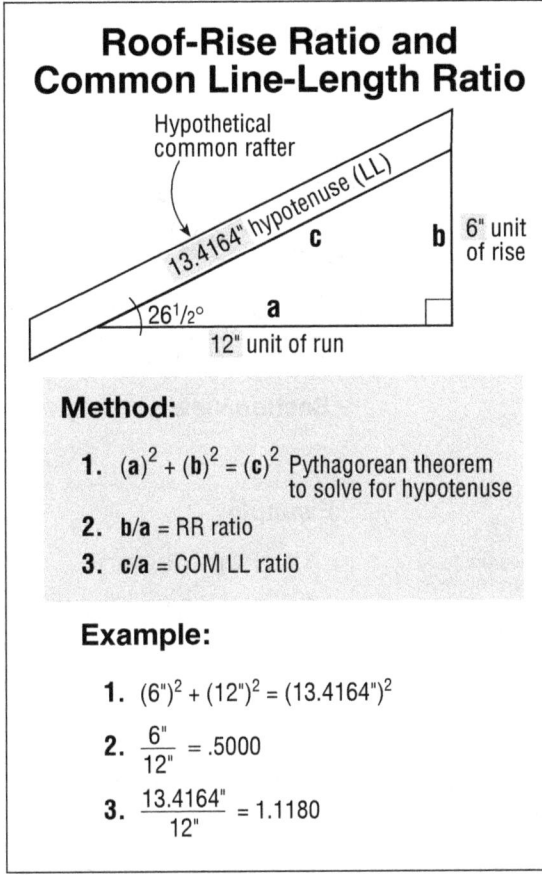

Figure 0-3. The roof-rise (RR) ratio represents the relationship of **b:a**, while the common line-length (COM LL) ratio represents the relationship of **c:a**.

In this book, the run and the effective run for hips and valleys are the same as the run and the effective run for commons. In other words, **run** always refers to half the span of a regular gable or hip roof. This may be a departure from traditional mainstream roof framing methods that teach that a hip or valley has a unit "run" of 17 in., but I believe it is confusing to give more than one meaning to the word. Therefore, when I use the word "run," it means only one thing: the horizontal side of a right triangle formed by the pitch of the roof. (This is also the way most rafter table books are set up.) I use the words **diagonal travel** or **hip travel** when referring to the horizontal distance directly under the hip or valley.

LL/RR method. There are many different methods to calculate rafter lengths: from the cave man cut-and-fit method, to stepping off using a framing square, to rafter table books, to specialized roof framing calculators like the Construction Master®, to computer programs. The method I use to find rafter lengths and various wall and beam heights requires only a regular low-budget handheld calculator and a few simple ratios. I call this system the LL/RR method. Each specific roof pitch has its own unique ratios which you will find listed in Charts 2 and 4 in Appendix A at the back of this book. These ratios are quite simple to calculate, and I will explain how they are computed.

With the right triangle formed by the pitch of the roof (6/12 in **Figure 0-3**), use the Pythagorean theorem to solve for the hypotenuse ($a^2 + b^2 = c^2$).

If we take the roof's unit of rise (6) and divide by the unit of run (12), we arrive at a ratio of **.5000**. I call this ratio the roof-rise ratio or the RR ratio. I use this ratio to calculate the change or "step" in gable stud lengths and to

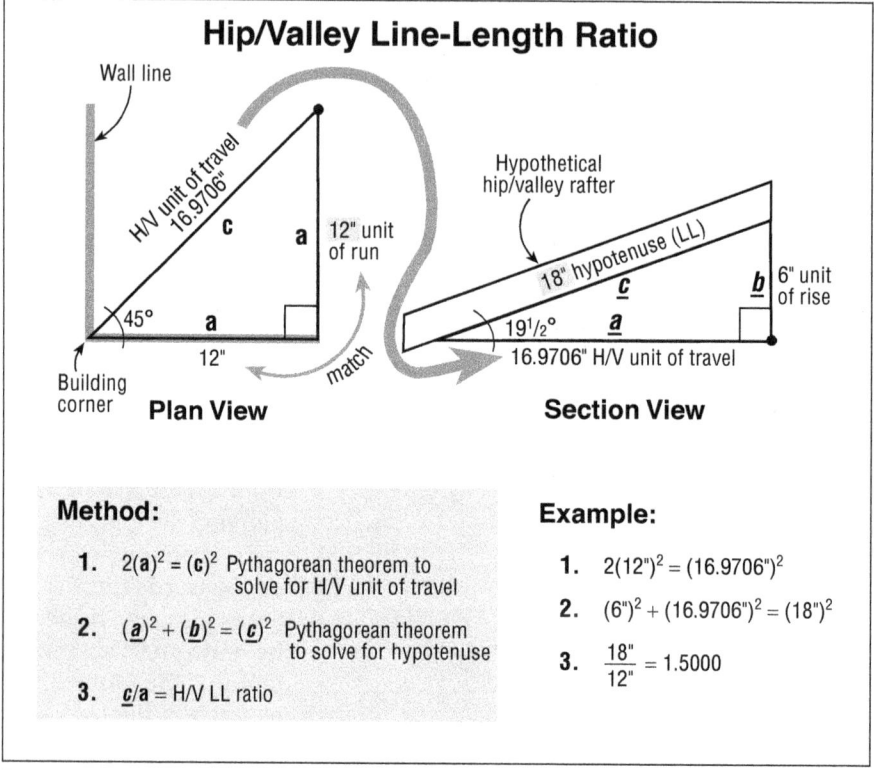

Figure 0-4. The hip/valley line-length (LL) ratio is found by using the diagonal of a 12-in. x 12-in. plan-view right triangle together with the unit of roof rise to create a section-view right triangle, and then solving the *c*:*a* relationship.

help determine the height of any tall walls, purlin beams, or ridges. In trigonometric terms, the RR ratio is the tangent of the roof-pitch angle (opposite side ÷ adjacent side).

If we take the hypotenuse of this same triangle (13.4164) and divide it by the unit of run (12), we arrive at a ratio of **1.1180**. I call this ratio the common rafter line-length ratio (COM LL ratio). I use this ratio to change any horizontal dimension into a rake measurement. Some examples would include the top plates for a rake wall, common rafter lengths, and jack-step lengths. In trigonometric terms, the COM LL ratio is the secant of the roof-pitch angle (hypotenuse ÷ adjacent side).

If a roof has any regular hips or valleys, we'll need one more ratio – what I call the hip/valley line-length ratio (H/V LL ratio). It's a little more complicated to find since it requires two separate sets of calculations (**Figure 0-4**). First, in the plan view, solve for the hypotenuse (unit of travel) on the isosceles right triangle created by the hip/valley traversing at 45° across the building through one unit of run. Then with the unit of travel (16.9706) as the base leg for a section-view right triangle and the unit rise (6) as the vertical leg, calculate the hypotenuse (18). Divide this number by the unit of run (12) to find the H/V LL ratio of **1.5000**. I use this ratio to help find the lengths of any hips or valleys.

These three ratios (RR ratio, COM LL ratio, and H/V LL ratio) express a relationship as a percentage to a known horizontal run distance. For a 6/12 pitch roof, the rise is 50% of the run value, the common rafter lengths are 111.8% of the run value, and the hip/valley rafter lengths are 150% of the run value. Since we can always find the horizontal dimensions off the prints or actual field measurements, determining the rise, rake, and diagonal rake involves simple multiplication.

In addition to the ratios, it is necessary to know the roof-pitch angle in degrees for cutting gable studs, rake walls, California valley jacks, etc. The degree for each common roof pitch is listed in the back of this book (Chart 3, Appendix A), or you can simply read them right off a rafter square. (When I use the term rafter square, I am referring to the triangular layout square such as the Speed® Square from Swanson Tool Co. or the Quick Square® from Stanley Tool Co. This is not to be confused with the age-old framing square that is shaped like a large "L".)

Throughout the book I have used 6/12 as the standard roof pitch with rafters spaced at 16 in. on-center; 2x material is figured as $1^{1}/_{2}$ in. thick; 4x material is figured at $3^{1}/_{2}$ in. thick; and 6x material at $5^{1}/_{2}$ in. thick. All exceptions are noted. Also, anytime I mention a Skilsaw®, I'm referring to a wormdrive circular saw, similar to the Skil® 77.

Chapter 1

Figuring and Framing Walls

SNAP

Snapping wall lines is one of the most important aspects of framing. To begin, check the foundation for parallel and square by measuring overall dimensions and comparing diagonals *(Figure 1-1)*. It is quicker to adjust

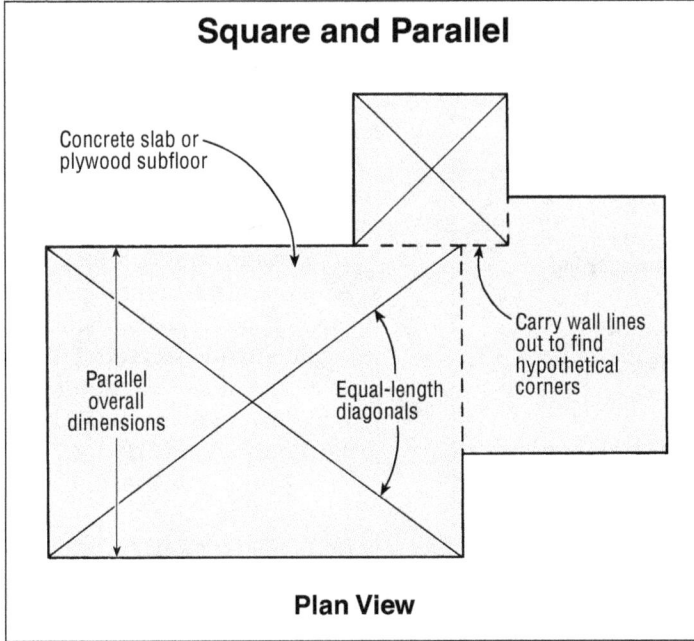

Figure 1-1. Before snapping, always check the foundation for parallel and square by measuring overall dimensions and checking building diagonals.

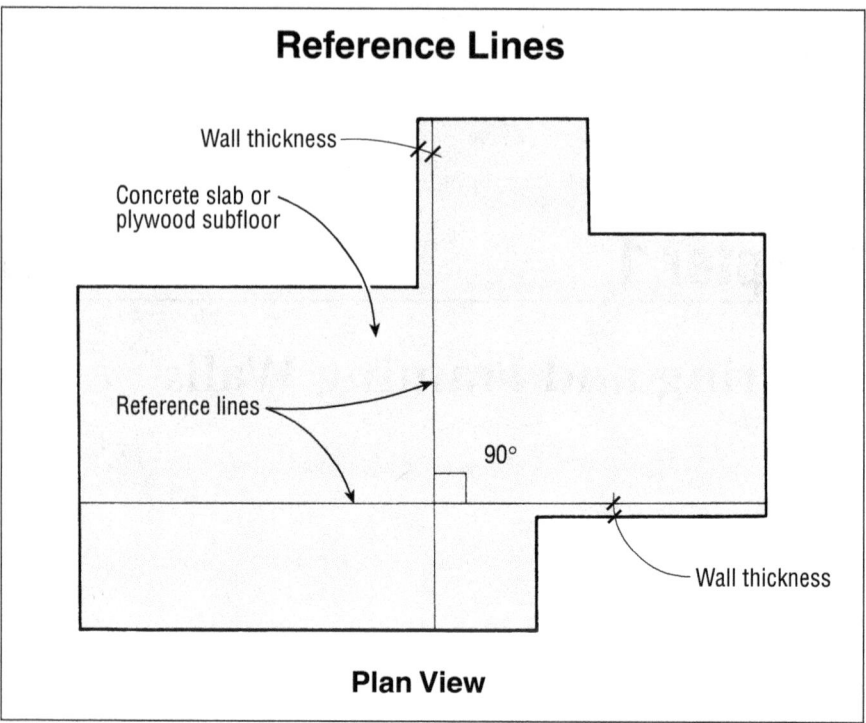

Figure 1-2. When snapping out wall lines for a chopped up house, start with a few reference lines.

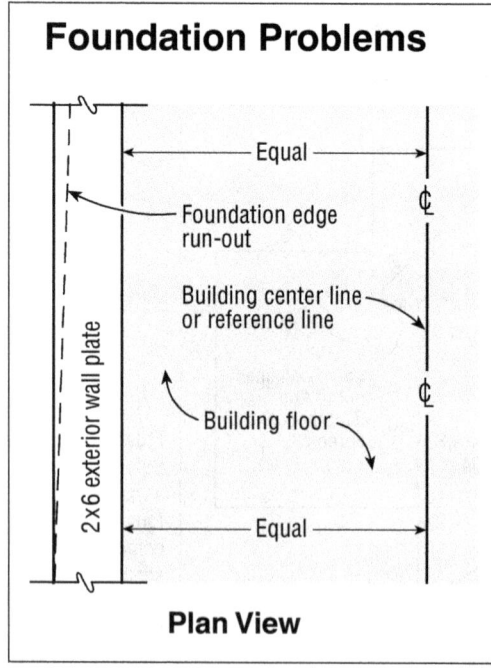

for poor foundation work now rather than after the walls are up. Homes that are chopped up with many different offsets are best begun with a few reference lines *(Figure 1-2)*. On houses with complicated roofs, snap centerlines for the ridges, hips, valley, etc. This makes it easier to place support posts, etc., for point loads when scratching (detailing the plates for studs, intersections, and openings) and gives the stacking crew a birds-eye view of the roof skeleton.

Figure 1-3. Correct for errors in the foundation by jogging the plate line in or out as required.

8   CHAPTER 1

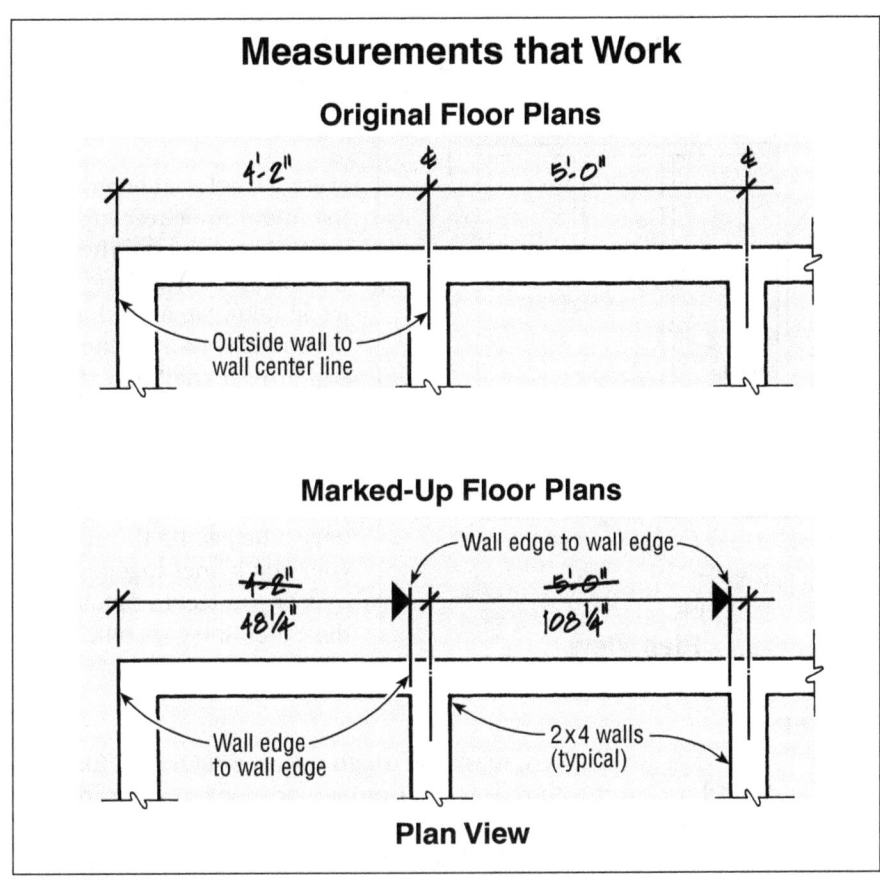

Figure 1-4. For layout purposes, change the dimensions on the prints to read from wall edge to wall edge, not to centerlines. Also, summarize all segment dimensions into an overall length from the building corner.

Snap the inside edge of the outside wall plates, and jog them in or out to correct for dimensional errors in the concrete *(Figure 1-3)*.

Change the wall-to-wall dimensions given on the blueprints to read to the edge of a wall rather than to a centerline, and summarize all small-segment dimensions into measurements from a building corner *(Figure 1-4)*. Change the feet-and-inch measurements to *inches only* (like a modified metric system) to avoid any visual translation errors (for example, 17' 4" = 208" not 174").

For best results when snapping lines, use a fast-reel chalk box fitted with a nylon fly fishing line and filled with Blackline's waterproof chalk-line compound (Blackline Manufacturing, Ltd., Langley, B.C.). Without the luxury of this indelible chalk, use a Hudson sprayer to apply a coating of water sealer (e.g., Thompson's or similar) to protect the lines from rain and foot traffic. Another option on wood floors is to make small 1/8-in.-deep saw kerfs on both sides of the wall snap-lines at each corner intersection and

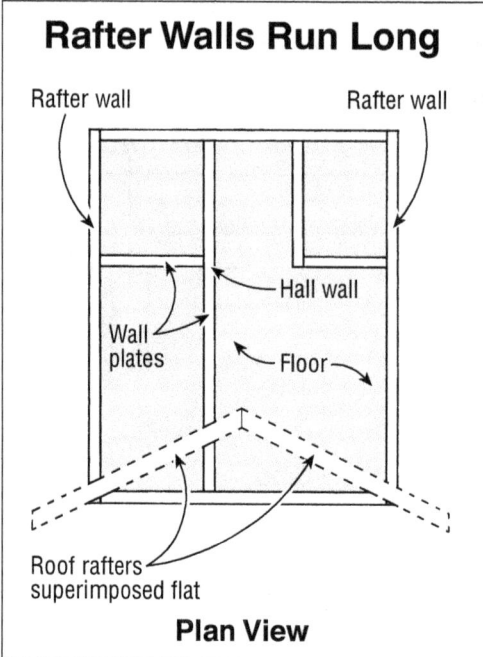

Figure 1-5. In a gable roof house, plate the two rafter walls to run through from end to end.

every 8 ft. of wall length so the lines can be resnapped if washed away by weather.

When working alone on a wood floor, tap an awl into the subfloor to hold the loose end of your chalk line. On a green slab, use a concrete nail driven in a similar fashion, or set a weight on the end of the line. When you have a helper, tie the ends of your chalk lines together so that as you reel in one line, the other line goes out.

PLATE

When all the walls are snapped, mark the rough opening (RO) sizes for doors and windows on the floor near their proper locations so you can see where to break the plates if necessary.

Plating should be done carefully. Take time to figure an order to frame and stand the walls. Good wall plating will avoid the need to shuffle walls around after they are stood to make room to frame other walls. Bearing

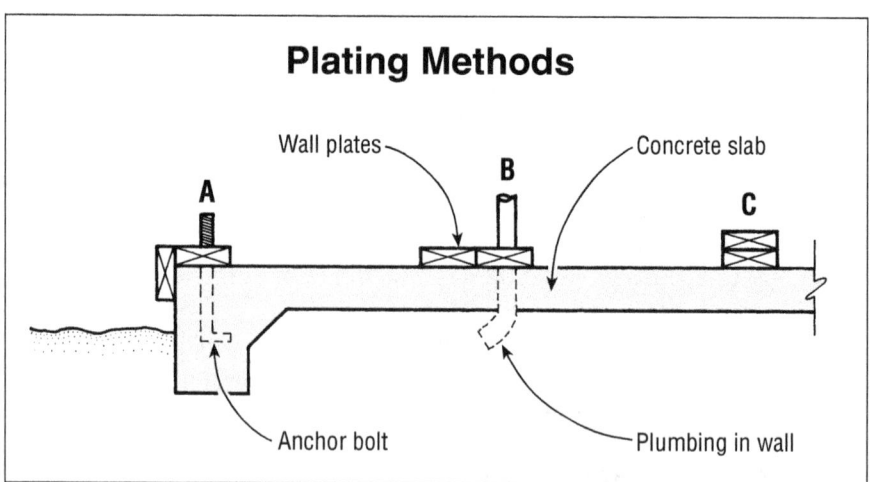

Figure 1-6. Exterior walls with bolts require the top plate to be hung off the side. Interior walls with plumbing must be plated side by side. Walls with no penetrations can be double-stacked.

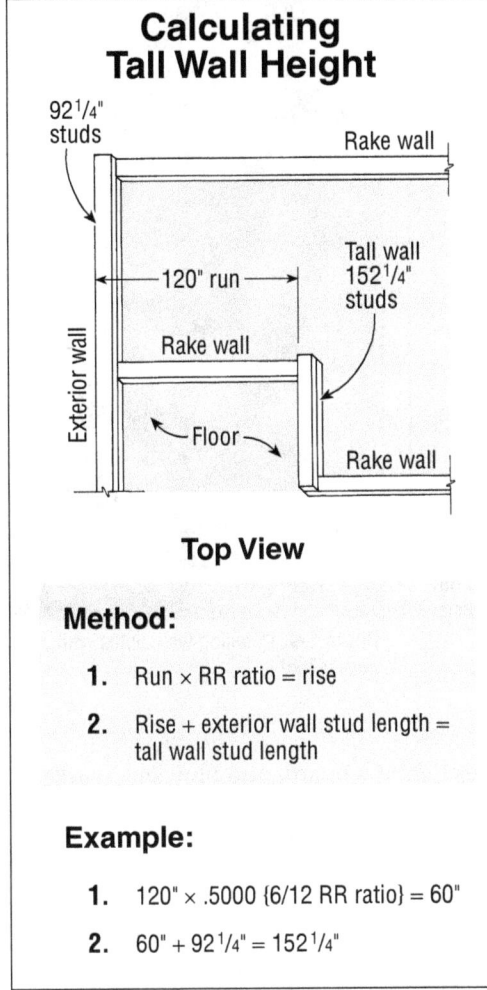

Figure 1-7. Use the wall rise together with the exterior wall stud length to find the tall wall stud length. The wall rise is calculated by multiplying the distance from the outside edge of the exterior wall to the tall wall by the RR ratio. Plate all rake walls with a single bottom plate; their top plates will be cut during assembly.

walls should run through without interruption. On a gable house, for example, plate all the outside rafter walls from end to end, and run hallway plates straight through as shown in **Figure 1-5**. Butt your plates tight, and use straight stock for the top plates so the house will be easy to plumb and line.

Three common ways of plating straight walls are shown in **Figure 1-6**. For walls with anchor bolts, drill the pressure-treated sill plate and place it over the bolts while tacking the top plate so it hangs over the concrete edge **(A)**. Plates for walls where plumbing vents are already in place must be stacked side by side **(B)**. Double-stack all plates where practical **(C)**.

Keep breaks in the top plate at least 4 ft. away from corners and intersections to provide a strong lap between the top plate and doubler.

A rake wall should be plated with a single bottom plate between the exterior wall and a tall wall **(Figure 1-7)**. Both top plates are cut during the framing stage. Rake walls should only be used with cathedral or open-beam ceilings. Use gable studs to close off the gable roof attic ends on homes with flat ceilings. (This is not only faster, but it is also stronger because the continuous top plates act as a building tie.)

SCRATCH

To detail the plates, mark all channels (T-shaped wall intersections) and corners first, followed by the window and door openings, and finally the

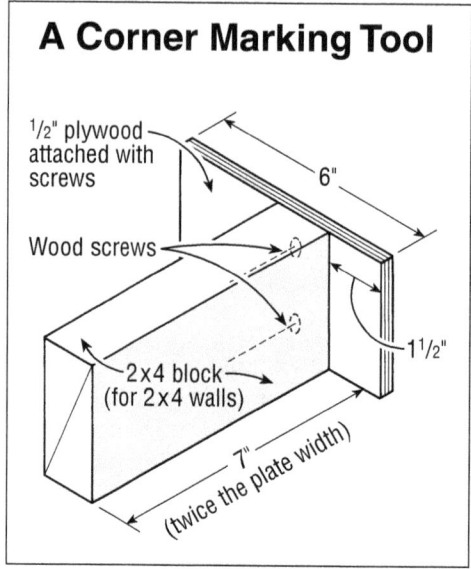

Figure 1-8. Using a corner tool makes laying out corners, intersections, and openings much easier. It acts like a 3-D rafter square.

Photo 1-9. Detailing wall plates with a corner tool.

studs. Use pencil lines to denote the edge of a board, and blue keel marks to identify special items such as wall intersections, king studs, posts, and RO dimensions. (Some folks prefer a single black keel slash denoting center of stud instead of the two pencils lines for edge of stud.) Openings are marked on the top and one side of the double-stacked plates; studs are marked only on one side, depending on which way the plates will be spread for framing purposes. Corners and intersections are marked on the top and both sides as a positioning aide when connecting walls.

A corner tool for marking intersections *(Figure 1-8* and *Photo 1-9)* and a layout stick *(Photo 1-10)* for marking studs make quick work of scratching the plates. These and other framer's tools are available from Big Foot Tools (Henderson, Nevada), or you can make your own.

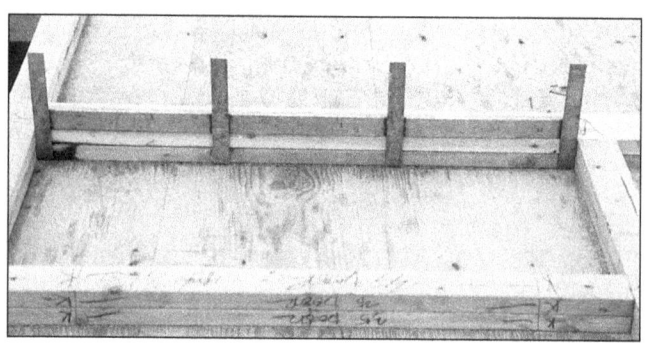

Photo 1-10. A layout stick offers a quick way to mark studs.

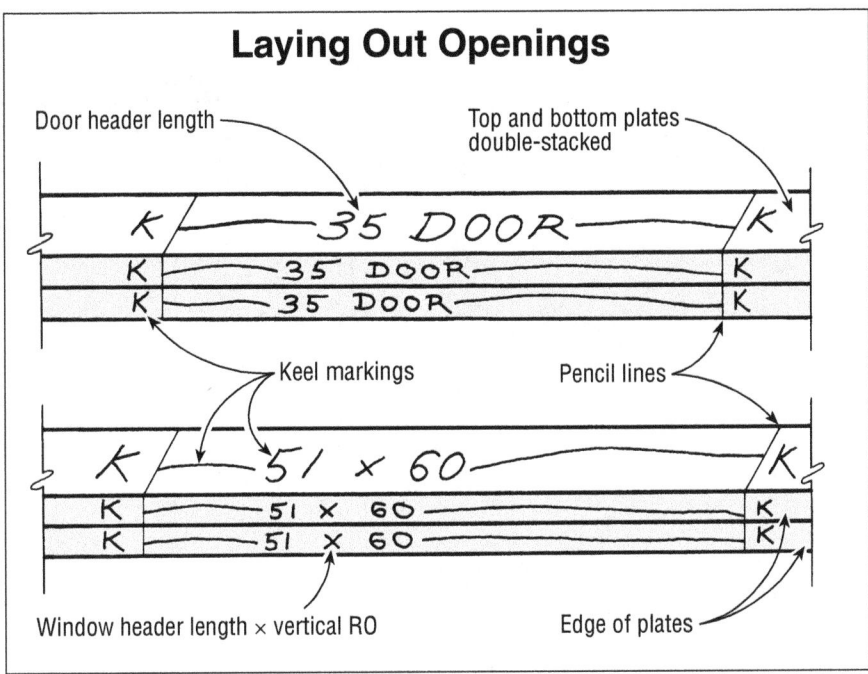

Figure 1-11. Mark openings using the header length as the width for both doors and windows. On windows, also mark the required RO height.

Mark the header size as the opening width when you lay out a window or door. For example, a window with a RO of 48 in. x 60 in. would be marked *51 x 60*, allowing 3 in. for the thickness of a trimmer on each side. A 30-in. regular door would be marked *35 Door*, allowing 3 in. for trimmers and 2 in. for jambs *(Figure 1-11)*.

Run double trimmers on openings 8 ft. wide or larger and double sills on any window 6 ft. wide or larger. Use $82^{1}/_{2}$ in. as the standard header height to allow room for a threshold or thick carpet. Header heights differing from the standard for the house should be noted on the plates (i.e., *35 Door @ $98^{1}/_{2}$* or *51 x 60 @ $98^{1}/_{2}$*). Pocket doors require the header to be set at 84 in., while a drywall return bypass door RO is framed at the actual sum of the two doors to allow for a 1-in. overlap.

Note stud lengths for tall walls in keel. (See the following section, "Figuring Tall Walls," for calculation.) Scratch rake wall plates with the shortest stud SP (short point of bevel-cut) length on one end, the longest stud LP (long point of bevel-cut) length on the other, and the length of the two top plates circled in the middle *(Figure 1-12)*.

Keep at least the 48-in. on-center stud layout consistent on the exterior if using 4x8 siding or shear panel; otherwise change the layout around wall intersections to avoid clumps of studs. (*Note:* I mark the 48-in. on-center stud layout for shear panel lap joints with a yellow keel so they will be obvious

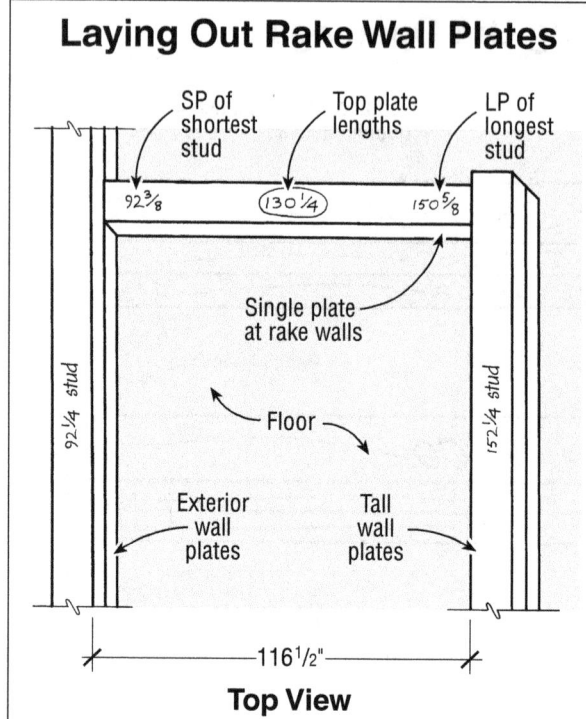

Figure 1-12. Mark rake wall plates with the SP of the shortest stud and the LP of the longest stud at opposite ends and the top plate lengths circled in the middle.

when sheathing.) In most single-story houses, stud bays up to 22 1/2 in. wide can be left open without the need for an extra stud. When marking studs, keep the space behind a toilet clear, and don't forget to mark the tub access and medicine cabinets. Also keep an eye out for such special areas as bathtub locations (minimum 60 1/2 in.) and toilet compartments (minimum 31 in. wide, minimum 24 in. clearance in front).

Use a story pole to determine top and bottom cripple studs or "crips" *(Figure 1-13)*. Spread the headers around the house where they will be used, and toenail on the top crips. Maximize preassembly by precutting the lower crips, windowsills, and window trimmers.

FIGURING TALL WALLS

To figure the height of a tall wall, measure from the outside edge of the exterior wall to the face of the tall wall nearest the exterior wall, and multiply that distance by the RR ratio (Chart 4, Appendix A) to find the rise. Add this rise to the length of the exterior wall studs (Figure 1-7) to find the length of the square-cut tall wall studs. This calculation allows for a birdsmouth connection at the tall wall. For nonbearing walls *(Figure 1-14)*, subtract the depth of the birdsmouth from the stud height to lower it below the rafter. (I leave out all intermediate birdsmouth notches when possible.) Remember that for walls 14 ft. and taller, the studs must be 2x6s

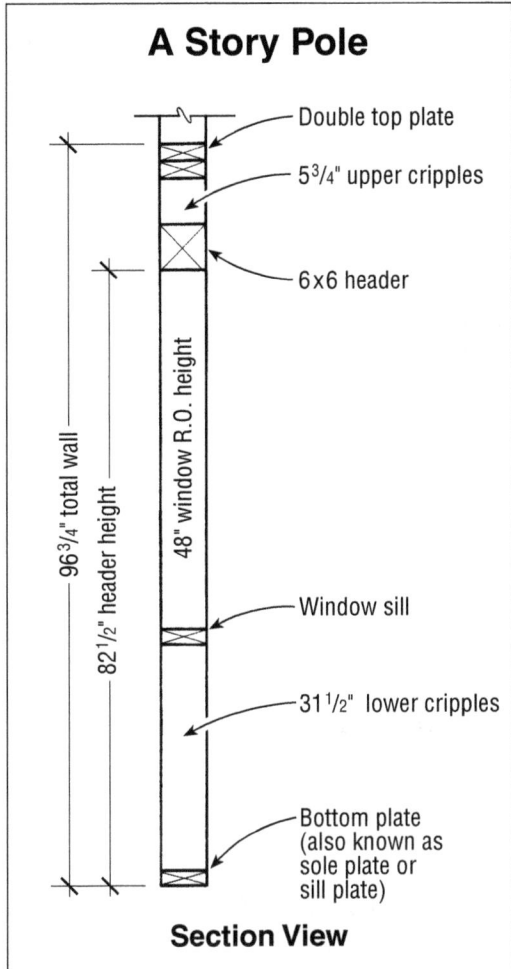

Figure 1-13. A story pole is used to determine top and bottom cripple lengths. To make a story pole, lay out the cross section of the wall on a long 2x4.

or double 2x4s. Fire-block tall walls at 10 ft. maximum. Mid-height blocking on any wall helps keep the studs from bowing.

Heights for ridge beams and purlin beams located below the rafters are calculated the same way as for tall walls, but rather than using the outside wall stud length, use the overall height of the outside wall together with the calculated rise. When rafters are butted to a ridge so they flush out at the top, add the heel-stand of a common rafter to raise the beam the proper amount.

FRAMING STRAIGHT WALLS

Standard-height wall framing is relatively straightforward and needs little discussion. Frame all the outside walls first, and raise walls only when there is no more room to work. (It is much easier to carry studs, plates, and headers over flat walls than around or through them.) Leave out the window sills in large windows to provide more access into the building, and finish fram-

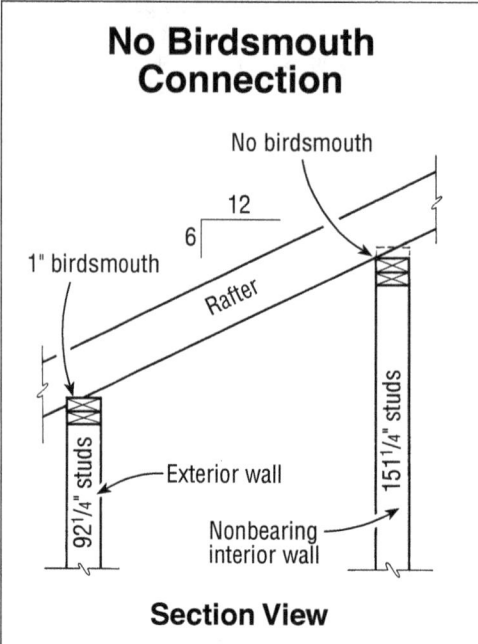

Figure 1-14. To lower a tall wall for a no-birdsmouth connection, subtract the depth of the birdsmouth from the tall wall stud length.

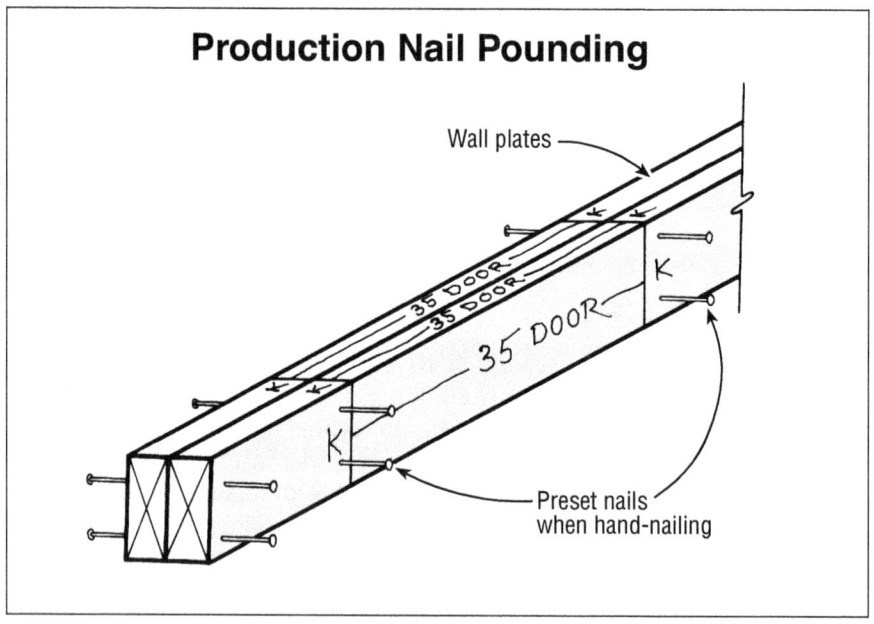

Figure 1-15. When hand-nailing walls together, some framers like to preset all the end-nails on the wall plates prior to placing the studs between them.

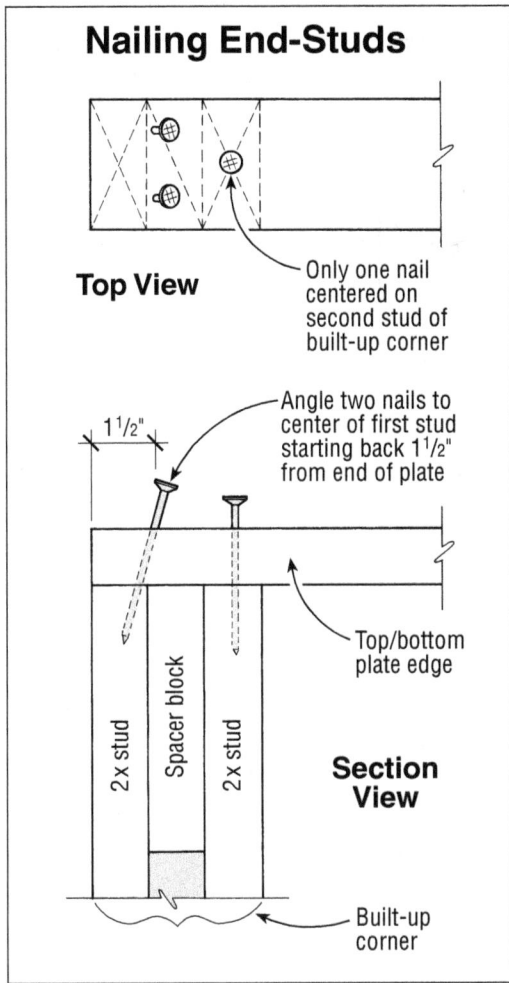

Figure 1-16. To help avoid splitting out the end of a plate, move the two nails for the first stud in from the end about 1½ in., and angle them towards the center of the stud. Use only one nail top and bottom on the second stud of a built-up corner (stud-block-stud).

ing these openings during pick-up. Frame all walls as close to their final location as possible.

When hand-nailing, some carpenters like to preset all the end-nails for the studs on both plates prior to spreading the studs between them. This keeps from jostling the wall during assembly *(Figure 1-15)*. Develop a systematic order of assembly to follow. For example, nail in sequence: 1) a stud on each end; 2) windows and doors; 3) wall intersections; 4) intermediate studs; 5) double plate; 6) block and brace. (I typically cut-in without measuring all door trimmers, oddball fire-blocking, and window trimmers.)

Proper nailing schedules can be found in the UBC nailing chart. Nailing in pairs is better than staggering to prevent twist on double plates, trimmers, and the like. Always add toenails back into the king stud in addition to the required end-nails on headers, window sills, etc., to resist any pull-apart force, unless a strap such as a Simpson Strong-Tie® 55L (small flat 90° angle) is used. Nail the end-studs as shown in *Figure 1-16* to avoid splitting the plates.

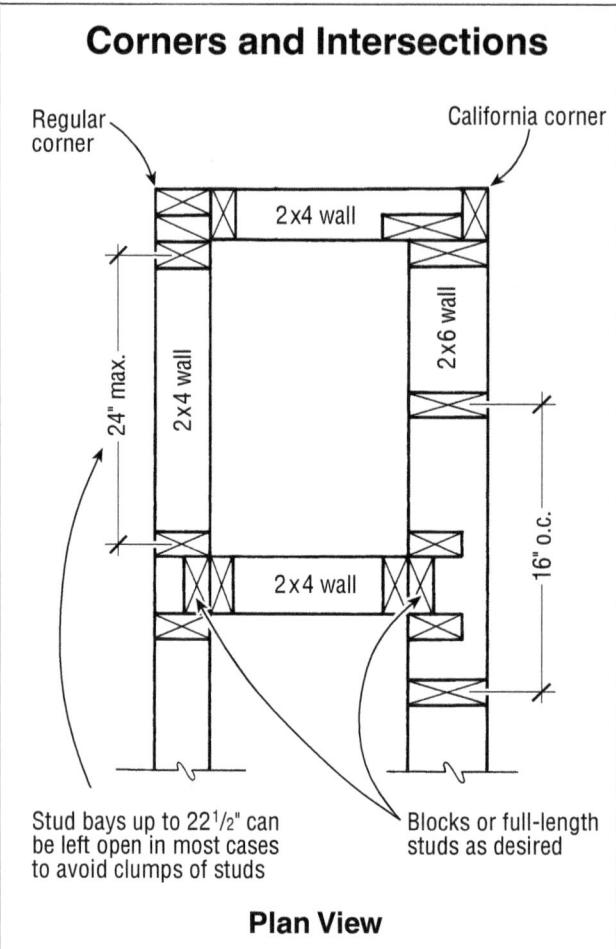

Figure 1-17. While a stud-block-stud works well for 2x4 walls, a California corner should be used on walls 2x6 or larger.

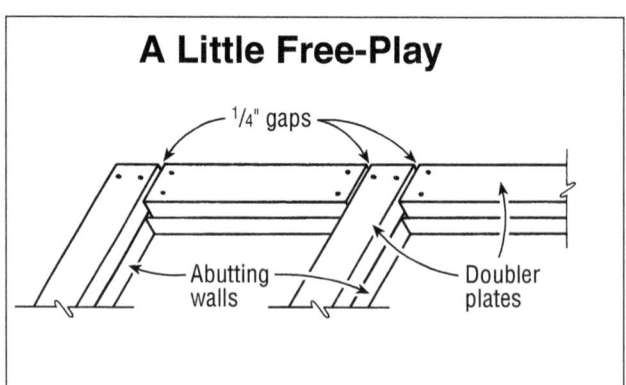

Figure 1-18. Leave a 1/4-in. gap at the corners and intersections when installing the doubler plate. This free-play allows the overlapping plates at wall intersections to fit together more easily when standing walls.

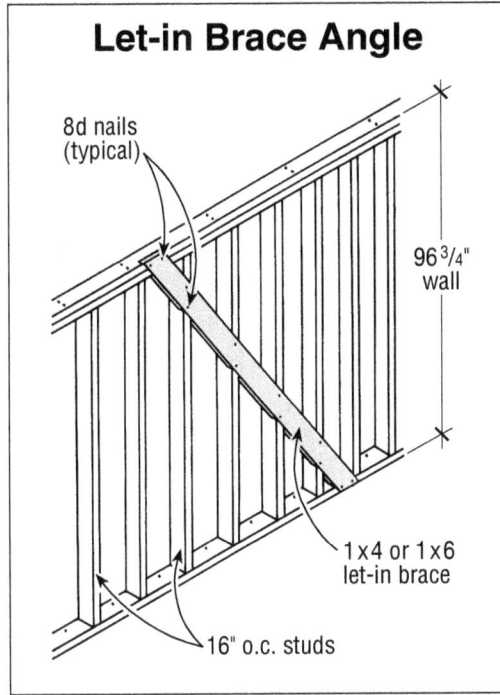

Figure 1-19. Although seldom used anymore due to rigid seismic and wind-loading criteria, the old 1x6 let-in brace should cross four studs or five bays in a standard 8-ft. wall.

Wall corners for walls sized 2x6 and larger should be framed using the California corner method *(Figure 1-17)*.

Don't forget to cut the doubler plate out at same-height wall intersections. Make the plate notches wider than the intersecting wall to facilitate assembly when standing walls *(Figure 1-18)*. Do not cut the doubler plate out at rake wall intersections; make this connection with a metal strap.

With the proliferation of shear panels to meet the latest seismic and wind-load requirements, the good old let-in brace is almost a thing of the past. They are still great for holding non-shear-paneled interior walls plumb. Put a let-in brace in any wall with more than five studs. Long walls should have one brace on each end and an additional brace every 25 ft. The proper brace angle for an 8-ft. wall is shown in *Figure 1-19*. Metal cut-in braces can be used to save time (Simpson Strong-Tie® CWB106 or similar).

Remember to lay out your floor joists or ceiling joists and rafters before you stand the exterior walls.

Figuring Rake Walls

Rake walls are a bit more involved. The fastest way to calculate the length of the LP and SP studs is to calculate down from the tall wall or ridge beam height *(Figure 1-20)*. From the tall wall stud length subtract:
1) the depth of the birdsmouth;
2) $1/4$-in. play to allow for irregularities in the floor ($1/2$ in. for steep-pitch roofs);
3) the dimensional difference between the plumb thickness of the angled top plates versus the regular top plates of a straight wall. (See "Angled Plate Dimensions," page 21.)

The result is the length of the longest stud to the LP of the bevel.

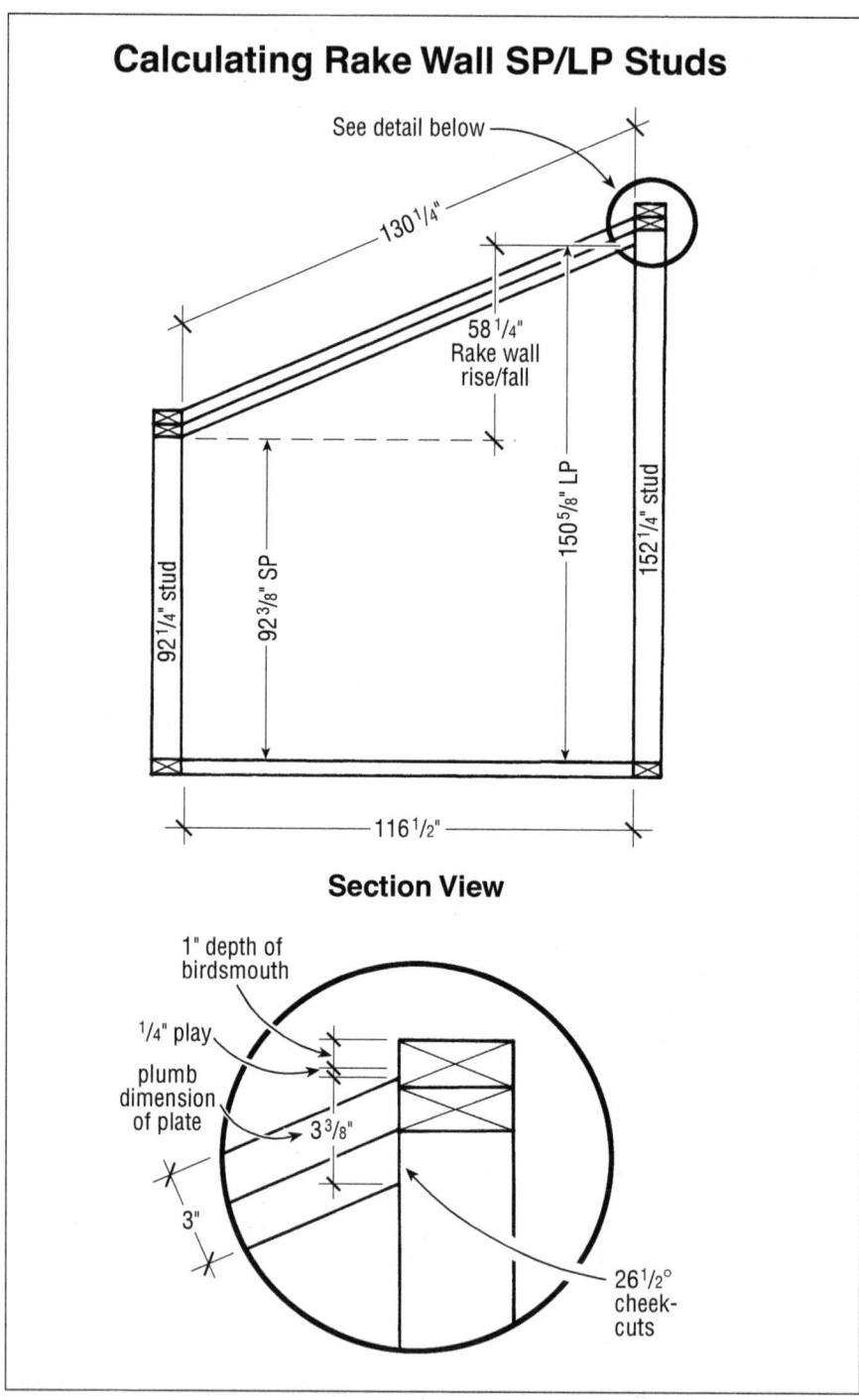

Figure 1-20. To calculate the shortest and longest studs in a rake wall, work down from the stud length of the tall wall into which the rake wall terminates. The rake wall bottom plate is 116 1/2 in.; therefore the drop is 58 1/4 in. (run × RR ratio). Subtract this amount from the tallest stud's LP measurement to determine the shortest stud's SP length.

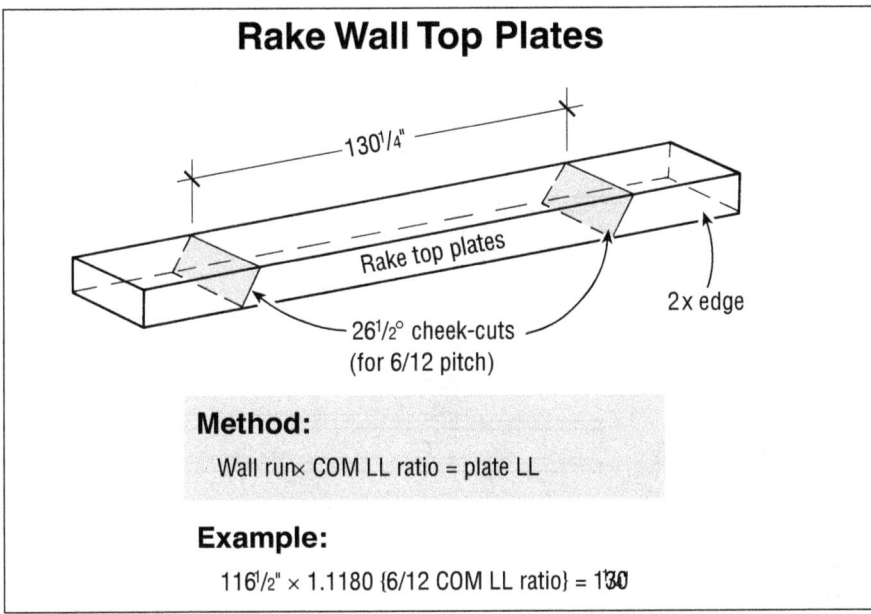

Figure 1-21. The lengths of the two top plates are calculated by multiplying the length of the bottom plate by the COM LL ratio. Each end is cut at the angle of the roof pitch (see Chart 3, Appendix A).

The shortest stud is found by subtracting the fall (rise) for the rake wall length from the longest stud. To calculate the fall, measure the rake wall bottom plate and multiply by the RR ratio. In Figure 1-20, the rake wall bottom plate is 116 1/2 in. Therefore, the fall is 58 1/4 in. (116 1/2" × .5000 {6/12 RR ratio} = 58 1/4"). Subtract this amount from the longest stud to find the length of the shortest stud to the SP of the bevel.

The lengths of the top plate and doubler are found by multiplying the bottom plate length by the COM LL ratio. Each end is cut at the angle for that roof pitch (see Chart 3, Appendix A, or consult a rafter square), as shown in ***Figure 1-21***.

To figure a rake wall that butts to a ridge or purlin beam instead of a tall wall as shown in Figure 1-20, simply subtract the thickness of the top and bottom plates of a straight wall from the total overall beam height, and use the results (equivalent to a hypothetical tall wall stud length) in the formula.

■ **Angled Plate Dimensions**
The plumb dimension of rake wall top plates can be found using a Speed® Square or Quick Square® set to the pitch of the roof to scribe a line drawn across two plate thicknesses and measuring that distance. It can also be calculated mathematically by multiplying the thickness of two plates by the COM LL ratio for that specific roof pitch (see Chart 2, Appendix A). (Example: 3" × 1.1180 {6/12 COM LL ratio} = 3 3/8")

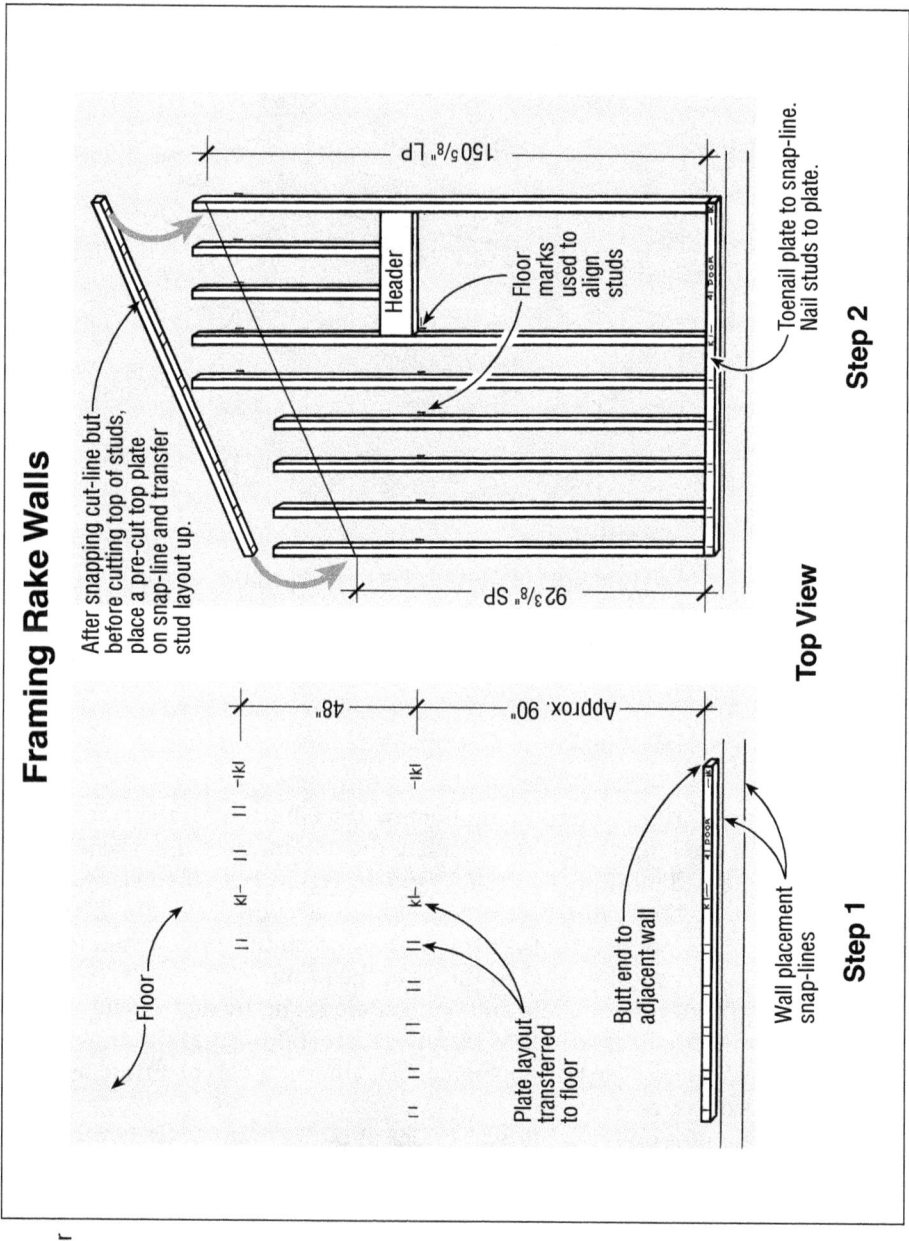

Figure 1-22. When framing rake walls, use the bottom plate as a template to transfer the layout marks to the floor at several locations. This layout keeps the studs straight until snapped for length. With the studs nailed to the bottom plate and everything aligned on the floor layout, measure and mark the shortest and longest studs and snap the cut-line. The studs are cut vertically in place. When the front of the saw foot hits the floor, pick up on the stud to finish the cut.

Photo 1-23. Left: Square-cut the stud at the LP. Right: Cut the angle by eyeballing the snap-line. Caution: The lower blade guard was removed in this demonstration for visual clarity.

FRAMING RAKE WALLS

With a good method, framing rake walls is quite satisfying. Use the rake wall bottom plate as a pattern to transfer the wall layout to the floor at the height of the shortest stud and every 4 ft. above this in the direction the rake will be framed *(Figure 1-22)*. Be sure to butt one end of the bottom plate to a perpendicular wall or snap-line to keep everything straight while you transfer the wall layout marks to the floor. When finished transferring the marks, return the bottom plate to the wall snap-lines (toenail to the floor inside the line if the floor is plywood), and nail uncut studs to the plate at each mark.

To cut the tops, check to make sure the bottom plate is aligned with the wall snap-line, and place each of the studs on the floor marks. Measure and mark the end-studs with the shortest or longest lengths written on the bottom plate, and snap a line between the two points. Using the measurement calculated earlier and also written on the bottom plate (Figure 1-12), cut the top plate and place it on the studs directly above the rake snap-line to transfer up your stud layout before making the bevel-cuts.

The rake wall in Figure 1-22 is angled so the studs can easily be cut if you're using a wormdrive circular saw. With the saw table set to the proper degree for the pitch of the roof (Chart 3, Appendix A), cut vertically until the front of the saw foot hits the floor. Then pick up the board, pulling it

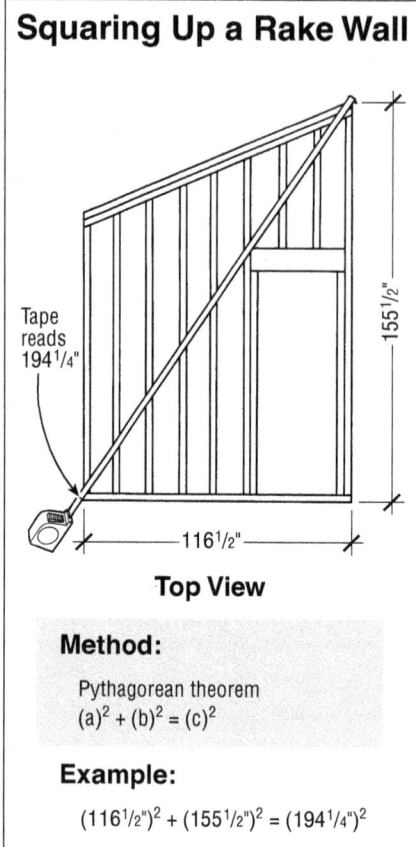
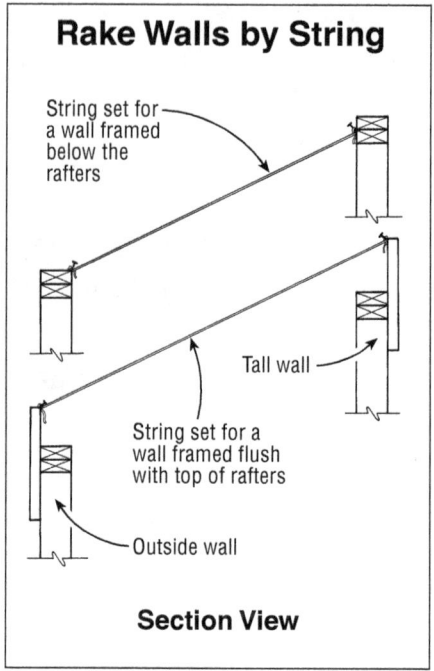

Figure 1-24. To shear-panel a rake wall on the ground, square up the wall using the hypotenuse of the right triangle formed by the long stud side and the bottom plate.

Figure 1-25. Some folks like to stick-frame rake walls to a string-line.

into and through the blade to finish the cut. However, if the wall is going the wrong direction for the saw angle, the studs must be square-cut first at the LP, then cut again (with the saw still set square) while eyeballing the angle of the snap-line. (See ***Photo 1-23***).

If you have trouble eyeballing this cut, run the saw set square at full depth across the edges of the studs, following the snap-line as if you were cutting in a wall brace. Then go back and cut the ends. This deep starter pass will serve as a guide when eyeballing the angle-cut.

To finish the rake wall, nail on the top plate and doubler, block, and brace.

Installing exterior plywood sheathing to tall rake walls on the ground prior to raising them will prevent having to work from scaffolding later. Square-up the wall by pulling a diagonal measurement using the length of the bottom plate and the total wall height at the LP end as the two legs of

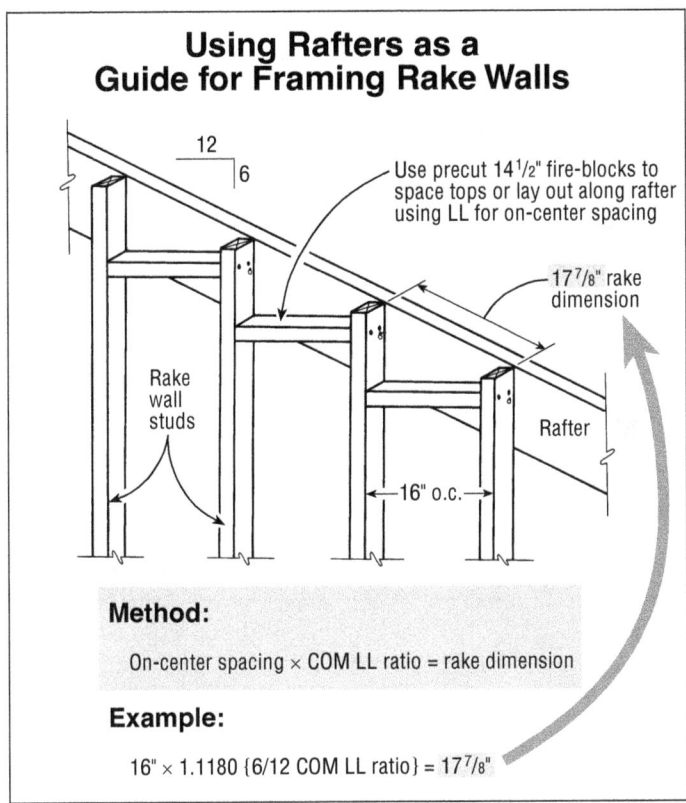

Figure 1-26. Sometimes, rake walls can be stick-framed behind or under the rafters after they are stacked.

Photo 1-27. Here a crew stands interior rake walls.

a right triangle *(Figure 1-24)*. Do not nail the bottom 2 ft. of a shear panel that overlaps a rim joist below. Leaving the bottom of the shear panel loose allows the wall to be easily pulled in to match it up with the wall snap-line.

Some folks like to stick-frame rake walls to a string as in *Figure 1-25*, or frame them behind or under the rafters after they are stacked, similar to *Figure 1-26*.

RAISING WALLS

Whereas 8-ft. to 10-ft. walls are relatively easy to raise *(Photo 1-27)*, taller walls can sometimes be a problem. A top-heavy wall as shown in *Figure 1-28* can be helped up by using long braces that nail to the outside ends

FIGURING AND FRAMING WALLS **25**

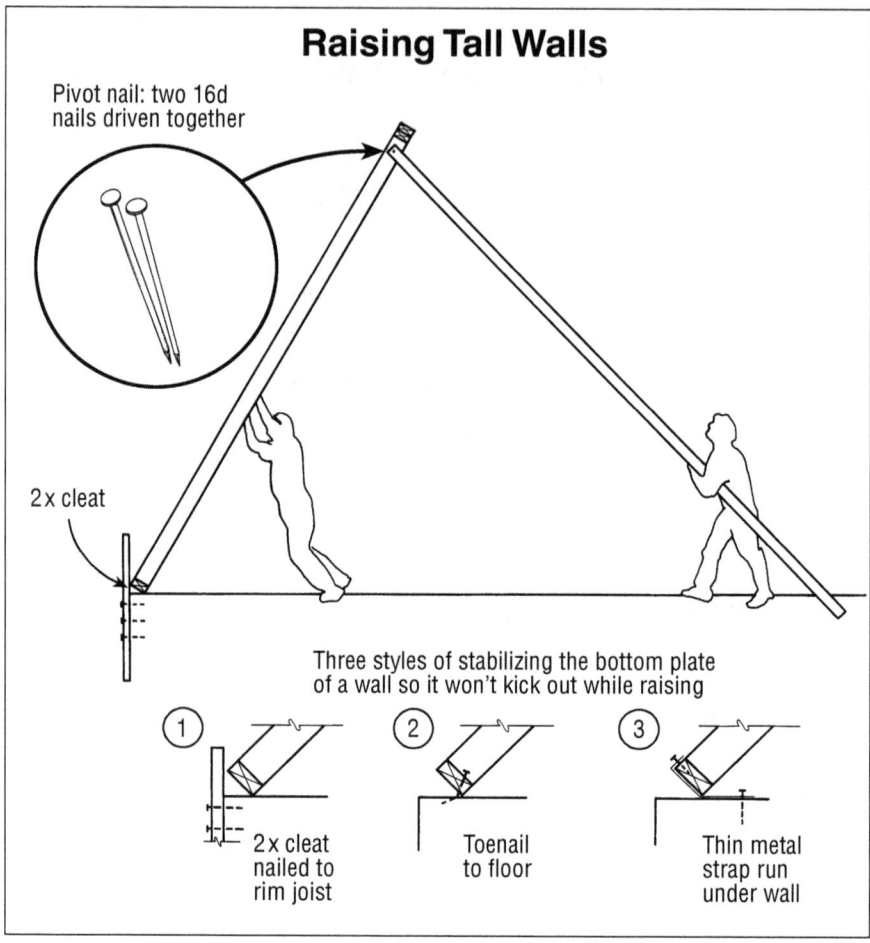

Figure 1-28. Use a long brace attached to the end-stud with a pivot nail (two 16d nails driven side by side) to help raise a top-heavy wall.

and pivot as the wall goes up. Use a pivot nail (two 16d nails driven together) to attach the braces. Use cleats, toenails, or thin metal straps (like lumber banding straps) nailed under the bottom plate and to the floor inside to keep the walls from sliding off a raised floor as they are tilted vertical.

Walls that are too heavy to lift by hand can be raised using wall jacks **(Photo 1-29)** or pulled up by a truck or winch. When using a truck or winch, the trick is to transfer the horizontal pull to a vertical pull in order to lift the wall. To do this, crisscross two studs as shown in **Figure 1-30**, and nail them vertically to the wall near the top. Another brace must be placed at 90° to hold them in this position. Run the cable or rope over the crisscross, and attach it to the top of the wall. Long sway braces should be nailed on each wall end to steady the wall as it is raised (Figure 1-28).

Photo 1-29. This shear-panel rake wall is raised using wall jacks. Notice that the bay window on the right wall section was fully framed before the wall was stood.

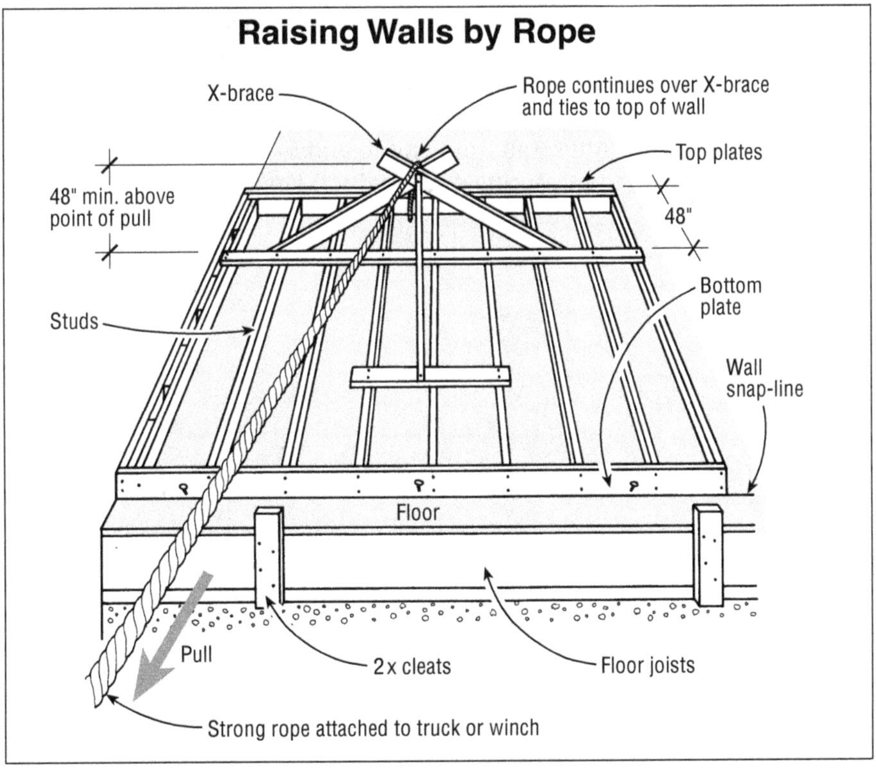

Figure 1-30. When standing walls using a truck or attached winch, redirect the horizontal pull into a vertical pull by changing the rope angle with a makeshift crisscross of braces.

FIGURING AND FRAMING WALLS 27

Underpinning For Hillside Lots

I have found the most accurate way to frame underpinning on steep hillside lots is to stick-frame the studs, letting the tops run wild. Then shoot an elevation mark for the top-of-stud height at each end, snap a line, and cut the studs in the air. (This negates any inconsistency in the foundation, which will throw off a standard progression.) Nail a horizontal 2x4 cleat outside the wall to keep the studs properly spaced and aligned until the top plate is on.

Dealing with extra-tall studs takes a little ingenuity. One time on the parallel bottom wall of a steep hillside foundation, the underpinning studs were over 22 ft. long, making it impractical to cut them in the air. The cripple wall was made of double 2x6s spaced 12 in. on-center and blocks spaced 48 in. on-center, making a prebuilt wall too heavy for two guys to lift without a crane. So we chose to stick-frame it in the air. We found the difference in height between the two ends and then framed a big box with just the two end-studs, a bottom plate, a single top plate, and a diagonal brace. Using push-sticks nailed to the outside of the end-studs with pivot nails, we raised our box *(Figure 1-31)*. We had set our push-sticks at a certain height so that after the wall was up and the braces were tied back horizontally to the concrete footing going up the hill, it was at the perfect height on which to throw a couple of scaffold planks to use for installing the intermediate studs. We prenailed 48-in. on-center fire blocks to each stud before standing them. The two push-braces also served as the flat positioning cleat along the side rake cripple studs that were to be cut later in the air. Since the concrete had quite a few ups and downs, we ran a level string-line along the bottom of the downhill wall from end to end as a reference to measure down from, rather than measuring each stud full length.

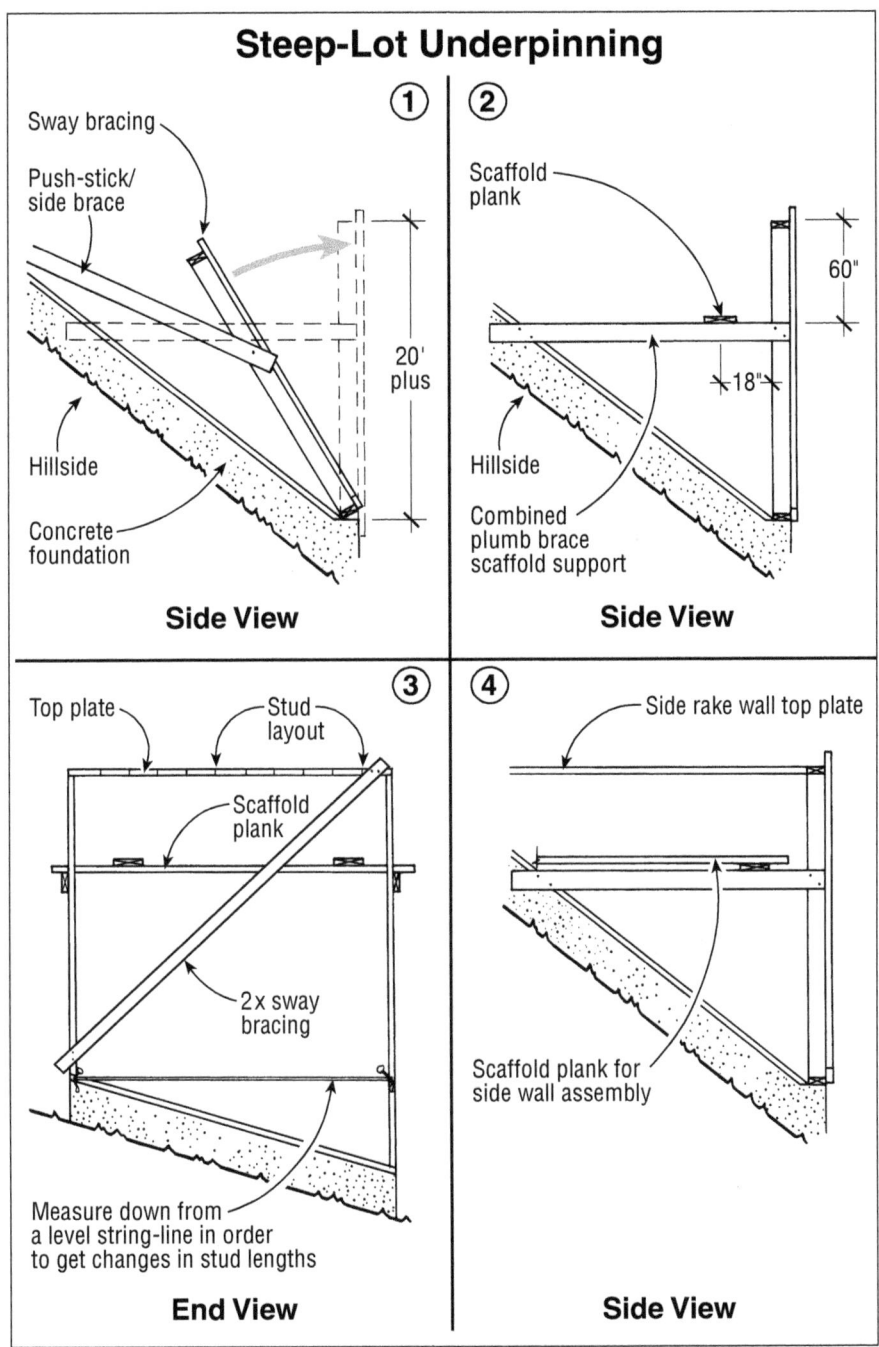

Figure 1-31. The skeleton for steep hillside underpinning can be built and raised similar to an inverted rake wall. Position the temporary side plumb braces to allow them to be used as supports for an assembly scaffold.

Chapter 2

Plumb, Line, and Joist

PLUMB AND LINE

Walls up to 9 ft. tall can be plumbed using a 6-ft. level attached to a straight stud *(Figure 2-1)*. Anything taller should be done with a minimum 32-ounce

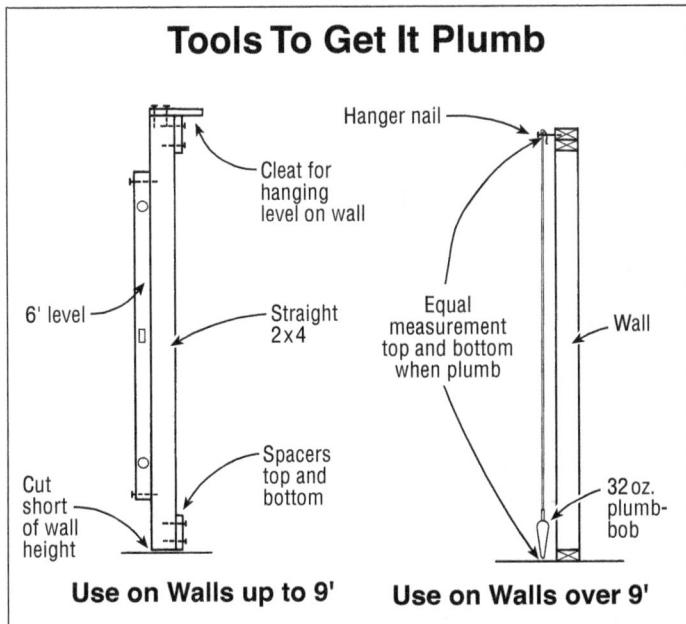

Figure 2-1. Walls up to 9 ft. tall can be plumbed using a 6-ft. level attached to a straight stud. Spacers at top and bottom negate any crown in the wall that may interfere with getting a correct reading. Walls over 9 ft. tall are best done with a plumb-bob.

Photo 2-2. Top and bottom measurements will be equal when using a "bob" to plumb tall walls.

Plumb and Line Basics

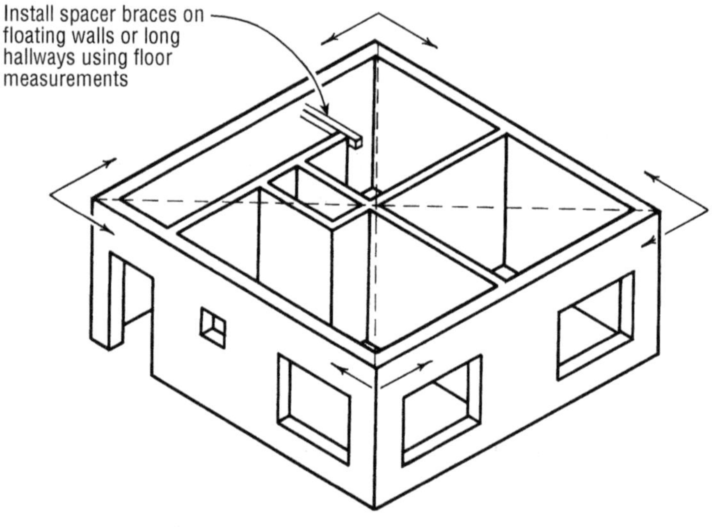

Install spacer braces on floating walls or long hallways using floor measurements

Method:

1. Tie all floating interior walls with spacer braces
2. Plumb outside corners
3. Check and adjust diagonals if roof is a hip
4. Line outside walls by eye or string

Figure 2-3. To plumb and line, always start by plumbing the outside corners. Then, if the roof is a hip, check and adjust diagonals before lining the outside walls.

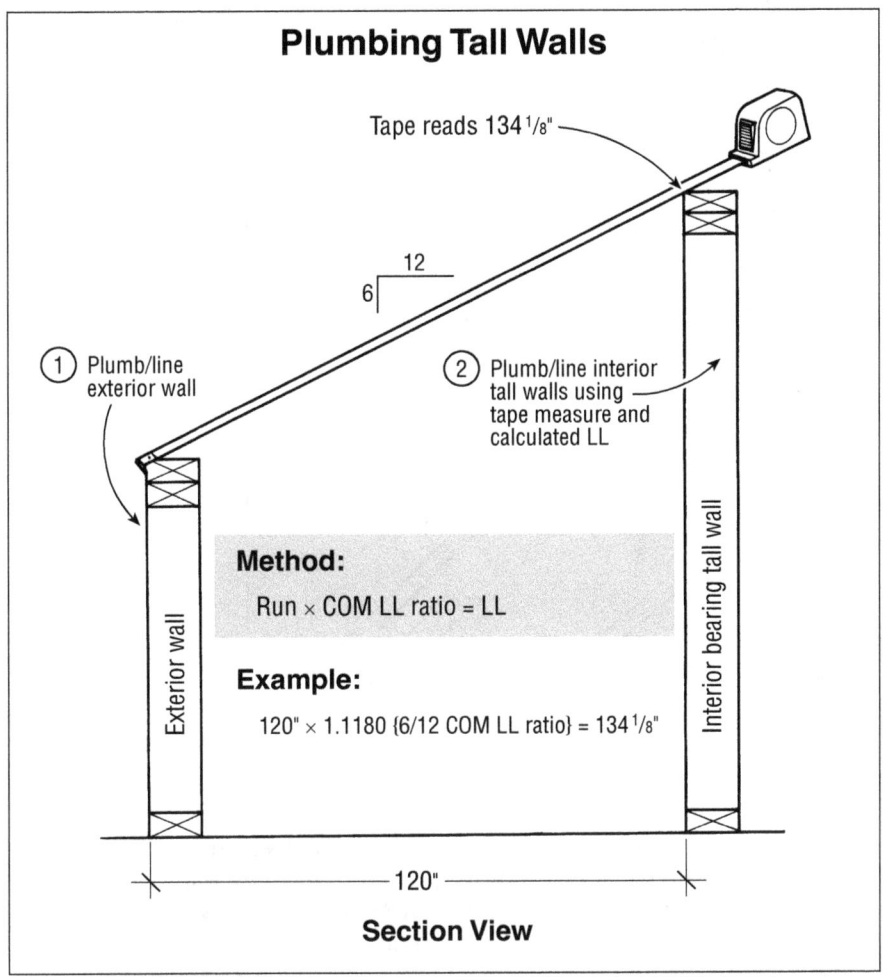

Figure 2-4. Short-run interior tall walls can be plumbed by measuring over from the exterior wall using the appropriate line length. If the tall wall runs the full length of the building, plumb and line in reverse starting with the tall wall.

plumb bob *(Photo 2-2)* or with one of the new-generation, pocket-size plumb/level lasers on the market.

Check both ends of a wall with the level before determining if it is okay. Plumb all the outside corners and adjust them out of plumb slightly if it is necessary to correct for bad diagonals *(Figure 2-3)*. Out-of-square buildings make roof framing difficult, particularly with hip roofs. Eyeball or use a string to line all walls including rakes. Always check overall house dimensions and LL measurements from exterior walls to tall walls. If the wall has been shortened for a no-birdsmouth connection, set a small piece of wood equal to the birdsmouth depth on the wall so an LL measurement can be taken accurately *(Figure 2-4)*. For balloon-framed walls, plumb, line, and brace at each floor line *(Figure 2-5)*.

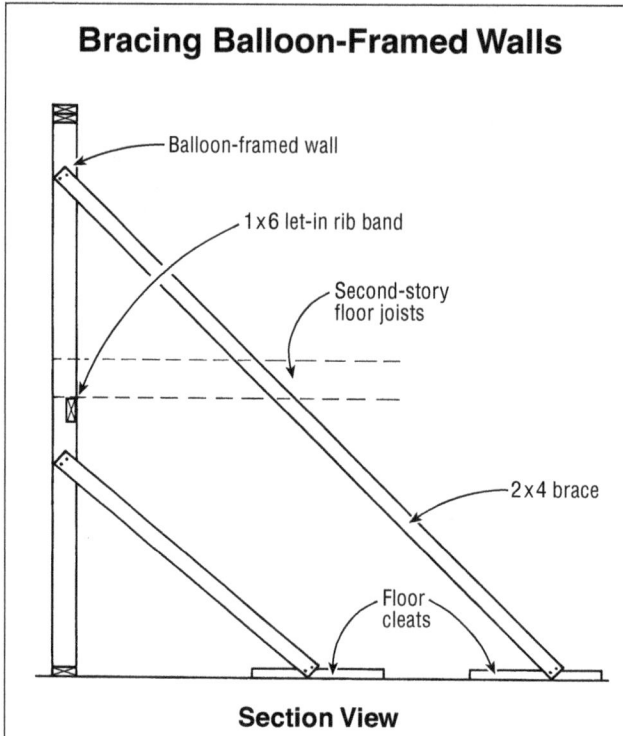

Figure 2-5. Balloon-framed walls may require a brace at each floor line.

There are many different methods for racking walls around. ***Figure 2-6*** and ***Figure 2-7*** illustrate methods for pulling or pushing walls when working on a wood floor. The method shown in ***Figure 2-8*** works well on both concrete and wood floors. With this technique, the push-brace is hooked flat under the top plates in the corner, bent like a bow, slid over, and expanded.

Another good method for either type of floor is to nail a temporary brace at the top in the corner of two intersecting walls and pry it at the bottom using a hatchet or flat-bar ***(Figure 2-9)***.

Install 2x4 let-in wall corner ties in a garage unless drywall will be installed on the ceiling ***(Figure 2-10)***. Bad wall dips and rises due to an uneven floor can be fixed as shown in ***Figure 2-11***. Wall dips over 1/4 in. are best corrected by placing shims under the sill plate rather than between the top two plates since a large gap severely weakens their connection.

Pre-snap 16-in. on-center nail gun lines on shear-panel sheets prior to installation. OSB is nice in this regard, as it generally comes premarked. When a lift of regular 4x8 plywood sheathing arrives on the delivery truck, jump up there and mark the ends of the lift at 16 in. and 32 in. on-center while they're still banded together. This eliminates the need to measure and mark each sheet individually later — just snap the lines.

To plumb a bay window section, precut a plywood top or corner pattern with the exact side angles as on the floor and set it on top. Rack the bay

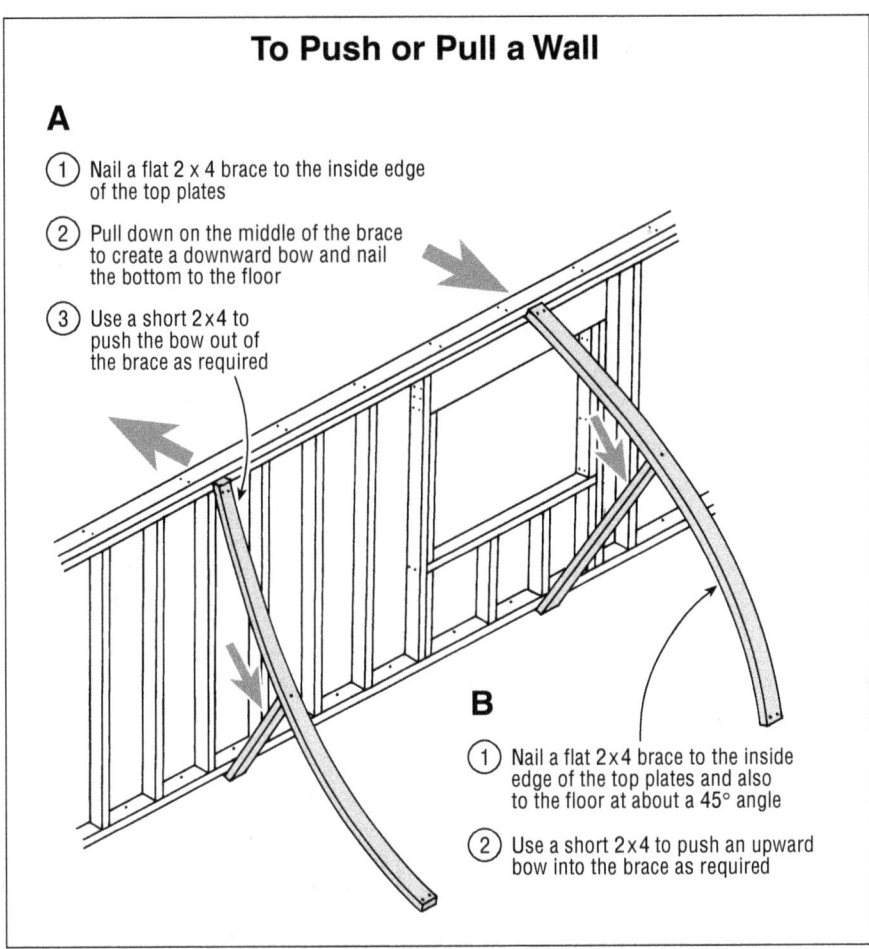

Figure 2-6. A flat 2x4 brace nailed top and bottom under pressure in a bow (**A**) will push a wall out when it is straightened with a short 2x4. A flat 2x4 brace nailed top and bottom while slack (**B**) will draw a wall in when pushed into a bow with a short 2x4.

around until it matches the top, and nail off the temporary wall braces. If the plywood top can stay permanently, nail it off to eliminate the need for any temporary wall braces at all *(Figure 2-12)*.

CEILING JOISTS

Always lay out the rafters before marking ceiling joists so you will end up with good building ties. Instead of precutting ceiling joists to length on the ground, cut them in place. With one end nailed, eyeball the outside wall, and cut vertically until the front of the saw-foot hits the doubler plate, then lift the joist slightly to finish the cut — similar to cutting studs for a rake wall *(Figure 2-13)*.

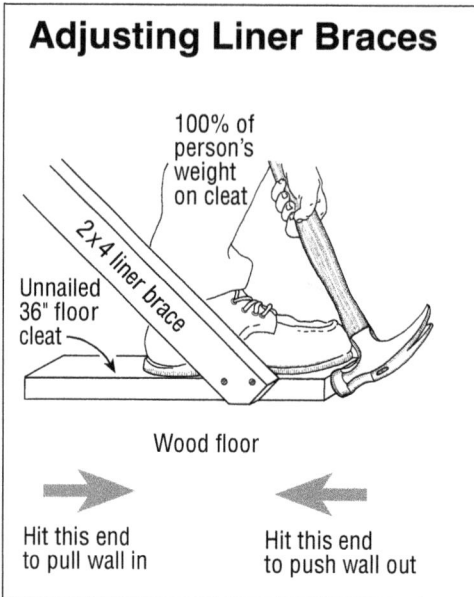

Adjusting Liner Braces

100% of person's weight on cleat

2x4 liner brace

Unnailed 36" floor cleat

Wood floor

Hit this end to pull wall in

Hit this end to push wall out

Figure 2-7. Nail the bottom end of a liner brace to a 3-ft. piece of flat 2x4. While standing on this block, drive it in or out as needed to line the wall before locking it off with nails to a floor joist below.

Figure 2-8. A favorite method of racking walls when there is a perpendicular wall nearby is to use a long 2x4 or 2x6 and tuck it under the top plate in the corner and against the perpendicular wall at the bottom. Bow the brace, slide it over, and pull it up to expand. ▼

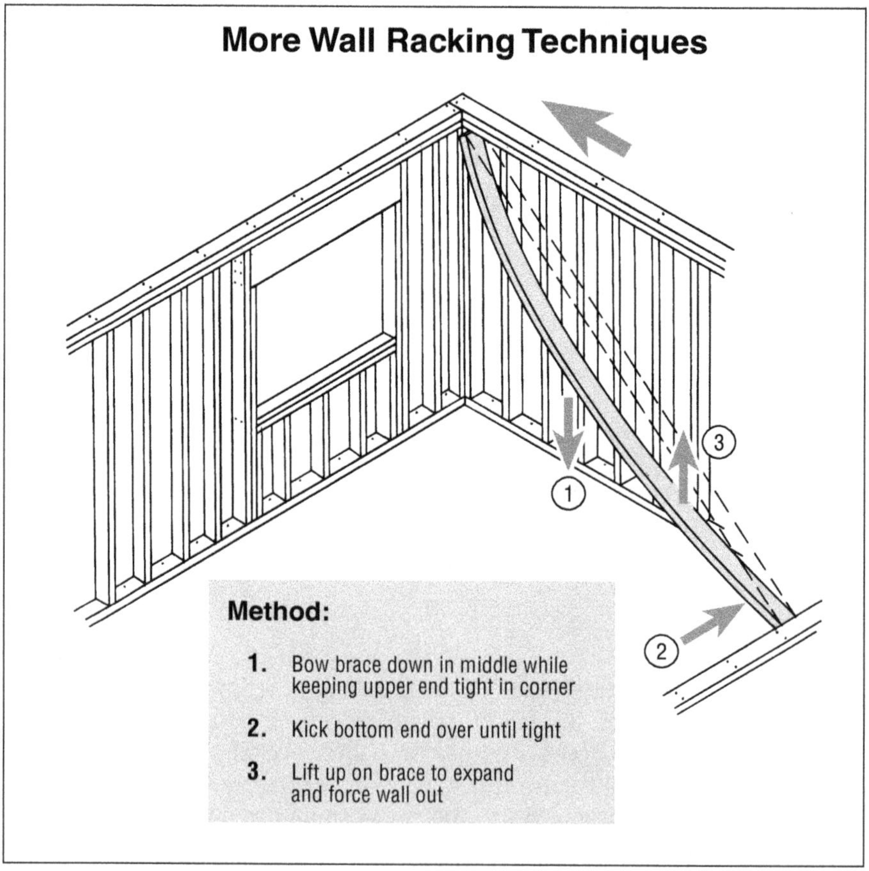

More Wall Racking Techniques

Method:

1. Bow brace down in middle while keeping upper end tight in corner
2. Kick bottom end over until tight
3. Lift up on brace to expand and force wall out

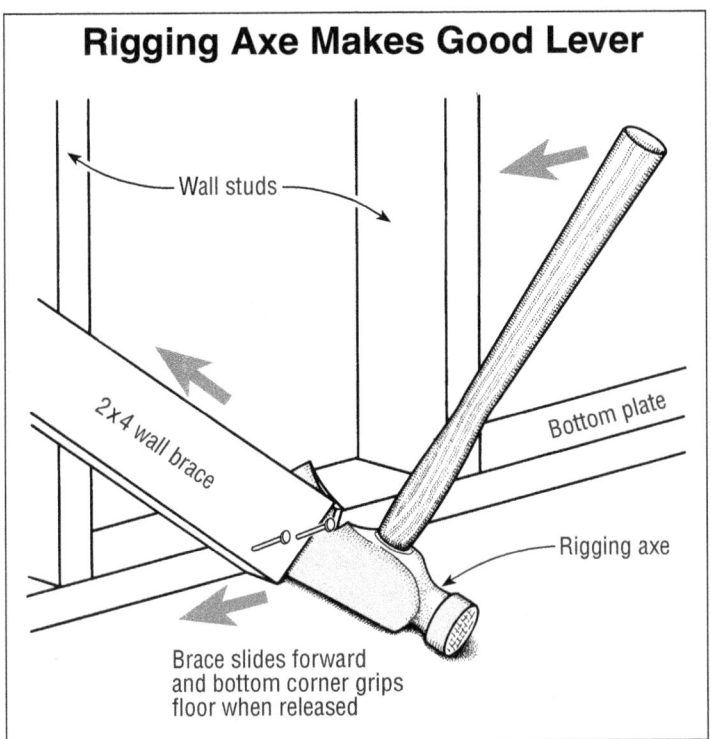

Figure 2-9. Use a rigging axe as a lever on the bottom of a brace to push a wall.

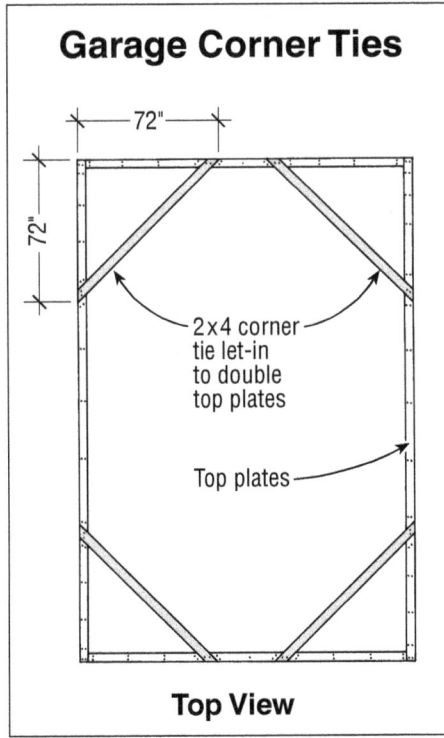

Figure 2-10. Install 2x4 let-in corner ties in a garage, unless drywall will be installed on the ceiling.

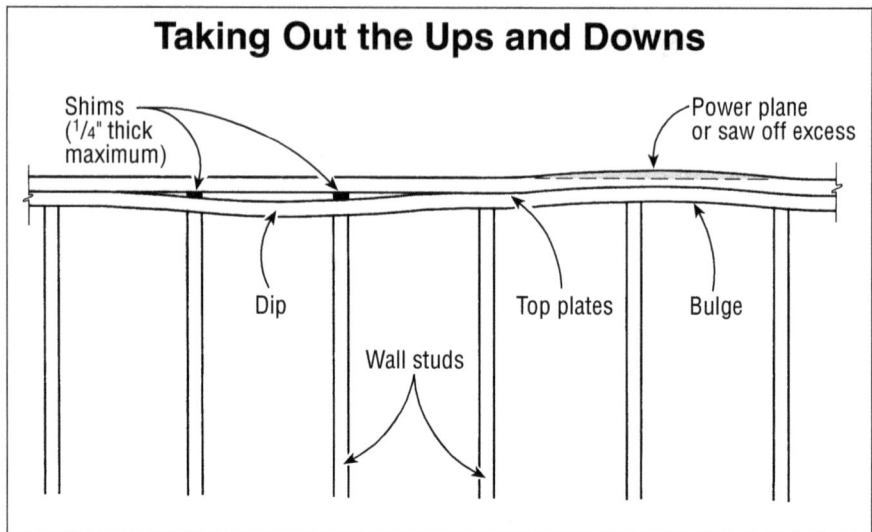

Figure 2-11. Raise a dip in a wall by shimming between the two top plates. A bulge in a wall can be removed with a power plane from the top or a circular saw run along the sides after the nails have been countersunk or pulled.

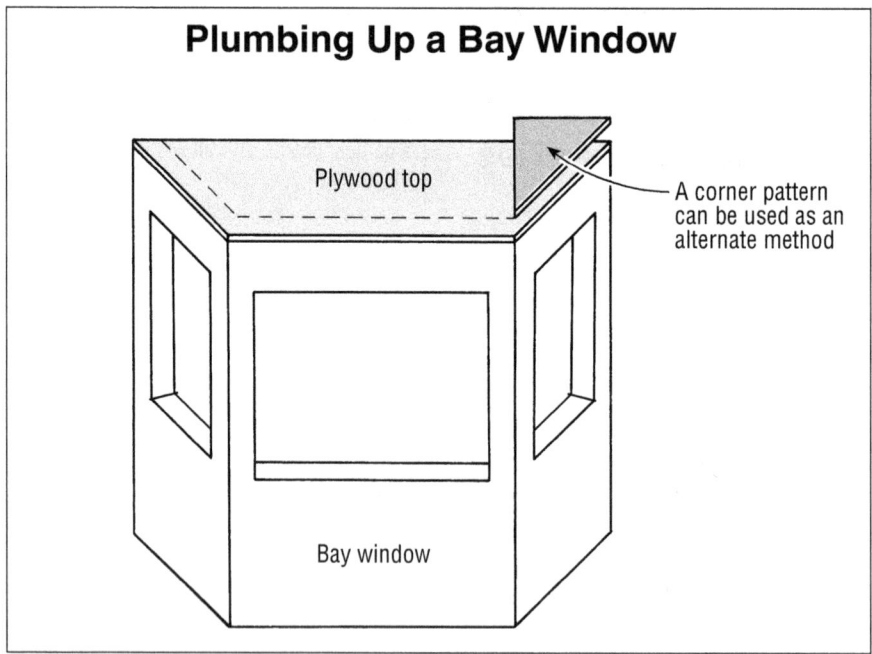

Figure 2-12. To plumb a bay window section, precut a plywood top with the exact side angles as on the floor. Rack the bay around until it matches, and nail off the interior braces.

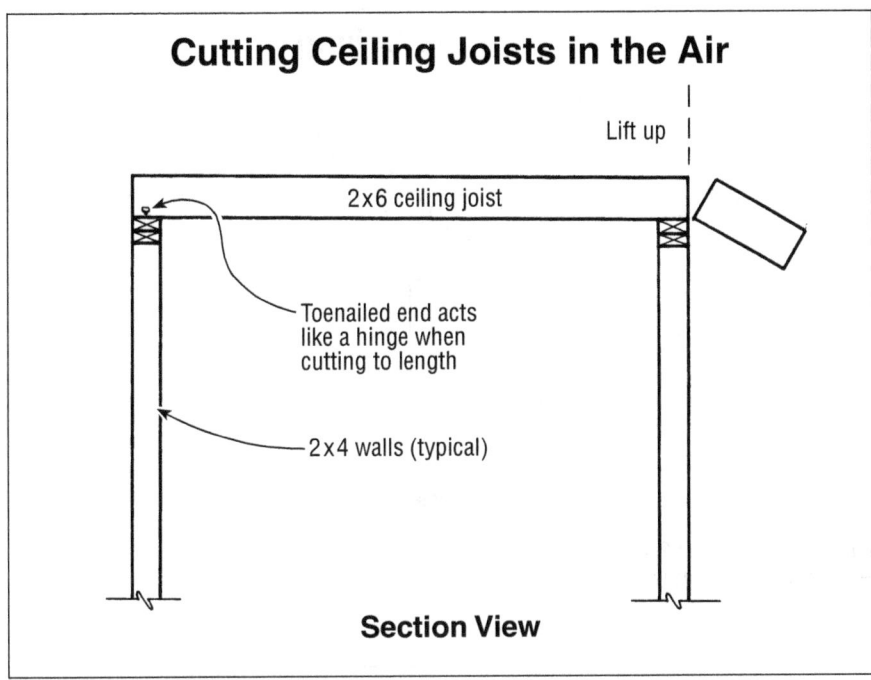

Figure 2-13. Cutting ceiling joists in the air saves time. With one end nailed to the plate, cut vertically — eyeballing the outside wall until the front of the saw-foot hits the wall. Then lift up the board to finish the cut.

To stiffen a run of ceiling joists, nail a strong-back *(Figure 2-14)* to the 2x catwalk or run vertical braces to the ridge after the roof is stacked.

Instead of heading ceiling joists into a beam to shorten their span, try raising the beam above the joists and hanging them with an extra deep hanger or a 2x4 cleat. With this method, the joists function as uninterrupted building ties, and less framing metal is required *(Figure 2-15)*.

Change the direction of the ceiling joists at the hip-end of a roof far enough back so they won't interfere with the hip rafters *(Figure 2-16)*.

When ceiling joists run parallel to a kitchen cabinet wall and the top cabinets run to the ceiling rather than a lowered soffit, add an extra joist for backing centered on $13^{1}/_{4}$ in. from the cabinet wall.

Figure 2-17 illustrates two different ways to build a bath or kitchen drop. In both methods, the soffit bottom is box-framed on the ground and raised into place. Use 2x4 verticals, plywood, or metal straps as support for the front. (Simpson Strong-Tie® CS22R cut into short lengths works well for this purpose.)

When stick-framing drop ceilings to a ledger, use 16d backing nails instead of pressure blocks, and toenail the ceiling joists to the ledger. (Hangers need to be used on ceiling joists over 10 ft. long or any time there is more

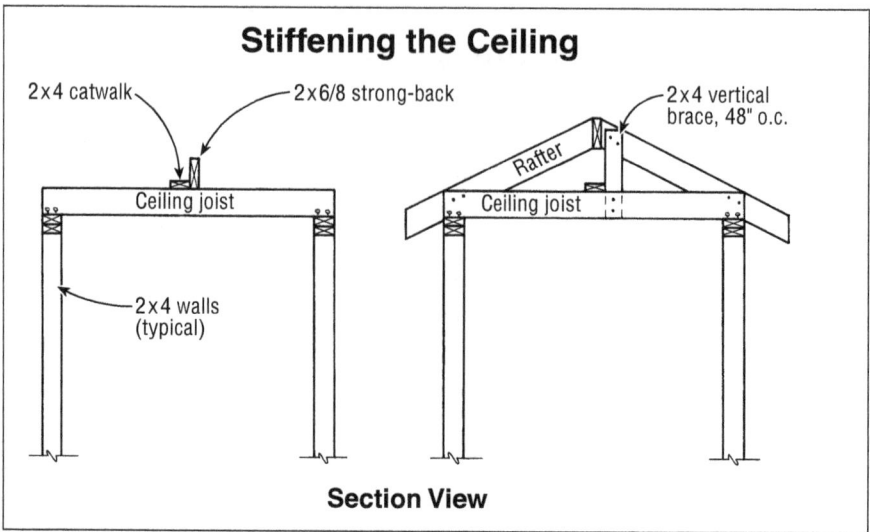

Figure 2-14. A 2x6 or 2x8 strong-back nailed to a 2x catwalk will stiffen a run of ceiling joists — as will vertical braces run to the ridge.

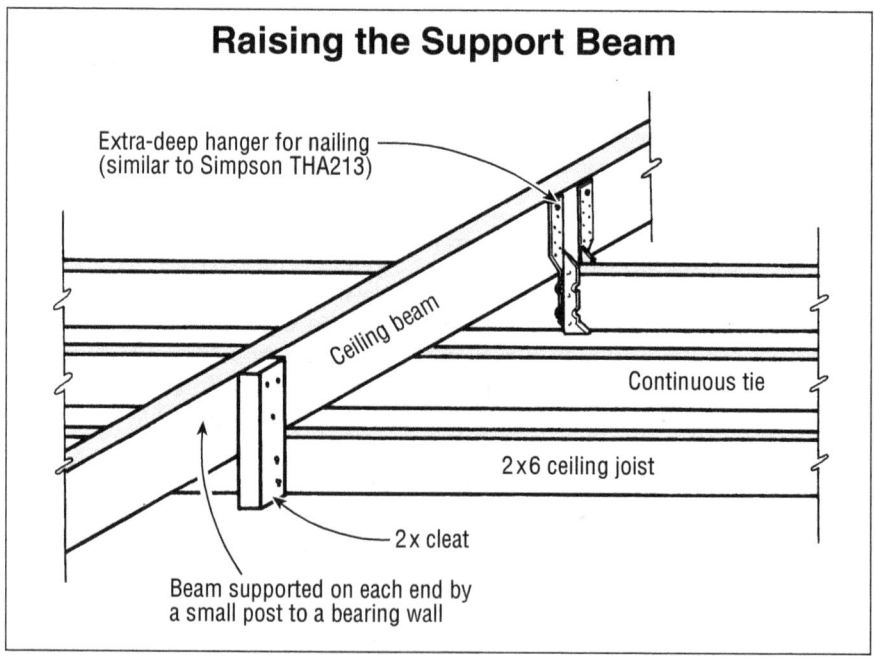

Figure 2-15. Instead of heading ceiling joists into a beam, try raising the beam above the joists and picking up the load with a 2x4 cleat or deep hanger.

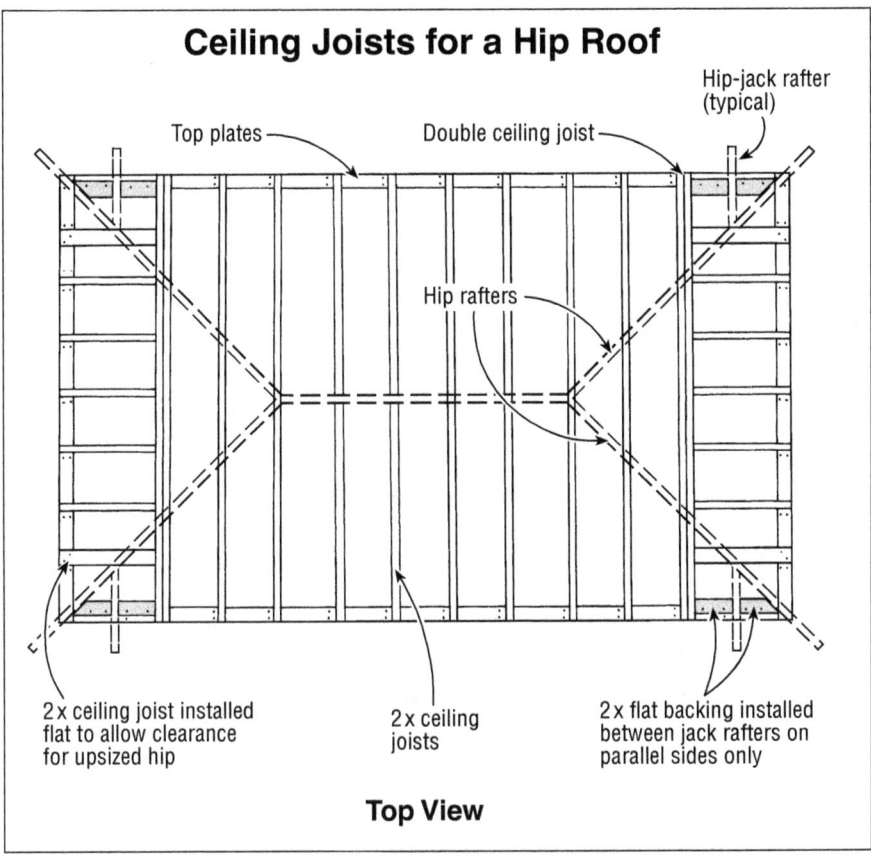

Figure 2-16. Change the direction of the ceiling joists at the hip-end of a roof far enough back so they won't interfere with the hip rafter.

than just a drywall ceiling load.) A bent nail as shown in **Figure 2-18** will help hold up the other end of the board if you're working solo.

FLOOR JOISTS

Like ceiling joists, floor joists are fast and easy. Remember the building code to avoid trouble: openings 4 ft. and larger require a double header, and tail joists (joists hanging from a header) longer than 6 ft. require hangers. If intermediate joists have been headed out more than 24 in. from a bearing point, double the side supporting joists when framing an opening.

By code, floor joists should be blocked at each end (using either solid blocks or a rim joist) and over each intermediate supporting wall or beam. Blocks installed in the clear span are possible squeakers and are best left out. If they are required for some reason, preset the top end-nails in the joists as shown in **Figure 2-19** to simplify installation.

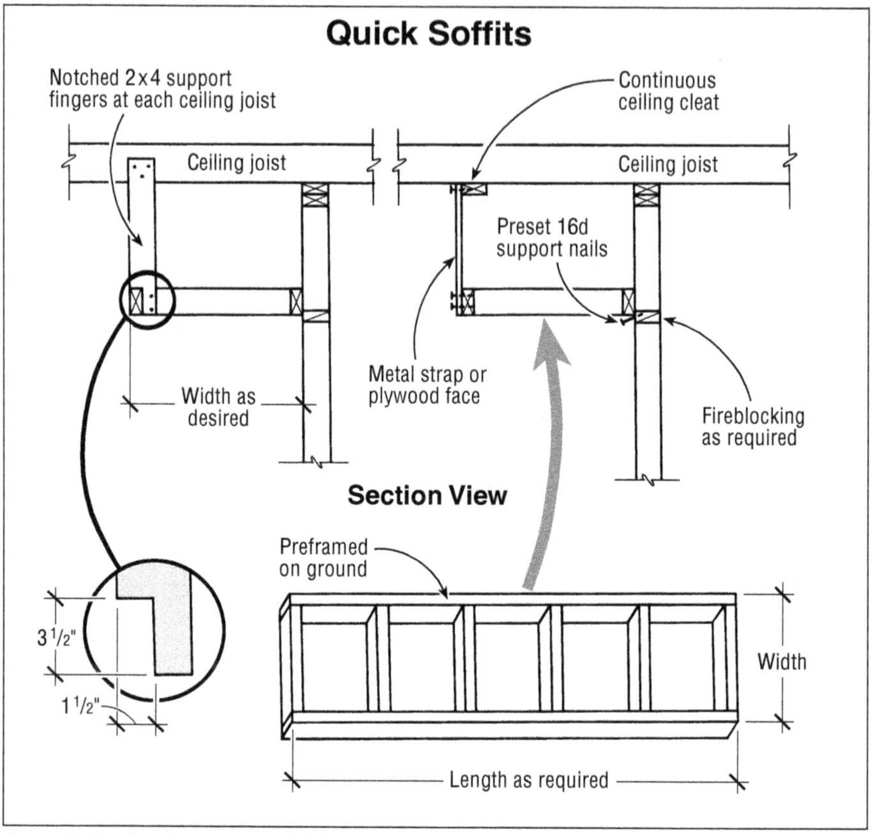

Quick Soffits

Notched 2x4 support fingers at each ceiling joist

Continuous ceiling cleat

Ceiling joist

Ceiling joist

Preset 16d support nails

Width as desired

Metal strap or plywood face

Fireblocking as required

3 1/2"

1 1/2"

Section View

Preframed on ground

Width

Length as required

Figure 2-17. Box-frame the soffit lid and hang it from the ceiling joists using notched 2x4 verticals, plywood, or metal straps.

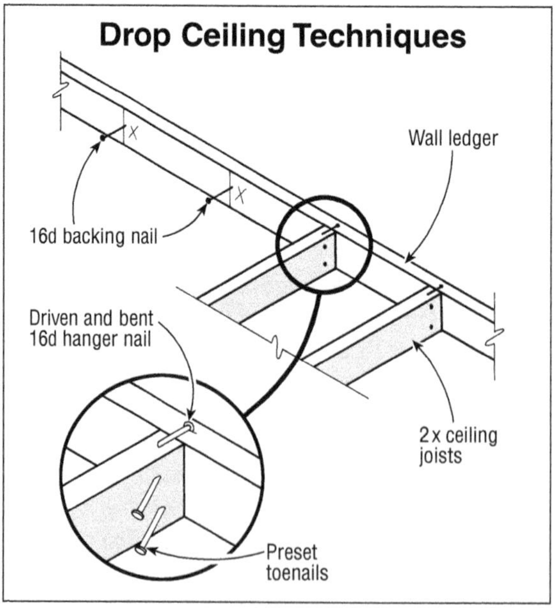

Drop Ceiling Techniques

Wall ledger

16d backing nail

Driven and bent 16d hanger nail

2x ceiling joists

Preset toenails

Figure 2-18. Preset toenails, bent hanger nails, and 16d backing nails help to make a drop ceiling installation go more quickly.

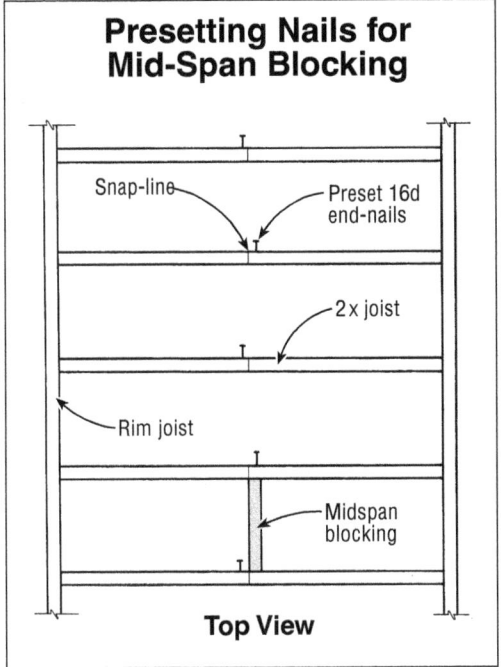

Figure 2-19. Preset the upper end-nails when installing midspan blocks for floor joists. Use staggered blocks as opposed to in-line blocks for ease of nailing.

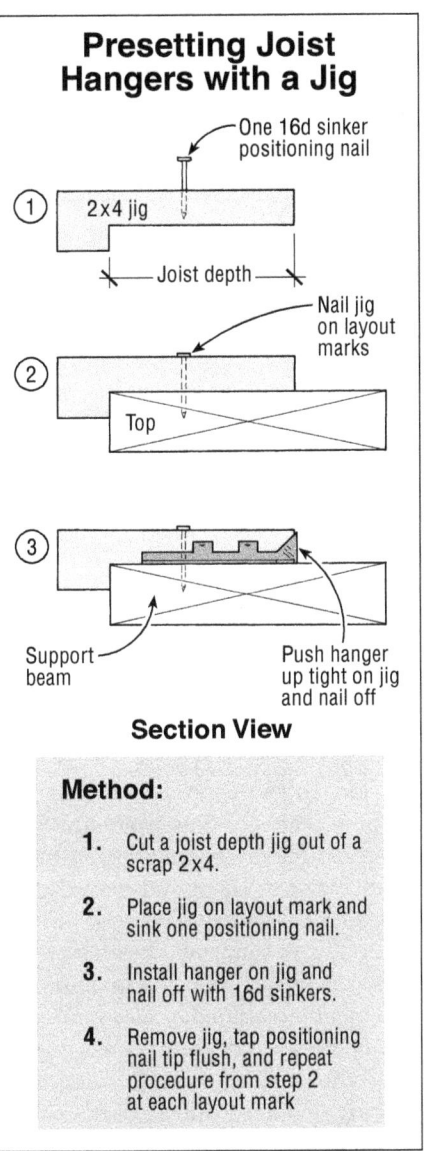

Figure 2-20. Install hangers on a flush-framed beam before raising it in place. When attaching hangers without a top flange, use a notched 2x4 jig as a position gauge.

Install hangers on a flush-framed beam while it is still on the ground. For hangers that do not have a top flange, use a notched 2x4 as a position gauge *(Figure 2-20)*. Toenail the joist into the beam with 16d sinkers *(Figure 2-21)* — instead of using those little hanger nails into the joist — or use Simpson Strong-Tie® LUS and HUS double shear hangers. The toenails prevent the joist from moving in the hanger and causing floor

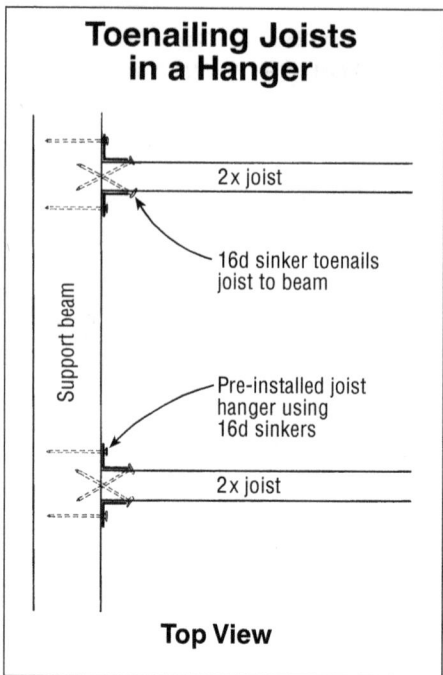

Figure 2-21. Instead of using short hanger nails from the hanger into the joist, toenail the joist to the beam inside the hanger with 16d sinkers. This helps eliminate floor squeaks. Where possible, it is always better to place support beams low and run joists over the top.

squeaks. In most cases, 16d sinkers can be used from the hanger into the support beam for better penetration. (As a general rule of thumb, I always use the biggest nail that will fit into the hole of the hanger flange. If in doubt, refer to the metal manufacturer's nailing schedule.)

A floor beam may be notched on the ends for one or both top plates as long as the structural tapered bearing area in **Figure 2-22** is not infringed upon. This same area is also the maximum allowable amount that can be removed in a taper-cut to make ceiling joists or roof beams fit below the roof plane.

One method of framing a curved floor section is shown in **Figure 2-23**. On some gentle curves, 2x material can be used instead of plywood by making saw kerfs on the back of the board approximately $7/8$ in. deep and $3/4$ in. apart.

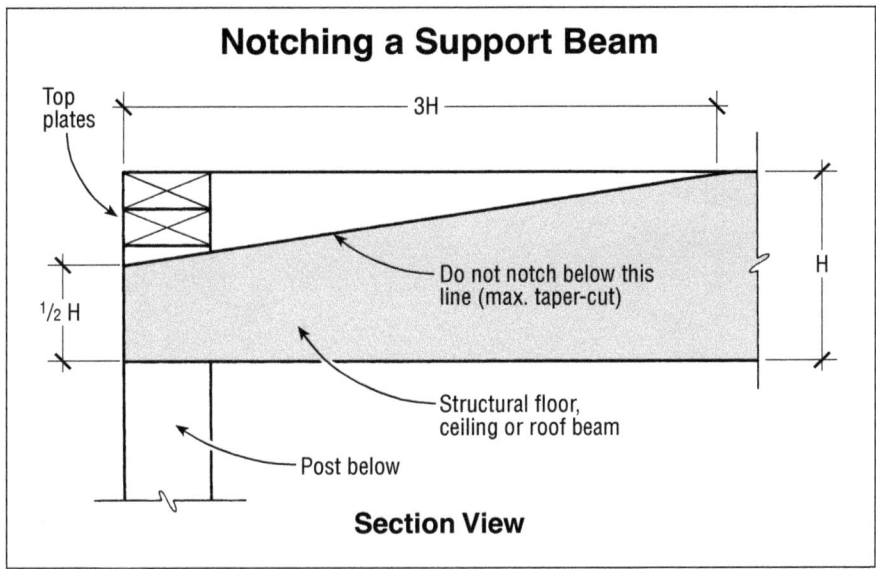

Figure 2-22. It's okay to notch the end of a beam for one or both top plates if it will not cut into the structural taper-shaped area. Running at least one top plate through allows the wall tie to stay intact without the need for a plate strap.

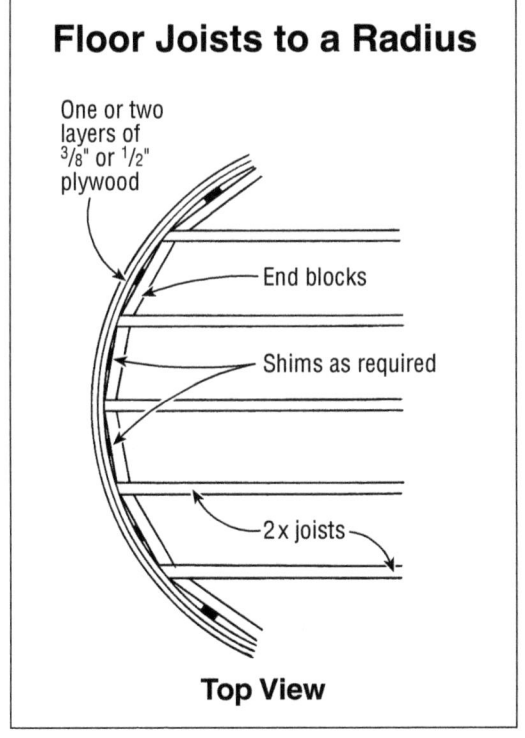

Figure 2-23. One or two layers of $3/8$-in. or $1/2$-in. plywood (or a 2x kerfed on the backside) — bent around like a rim joist — help to finish off a curved floor section.

Chapter 3

Gable Roofs/Production Roof Cutting

RACKS FOR GANG-CUTTING RAFTERS

The first step in production roof cutting is to set up some racks so the rafters can be gang-cut. All of the roof's rafters, including hip and valley jacks, will be marked and cut at one time on these racks *(Photo 3-1)*. A good set of racks doesn't need to be exactly level, but it must be horizontally parallel. Check this by eyeballing the tops of the racks to see if they both plane together. A pair of 2x12s placed on some 4x sleepers works well as a cutting rack (shown in *Figure 3-2*) and raises the top of the rafter

Photo 3-1. Cutting birdsmouths on lapping common rafters using a dado-saw.

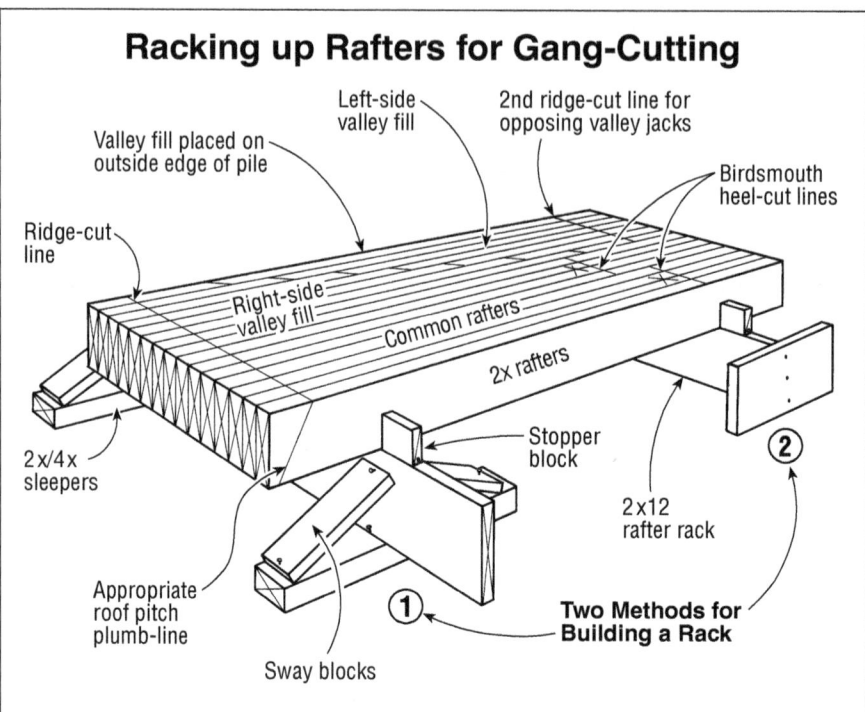

Figure 3-2. A good rafter rack raises the top of the material to a working height of 24 in. to 30 in. A 2x12 on edge set on 4x sleepers works well. One rack is placed 12 in. in from the ridge-cut, and the second rack is positioned under the birdsmouth. A rack holding several different length common rafters will require a compromise position under the birdsmouth end. Generally, the ridge-cut ends are always kept aligned with sets of different length rafters. Valley fill is placed on the outside edge of the rack to enable both ends of the stack to be cut with a saw (far side for a sidewinder as illustrated, near side for a Big Foot® Headcutter).

material to a good working height (24 in. to 30 in. above the ground). Many times the ridge stock can be used for racks. Always brace the middle of a long rack, and wax the top edge to make it easier to slide large beam rafters around.

Keep the racks spaced about 12 in. to 18 in. less than the rafter LL. If you have sets of different length rafters on the same rack, space the racks for the best compromise of positions to support all rafter lengths. Stack the rafter material crown down and leave about 12 in. overhanging one rack. The second rack will sit approximately under the outside wall birdsmouth notch. Nail some stop-blocks positioned like bookends on the rack to keep the rafters together. When drywall will be installed on the underside edge for a cathedral-style ceiling, rafters that are low when racked together can be raised and toenailed to stay flush up top for cutting purposes *(Figure 3-3)*.

When racking the rafters, position the jack-fill on the outside of the pile (Figure 3-2) so it will be easy to make the head-cuts on each end and the

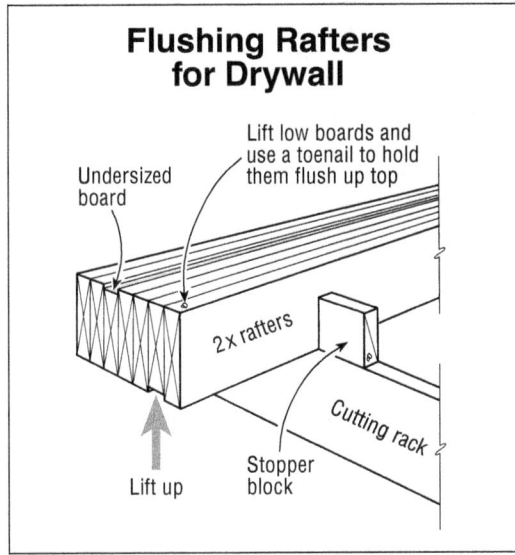

Figure 3-3. With only one exception (valley jacks), all rafter material is placed crown down on the racks. If drywall will be installed on the bottom edge of the rafters, flush this edge before gang-cutting the birdsmouths.

cheek-cuts in the middle as described in the Chapter 5 sections, "Regular Valley Jacks," page 89, and "California Valley Jacks," page 97.

COMMON RAFTERS TO A RIDGE BOARD

With the rafters racked and crowned, determine the common rafter LL in order to snap the ridge-cut and birdsmouth heel-cut lines. The LL calculation for a straight gable is shown in *Figure 3-4*. Subtract the thickness of the ridge from the span and divide by 2 to find the effective run, and then multiply by the COM LL ratio (Chart 2, Appendix A) to find the actual rafter length (LL).

To mark a line for the ridge-cut, come in far enough from the end of the material so the ridge-cuts will remain on the board as they angle down and away (verify this with a Speed® Square). Adjust the chalk line until it is perpendicular to the rafters and snap. From this line, measure towards the tail the calculated rafter LL distance on each side of the pile and snap the heel-cut line. For exposed rafter beams, check diagonals across the pile from heel-cut line to ridge-cut line to be sure the birdsmouths will be square.

Birdsmouth. The birdsmouth notch can be cut with either a dado-saw or a swing-table saw (*Photos 3-5* and *3-6*). The dado-saw cuts the birdsmouth in one easy pass, whereas the swing-table saw requires two passes: one to make the heel-cut and the other for the seat-cut. Use a board as a guide-fence when cutting exposed birdsmouths to get a perfectly straight cut (*Figure 3-7*).

Ridge-Cuts. The most common methods of making ridge-cuts are with either a giant portable circular saw like the Makita 16-in. beam saw (which is limited to 2x6 or smaller rafter stock) or some type of chainsaw device (see the following section, "The History and Tools of Production Roof Cutting"). Both styles of tools are set to the appropriate roof-pitch angle and

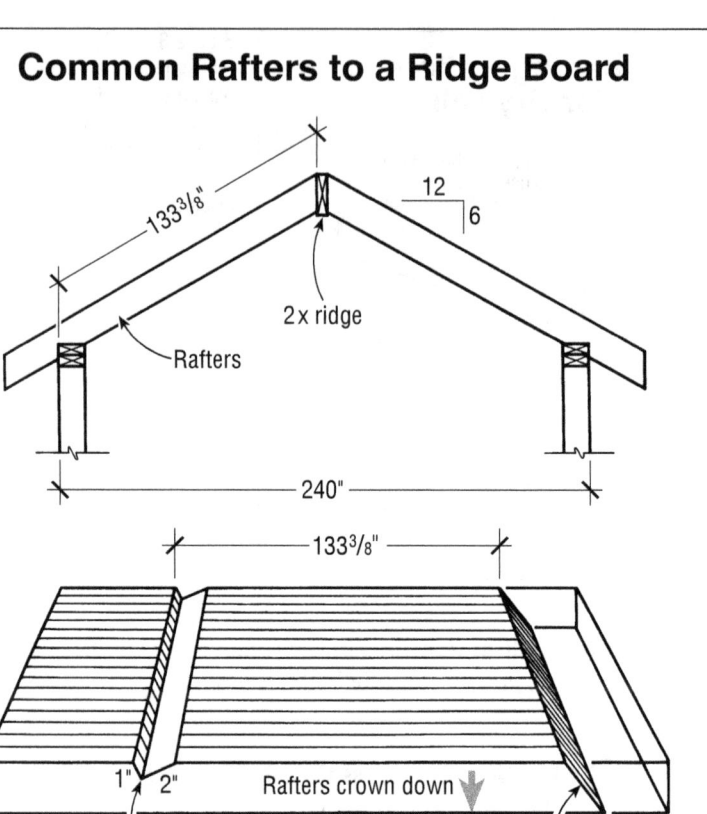

Figure 3-4. Lengths for common rafters that butt a ridge board are calculated in two steps: the first step is to find the effective run, and the second step is to convert that horizontal distance into a rake measurement using a ratio. The appropriate COM LL ratio for each pitch is found in Chart 2 in Appendix A.

See Appendix B

Photo 3-5. This dado-converted Skil® 107 gang-cuts the whole birdsmouth in one pass.

Photo 3-6. Making the birdsmouth seat-cuts with a swing-table installed on a Skil® 77.

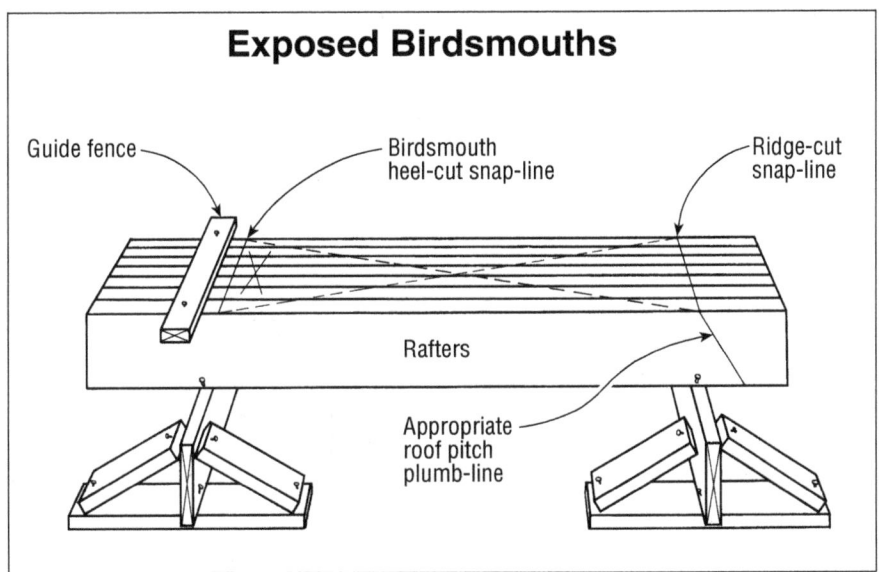

Figure 3-7. Check diagonals across the pile and use a straight board as a guide fence when gang-cutting exposed birdsmouths.

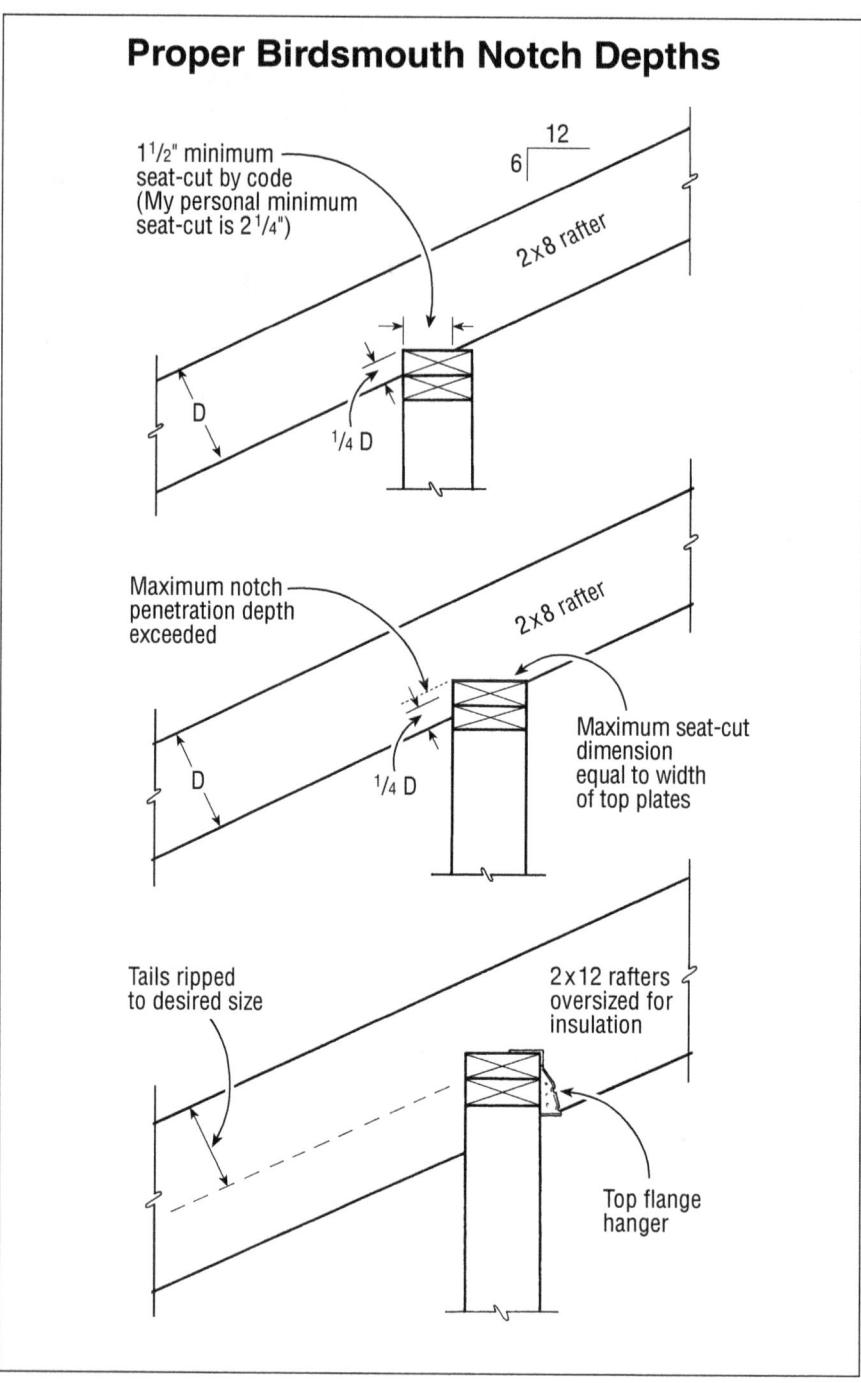

Figure 3-8. Rafter birdsmouths should have a minimum seat-cut dimension of 1½ in. and a maximum dimension no greater than the width of the top plate. Additionally, the birdsmouth notch should not penetrate deeper than one-quarter the distance across the dimensional width of the rafter material for sufficient tail strength on larger overhangs.

■ So what is the proper birdsmouth depth?

This is a common question for which I've heard all kinds of answers. Here's my take: The building code requires a minimum of 1 1/2-in. bearing for load transfer with 2x material. This measurement carries a 100% safety factor over the minimum engineering requirement of 3/4 in. If you've ever noticed, all metal joist hangers for 2x material have a 2-in. to 2 1/4-in. supporting saddle. I figure if it is good enough for the metal manufacturers, it's good enough for me. So for 2x material, I make the birdsmouth seat-cut in the range of 2 1/4 in. to 2 3/4 in. wide, which conversely determines the depth of my birdsmouth heel-cut *(Figure 3-8)*. Drywall can easily span any wall-to-cathedral-ceiling gap caused when the birdsmouth seat doesn't reach all the way across the plate.

David Utterback, a wood specialist with the WWPA, informed me that the building code also limits the birdsmouth notch to a maximum depth of **one quarter the dimensional width** of the material for tail strength. For example: With a 2x6 rafter, the birdsmouth notch should go no farther than 1 3/8 in. across the width of the board (5 1/2" ÷ 4 = 1 3/8"), or converted into roof cutting measurements for a 6/12 pitch roof, a maximum heel-cut depth of 1 1/2 in. with a seat-cut width of 3 in. So watch out for those full-plate-width-style birdsmouths — especially on steeper pitches, as they can easily exceed the maximum notch limitation.

In a cathedral-style gable-roof ceiling where the rafters have been oversized to create more space for thicker insulation, a deeper birdsmouth may be cut, but not so deep as to allow the seat-cut to extend past the inside plate — where it would remain unsupported. This is true even when using 2x12 rafters where 2x6s would suffice due to lumber grading technicalities.

Another area where seat-cut bearing can be a problem is with structural beam hip and valley rafters on low-slope roof pitches. If the seat-cut will extend beyond the wall plate, cut a birdsmouth notch that fits over the wall like the open end of a wrench, and support that part of the rafter inside the building with a joist/beam hanger. In rooms with a flat ceiling height at the top of the exterior walls, the "open-end-wrench" type joist hanger support will not work. For these situations where over-extensions are necessary, try wrapping a metal strap like a band around the rafter just above the inside edge of the seat-cut, or try upgrading the member to TimberStrand® LSL engineered lumber (manufactured by Trus Joist), which is ten times stronger across the grain than dimensional lumber.

---

run through the racked rafter stock following the ridge-cut snap-line. The sidewinder blade was very popular in the 1960s – 1970s to finish off ridge-cuts made by saws that were unable to reach all the way through rafter material racked on edge (see ***Photo 3-9***).

An alternative to using these tools — when all you've got is a regular Skilsaw® — is to make a starter pass following the ridge-cut snap-line with the saw set to maximum depth at the appropriate roof-pitch angle (Chart 3, Appendix A). Return the saw to square and change the depth to 1 3/4 in. On the right side of the pile (looking at the ridge-cut end), draw a plumb ridge-cut line down from the starter pass with an adjustable Quick Square® and saw vertically to finish the cut. The saw blade will leave a kerf-line on the second board. Push the cut board back toward the tail and out of the way of the saw table. Now, use the saw-kerf line as a guide to cut the second board,

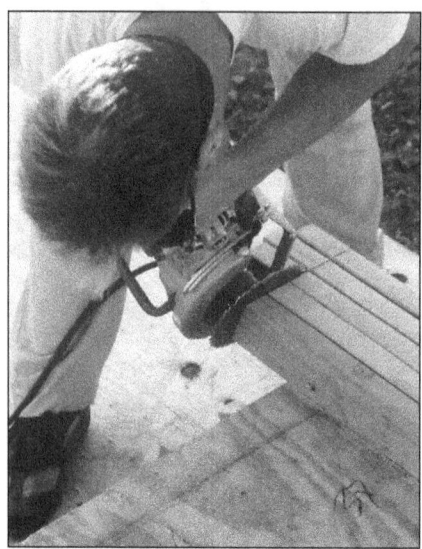

Photo 3-9. Using the sidewinder blade to finish off the ridge-cuts was a technique used in the California tracts during the 1960s-1970s.

and so forth. (With the sidewinder blade there was no need to push each board back to make room for the saw foot since the blade was outside the guard.) Check the cuts every so often with a rafter square to make sure the cut is not getting off, or snap a top-of-ridge-cut line under the pile and peek below to see if the ridge-cuts are staying true. If the roof pitch is extremely steep, it may be necessary to lay each board flat and cut each ridge-cut individually.

To help your roof cutting tools last, always keep the blades sharp and lightly coated with silicone spray. A little paraffin wax on the bottom of the saw table makes it easier to push the saw across a rack of lumber by lessening the friction between the saw foot and the wood.

THE HISTORY AND TOOLS OF PRODUCTION ROOF CUTTING

Before the late 1950s, production roof cutting was virtually unheard of. But when the building boom hit the Los Angeles basin in the late 1950s and early 1960s, house building methods changed radically. Contractors began throwing up whole tracts of houses in record time. It seemed that a field stood empty one day, and the next day it was filled with houses. Tract carpenters were paid by the piece — so much money per square foot to do a certain task. For example, 5¢ a square foot to snap, plate, and scratch; 8¢ a square foot to stand walls; 4¢ a square foot to cut rafters, etc. (mid-1970s prices). With pay for performance as the incentive, carpenters began to specialize in only one specific assembly skill. To save time, they constantly thought up new techniques and short-cuts, and they invented and modified tools. From these "piece work" days came most of the specialty framing tools that we use today (bolt markers, layout sticks, rafter squares, framing hammers, saw hangers, etc.).

Production roof cutting reached its peak during the late 1960s and early 1970s and died almost overnight when roof trusses gained prominence in the late 1970s.

Although gang-marking racked lumber dates back to the Middle Ages, rafters were still laid flat and cut one at a time up until the late 1950s. The Skil® 117 Groover changed that forever. The Groover was a 2-in. dado-saw manufactured by Skil Power Tools from the late 1940s to the mid 1950s.

Photo 3-10. The historical sidewinder blade stuck out past the saw foot and the blade guard, making it inherently dangerous. It was forced out of production by OSHA in the 1990s.

(See the photo in "About the Author," page vi.) It was based on the Skil® 107 (10-in. wormdrive circular saw) and was originally designed to cut a square notch in beams or joists to run electrical wiring. With a little modification to the blade guard, it was able to tilt sideways, making the Skil® 117 the perfect tool for gang-cutting birdsmouths on racked lumber.

By the mid 1960s when the supply of "Groovers" had dried up, saw shops in the Los Angeles area were already busy modifying the standard Skil® 107 with wider $3^{1}/_{2}$-in. dado sets. Nate Fletcher, formerly of Nate's Saw Shop (Anaheim, Calif.) was one of the primary innovators behind this and several other tool modifications. Nate modified close to two hundred Skil® 107s, including one for me.

When the supply of 107s dwindled, several saw shops around California began modifying the newer Skil® 77 and 87 ($7^{1}/_{4}$-in. and $8^{1}/_{4}$-in. wormdrives) with dado sets. Pairis Products, Inc. (Phelan, Calif.) made a dado kit for the 77, while Furber Saw (Martinez, Calif.) made a dado kit for the 87. Both kits were available up until the early 1990s.

While the dado-saw required quite an investment, the swing-table was inexpensive and simple. It has been around almost as long as the dado-saw, having its beginning in the early 1960s, and it is favored by most everyone other than the dedicated roof cutter. A swing-table installed on a standard circular saw allowed it to swing well past 45° and get the shallow angle required for the seat-cut. Both Pairis Products and Big Foot® Saw Adapters (Las Vegas, Nev.) make models for various saws.

While the dado-saw and swing-table saw made quick work of the birdsmouth, a fast method was needed for the ridge-cut. The largest portable circular saw in the early 1960s was the Skil® 127 (12-in. wormdrive circular saw), which could cut 2x4 rafters racked on edge (the common rafter size in those days) but fell short of reaching through a rack of 2x6s. The method developed for larger material was to use the Skil® 127 (or even a standard $7^{1}/_{4}$-in. Skil®) to make a starter ridge-cut pass, and finish off the cut with a sidewinder blade *(Photo 3-10)*.

While inherently dangerous, the sidewinder in the right hands proved to

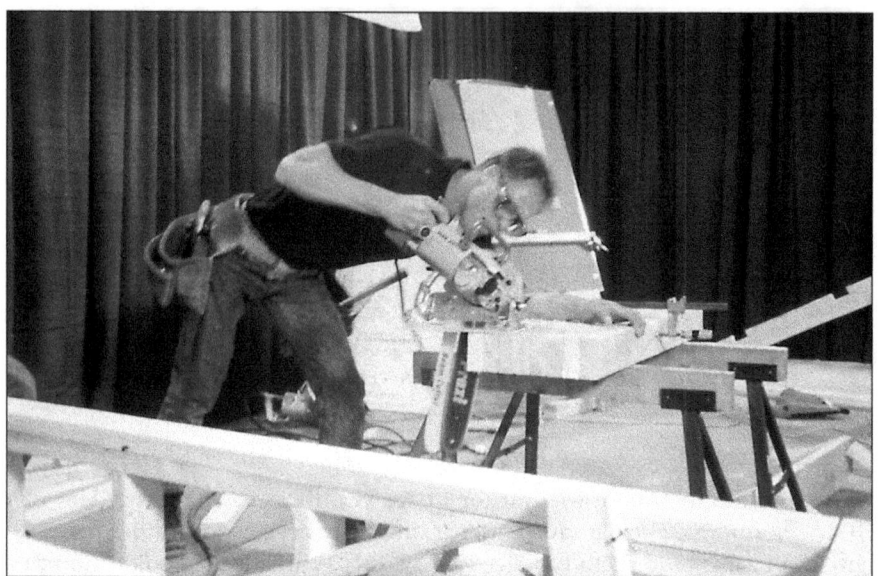

Photo 3-11. Using the Prazi® Beam Cutter to make ridge-cuts at the 1996 JLC-Live show.

be a very efficient tool for roof cutting. OSHA eventually pressured the blade out of manufacture in the 1990s.

In the mid 1960s, Nate Fletcher began modifying the Skil® 127 with 18-in. or 20-in. blades, which allowed roof cutters to make the ridge-cut in one pass. The 20-in. saw could cut through 2x8 rafters on edge up to a maximum pitch of around 5/12. In the late 1970s, Makita introduced the 16-in. beam saw (model 5402). It was able to cut 2x6s on edge up to a pitch of 5/12 but lacked the power for long, continuous rip-style cutting as it was designed more as a crosscut cutoff saw.

In the late 1980s, the Linear Link® saw (Muskegon Tools, North Muskegon, Mich.) arrived on the scene with a self-oiling 14-in. chainsaw bar attached to a Skil® 77 motor body. Because it could be tilted sideways, many carpenters used it to make the ridge-cut, but it was underpowered and not nearly as precise as a circular saw. Another similar device, the Prazi® Beam Cutter (Prazi USA, Plymouth, Mass.), came along in the mid 1990s *(Photo 3-11)*. The Prazi® Beam Cutter was less expensive and much easier to attach to a circular saw motor body, but it had no provision for self-oiling. In 1997, Big Foot Saw Adapters made available the "Headcutter," an adjustable saw table that attaches to a gas-powered chainsaw. I believe it is the best option available today for gang-style cutting the heads of common rafters. It combines a powerful gas motor, a self-oiling chain system, and a large saw foot for making very accurate cuts *(Photo 3-12)*. Together with a chisel-tooth ripping chain, it is hard to tell the cut made with the Headcutter from one made with a circular saw. (The Headcutter also works well for precutting bundled I-joists to length for floor spans or even large birdsmouth seat-cuts when the swing-table version is coupled with a "stubby" solid chain bar.)

To be totally fair in my reporting of history, there were also some early attempts to use the old Comet and DeWalt radial-arm saws to cut rafters, but the technique never really caught on because only small bunches of rafters could be gang-cut together. Two saws were used in assembly-line fashion, one with a dado for the birdsmouth and the other with a circular blade for the ridge-cut.

European Cutters. The Europeans have been gang-cutting timber-frame beams since the late 1950s or early 1960s. Mafell AG (Germany) began manufacturing a 16-in. diameter portable circular saw in the early 1950s. They added an adjustable vertical cutting electric chainsaw and a dado-saw to their selection in the late 1950s/early 1960s. Today Mafell offers a wide variety of specialty timber framing tools including a $4^1/2$-in. dado-saw called a skew-notch and tenon cutter. Their tools are very well made, but a bit pricey for most carpenters to have in their toolbox.

Photo 3-12. Making ridge-cuts with a gas-powered chainsaw and an adjustable table attachment.

My Tools. Since I learned roof cutting in the Southern California tracts during the mid 1970s, I was weaned on the old dado-saws and the sidewinder. When I switched to building custom homes, I kept these tools and added a Makita 16-in. beam saw and a swing-table for my Skil® 77. I use the Makita beam saw on exposed beam work when I absolutely cannot use a Skil® 77 or a chainsaw. I use the swing-table on steep-pitched roofs (over 8/12), since my old dado-saw has to work hard to chew through all that wood, and I want it to last my lifetime at least. The most recent addition to my roof cutting saw line-up is an adjustable table for my gas-powered chainsaw (from Big Foot® Saw Adapters), which I now use instead of the sidewinder blade. For rafter layout, I use Stanley's 6-in. and 12-in. adjustable Quick Squares® (Stanley Tool Co., New Britain, Conn.).

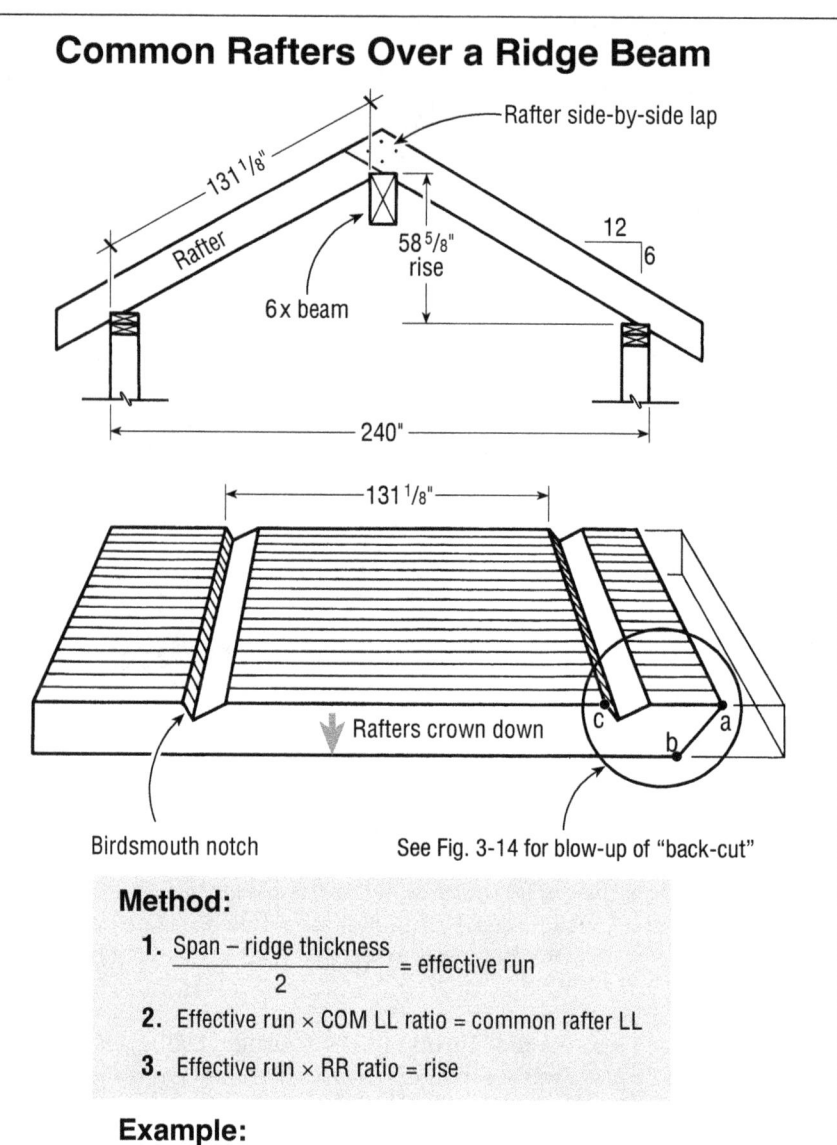

Figure 3-13. For common rafters lapping over a center ridge beam, the LL between the outside wall and ridge birdsmouth is calculated using the effective run to the ridge beam. The rise to the top of the ridge beam above the outside wall is found by multiplying the effective run by the appropriate RR ratio.

COMMON RAFTERS LAPPING OVER A CENTER RIDGE BEAM

Figure 3-13 illustrates a gable roof with common rafters sitting on a ridge beam and lapping — instead of butting — a ridge board. There is no ridge-cut, but a birdsmouth notch is cut for the ridge beam. The rise for the ridge beam and the rafter LL are both figured using the same effective run. To find this, subtract the thickness of the ridge beam from the span, and divide by 2. To find the rise to the top of the ridge above the outside wall, multiply this effective run by the RR ratio. To find the LL between the top and bottom heel-cuts, multiply the effective run by the COM LL ratio. Common rafters for a shed roof are calculated similarly, with the effective run being measured from the outside edge of the shorter wall to the inside edge of the taller wall.

To lay out lapping common rafters (Figure 3-13), start at the tail-end of the racked rafter stock and — leaving enough tail length for the overhang — snap a line for the heel-cut of the exterior birdsmouth. From that line, measure towards the ridge end of the racked rafter stock the length of the calculated LL, and snap a second heel-cut line (Figure 3-13, line **c**) for the ridge beam. Then, referring to ***Figure 3-14***, draw a 6/12 plumb-line down the side of the rafter from heel-cut line **c** at the head. From this first plumb-line, measure over perpendicular 1/2 thk. of the ridge beam to draw a second plumb-line, denoting the center of the ridge beam. Place a small scrap of rafter stock with a 6/12 ridge-cut tangent to this line to mark the back-cut **a-b** (Figure 3-14). This back-cut is necessary to keep the common rafter from protruding through the opposite plane of the roof.

Some folks prefer to cut the lap in the air, but you can also gang-cut the back-cut on the rack similar to making an inverted ridge-cut using a chain-saw-type angle cutter. Make this cut following the line snapped across the pile at **a** in Figure 3-14. The correct saw-blade angle setting to make the back-cut at **a** is 90° less twice the degree of roof-pitch or 37° for a 6/12 pitch roof (90° − 2[26.5°] = 37°). If the roof pitch is less than 5/12, the back-cut angle will be greater than 45° and outside the angle limitations of the saw. In this case, square-cut the end of the racked lumber just inside snap-line **a** to create a uniform vertical surface, and snap a horizontal line along the ends at **d** where the ridge-cut pattern intersects the square-cut ends. Make a saw pass following this line with a Skilsaw®, or chainsaw-type cutter set to twice the degree of the roof pitch as the blade angle. A line snapped across the bottom of the rafters at **b** will verify if the back-cut is staying true.

GABLE STUDS

To cut gable studs, begin by calculating the number needed for half the gable-end span. This is done by dividing the run in inches by the on-center spacing and dropping the fraction (round down, because typically the vertical brace under the ridge will also serve as the tallest gable stud). Stack this amount of 8-ft. studs — plus one extra — flat on top of each other with one end against a wall to keep them aligned. The extra stud on the bottom of the pile serves as a buffer to keep the saw blade from slicing into the slab

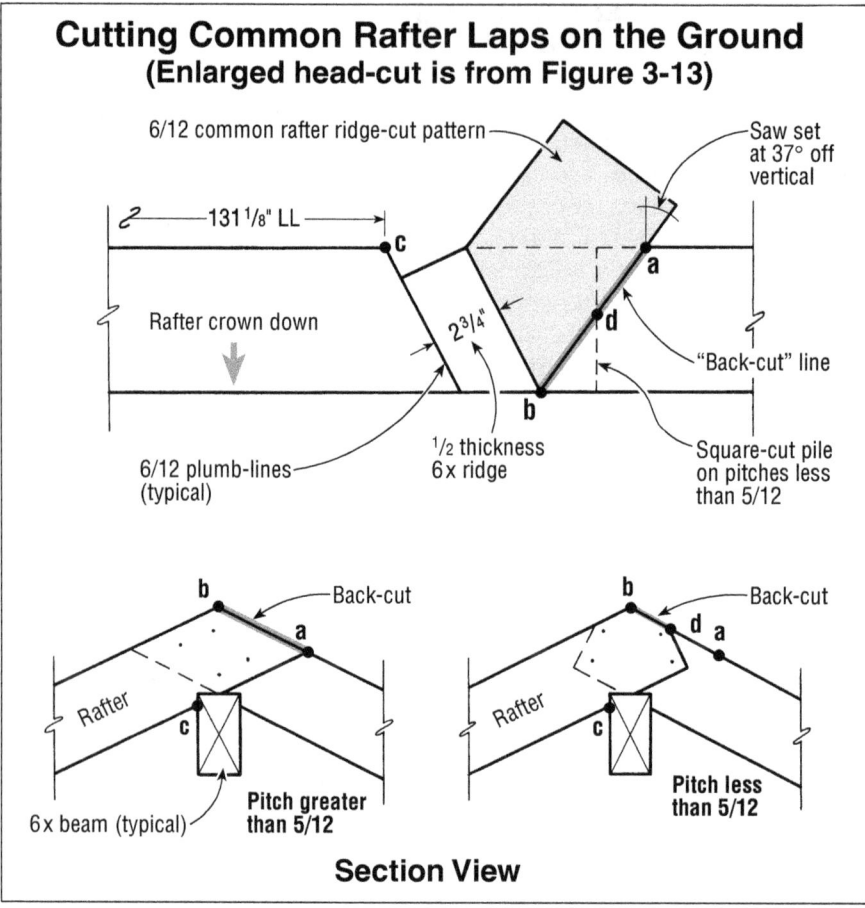

Figure 3-14. The lapping common rafter back-cut at the ridge is made at point **a** with the saw angle set to 90° less twice the degree of the roof pitch. On roofs with a pitch of 5/12 or less, the back-cut angle is greater than 45° and, therefore, outside the angular adjustment of most saws. In this case, square-cut the pile inside point **a** to create a flat vertical surface on which to make a horizontal saw-cut along the end of the pile at **d** with the saw bevel set to twice the pitch of the roof.

or subfloor *(Figure 3-15)*.

Multiply the on-center spacing by the RR ratio to find the gable stud step measurement (16" × .5000 {6/12 RR ratio} = 8"). Then starting on the top of the pile, progressively mark the top edge of each stud longer by the step amount until the required number has been laid out. (A small scrap of wood cut to the length of the 8-in. step is helpful when marking.) When it is required to line up the gable studs with the wall studs below, field measure the shortest one, and step up from it.

Now with one-half the gable end marked, set up the cutoffs as the second half. To do this, pair up the shortest in one set with the longest in the other set and work backwards. The layout marks denote the SP of the first

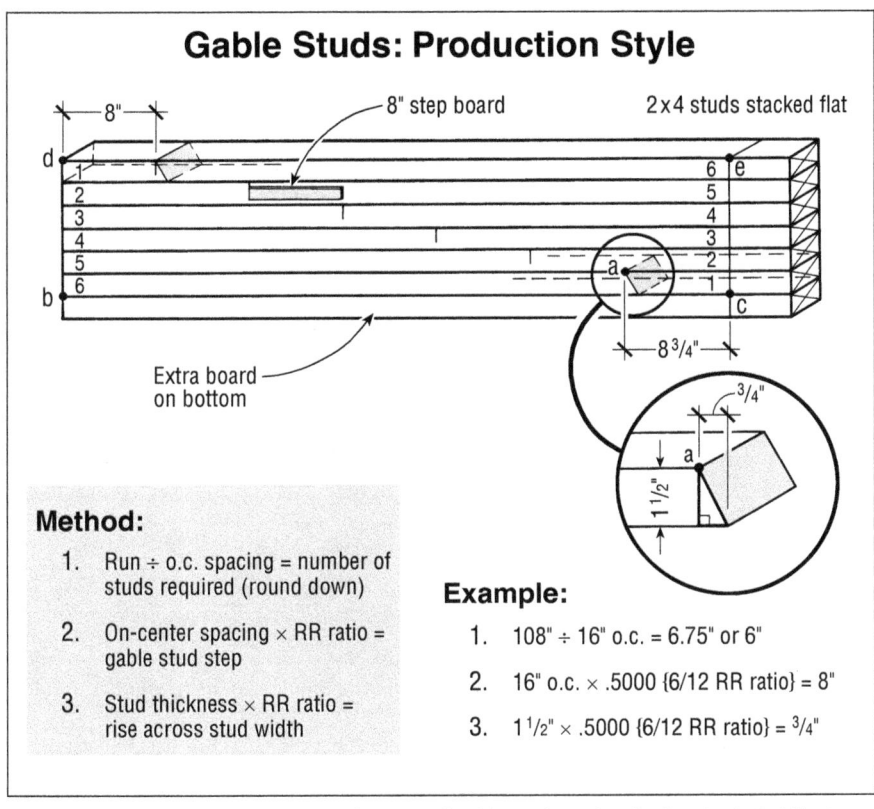

Figure 3-15. To pair up the two opposing sets of gable studs at the cheek-cut, start at the top of the pile and progressively mark each board one step longer until the required number of studs for one-half the span is reached. Use the cutoffs from the first set for the studs of the second set by pairing the shortest of the second set with the longest from the first set similar to what is shown in the upcoming Figure 5-6 for valley jacks. See Appendix B

set and the LP of the second set as shown at **a** (Figure 3-15). The LP measurement of a gable stud can be determined either by making a trial saw pass at the roof pitch degrees on the first gable stud and measuring the change across the thickness of the board, or mathematically by multiplying the stud thickness by the RR ratio. Add this rise to the first gable stud length to find an LP measurement (8" + 3/4" = 8 3/4"), which is then combined with the longest gable stud from the first set **(a)** to mark the location for the square-cut end of the second set at **c**. Transfer the combined measurement of the two sets **(b-c)** to the top of the pile **(d-e)** and connect the two points with a straight line **(e-c)**. Both sets are now laid out to be identical.

Gang-cut the square-cut ends **(e-c)** with a chainsaw (in the old days, a sidewinder blade was used instead) before making the cheek-cuts at each step mark with a circular saw's bevel set to the degrees of the roof-pitch. Multiple sets (for houses with several gable ends) can be cut at once by stacking several rows of 8-ft. studs side by side and cutting across all the rows at each step layout mark.

Chapter 4

Regular Hip Roofs

Calculating the lengths of common rafters in a hip roof is identical to calculating those in a gable roof, so refer to Chapter 3 if a review is needed. The name "king common" is given to the regular common rafters that sandwich the hip rafters.

HIP ROOF RIDGE LENGTHS

The theoretical ridge length for a full hip roof (i.e., hip-end at each end of the ridge) is the length of the building less its width. When framing with 2x rafters and a 2x ridge, the actual ridge length would be the theoretical ridge length plus the thickness of the ridge board (1$\frac{1}{2}$") to allow a common rafter (king common) to stack directly off each end of the ridge *(Figure 4-1)*.

The actual and theoretical ridge lengths for an intersecting hip roof section are the same, and they match the length of the intersecting building section when a common rafter (king common) is stacked directly off the hip-end of the intersecting ridge. The centers of the two valley rafters will connect directly opposite each other at the interior end of this ridge length. A broken hip running off the interior end of the ridge necessitates extending the ridge board by at least an amount equal to the thickness of the ridge and $\frac{1}{2}$ 45° thk. of the broken hip to allow for the connection.

THE HIP RAFTER

To calculate the LL of the hip rafter, take the span, subtract off the thickness of the ridge, divide by 2 to find the effective run, and multiply by the

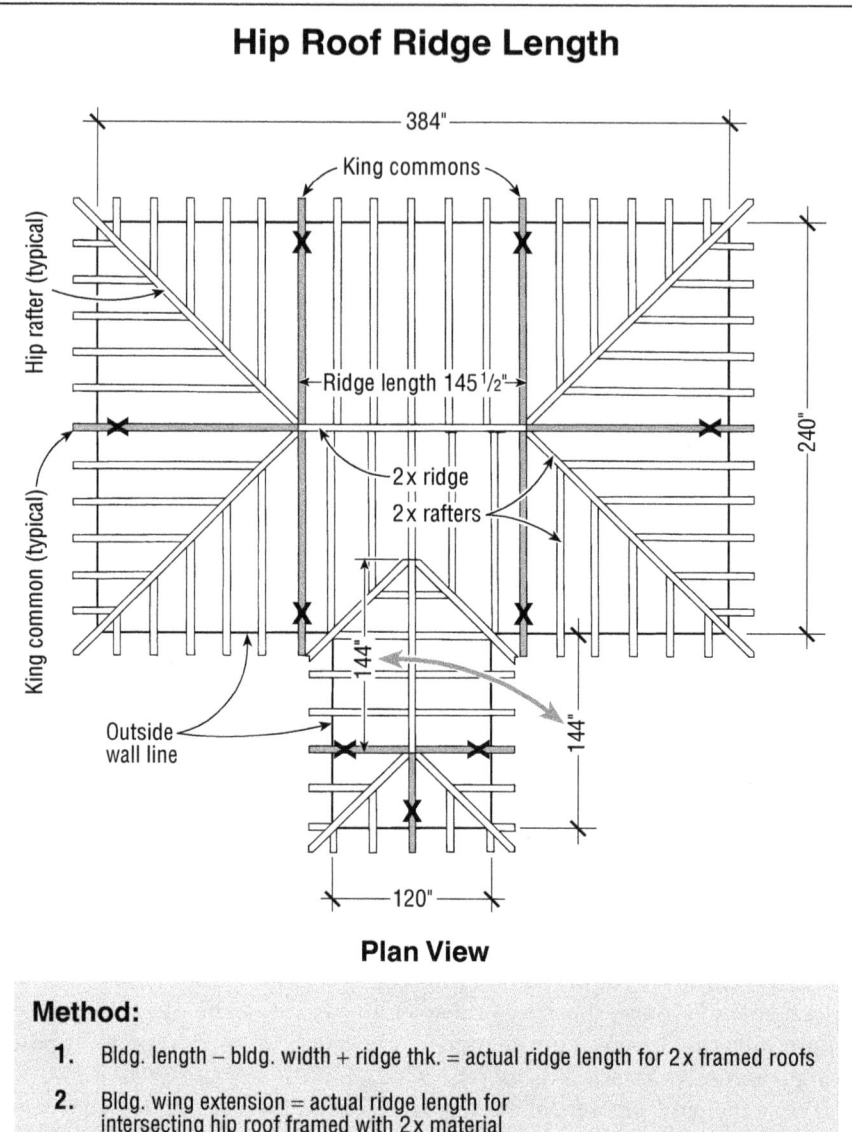

Hip Roof Ridge Length

Plan View

Method:

1. Bldg. length − bldg. width + ridge thk. = actual ridge length for 2x framed roofs

2. Bldg. wing extension = actual ridge length for intersecting hip roof framed with 2x material

Example:

1. 384" − 240" + 1 1/2" = 145 1/2"
2. 144" = 144"

Figure 4-1. When the ridge and rafters are made from 2x material, frame a king common rafter straight off each end of the ridge. The ridge length for the full hip in this situation is the building length less the building width plus the ridge thickness. The ridge length for an intersecting hip roof section is the length of the building wing extension.

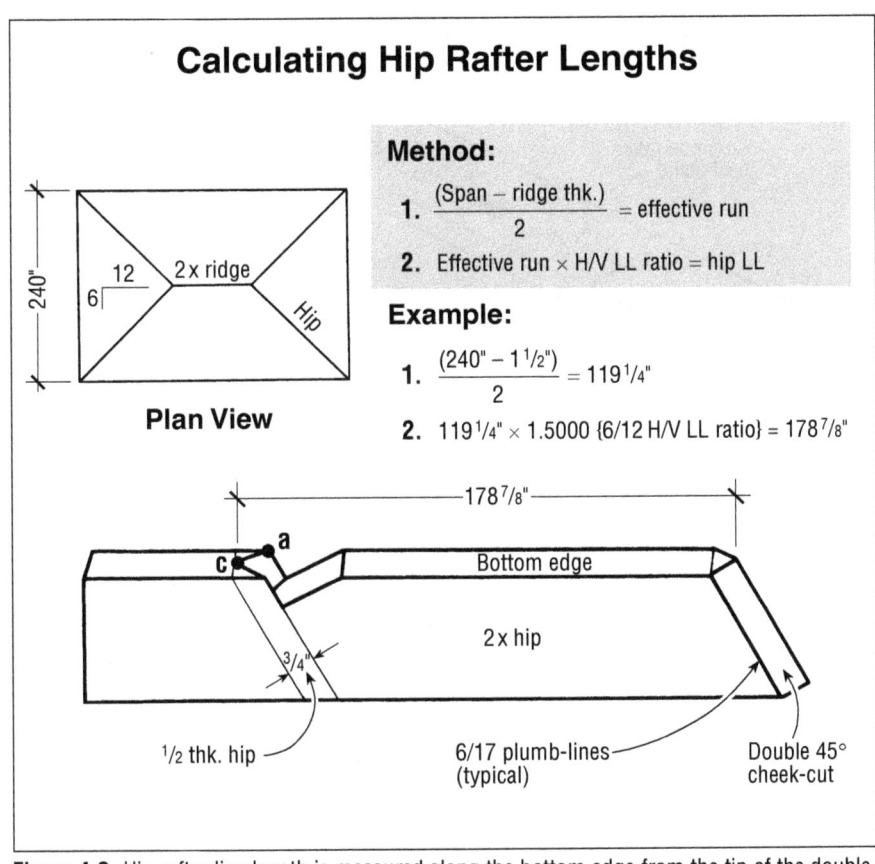

Figure 4-2. Hip rafter line length is measured along the bottom edge from the tip of the double 45° cheek-cut at the head to the point of the V-notch at the birdsmouth. See Appendix B

appropriate H/V LL ratio (See Chart 2, Appendix A). The result is measured along the bottom edge of the board from the tip of the double 45° cheek-cut at the head to the point of the V-notch at the birdsmouth *(Figure 4-2)*. Don't forget to set the Quick Square® for the hip/valley plumb-cut. (I often keep two adjustable rafter squares painted different colors — one for hips and one for commons — so I won't screw up.)

If the hips and ridge are beams and the rafters are 2x material, calculate the hips for the full theoretical run so they will butt head to head against the end of the ridge. For this situation, the ridge length is shorter by half its thickness at each hip end as opposed to the standard condition of king common to end of ridge.

To lay out the hip seat-cut, mark the heel-stand of a common rafter **(b)** down from the top edge of the hip rafter on a plumb-line drawn 1/2 thk. of the hip uphill **(a)** from the LL plumb-line **(c)**. The 1/2 thk. dimension is

REGULAR HIP ROOFS   **65**

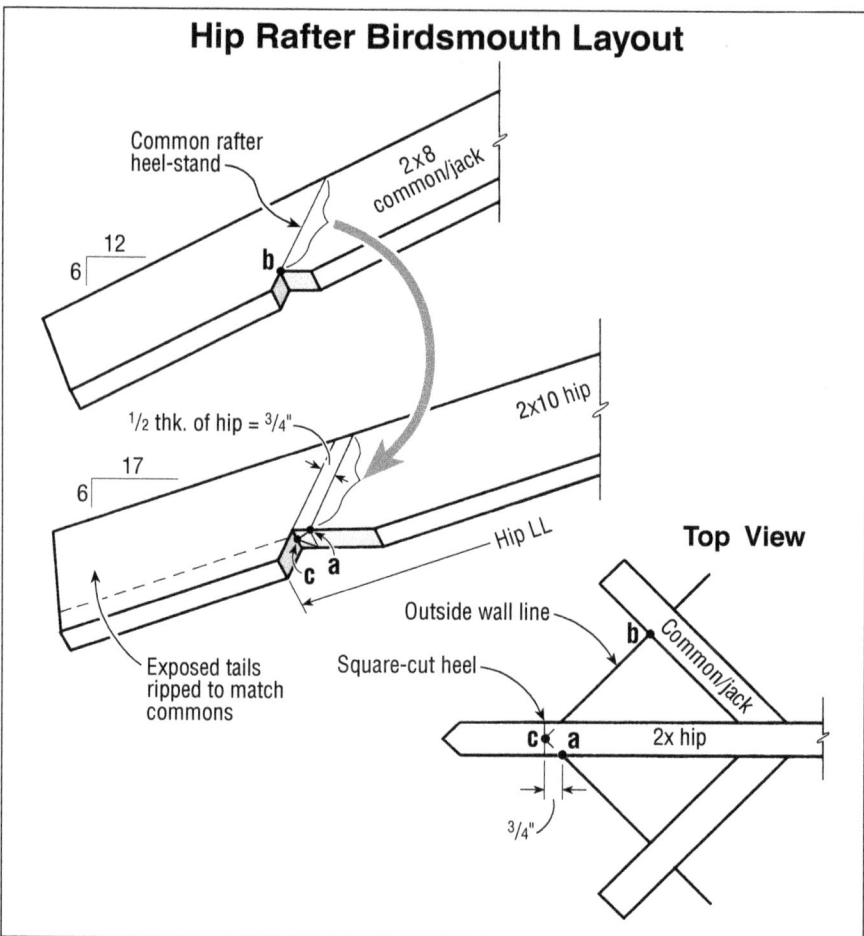

Figure 4-3. To lay out the hip rafter birdsmouth seat-cut line, mark the heel-stand measurement from a common rafter on a plumb-line drawn 1/2 thk. of the hip uphill from the lower LL plumb-line. For 2x material, square-cut the heel at **c**, and butt to the outside corner of the building.

measured perpendicular to the LL plumb-line. Draw the level seat-cut line through this mark *(Figure 4-3)*. (*Note*: Plumb-line **a** is where the side of the board crosses the outside wall line.)

On a 2x hip, square-cut the heel-cut at the LL mark (**c**), and butt it right to the corner of the building. When a beam is used as a hip and the tail is exposed, the V-notch heel-cut must be chiseled or cut with a chainsaw. One way to avoid cutting the exposed V-notch is to square-cut the heel-cut at **a**

■ Calculating the Heel-Stand

While measuring the heel-stand of a common rafter is simple, it can also be found mathematically by multiplying the width of the common rafter by the COM LL ratio to find the total plumb dimension, then subtracting the depth of the birdsmouth. For example, a 2x8 rafter at 6/12 pitch with a 1-in. birdsmouth has a heel-stand of 7 3/8 in.: (7 1/2" × 1.1180 {6/12 COM LL ratio} − 1" = 7 3/8").

and clip the corner of the wall plates as shown in ***Figure 4-4.***

If the top of the hip will be backed after it is laid out, mark the common rafter heel-stand measurement ($7^3/8$" in Figure 4-3) at the LL plumb-line **(c)** where the centerline of the hip crosses the outside wall line, instead of the uphill position that's shown. If the hip board is backed prior to rafter layout, mark the heel-stand at **a**.

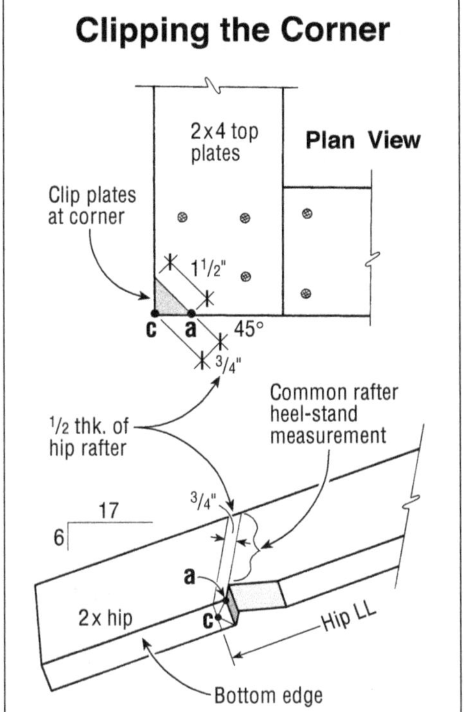

The ridge end of the hip is cut with a plumb double 45° cheek-cut. To mark the cut-lines for these angles, measure downhill $1/2$ thk. of the hip perpendicular to the LL plumb-line at the head. When a hip runs up to the outside corner of a flat roof section, the head-cut must be made with a double 45° V-notch rather than the standard wedge-shaped double 45° cheek-cut (see ***Photo 4-5***). To find the cut-lines in this case, measure uphill $1/2$ thk. of the hip from the LL plumb-line at the head.

Clipping the Corner

Figure 4-4. An alternative to V-notching an exposed hip birdsmouth is to clip the top plates at the building corner and square-cut the heel-cut at the uphill end of the V-notch.

BACKING A HIP

Backing can be done on the top and/or the bottom of a hip as illustrated in ***Figure 4-6***. To find the rip-angle and the distance down perpendicular from the upper edge of the hip to the top rip-cut lines, use a framing square set to the unit of roof rise (6" for 6/12 pitch) and the LL for 12 in.

■ **Laying Out Hip/Valley Birdsmouth Depth**

I do not use or like the term "dropping a hip." It is an extremely confusing and misleading expression. No board is "dropped," rather the birdsmouth depth is positioned depending on whether you want an edge or the centerline of a hip/valley to plane in with the top of the adjoining common rafters. If you want to plane in an outside top edge of a hip/valley, position the heel-stand of a common rafter where that hip/valley edge crosses the exterior plate-line (unbacked hips, backed valleys). If you want to plane in the centerline of a hip/valley, position the heel-stand of a common rafter where a hip/valley centerline crosses the exterior plate-line (backed hips, unbacked valleys). Centerline measurements are marked on the side of the board by squaring out to the edge. These principles work with both regular- and irregular-pitch hip/valleys.

Photo 4-5. Shown here is a hip from an inside 45° corner wall to an outside 90° ridge corner. Two broken hips are located beyond to the left, and another one is located on the right. The 2x spacer at the lower end of a broken hip facilitates correct positioning. The two rafters directly above the 45° corner wall are actually two hips since they are at 45° to the roof plane.

of hip run (12" × 1.5000 {6/12 H/V LL ratio} = 18") to mark a line across the width of the hip rafter board (shown in **B**). Divide this line in half (since the hip is backed to its centerline) with a second line drawn perpendicular to the edge of the board to find the backing distance ($1/4$"), and note the angle formed with a Speed® Square (or found in Chart 6, Appendix A) to set the saw-blade angle ($18 1/2°$).

To locate the rip-cut lines for backing the bottom edge, place the plumb dimension of a common rafter (shown in **A**) on a hip plumb-line (shown in **B**), and measure square across the hip to that point. This measurement is the perpendicular distance between the top and bottom rip-cut lines ($7 7/8$"). Rip the bottom edge in an inverted V-shape with the same rip-angle calculated for the top edge. (Rip-angles and rip-cut lines can also be found using the technique shown in the Chapter 8 section "Backing Bastard Rafters," page 183.)

HIP JACKS

The production method of cutting hip jacks pairs the opposing sets of jacks together on the same board. To find the number of boards required for each paired set of hip jacks, divide the appropriate run by the on-center spacing (example: 120" ÷ 16" o.c. = 7.5). Round down if using material 2 ft. longer than the common rafters, or round up if using material of the same length. For overhangs greater than 2 ft., an extra board will probably be required for each paired set. Don't forget to place them crown down on the rack. (*Note:* To keep everything simple, I always use material the same length as the common rafters and just add the necessary extra boards.)

There are two common ways to cut hip jacks. One method starts layout from the king common and moves towards the outside building corner; the second method starts layout from the outside building corner and moves towards the king common.

The key to cutting hip fill laid out from the king common is to find the LL of the longest hip jack to the SP and progressively step down the remaining jacks. This is done by shortening the adjacent king common

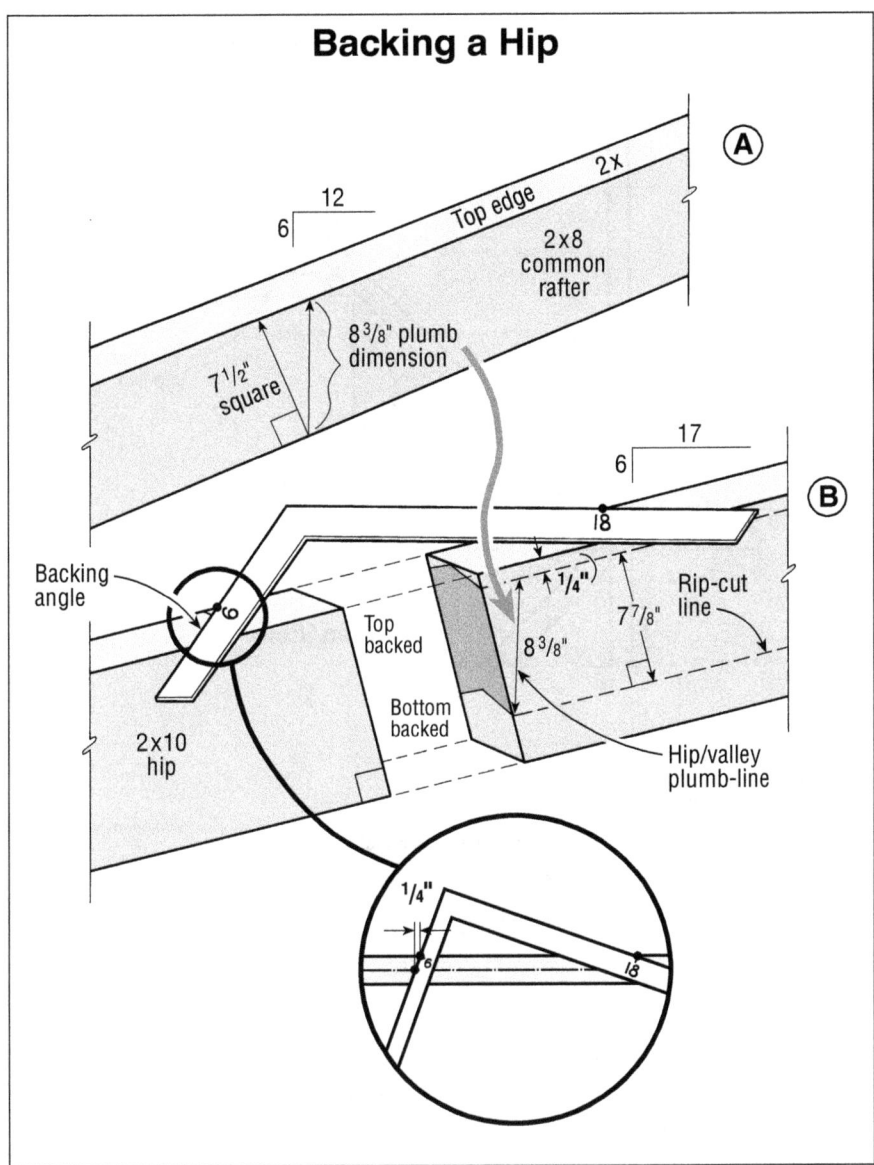

Figure 4-6. A framing square positioned correctly across one-half the edge of the hip material will find the measurement for locating the backing rip-cut line and the rip-angle.

■ Calculating the Jack-Step

The "jack-step" is the amount that each jack rafter is shortened or lengthened in sequence to continue the on-center spacing. It is calculated by multiplying the on-center spacing by the appropriate COM LL ratio (example: 16" o.c. × 1.1180 {6/12 COM LL ratio} = 17 7/8").

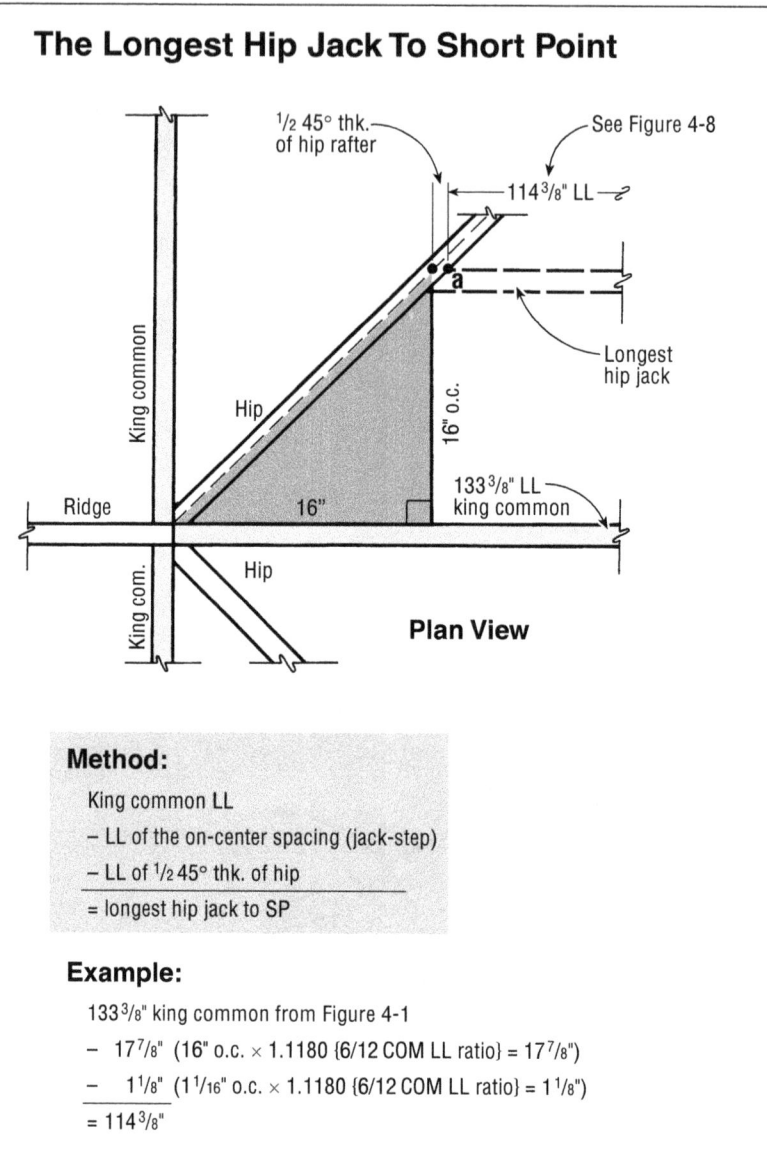

Figure 4-7. To calculate the longest hip jack measurement from the birdsmouth heel-cut to the SP of the 45° cheek-cut at the head, subtract the LL of both the on-center spacing and 1/2 45° thk. of the hip from the adjacent king common rafter's LL. See Appendix B

rafter length by one jack-step measurement plus the LL of 1/2 45° thk. of the hip *(Figure 4-7)*. The result is the longest jack length from the birdsmouth heel-cut to the SP of the cheek-cut at the head measured along the bottom.

The 1/2 45° thk. of the hip measurement can be found by using a Speed® Square to mark a 45° line across the width of the hip material and measuring

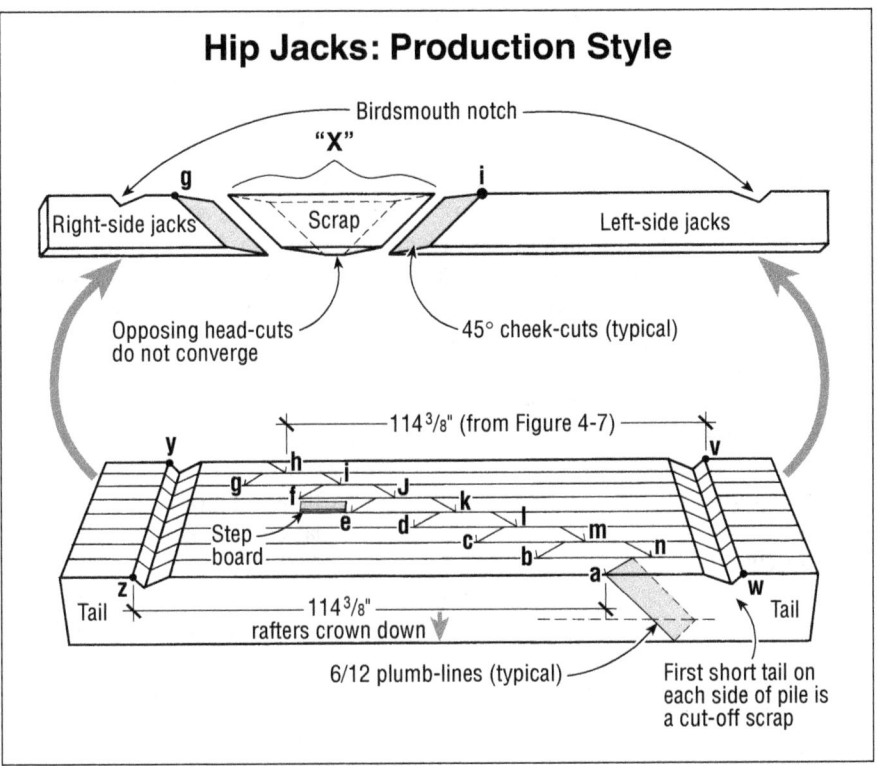

Figure 4-8. Snap a heel-cut line allowing for the required overhang on each end of the rafter pile before marking the opposite sides of the pile with the longest hip-jack SP measurement as figured previously. Progressively mark each board one jack-step shorter. The head-cut plumb-lines for each jack rafter must match the appropriate birdsmouth heel-cut direction, and the 45° cheek-cut must angle away from the corresponding birdsmouth notch. The distance between the opposing fill sets at "**X**" must be large enough so the converging head-cuts do not overlap. If they do overlap, the sets must be moved one board apart and paired up with the next shorter jack in succession to allow sufficient space between the two cuts.

half of that distance, or it can be calculated mathematically by multiplying 1/2 thk. of the hip by 1.4142. Either way, the results must be multiplied by the COM LL ratio to convert to an LL measurement.

Lay out the hip jacks by starting at the tail *(Figure 4-8)*. Measure the LL amount required for the overhang (OH × COM LL ratio), and snap a line for the exterior birdsmouth heel-cut (**y-z**). Measure from that line the longest hip jack length found in Figure 4-7, and place a mark at **a**. Make a keel-slash going away to remind you that this is an SP measurement and that the 45° cheek-cut must be made in that direction. Next, beginning from point **a**, use a step pattern (a small stick cut to the length of the jack-step) to mark each successive board one step less than the previous one until you reach the birdsmouth heel-cut line (**b** through **g**). The right-side hip jack fill is now marked. (Sides refer to looking up a hip from the outside corner.)

The left-side hip jacks are made from the cutoffs. At the other end of the pile, set up another tail and birdsmouth heel-cut line just as before (**v-w**). Mark off another longest jack on the far side of the pile at **h**, and step down from it to the second birdsmouth heel-cut line (**i** through **n**). Make the keel-slash indicating cut direction using a different-color keel this time, so the two opposing cheek-cuts won't get confused when they are cut.

The two opposing hip jack head-cut SP marks must be placed on the same edge of the board to make two hip jack sets with opposite-direction 45° cheek-cuts at the head. The distance "**x**" between the marks must be large enough so the two opposing head-cuts do not converge (see Figure 4-8). If you notice that they will run into each other, move the sets farther apart by adding one extra rafter to the far end of the pile, and remark the second set beginning from there. For example: Looking closely in Figure 4-8, notice that if **h** were on the same board as **g**, the space between the two opposing jack head-cuts would be too small and the cuts would converge. By adding one extra board, **h** moved over and now the next shorter jack **i** is paired with **g**.

After cutting the birdsmouth on each end of the pile, roll the set of hip jacks on their side so they are stacked vertically to make the 45° cheek-cuts one at a time in the middle. Be very careful to mark and cut each plumb-line and cheek-angle going the correct direction.

The second method of cutting hip jacks begins layout from the building corner and works towards the king common. It is used on large custom homes or in a tract situation with many different hip spans. One advantage of using this method is that the various sets of hip jacks are all the same, making it impossible to mix them; whereas with hip jacks spaced from the king common, each particular span has a different set, and each set must be kept separate. Also, starting the layout from the building corner makes the ceiling-joist layout easier since the rafters are "mark-and-go," while the ceiling joists are "mark-and-back." Still another advantage comes when it is necessary to install square-hung frieze blocks. Because a hip jack flyer is always positioned right on the outside building corner, the compound-mitered frieze blocks from the last hip jack to the hip are not necessary (see

Photo 4-9. Positioning a jack flyer on the building corner with open eaves eliminates the compound-mitered frieze blocks to the hip.

Photo 4-9). On the negative side, you often end up with two nonstandard rafter bays adjacent to the king commons and a little more work sheathing the roof.

To lay out jacks this way, multiply the number of hip jacks required for one side of the hip with the jack-step measurement. Then subtract the LL of $1/2$ 45° thk. of the hip to calculate the longest hip jack from the birdsmouth heel-cut line to the SP of the cheek-cut at the head. Substitute this measurement for $114^{3}/8$ in. (Figure 4-8), and step down accordingly.

Note: Hip jacks can also be paired together at the cheek-cuts similar to what is shown in the regular valley jack section (see Chapter 5), but each set of fill must be clamped together and rolled 180° in order to put a birdsmouth on the bottom of the stack before the single 45° cheek-cut is made in the middle. While this method has fewer 45° saw-cuts, longer racks and more shuffling around is required. I did this a lot when I was younger and 2x6 rafter material was the norm.

Book Guideline: *Unless noted otherwise, throughout this book regular hip jack rafters will be spaced starting from the king common and progressing towards the outside building corner.*

HIP-VALLEY JACKS

Hip-valley jacks for parallel running hips and valleys are found as shown in *Figure 4-10* by taking the distance between the inside and outside corners of the building and subtracting $1/2$ 45° thk. of both the hip and the valley, before multiplying the result by the COM LL ratio. The jacks are then cut using common rafter plumb-lines and 45° cheek-cuts. Make sure the cheek-cuts run parallel to each other. *(Note:* There is no difference between right- or left-side parallel running hip-valley jacks as there is with converging hip-valley jacks. They can be flipped around for either left or right side unless the board's crown must be taken into consideration on long jacks.)

The LL of the king hip-valley jack spanning between a parallel running hip and valley as shown in Figure 4-10 is calculated similarly. Use the same inside-corner-to-outside-corner measurement, but subtract only $1/2$ 45° thk. of the valley before multiplying the result by the COM LL ratio. Lay out the rafter using the calculated LL measured from a square-cut common rafter head-cut to the LP of a single 45° cheek-cut.

Note: I rarely cut king hip-valley jacks. Whenever there isn't a full-length king common running directly off the end of a ridge, I run the ridge wild and install one of the regular hip-valley jacks at the upper end of the hip rafter, slapped against the extended ridge (see **Photo 4-11**). The ridge is then taper-cut with a chainsaw using this jack as a guide. This is much simpler than messing around with a special rafter that will probably get lost by the time it is stacked anyway.

Hip-valley jacks for a diverging broken-hip-to-valley situation (example shown in *Figure 4-12)* increase in length by two step measurements instead of one as a normal hip-valley jack. Start with the shortest jack as two steps in

Hip-Valley Jacks for Parallel Situations

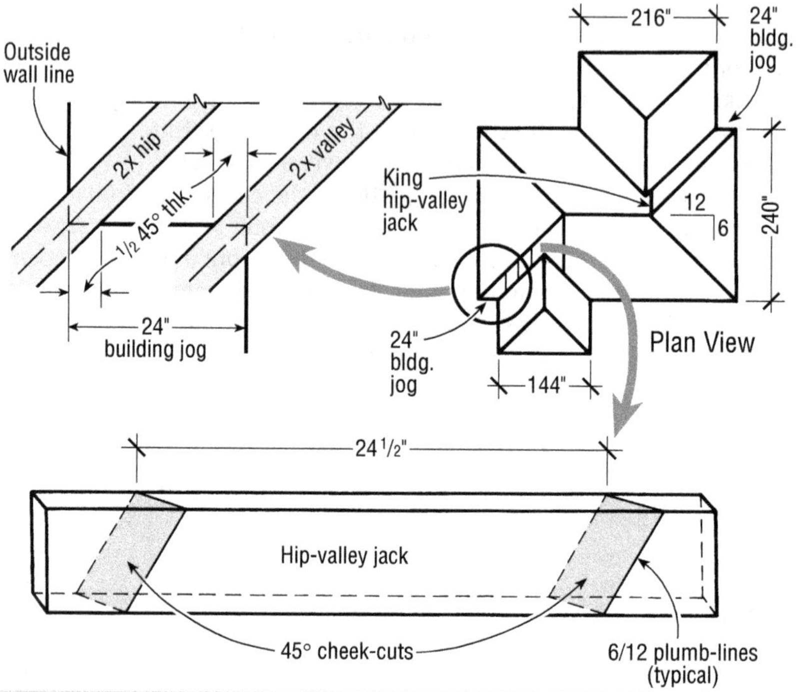

Method:

1. Bldg. jog − 1/2 45° thk. of both hip and valley = effective run of hip-valley jack
2. Effective run of hip-valley jack × COM LL ratio = hip-valley jack LL

Example:

1. 24" − 1 1/16" − 1 1/16" = 21 7/8"
2. 21 7/8" × 1.1180 {6/12 COM LL ratio} = 24 1/2"

Figure 4-10. The effective run of a hip-valley jack rafter for parallel situations is found by subtracting 1/2 45° thk. of the hip and 1/2 45° thk. of the valley from the building jog.

See Appendix B

length from LP to LP and increase by two step measurements on each successive jack. All sets of converging hip-valley jacks will be the same length, but the cheek-cuts will be opposite for right- and left-side jacks unless they are made universal by cutting a double 45° cheek-cut on both ends. *(Note:* As with the upcoming "California Valley Jacks" section, I start my on-center progression for hip-valley jacks from the intersection of the valley and broken hip to the ridge. I do not waste time trying to carry through the on-center spacing from the adjacent common rafters. I just make sure there isn't an over-span

Photo 4-11.
The top hip-valley jack slaps to one side of the extended ridge. Afterwards, the ridge end is taper-cut with a chainsaw using this jack as a guide.

rafter bay at the transition between the common rafters and the jacks.)

The LL of the diverging king hip-valley jack rafter that would run to the valley of the 144-in. secondary span shown in Figure 4-12 is calculated by finding the difference between the major and minor spans, then subtracting $1/2$ thk. of the top ridge and $1/2$ 45° thk. of the valley, and finally multiplying the result by the COM LL ratio. The rafter is laid out with the calculated LL measured from a square-cut common rafter head-cut to the middle of a single 45° cheek-cut at the lower end. The diverging king hip-valley jack that would run to the valley of the 144-in. secondary span shown in Figure 4-10 would be calculated similarly, but the overall length would be shortened by the LL for the 24-in. building jog on the left side.

To help position either type of hip-valley jacks, convert the rafter on-center spacing to a hip/valley LL measurement and use this to layout along the hip or valley rafter. To find this measurement, multiply the on-center spacing by the H/V LL ratio. (Example: 24" o.c. × 1.5000 {6/12 H/V LL ratio} = 36")

HIP (OR VALLEY) HEAD-CUTS FOR RAFTERS THAT SIT ON A RIDGE BEAM

Since there are only minor differences between a hip and valley in this situation, both are included together. When the head-cut of a hip (or valley) rafter sit on a ridge beam, a special birdsmouth is required. In these instances, the LL would be figured full-span without subtracting for the thickness of a ridge board. Ridge-beam height is calculated as shown in the Chapter 3 section "Common Rafters Lapping Over a Center Ridge Beam" page 59.

Lay out the special birdsmouth on the side of the rafter board facing the ridge, as shown in ***Figure 4-13***. From the top LL plumb-line **a**, measure perpendicular downhill $1/2$ 45° thk. of the ridge, and draw a reference plumb-line at **b**. (Remember to set the Speed® Square for hip/valley.) Draw plumb-lines **c** and **d**

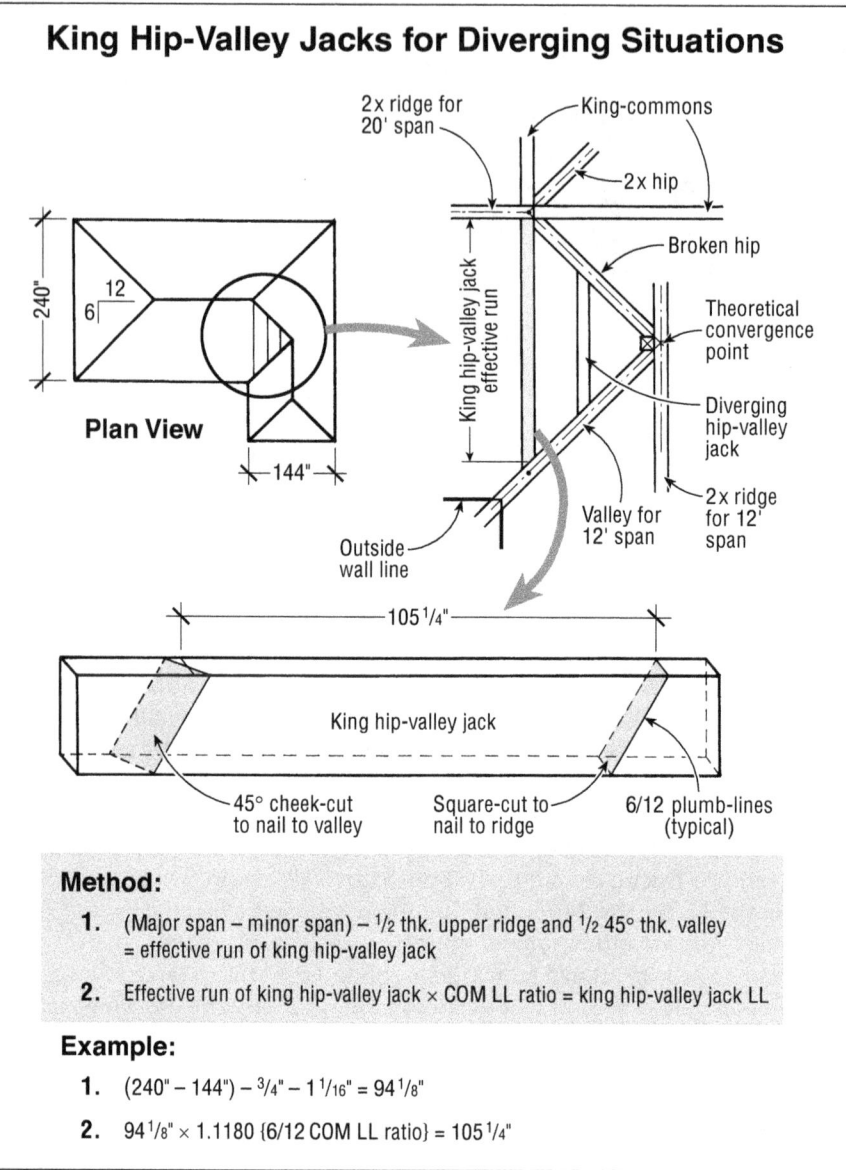

Figure 4-12. The king hip-valley jack rafter length in a diverging situation is calculated by subtracting 1/2 thk. of the ridge plus 1/2 45° thk. of the valley from the span difference between the major and minor roofs and multiplying the result by the COM LL ratio. The rafter is laid out from a square-cut common rafter head-cut to the middle of a single 45° cheek-cut. Diverging hip-valley jacks increase in length by two step measurements instead of one as a regular jack does.

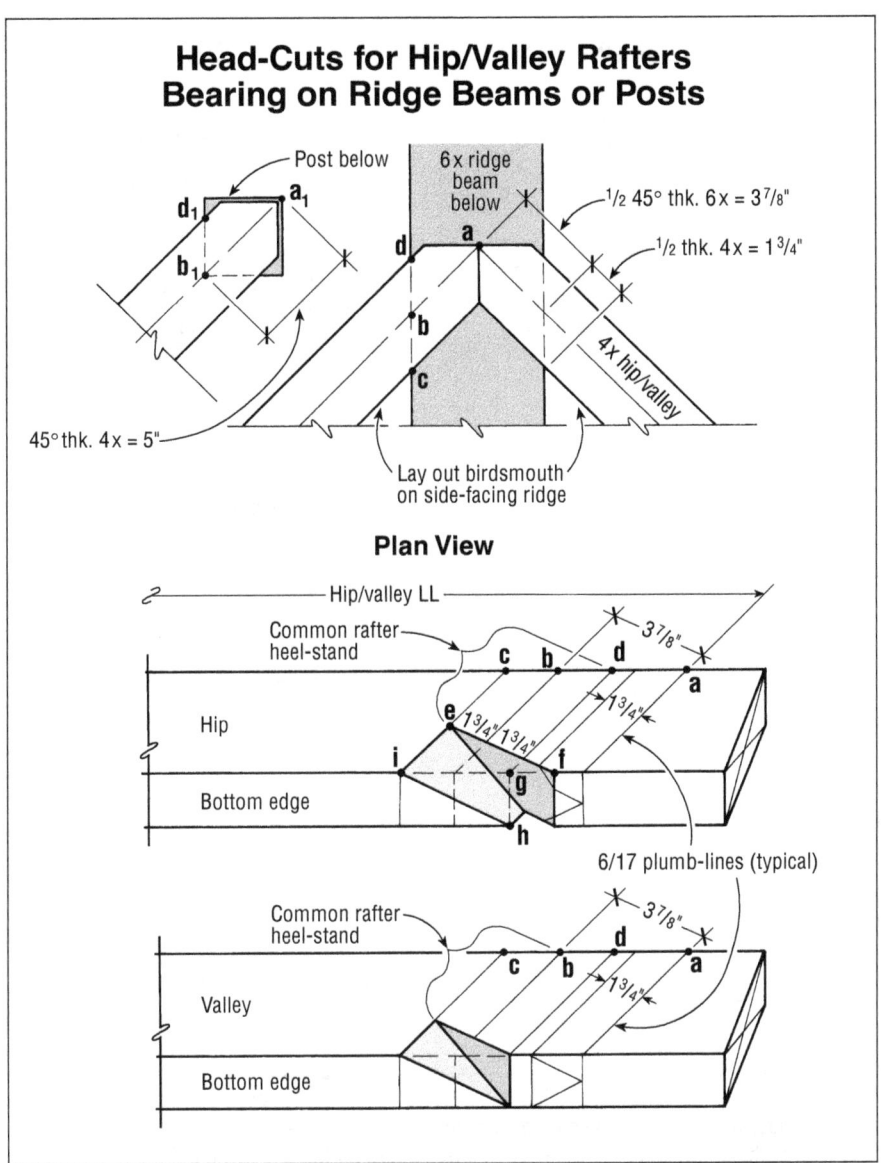

Figure 4-13. Hip and valley heads that bear on a ridge beam have similar birdsmouths but differ in depth. The heel-stand of a common rafter is placed at **d** for a non-backed hip, **b** for a non-backed valley or a backed hip, and **c** for a backed valley.

REGULAR HIP ROOFS

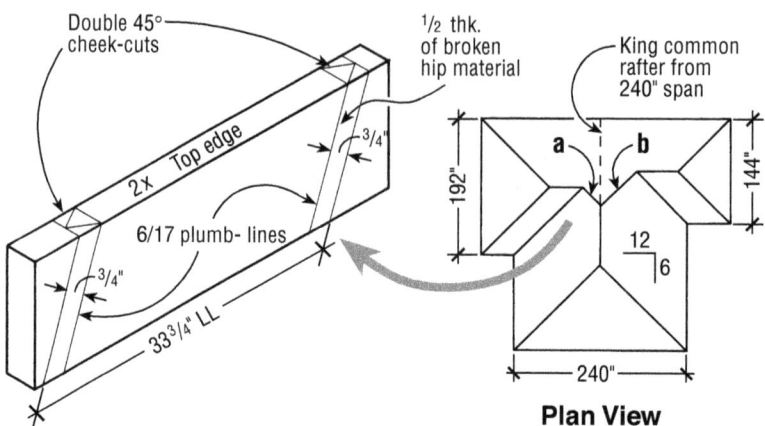

Figure 4-14. Broken or continuation hip rafters are common on chopped-up hip roofs. To calculate these rafters, divide the difference between the two hip spans in half, then subtract ½ thk. of both the top and bottom ridges before multiplying by the H/V LL ratio. The cut-lines for the double 45° cheek-cuts at each end of the broken hip are found by measuring inboard ½ thk. of the broken hip material perpendicular to the LL plumb-lines.

by measuring both up and downhill ½ thk. of the hip perpendicular to plumb-line **b**. Mark the heel-stand of a common rafter at **d** for a non-backed hip (**b** for a non-backed valley or a backed hip, **c** for a backed valley) and draw the level seat-cut line (**e-f**) through this point. Next, square line **d** across the bottom edge of the board (**g-h**), and draw the diagonal heel-cut line **h-i** as shown. This diagonal line would go the other direction on the opposing hip since the birdsmouth is laid out on the opposite face. The cut-lines for the double 45° cheek-cut at the head are laid out by measuring downhill 1/2 thk. of the hip perpendicular to the top LL plumb-line **a** on each side.

The diagonal heel-cut along the underside of the beam can be cut using a Skilsaw® (with the proper angle found by making a trial pass on a scrap of beam) or freehand with a chainsaw.

A birdsmouth that is cut for a post positioned at the upper end of a hip or valley (see upper right corner in Figure 4-13) would be laid out identically except a V-notch would be made for the heel-cut rather than a single-cheek heel-cut as shown. The run is calculated to the far side of the post (a_1), and the tip of the V-notch birdsmouth (b_1) is found by measuring the **full** 45° thk. of the post downhill perpendicular to the top LL plumb-line when laying out.

BROKEN HIPS

To calculate broken hips **a** and **b** illustrated in ***Figure 4-14***, find the difference between the major and minor spans, divide the result by 2, subtract 1/2 thk. of both the top and bottom ridges, and multiply by the H/V LL ratio. The result is the LL from the tip of the double 45° cheek-cut on one end to the tip of the 45° cheek-cut on the other end. Don't forget to use hip/valley plumb-lines to mark the cut-lines. Correct stacking position for this rafter is shown in Figures 4-12 and 6-20 and discussed in the Chapter 6 section "Stacking a Complex Hip Roof," page 124.

Another way to think of the broken hip is as an additional piece added to the upper end of the minor-span valley to make it the same length as the major-span hip with the two pieces separated by the minor-span ridge slicing through at 45°. In other words, find the difference between the LL of the major-span hip and the LL of the minor-span valley, and shorten it by the 45° thk. of the minor-span ridge. (Remember, we are working at 45° to the roof span in this explanation as opposed to working parallel with the roof span in the broken hip calculation formula.)

When calculating a broken hip between roof sections that originate from different plate heights, translate the difference into a modified span so both roofs will originate from a common plate line. For example: If the 12-ft. span wall heights in Figure 4-14 were 6 in. taller than the rest of the house, that difference would translate into a 2-ft. increase in the 12-ft. span to theoretically lower its plate height to the same level as the others ([6" ÷ .5000 {6/12 RR ratio}] × 2 = 24"). Therefore, 20-ft. and 14-ft. spans would be used in the broken-hip calculation formula. (See the Chapter 12 section, "Equal-Pitch Roofs from Varying Plate Heights," page 241, for a more detailed explanation of this procedure.)

Still another method for calculating broken hips in all situations is to find the difference in theoretical ridge heights and work backwards to find the run. Then insert this run dimension into the formula at the second step, and continue by subtracting 1/2 thk. of both top and bottom ridges and multiplying by the H/V LL ratio to calculate the rafter LL. For example:

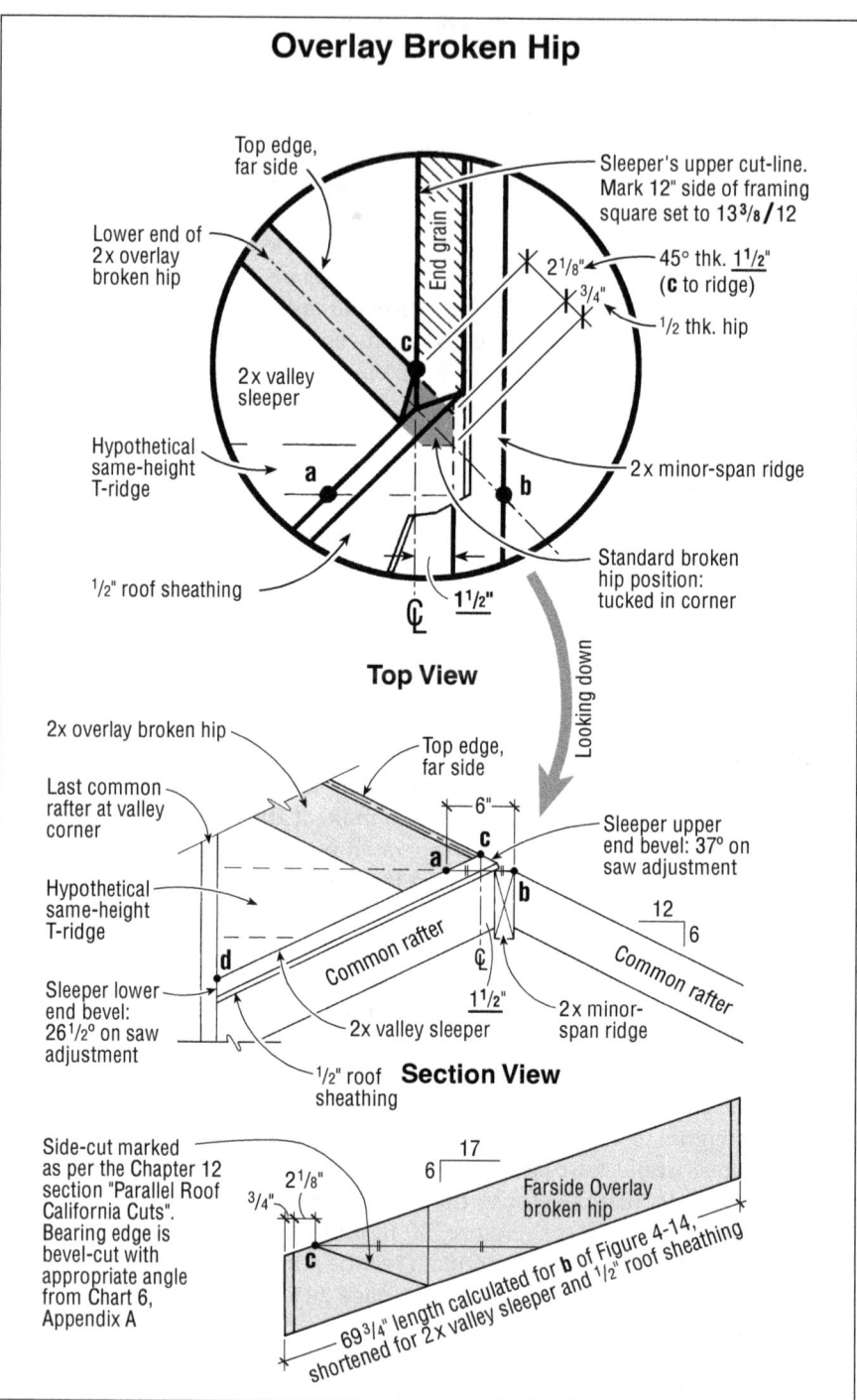

Figure 4-15. Both a cross-section and a top view of the overlay broken hip's connection to the valley sleeper are used to determine the shortening amount for modifying a regular broken hip to fit this condition.

Using the same situation noted in the previous paragraph, the rise for the 20-ft. span (60") less the rise for the 12-ft. span (36") equals 24 in. Next, subtract the wall step-up (6") from this 24 in. to net the theoretical ridge height difference (18"). Dividing this difference by the 6/12 RR ratio (.5000) results in a run of 36" which is inserted back into the formula at the second step ([36" – $3/4$" – $3/4$"] × 1.5000 {6/12 H/V LL ratio} = $51^{3/4}$" LL). Of course, in a pinch the trusty level can always be used to find the height difference between stacked ridges of equal thickness, which would be the same as the computed theoretical ridge-height difference.

Occasionally (as shown in **Figure 4-15**), a broken hip is framed to sit on a California valley sleeper rather than attaching to a minor-span ridge. (California valley sleepers are discussed in Chapter 5.) Compared to the standard broken-hip situation, this rafter will need to be shortened, marked with a special side-cut (or a seat-cut, in effect), and bevel-cut along this line.

Begin the lay-out procedure for this overlay broken hip as if it were to be installed in a standard situation where the rafter is framed from a major-span ridge to a minor-span ridge (as shown in Figure 4-12), and calculate its length as outlined in Figure 4-14. Next, referring to Figure 4-15, determine the distance from **a** (top edge of the sleeper level with the minor-span ridge) to **b** (far side of minor-span ridge) by drawing a full-size section view on a piece of plywood* and dividing this distance in half to find how far the centerline through point **c** is located from the inside or rear edge of the minor-span ridge. Plot this dimension on a similar full-size top view (Figure 4-15) to locate where centerline **c** will intersect a regular full-length broken hip on the far top edge (the top edge away from the valley), and transfer this to the rafter layout as shown.

Refer to the Chapter 12 section, "Parallel-Roof California-Cuts," page 242, for more detail on marking the side-cut and determining the bottom edge's bevel-cut angle.

SNUB-NOSE HIPS

Figures 4-16 and **4-17** illustrate a snub-nose hip. Calculate the height of the snub-nose tall wall section as shown in Chapter 1 using the 96-in. run. When using 2x roof framing material, calculate the main ridge length as shown at

---

* *For you math wizards out there, use rise/run and LL equations to solve the imaginary little roof-pitch right triangle formed when the sum of both the sleeper and the roof's sheathing thickness is the rise leg and the distance from point **a** to the nearside top edge of the ridge is the hypotenuse ([2" ÷ .5000 {6/12 RR ratio}] × 1.1180 {6/12 COM LL ratio} = $4^{1/2}$"). Also change the $1^{1/2}$-in. point **c** centerline to inside edge of the minor-span ridge distance into a hip-travel length using the Pythagorean theorem or into an LL measurement deduction by multiplying this $1^{1/2}$-in. distance by the appropriate H/V LL ratio. Remember, the result is a rafter centerline length and must be brought out to the edge via a $1/2$ thk. setback line to position point **c** correctly. (This is the same procedure done to the head-cut of a hip or valley to find the cheek-cut lines on the side of the board.)*

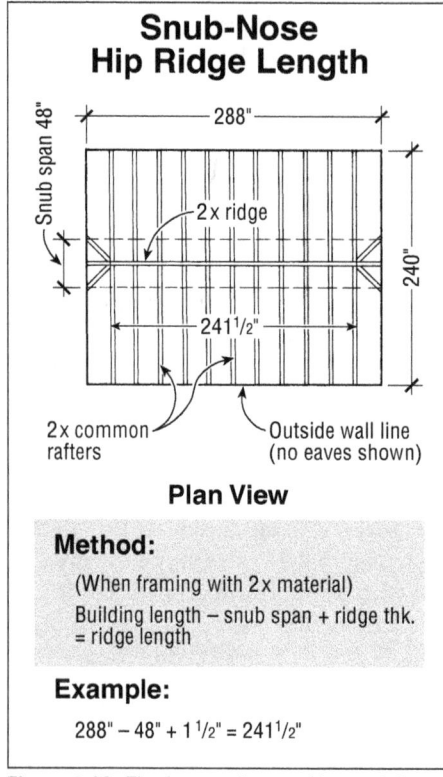

Figure 4-16. The four snub-nose hips and the two end-of-ridge snub-nose king commons are calculated using the 48-in. span.

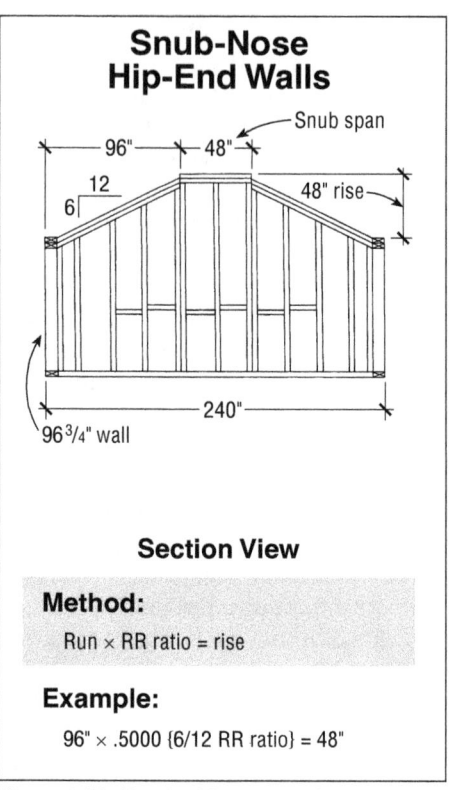

Figure 4-17. Use the 96-in. run to figure the height of the snub-nose tall wall section.

the beginning of this chapter by substituting the span of the snub section for the building width. The hips are obviously figured using the snub span. The gable-end hip jacks (positioned on top of the outside rake walls) are figured for the 96-in. run less 1/2 45° thk. of the hip. This will be an SP measurement.

DUTCH HIPS

A Dutch hip, as shown in *Figure 4-18*, is a cross between a gable and a hip-roof end. The quickest way to build this style roof is to cut two special full-length common rafters (**a** and **b**). These two rafters are calculated by multiplying the Dutch hip setback (run) by the COM LL ratio. The common rafters framed between the two specials (**e** and **f**) are calculated by subtracting the thickness of the ridge from the Dutch hip run and multiplying the result by the COM LL ratio. The length of the hips (**g** and **h**) are calculated using the full setback as their run.

The Dutch-hip ridge length is determined by subtracting the thickness of the two special rafters and twice the Dutch-hip run from the main roof span.

When stacking this roof, place the special common rafters flat against the

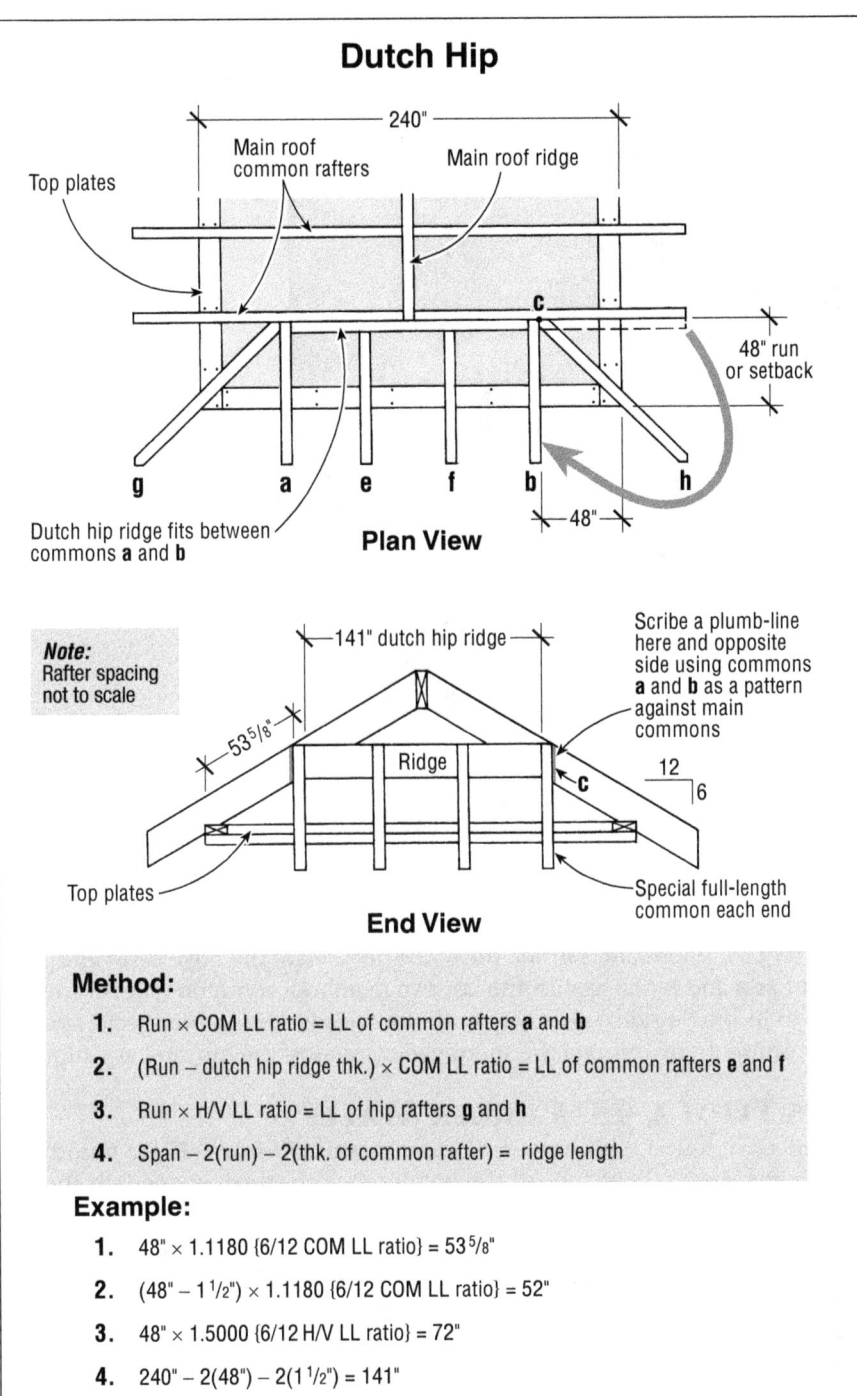

Figure 4-18. When stacking a Dutch hip, place the special full-length Dutch commons flat against the last two main roof gable commons and scribe the ridge-cuts as noted by **c**. When returned to their proper locations, nail them to the main roof commons inside the scribe-lines.

Photo 4-19. An example of a hip from an outside 45° corner wall.

two last main roof gable commons, and scribe their ridge-cuts as noted by **c**. When returned to their proper location off the front end, nail them to the main roof common rafters inside the scribe-lines. Place the ridge between special rafters **a** and **b** (flat against the last two main roof common rafters), and plane in its top outside corner edge with the top edge of the two special commons. Finish up by running the shortened commons, the hip, and any hip fill.

HIPS FROM A 45° CORNER WALL

The effective run of a hip from a 45° corner wall *(Photo 4-19)* is found by shortening the effective run for the building width (**o-p**) by one-half the distance from one corner of the 45° wall to the theoretical outside 90° corner (**p-q**) as shown in *Figure 4-20*. The post height at **s** is also calculated using the **p-q** distance and multiplied by the appropriate RR ratio. Position the post parallel in the 45° corner wall. Mark out a regular hip V-notch type birdsmouth at **s** on the hip rafter as if that point were the outside corner (refer back to the earlier section in this chapter, "The Hip Rafter") and square-cut the heel-cut at the LL mark. If required by design, wall-end rafters at (**r-s**) and (**s-t**) are both calculated as if they were hip/valleys because they run 45° to the plane of the roof (see Photo 4-5).

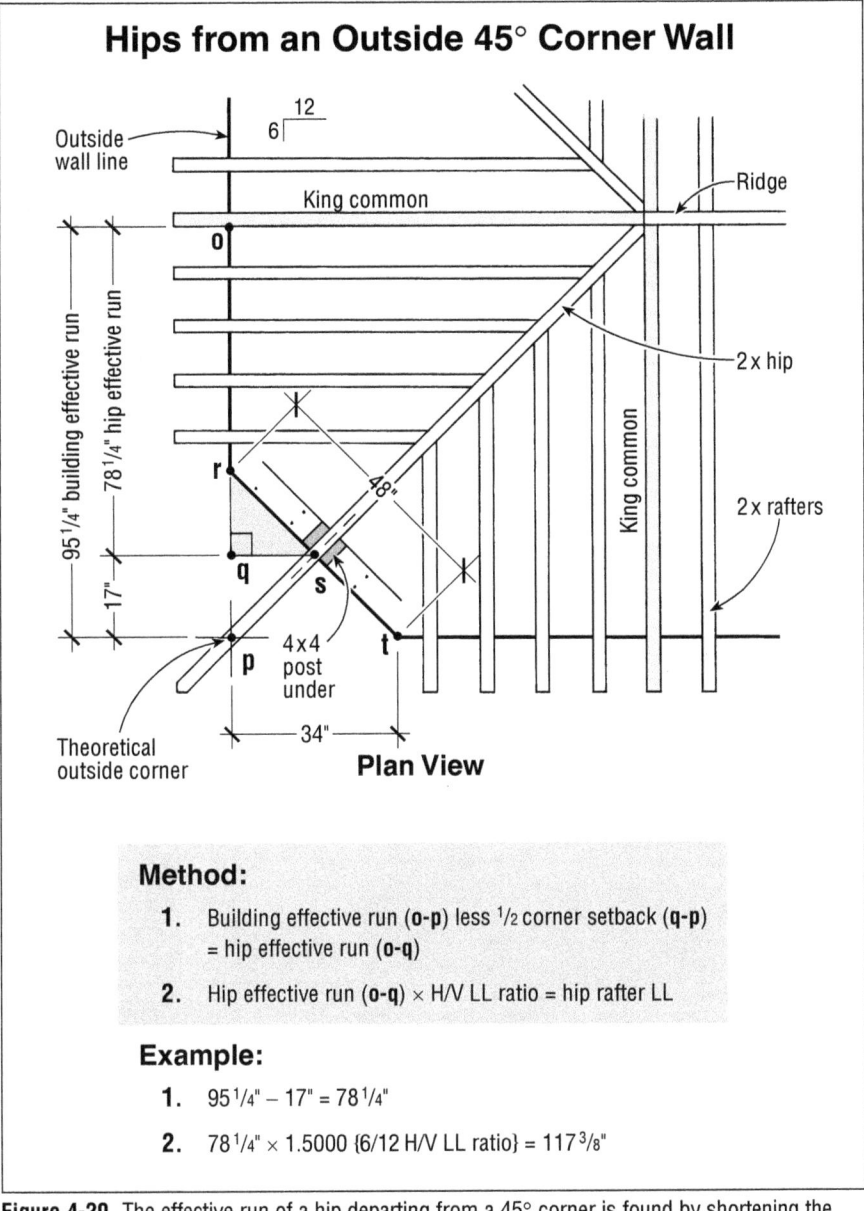

Figure 4-20. The effective run of a hip departing from a 45° corner is found by shortening the building's effective run by half the distance from one corner of the 45° wall to the theoretical outside 90° corner **(p-q)**.

Chapter 5

Regular Valley Intersections

THE VALLEY RAFTER

Valley rafter LL is figured in exactly the same way as a hip: Span less the thickness of the ridge, divided by 2, and multiplied by the H/V LL ratio *(Figure 5-1)*.

In actual layout, the only difference between a hip and a valley is at the birdsmouth since both ridge-cuts are identical. From the lower LL plumb-line **a** *(Figure 5-2)*, measure perpendicular 1/2 thk. of the valley towards the tail and draw another plumb-line **(b)**. Mark the heel-stand of a common rafter at **a** if the valley is not backed on the top, or at **b** if the valley will be backed on the top. Draw the level seat-cut line through this point. With a 2x valley, square-cut the heel-cut at **b** and butt it right to the corner of the building — since, even on open eaves, the square-cut heel-cut will be hidden *(Figure 5-3)*. When a beam is used as a valley and the tail is exposed, the V-notch heel-cut must be chiseled or cut with a chainsaw.

To back a valley, figure the rip-angles (and rip-cut lines if the bottom edge is to be backed) exactly as on a hip (see the Chapter 4 section, "Backing a Hip," page 67), except the backing cuts are reversed. Backing the top of a valley is quite common with exposed beam tails; otherwise there would be a large gap along each side of the valley at the eaves since the starter board would only touch at the center of the valley. *(Photo 5-4)*.

Calculating Valley Rafter Lengths

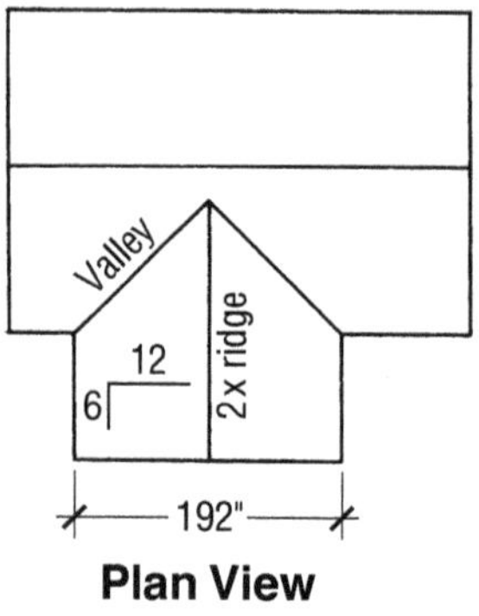

Method:

1. $\frac{\text{Span} - \text{ridge thk.}}{2}$ = effective run
2. Effective run × H/V LL ratio = valley LL

Example:

1. $\frac{192" - 1\,1/2"}{2} = 95\,1/4"$
2. $95\,1/4" \times 1.5000$ {6/12 H/V LL ratio} = $142\,7/8"$

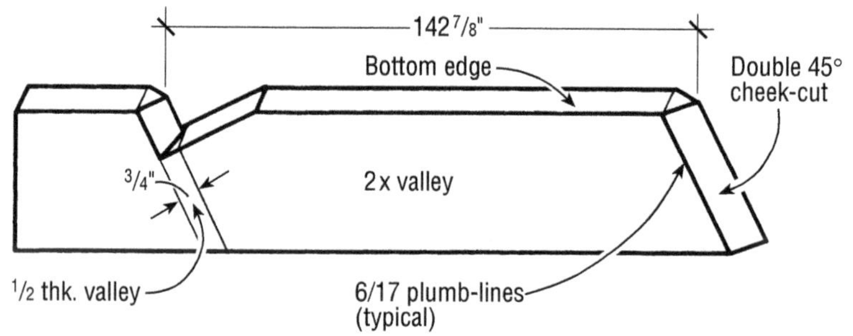

Figure 5-1. The valley rafter LL is calculated the same way as a hip. The difference between the two is in the birdsmouth notch.

Valley Rafter Birdsmouth Layout

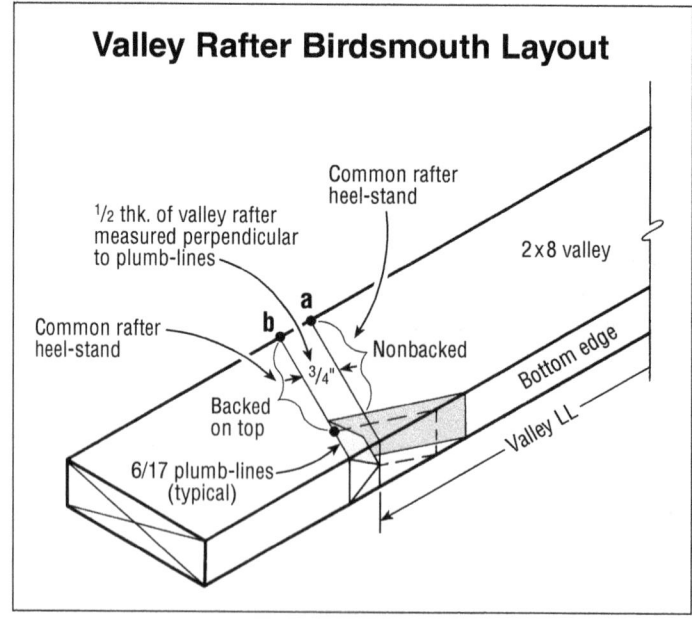

Figure 5-2. To lay out the valley rafter birdsmouth seat-cut line, mark the heel-stand measurement from a common rafter at position **a** for the standard nonbacked situation, or at position **b** if the rafter will be backed along the top edge.

REGULAR VALLEY JACKS

As shown in the hip jack section, valley jacks from opposing sides are paired up according to length, and cut from the same board. Whereas hip jacks (Figure 4-8) have a small scrap of wood between the opposing head-cuts when paired together (unless the set was rolled to put the second birdsmouth on the bottom of the pile as mentioned at the end of the "Hip Jacks" section in Chapter 4, page 68), valley jacks can be paired at the cheek-cut, thereby eliminating this scrap piece. Count the number of jacks needed on one side of the valley either from the prints or by dividing the valley run by the jack rafter's on-center spacing, and rounding down to the next whole number. Rack up only as many boards as there are jacks for one side of the valley since the cutoffs will be used for the opposing side. Use material that is the same length as the corresponding commons and add one extra board per each paired opposing jack set when the building's overhang is less than the jack rafter's on-center spacing.

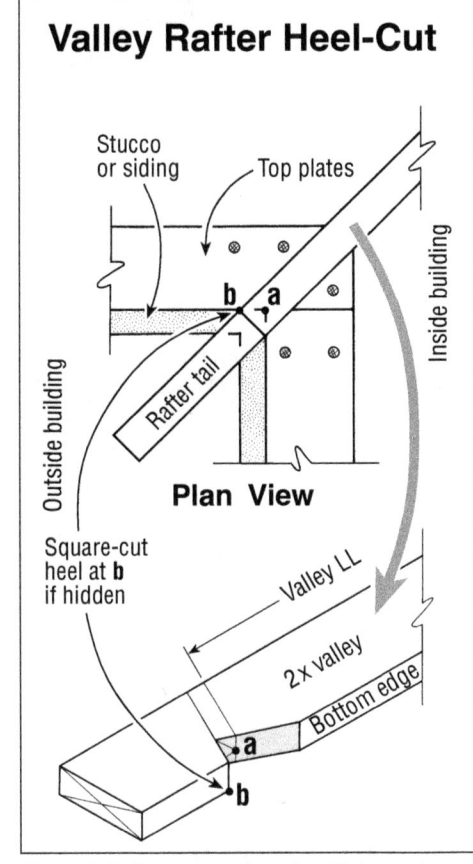

Figure 5-3. Square-cut the valley birdsmouth at the outside heel-cut line when using 2x material if the V-notch will be obscured by exterior siding or stucco.

As with hip jacks, there are two common ways to cut valley jacks depending on whether the job is a small single house or a large tract situation. One method starts layout from the valley birdsmouth at the inside building corner and moves towards the valley-to-ridge intersection. The second method starts layout from the valley-to-ridge intersection and moves towards the valley birdsmouth corner.

With the first method, the longest valley jack has the same LL (to the LP) as a common rafter for a given run and progressively shortens. (The longest valley jack from each set will require a seat-cut to sit on the exterior wall plate.) In **Figure 5-5** the opposing valley jack sets **a** and **b** are shortened from the 192-in.-span common rafter, while the opposing valley jack sets **c** and **d** are shortened from the 240-in.-span common rafter.

Start your layout by snapping a ridge-cut line on the right end of the rack of lumber and measuring to the left the LL of the common rafter for both

Photo 5-4. Above: Back an exposed valley beam tail to eliminate the sheathing gap along each side of the top edge. Left: Backing the top edge of a valley is simplified with the help of a rip guide.

the 16-ft. and the 20-ft. spans, as shown in **Figure 5-6**. Step down to mark sets **a** and **d** (to review how to calculate the step, refer back to the "Hip Jacks" section in Chapter 4, page 68). Place a slash in keel at each step layout going the direction of the 45° cheek-cut. Since our marks are LPs, your keel slash will angle back towards the ridge-cut line.

To pair set **b** with the cutoffs from **a**, and set **c** with the cutoffs from **d**, begin by calculating the LL of a 45° cheek-cut. (Math for this calculation is noted in Figure 5-6.) Locate points **v** and **w** by measuring back towards the right-side ridge-cut line the calculated amount (1 3/4"), and marking the opposite edge of the board as shown. These two points (the SPs of the shortest jacks in sets **a** and **d**) will be the LPs of the longest jacks for the sets **b** and **c**. From points **v** and **w** measure the common rafter LL distance for each span and mark the ridge-cut lines for the second sets. Be sure this ridge-cut line parallels

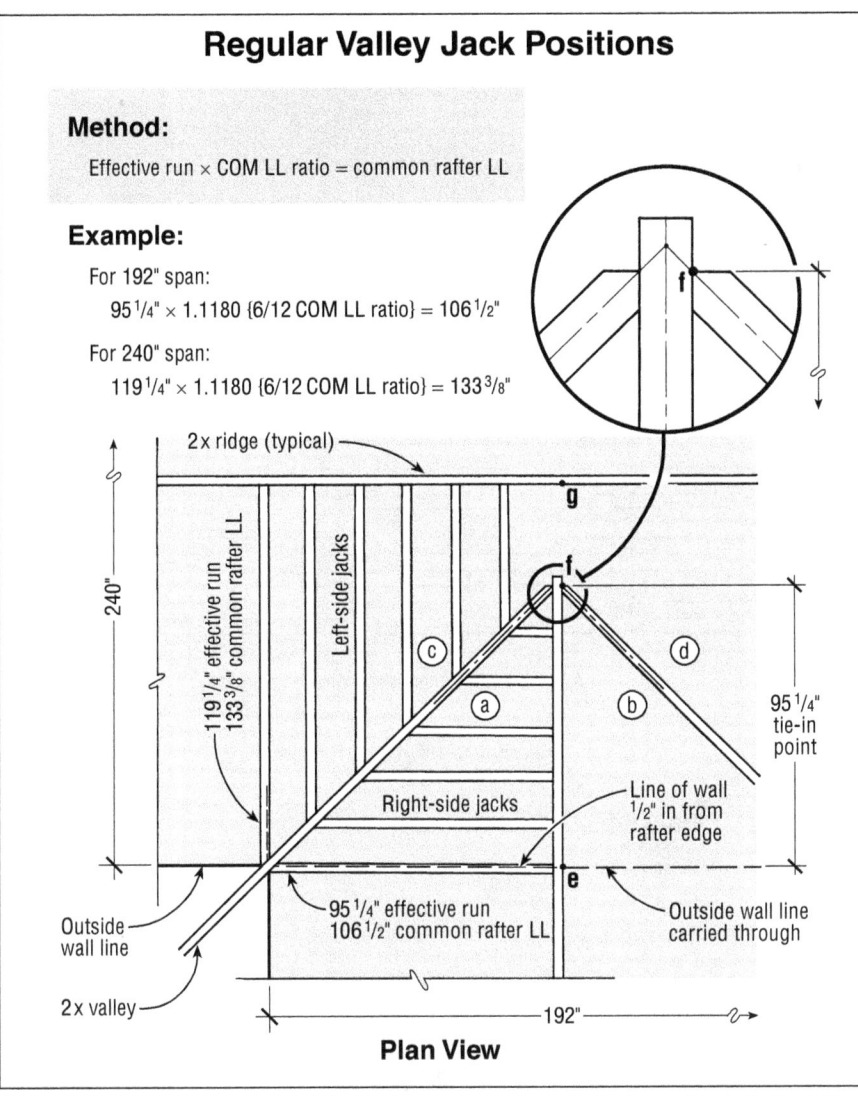

Figure 5-5. One method to cut and stack valley jacks begins with the longest jack (to the LP) equal to the common rafter LL for a given span, and each successive jack shortens one step measurement.

the one at the other end of the set. Notice in Figure 5-6 that all ridge-cut and cheek-cut lines angle down the same direction. This style of cutting requires all the jack rafter material to be straight boards; otherwise, half of each set must be crowned down, while the other half is crowned up to correspond to the longer jacks from each opposing set. (To help visualize the reason for this, compare the pairing of the cheek-cuts from opposing valley jack sets to placing the palms of your hands together vertically in front of your face with the fingers pointing in opposite directions. Notice how one thumb is pointed up and

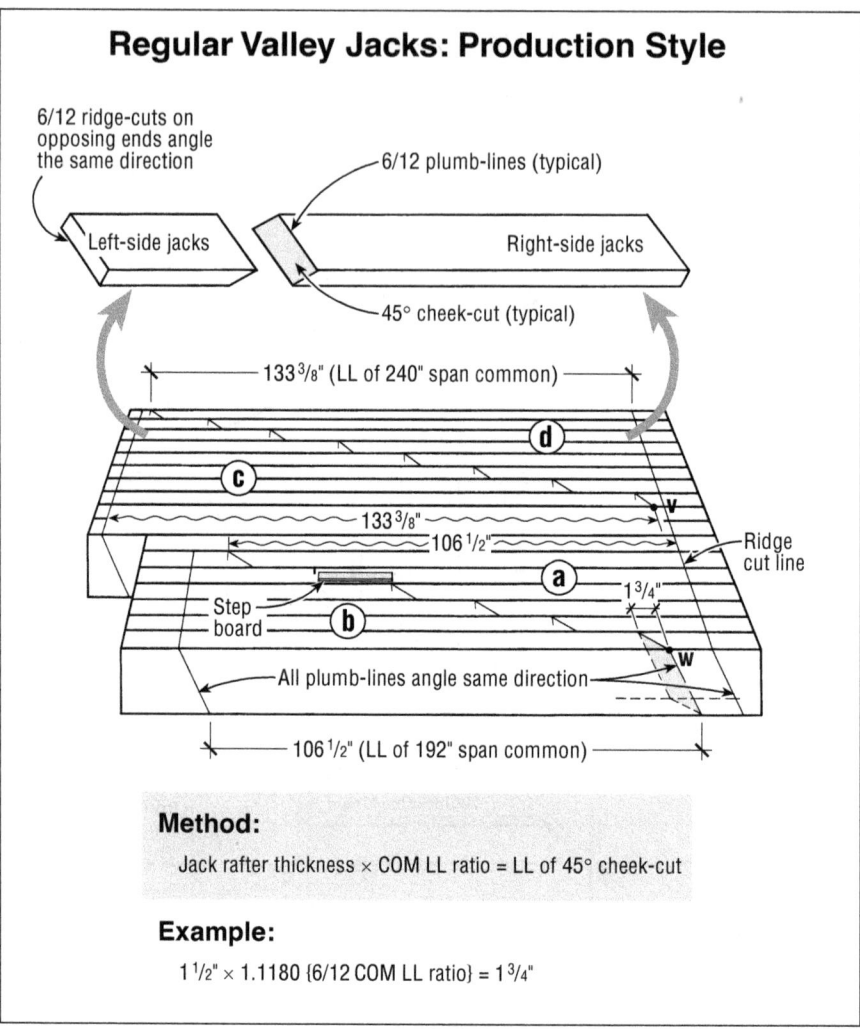

Figure 5-6. Pairing the cheek-cuts from opposing valley jack sets is like putting the palms of your hands together in front of your face with the fingers pointing in opposite directions. Notice how one thumb is pointed up and the other is pointed down just as the two sets of jacks will be. Therefore, crown the long jacks from sets **b** and **c** up accordingly. Locate points **v** and **w** by measuring back 1 3/4", the LL of the 45° cheek-cut.

the other is pointed down, just as the longest boards should be crowned for the two sets of valley jacks).

Gang-cut the ridge-cuts on each end of the pile before making the single 45° cheek-cuts one at a time in the middle. If the roof pitch is shallow, you can make the 45° cheek-cuts in a vertical manner with the boards racked on edge, rather than rolling the whole paired set of jacks flat and cutting the cheek-cuts horizontally across the top of the pile.

■ **Matching Rafter Layout**
While lining up common rafters (staggered by no more than 1½ in. for 2x material) across a 2x ridge board (or hip jacks across a 2x hip) is structurally beneficial when ceiling joists serve as a tension tie, lining up valley jacks across a 2x valley serves little purpose. There again, if the ridges and hips are structural beams or have been vertically braced, matching layout across the member serves no purpose except to facilitate the installation of any over-the-ridge tie straps between common rafters.

The second way of cutting valley jacks — layout starting from the intersection of the valley and ridge — keeps all sets of valley fill the same length, but the number of jacks in each set will vary depending on the span. This method is often used on large custom homes or in a tract situation with many different valley spans. With this method, the shortest jack to its LP is equal to one jack-step measurement, and each additional jack is sequentially one step longer. Therefore, multiply the number of jacks required for one side of the valley by the jack-step measurement. Then substitute that number for the 133³/₈-in. and 106¹/₂-in. dimensions in Figure 5-6 (example: 6 jacks × 17⁷/₈" {6/12 16"o.c. jack-step} = 107¹/₄"). Jacks cut using this method will not line up across from each other at the valley as they do in the first method, so it may not look as "pretty." But it makes no difference structurally.

The length of the special upper ridge to lower ridge jack in Figure 5-5 **(f-g)** is the difference in length between the two common rafters involved in the intersection (133³/₈" − 106¹/₂" = 26⁷/₈"). This rafter can be square-cut plumb on both ends to nail to the side of the lower ridge abutting the head-cut of one valley, or it can be level-cut square on the bottom end to stack on top of the lower ridge if this ridge was run long.

> **Book Guideline:** *Unless noted otherwise, throughout this book valley jacks will be spaced starting from the inside building corner stepping towards the valley-ridge intersection.*

CALIFORNIA VALLEY SLEEPERS

A California valley (CV; also known as a blind valley or an overlay/layover intersection) is an intersection where one roof's rafters are cut to sit upon another roof instead of running to a shared valley rafter *(Photo 5-7)*. It is most often used when a cathedral ceiling is desired through that section of the building where the valley is normally located, or for ease of construction. (It is also an excellent way to handle an unequal-pitch intersection, as discussed in the Chapter 8 section, "Unequal-Pitch Valleys," page 177.)

The level-cut end of CV jacks are sometimes nailed directly to the sheathing at the valley snap-line, but more often they are nailed to a sleeper or toe-board positioned to allow the sheathing to plane in at the snap-line.

Typically a CV sleeper is cut to length while stacking, but it is possible to precut valley sleepers to length and even avoid the snap-line procedure if the

Photo 5-7. A California (or blind) valley connection. Note the building and collar ties in the roof section on the left.

last set of opposing rafters on an intersecting equal-pitch/equal-heel-stand minor span are cut tailless and placed at the building's valley corner just outside the main span's wall line (as shown by the dash line through point **e** in Figure 5-5).

For this situation, the CV sleeper lengths are calculated similar to regular valleys but must be shortened to take into account the thickness of both the intersected roof's sheathing and the valley sleeper. Additionally, since the sleepers will butt head to head when placed on the intersected roof's sheathing, no allowance is made for the thickness of the ridge.

If the roof intersection shown in Figure 5-1 was framed CV style with $1/2$-in. plywood sheathing installed on the main span's roof section in combination with a 2x sleeper valley, the length would be $137^{1}/4$ in. This is measured from the square-cut LP at the head along the uphill top corner edge (the corner edge where the tail end of the CV jacks will terminate) to the short side of the bevel-cut LP at the tail (similar in effect to the exploded CV jack shown in Figure 5-8 if measured from the LP end at **u** to point **f**.

The calculator process is as follows:
1. Convert the thickness of both the roof's sheathing and the valley sleeper into a plumb dimension by multiplying by the roof's COM LL ratio. ($2" \times 1.1180$ {6/12 COM LL ratio} = $2^{1}/4"$)
2. Divide the sheathing/sleeper plumb height by the roof's RR ratio to determine the run value for that rise. ($2^{1}/4" \div .5000$ {6/12 COM LL ratio} = $4^{1}/2"$)
3. Subtract the resulting run value from the intersecting roof's theoretical run to determine the valley sleeper's effective run. ($96" - 4^{1}/2" = 91^{1}/2"$)
4. Multiply the sleeper valley's effective run by the roof's H/V LL ratio. ($91^{1}/2" \times 1.5000$ {6/12 H/V LL ratio} = $137^{1}/4"$)

In determining the length of the valley sleeper, variations in rafter heel-stands and plate heights between the major and minor spans can be compensated for by adding or subtracting, as appropriate, that difference to the plumb height dimension determined in Step 1 above. (Add that difference if the minor-span roof comes in lower; subtract that difference if the minor-span roof comes in higher.)

To mark out the cut-lines at the head and tail of the sleeper, set up a framing square with the unit of roof run (12") on one leg and the given roof's LL for the unit of run on the other (12" × appropriate COM LL ratio). Thus, for a 6/12 pitch roof, a framing square would be set to **12 in.** on one leg and **13^3/$_8$ in.** (12" × 1.1180 {6/12 COM LL ratio} = 13^3/$_8$") on the other, or a rafter square set at 13^3/$_8$ in. on the common rafter scale. (Framing square settings for the most common roof pitches are also listed in Chart 8, Appendix A.) Always mark the head-cuts on the longer leg (sleeper angle) and the tail-cuts along the 12-in. leg (shallower angle). The head-cut is made with the saw set square to be butted together, while the tail-cut is made with the saw's bevel set at the roof pitch in degrees, which allows it to fit against the tailless common rafters positioned at the valley corner.

Remember, the two valley sleepers are mirror images of each other, so take care during layout to mark them as opposites.

Note: When stacking, position the valley sleeper on the roof's sheathing by lining up its outside top corner edge at the tail with the top edge of the tailless rafters installed at the valley corners. The sleeper's head-cut LPs will flush together.

Another California valley situation seen less frequently than the previously described instance (a minor-span roof over-framed onto a major-span roof) is one where a major-span hip roof is over-framed onto a minor-span roof in an "L" or "T" configuration. This could be the case in Figure 4-12 if the minor span's common rafters on the valley side were continued tailless inside the building through the valley section for either a cathedral ceiling or for some structural reason.

As with the minor-to-major-span valley sleeper, a tailless rafter of the intersecting roof is positioned just outside the valley corner to provide a termination point for the valley sleeper at the lower end.

To calculate the length of this unique valley sleeper, use a full-size cross-section drawing of the top end of the sleeper at the minor-span ridge as shown in Figure 4-15 to find the dimension from the centerline at **c** to the inside face of the minor-span ridge. Then subtract this length from the effective run of the minor-span roof and multiply the result by the appropriate H/V LL ratio. For example, if the valley situation shown in Figure 4-12 was framed using a CV sleeper, the length would be 104^5/$_8$ in. ([71^1/$_2$" minor-span effective run less the 1^1/$_2$" ridge face to centerline offset] × 1.5000 {6/12 H/V LL ratio} = 104^5/$_8$")

As was done in the earlier discussion of minor-to-major-span sleepers, mark out this valley sleeper's length along the top outside edge (as indicated by point **d** to **c** in the cross-section view of Figure 4-15. What is different from the minor-to-major-span valley sleeper is that the cut-line placed across the top end of the board parallels the lower cut-line. The upper end is

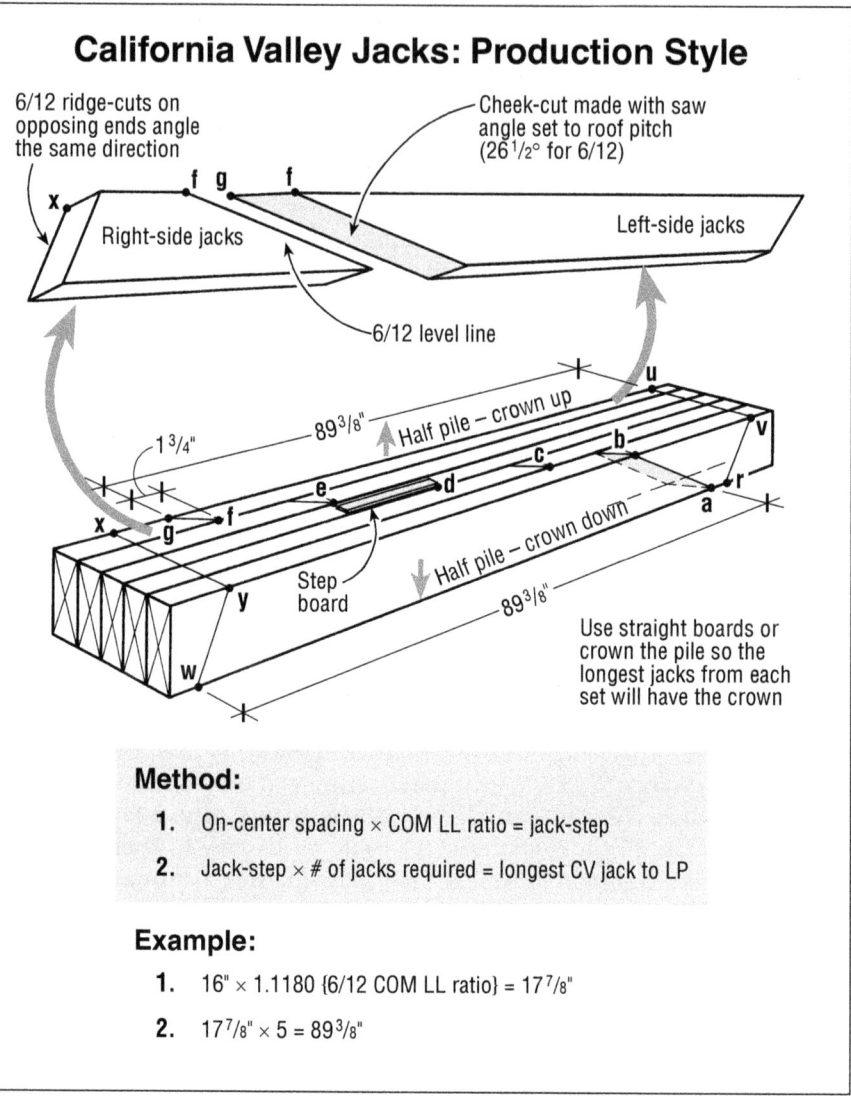

Figure 5-8. California valley jacks are paired together at the long, level California-cuts similar to the pairing of the 45° cheek-cuts for regular valley jacks. CV jacks are laid out from the intersection of the CV ridge and the main roof and progressively lengthen by one jack-step measurement.

cut with the saw set at 90° less twice the roof pitch in degrees, or 37° for a 6/12 roof pitch (90° − 26 1/2° − 26 1/2° = 37°) as shown in Figure 4-15, while the bottom end matches what was discussed previously.

Note: When stacking, position the lower end of the valley sleeper against the intersecting roof's last common rafter at the valley corner so the top edges line up as discussed earlier. Position the top end where the bevel-cut planes in with the far side of the minor-span ridge and adjoining common rafters.

CALIFORNIA VALLEY JACKS

Opposing CV jack rafter sets are paired together at the long, level California-cuts similar to the pairing together of the 45° cheek-cuts for regular valley jacks. The length of rafter stock needed and the number of boards required, etc., is the same as for regular valley jacks. CV jacks are laid out from the intersection of the CV ridge and the main roof and are progressively lengthened by one jack-step length. (Once again, it is not necessary to carry through any on-center spacing from the adjacent common rafters, but make sure there isn't an over-span rafter bay at the transition when stacking.) At the left end of the rafter stock *(Figure 5-8)*, draw a plumb-cut line **(y-w)** extending down the side of the board from the ridge-cut snap-line **(x-y)**. Calculate the longest jack length by multiplying the number of jacks required by the jack-step length (5 jacks × $17^{7}/_{8}$" {6/12 16"o.c. jack-step} = $89^{3}/_{8}$"), and measure from **w** along the bottom of the board this distance to mark **a**. This is the LP of the longest jack. Now, using the CV-cut pattern from *Figure 5-9*, draw a line back up the side of the board, and mark **b**. From **b**, step each rafter shorter sequentially towards the ridge-cut line **x-y** until you have marked the required number of jacks (**c**, **d**, **e**, and **f**). A small board cut to the step length makes marking the jacks much easier. Make a slash with keel at each step layout to mark the direction of the cut-angle. Since our marks are LPs, the keel slash will angle back towards ridge-cut line **x-y**.

Note: For you math-wizard types, the **y** to **b** dimension can also be calculated by solving for the hypotenuse in the right triangle formed with the plumb dimension of the rafter stock as the rise leg and the level-cut dimension as the run leg. (Remember: To find the plumb dimension of a rafter, multiply the board height by the appropriate COM LL ratio. To find the level-cut or run dimension, divide the plumb height by the appropriate RR ratio. And lastly, to find the hypotenuse or rake dimension, multiply the run by the appropriate COM LL ratio.) Subtract the resulting hypotenuse from the longest jack length and plot as a **y** to **b** length. For example, using 2x6 rafters in Figure 5-8 at a 6/12 pitch, the plumb dimension of the rafter is $6^{1}/_{8}$ in. so the hypotenuse calculates to $13^{3}/_{4}$ in. Subtracting this from $89^{3}/_{8}$ in. results in a **y** to **b** length of $75^{5}/_{8}$ in.

Now all the right-side CV jacks are marked. The cutoffs will be used for the left side.

> **Book Guideline:** *"Sides" refer to looking up a hip/valley from outside the building.*

On the longest jack from the first set, find the SP for the beveled bottom cut at **f**. This new point **g** will be the LP of the beveled bottom cut on the longest jack of the opposing set. The $1^{3}/_{4}$ in. noted in the drawing is found by multiplying the jack thickness by the COM LL ratio, or by making a sample California-cut on a scrap board with the saw angle set to the degrees of the roof pitch and noting the change. This $1^{3}/_{4}$-in. measurement is a LL measurement and is therefore measured along the rafter edge between the two lines shown. From **g**, measure to the right the length of the longest jack and snap

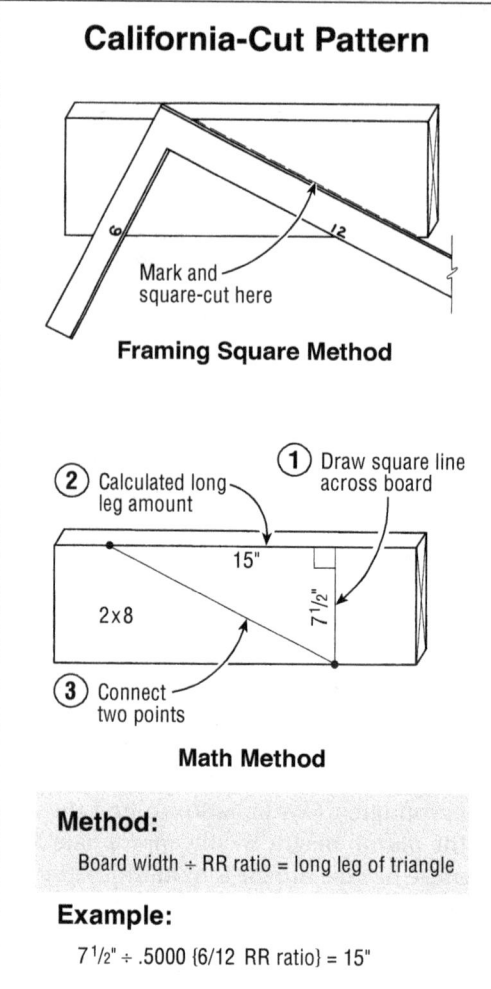

Figure 5-9. Mark the long side of a framing square set to the pitch of the roof to make the CV-cut pattern. Without a framing square, use the equation as shown to calculate the second leg of the right triangle and draw the hypotenuse across the board.

the ridge-cut line **u-v** for the second set. Be sure that this ridge-cut line is parallel to the ridge-cut line **x-y**. The plumb-cut line **v-r** will angle the same direction as **y-w**. (Remember: As with regular valley jacks, always use straight boards or crown half of the pile up to correspond to the long jacks of the set where the ridge-cut is **u-v** in Figure 5-8.)

Gang-cut the ridge-cuts at each end of the pile before rolling the paired set of CV jacks flat on their side to make the long California bevel-cut on each board one at a time. Using the CV pattern from Figure 5-9, scribe a cut-line from the step mark on each board parallel to **a-b**. Cut each board with the saw angle set to the roof pitch in degrees (Chart 3, Appendix A) and angled the same direction indicated by the keel slash.

OVER/UNDER INTERSECTIONS

When a long hip roof run has a change in wall heights as shown in *Figure 5-10*, the span for the two tailless valleys (**e-b** and **e-c**) is calculated by dividing the difference in plate heights (12") by the appropriate RR ratio to find the run distance **a-b**. Subtract twice this run from the building span to determine the tailless valley span *(Photo 5-11)*.

California-style framing is very common in this type of situation. The theoretical ridge length for the lower intersecting hip roof section in Figure 5-10 would be the distance from **a** to the building corner **d**, less the **a-b** run distance (run distance **a-b** = **a-f**).

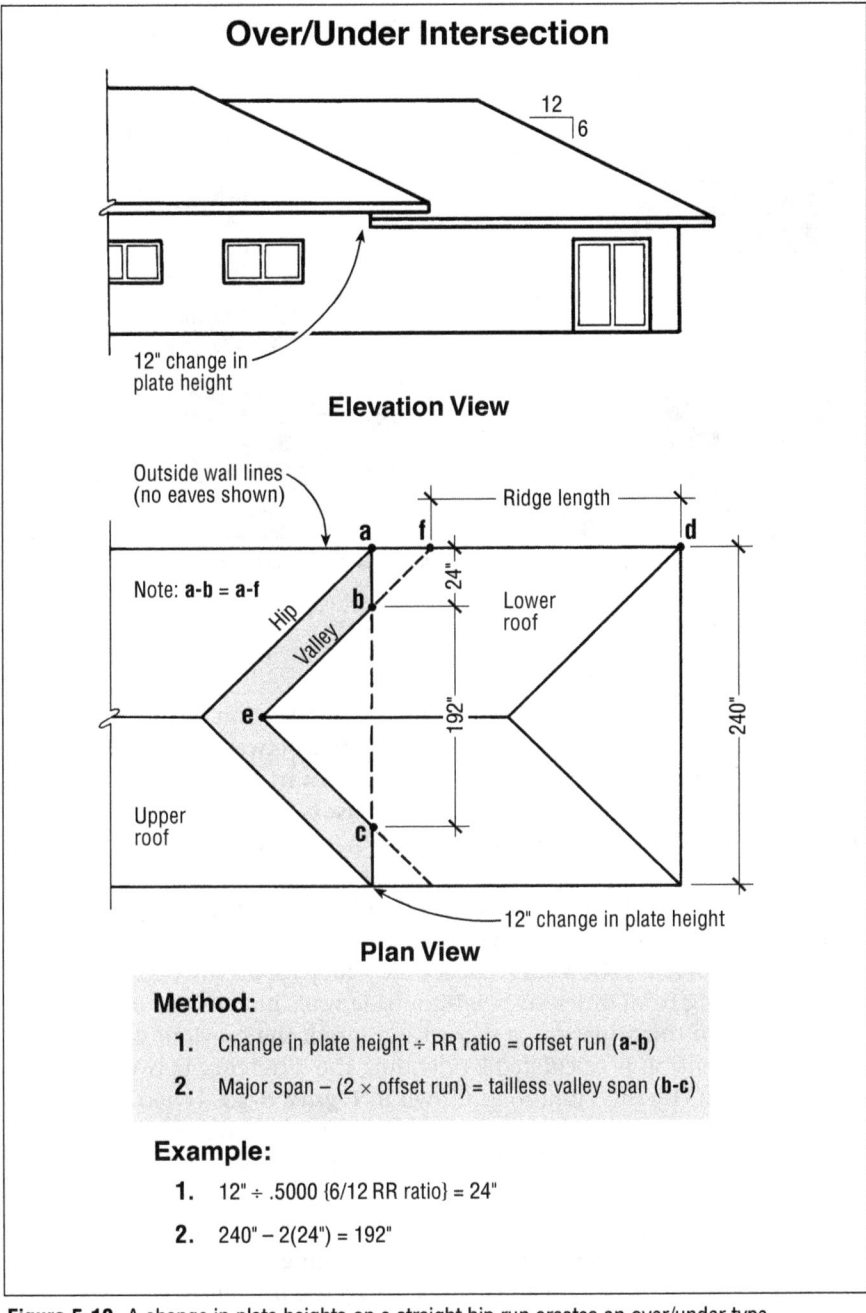

Figure 5-10. A change in plate heights on a straight hip run creates an over/under type intersection. Divide the change in plate height by the RR ratio to calculate the offset run distance (**a-b**) and subtract twice this amount from the major span to find the tailless valley span.

Photo 5-11. Top view of an over/under valley. The tailless valley nails to the common rafter from the lower section at the wall step-up.

OFFSET VALLEYS

The location of an offset valley caused by the intersection of two different size rafter stocks is found by taking the difference between the two rafter heel-stands and dividing by the RR ratio as shown in **Figure 5-12**. The overhang of the larger dimension material must be lengthened by the offset amount to have a consistent fascia height. When the valley rafter originates from the ridge of the rafters with a taller heel-stand, its effective run must also be increased by the amount of the offset to calculate LL. Its birdsmouth depth is set using the shorter rafter heel-stand measurement.

A similar problem is how far to offset the valley for an intersection of two roofs originating from different-height outside walls but sharing a common fascia height. In this situation (a slight variation of the previous example), the offset dimension is calculated by dividing the difference between the two wall heights by the RR ratio as shown in **Figure 5-13**. When the valley rafter originates from the ridge of the taller wall section, its effective run must be increased by the amount of the offset if it will sit on the lower height wall plate as shown.

Figure 5-14 illustrates the birdsmouth notch for an offset nonbacked valley. Since the valley is not located at the building corner, the appropriate half of the V-notch is carried all the way across the birdsmouth.

SUPPORTED VALLEY SITUATIONS

SupportING valley/supportED valley. A supporting valley is used when a secondary span intersects a primary span and there isn't a bearing wall or support beam below onto which the intersecting end of the secondary span

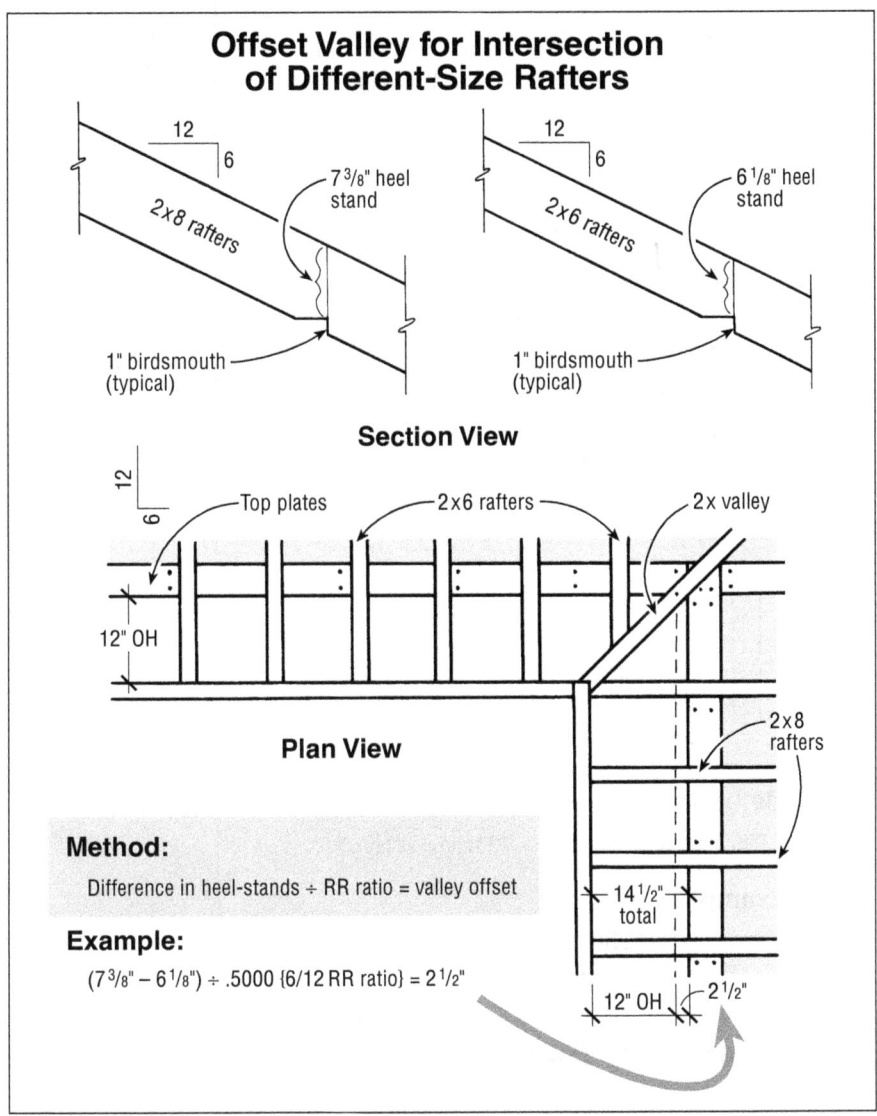

Figure 5-12. Divide the difference in heel-stands by the RR ratio to find the valley offset distance. Extend the overhang on the side with the taller heel-stand by this amount to match fascia heights.

ridge can be braced.

In **Figure 5-15**, support*ING* valley **c** is calculated for the 20-ft. primary span and connects to the main ridge. Support*ED* valley **d** is calculated for the **full** 16-ft. secondary span (without subtracting off the thickness of the ridge), shortened for 1/2 thk. of support*ING* valley **c** (remember to always shorten perpendicular to the LL plumb-line), and square-cut plumb similar to a common rafter ridge-cut (only the plumb-line is drawn for the hip/valley pitch). Back the top edge of the support*ING* valley above the intersection

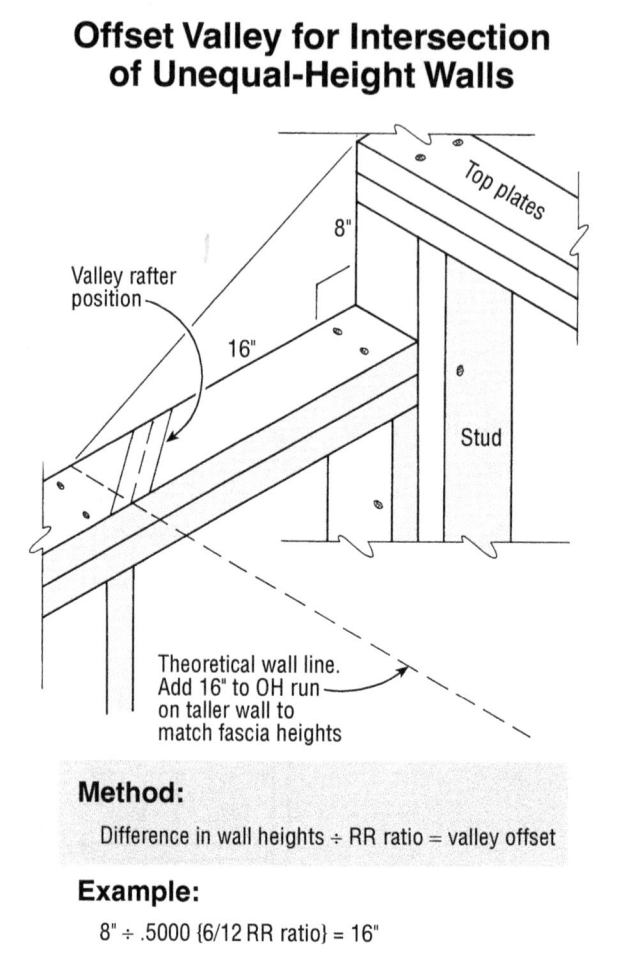

Figure 5-13. A valley offset for rafters with equal heel-stands but originating from walls of different heights is calculated by dividing that difference by the RR ratio.

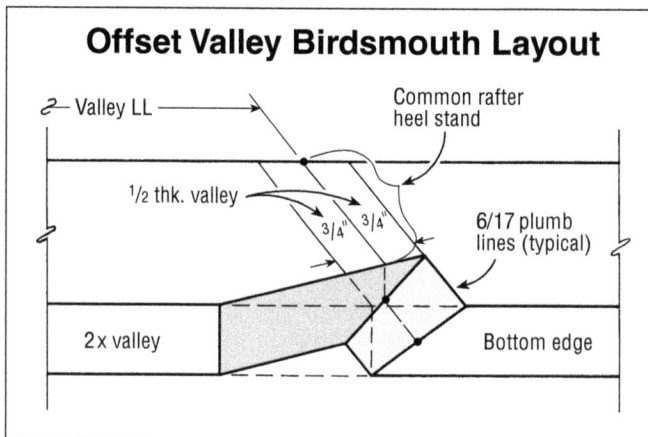

Figure 5-14. When the valley is not located at the building corner, the appropriate half of the V-notch heel-cut is carried all the way across the birdsmouth.

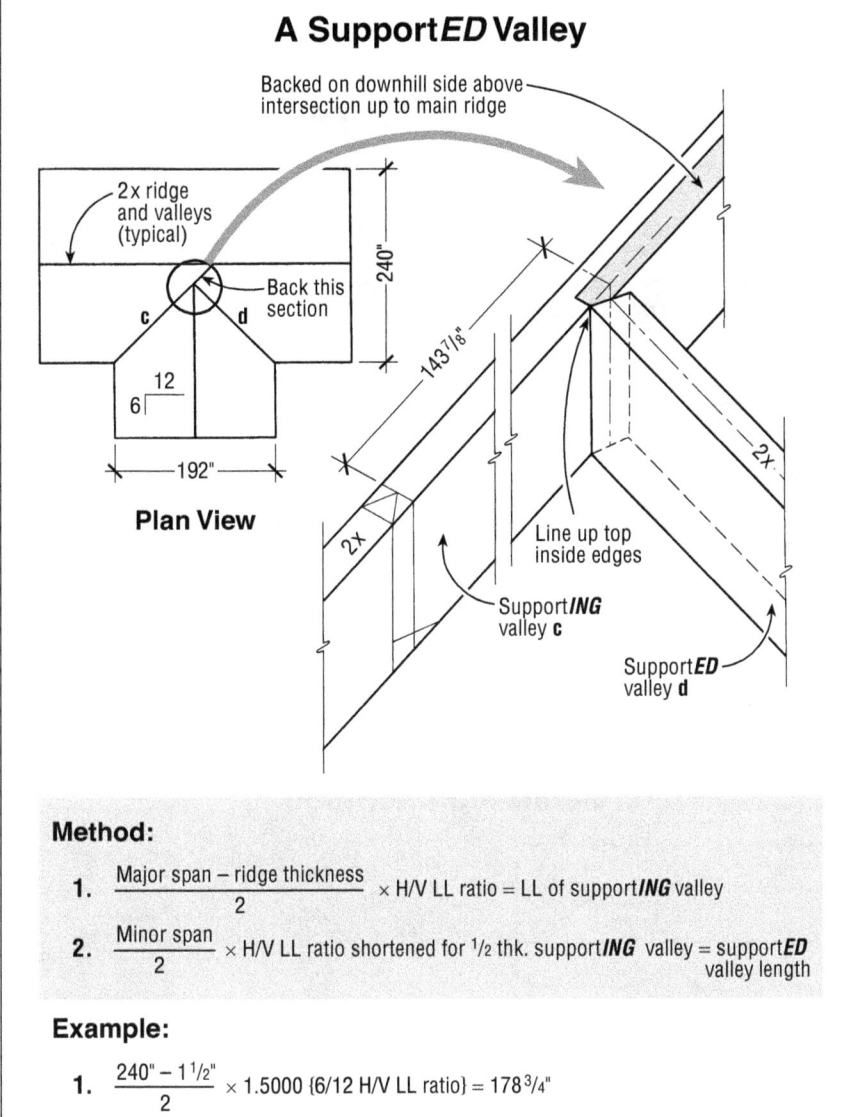

A SupportED Valley

Method:

1. $\dfrac{\text{Major span} - \text{ridge thickness}}{2} \times \text{H/V LL ratio} = \text{LL of support}\textbf{\textit{ING}}\text{ valley}$

2. $\dfrac{\text{Minor span}}{2} \times \text{H/V LL ratio shortened for } 1/2 \text{ thk. support}\textbf{\textit{ING}} \text{ valley} = \text{support}\textbf{\textit{ED}} \text{ valley length}$

Example:

1. $\dfrac{240" - 1\,1/2"}{2} \times 1.5000 \ \{6/12 \text{ H/V LL ratio}\} = 178\,3/4"$

2. $\dfrac{192"}{2} \times 1.5000 \ \{6/12 \text{ H/V LL ratio}\} = 143\,7/8"$ shortened $3/4"$

Figure 5-15. The supportING valley is a regular valley figured for the primary span. The supportED valley is figured for the secondary span using the theoretical run and shortened 1/2 thk. of the supportING valley. To mark the location where the center of the supportED valley connects to the supportING valley, measure up from the LL plumb-line at the birdsmouth the unshortened LL of the supportED valley. Position the supportED valley on a supportING valley by aligning the inside top edge with the top edge of the valley it hangs from.

REGULAR VALLEY INTERSECTIONS

Photo 5-16. Position the offshooting ridge from a supporting valley connection so both top edges plane into the center of the valley on each side. This supporting valley disappears in the roof plane from the lower ridge to the middle ridge and reappears as a hip from the middle ridge to the upper ridge.

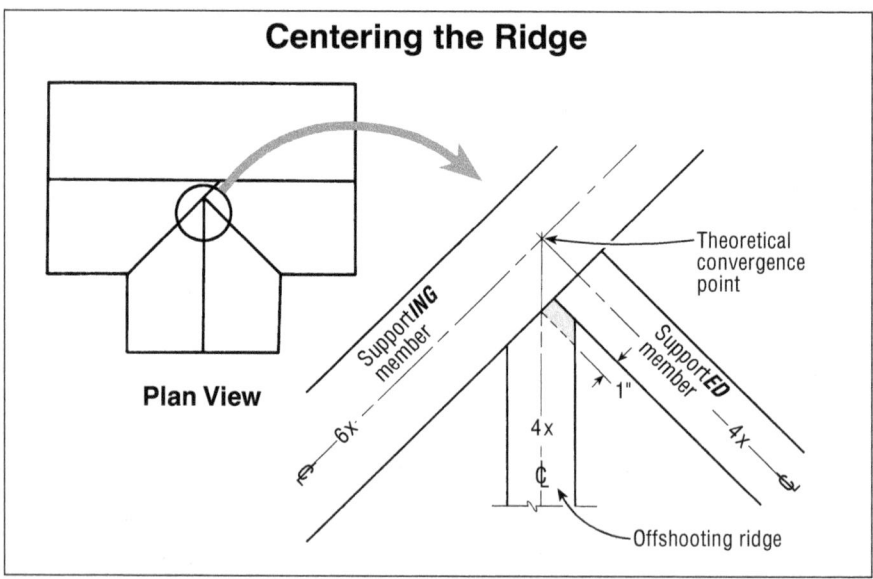

Figure 5-17. An adjustment to the cheek-cut is required to align the ridge between supportED and supportING beams of different thickness. First, lay out a standard double 45° cheek-cut on the end of the ridge, then add half the difference between the two beam thicknesses to the side towards the thinner material.

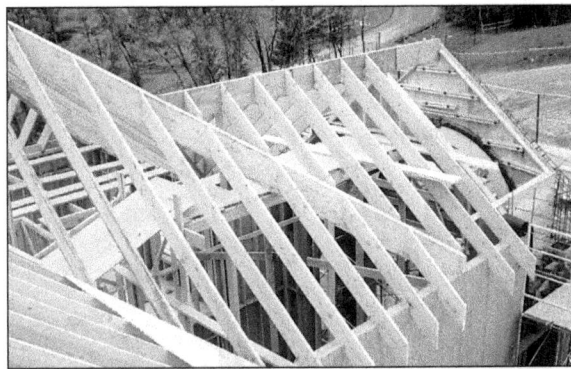

Photo 5-18. Top: A support*ING* hip with continuation jacks. Bottom: A close-up view of the offshooting ridge from a support*ING* hip/support*ED* valley connection. The continuation jacks are held high to plane in with the outside top edge of the support*ING* hip.

on the downhill side to keep it inside the roof plane (see the Chapter 4 section, "Backing a Hip," page 67, for proper set-up).

Before stacking these two rafters, measure up support*ING* valley **c** from the birdsmouth the unshortened span LL of support*ED* valley **d** (143⁷/₈") to locate the centerline of where they will connect. Flush the top inside edge of the support*ED* valley head-cut with the edge it is hanging from (see Figure 5-15).

Note: An optional method for calculating the actual length of the support*ED* valley — without the need to shorten for the support*ING* member — is to subtract ¹/₂ 45° thk. of the supporting member from the secondary span, then divide by 2 and multiply by the H/V LL ratio. Applying this method to Figure 5-15, the result would be 143¹/₄ in. ([192" − 1¹/₁₆"] ÷ 2, then × 1.5000 {6/12 H/V LL ratio} = 143¹/₄"). Remember to position the support*ED* valley on the support*ING* valley using the theoretical run LL of the secondary span (143⁷/₈") as shown.

The offshooting ridge is cut with a double 45° cheek-cut and positioned so both top edges plane into the centers of the valley on each side (see **Photo 5-16**, lower left). When the support*ING* member is larger than the support*ED* valley, it is necessary to offset the ridge slightly to center it in the span. Add one-half the difference between the two beam thicknesses to the 45° cheek-cut abutting the thinner material, as shown in **Figure 5-17**.

Support*ING* hip/support*ED* valley. A support*ING* hip **(Photo 5-18)** is identical to the matching hip which frames to the building corner (for the

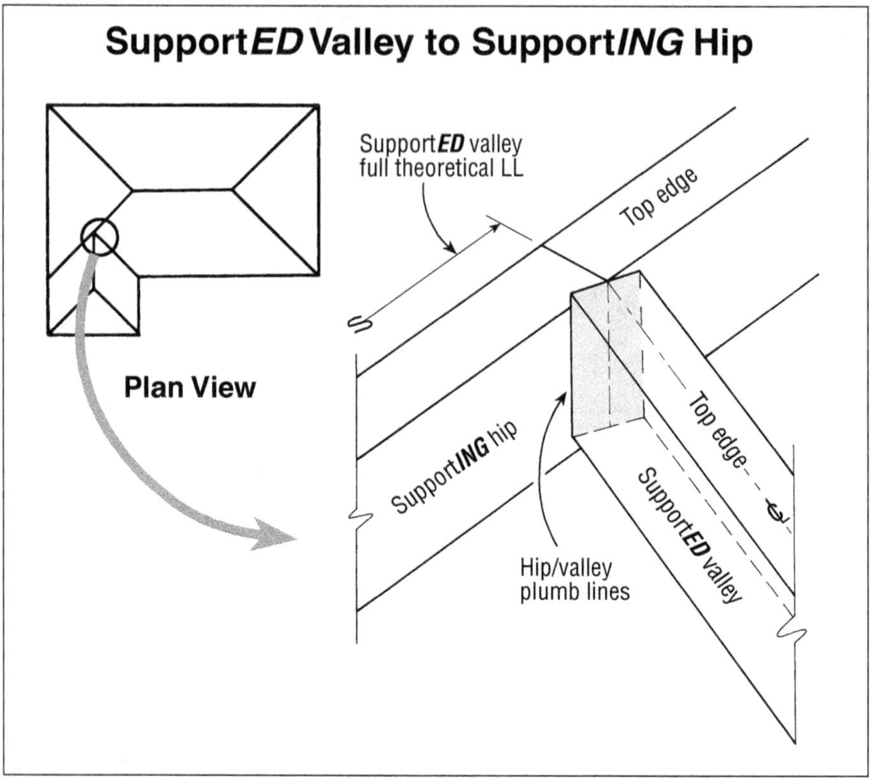

SupportED Valley to SupportING Hip

Figure 5-19. Position the supportED valley on a supportING hip by aligning the center of the valley with the top edge of the hip it hangs from.

Photo 5-20. The far edge of the offshooting ridge planes into the outside top edge of the supportING hip.

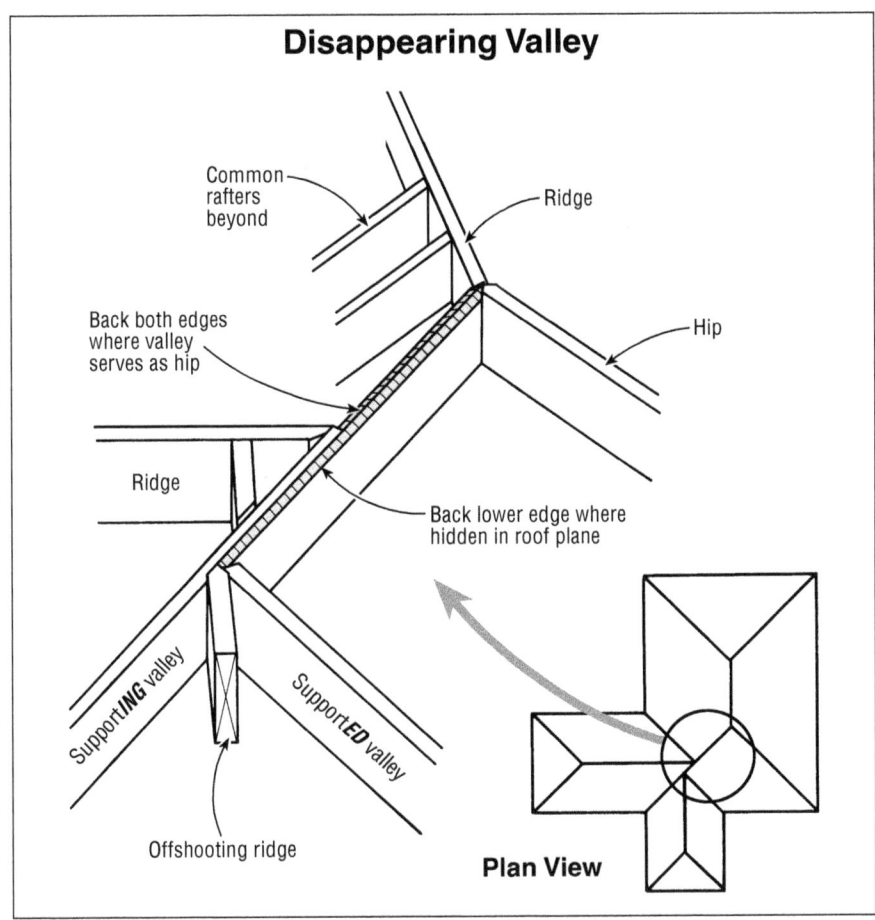

Figure 5-21. Here is an extreme example of the support*ING* valley doing double duty as a hip on its way to the ridge.

same span) except the appropriate half of the V-notch heel-cut is carried all the way across the birdsmouth. When stacking, locate this support*ING* hip directly across the span from the matching hip, which is framed to the corner. Position a support*ED* valley head-cut on a nonbacked support*ING* hip by aligning the center of the valley flush with the edge of the hip it hangs from *(Figure 5-19)*. The correct ridge height for the offshooting ridge is when the top corner edge abutting the hip planes in with the far edge of the hip *(Photo 5-20)*. Continuation jacks are held high to plane in with the outside top edge of a nonbacked support*ING* hip (Photo 5-18, bottom).

Disappearing valley? On rare occasions, you may run into what may seem to be a "disappearing" valley (Photo 5-16). It is really a support*ING* valley that has been backed on the lower side of the top edge where it disappears into the roof (like a normal supporting valley) and on both sides of the top edge where it reappears as a hip above the second ridge *(Figure 5-21)*.

Chapter 6

Roof Stacking

If you want a roof to go together nicely, keep all the building dimensions consistent and the diagonals on each section equal. On steep-pitched roofs small building dimensional errors that are unimportant when stacking shallower pitches get magnified.

When doing a lot of stacking, replace the 8-ft. electric cord on your saw with a 60- to 80-ft. (14-gauge) cord to keep the plug end from getting hung up or disconnected accidentally, and install a Saw Hanger (Tool Hangers Unlimited, Castle Rock, Colo.) for "hanging" a wormdrive-type circular saw on rafters and joists.

STACKING A GABLE ROOF

Common rafters lapping on a ridge beam can easily be set with a crane and are rolled similar to floor joists *(Photo 6-1 a & b)*.

Roofs with rafters butting to a ridge board may need some type of scaffolding unless there are ceiling joists to walk on. On a normal garage, for example, wall ties are typically spaced 48 in. on-center. In this case, tack a 2x8 scaffold plank up top like a catwalk. Place it 16 to 18 in. away from one side of the ridge to allow room to move around. Support the ends of the scaffold with a block the same height as the ceiling joists nailed to the top of each end wall or a vertical cleat nailed to the outside of the wall. Run a vertical brace to the floor from each garage tie *(Figure 6-2)*. The best working height for a scaffold at the ridge seems to be about the height of an individual's mouth (or 67 in. for me at 75 in. tall). *Figure 6-3* is one example of a raised scaffold.

Photo 6-1a. Pre-positioning rafter packs with a crane makes stacking even more of a treat.

Photo 6-1b. Lapping rafters are run just like rolling floor joists.

Once the scaffold is in place, nail a sway-stick on one end of the building to help line up the gable-end rafters with the outside wall edge and give the roof skeleton some longitudinal support until the roof can be properly braced. The sway-stick is a long 2x4 nailed on edge against the outside of the building slightly off-center from the ridge. It should extend above the ridge and at least twice that distance below the plate line for strength *(Figure 6-4)*.

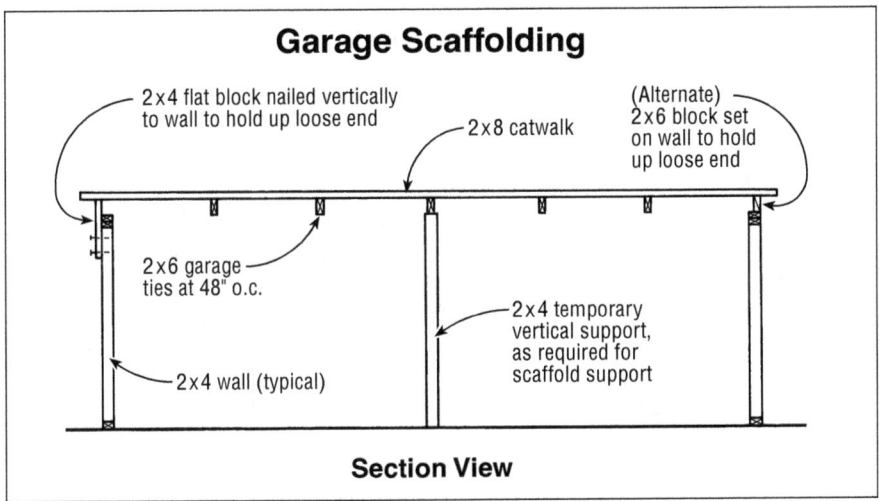

Figure 6-2. A 2x8 catwalk across the top of supported garage ties will work as a scaffold for most open garage situations. Support loose ends with 2x4 scabs or 2x6 blocking.

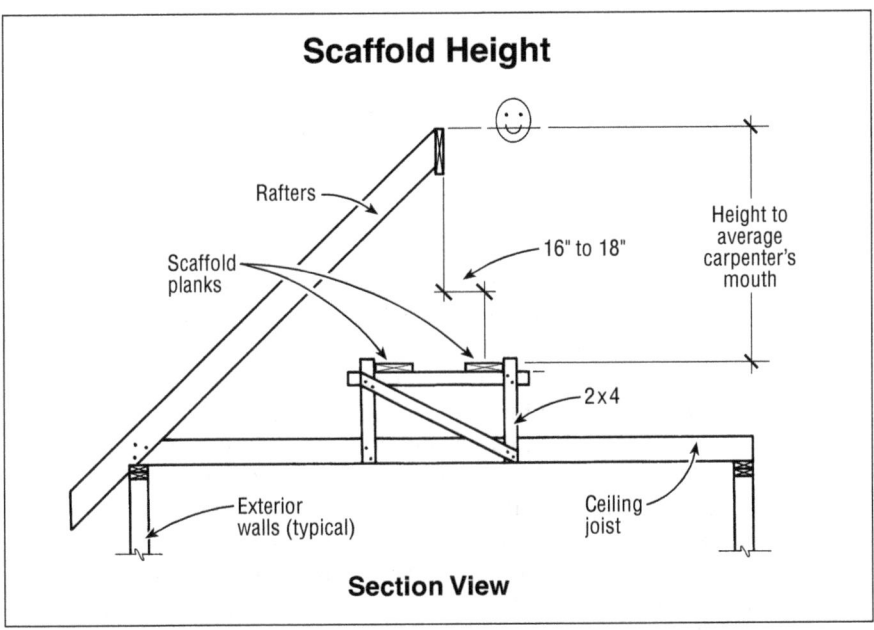

Figure 6-3. Install a scaffold 16 in. away from one side of the ridge and at a height so the top of the ridge is equal to the carpenter's mouth level for the best working position.

Next, lean up all the rafters around the outside near their layout marks and pull them up, putting the ridge-cut ends on the scaffold. Lay out the ridge board and move it up top. (*Note:* The ridge board should be of tall enough material to extend to the bottom of a rafter's ridge-cut. Except for extremely steep pitches, this is normally one size larger than the rafter stock.)

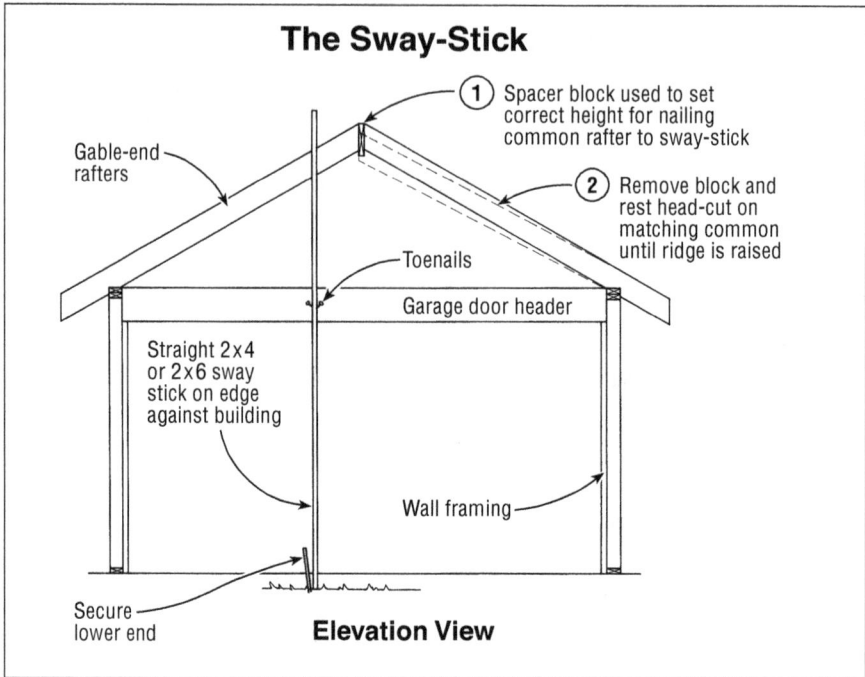

Figure 6-4. A temporary sway-stick nailed to one end of a gable run aligns the first two rafters with the edge of the building while providing longitudinal support until the roof skeleton can be properly braced.

On the end of the building with the temporary sway-stick, set up the two opposing gable-end common rafters. Use a helper to hold up the ridge-cut ends and toenail the birdsmouth flush on the building's edge. (Make sure your toenails are angled steep enough to come out the center of the board as shown in *Figure 6-5*). Place a block the same thickness as the ridge between these two rafters and tack the adjacent rafter to the sway-stick (Figure 6-4). Once the rafter is tacked, remove the block and let the second rafter sit down on the ridge-cut of the tacked rafter. Move to the other end of the building with your helper (consider this building to be a 20-ft.-long garage), and set up the opposing gable-end common rafters. Since there is no sway-stick on that end, have your helper steady these two rafters while holding one end of the ridge. Walk back to the far end of the building by the sway-stick and grab the other end of the ridge. Acting in unison, raise the ridge board between both sets of rafters and nail them off. (*Note:* I prefer using toenails when nailing rafters to the ridge in most situations because they resist a pull-apart force much better.) For a long ridge, install another set or two of opposing rafters in the middle to keep the ridge board straight.

Install diagonal sway-braces on each end of the roof skeleton and every 25 ft. in between *(Figure 6-6)*. Vertical braces to the ridge should be installed at each gable end and at 72 in. on-center to a bearing wall when the ceiling-

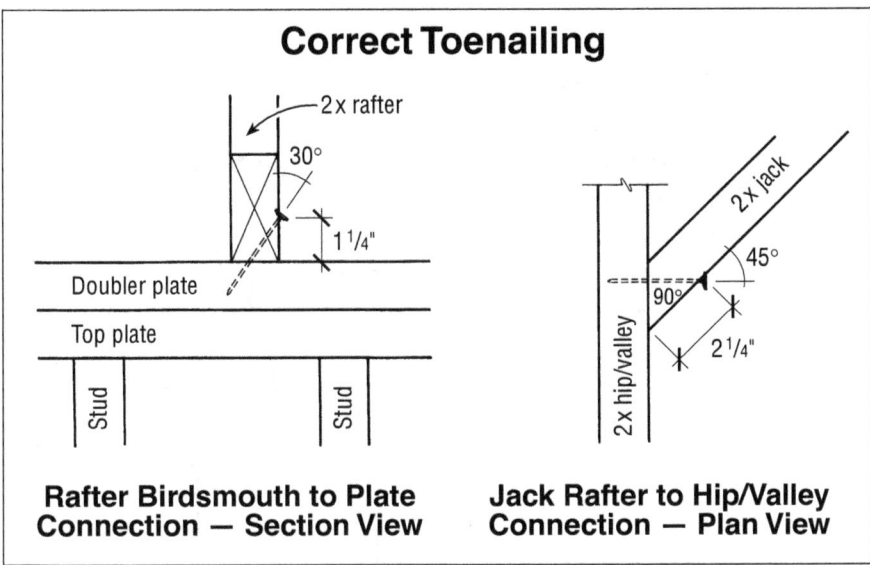

Figure 6-5. Correct toenail positions for various stacking situations using 16d sinkers.

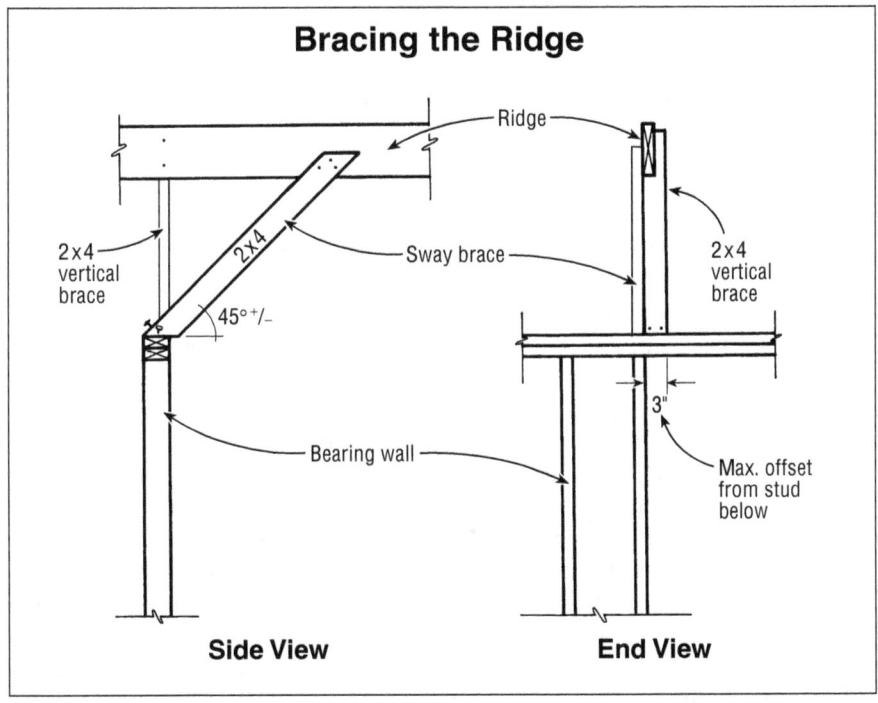

Figure 6-6. Install permanent sway-braces on each end of a gable run and every 25 ft. on-center in between. Also, if ceiling joists do not serve as a house tie, install vertical braces to the ridge at each end of a gable run and every 6 ft. on-center (to a bearing wall).

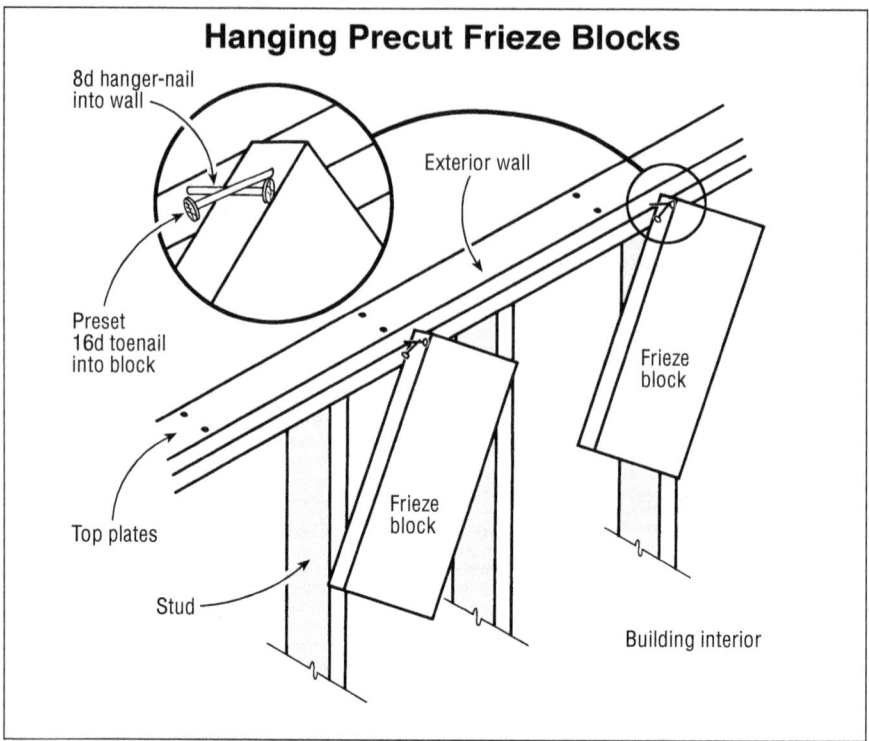

Figure 6-7. Frieze blocks prenailed with a 16d toenail are hung from 8d nails driven into the inside edge of the top plates along the outside wall.

joist-to-rafter lap doesn't carry through across the span and serve as a house tie (48 in. on-center). Double-up vertical braces that are 6 ft. and longer. (*Note:* On building sections where there are no house ties and the ridge is supported by vertical bracing or a purlin, always install metal straps over the ridge from rafter to rafter at 48 in. on-center to keep the rafters from pulling away from the ridge and the walls from spreading. This also holds true for rafters that butt to a supporting ridge beam [Figure 13-8] or sit on top with the head-cuts butting [Figure 12-6] rather than lapping as shown in Figure 3-13.)

After the bracing is completed, run the gable studs on each end and put up the rest of the commons. Nail the commons at the ridge and let the tails float to be nailed off later when the frieze blocks are installed. If there are no vertical braces because the ceiling joists will lap the rafters every 4 ft. on-center, opposing common rafters must be installed every 8 ft. on-center to brace and position the ridge before running the intermediate common rafters. Hang precut frieze blocks by a 16d toenail set on one corner from 8d nails driven into the inside edge of the exterior wall top plates ***(Figure 6-7)***. When running blocks, simply reach down and grab a block as needed. With proper planning there should be no need to get up and down from the roof. When there isn't a ladder on the job, lean one or two rafters against the wall and shimmy up as if it were a coconut tree in the South Pacific.

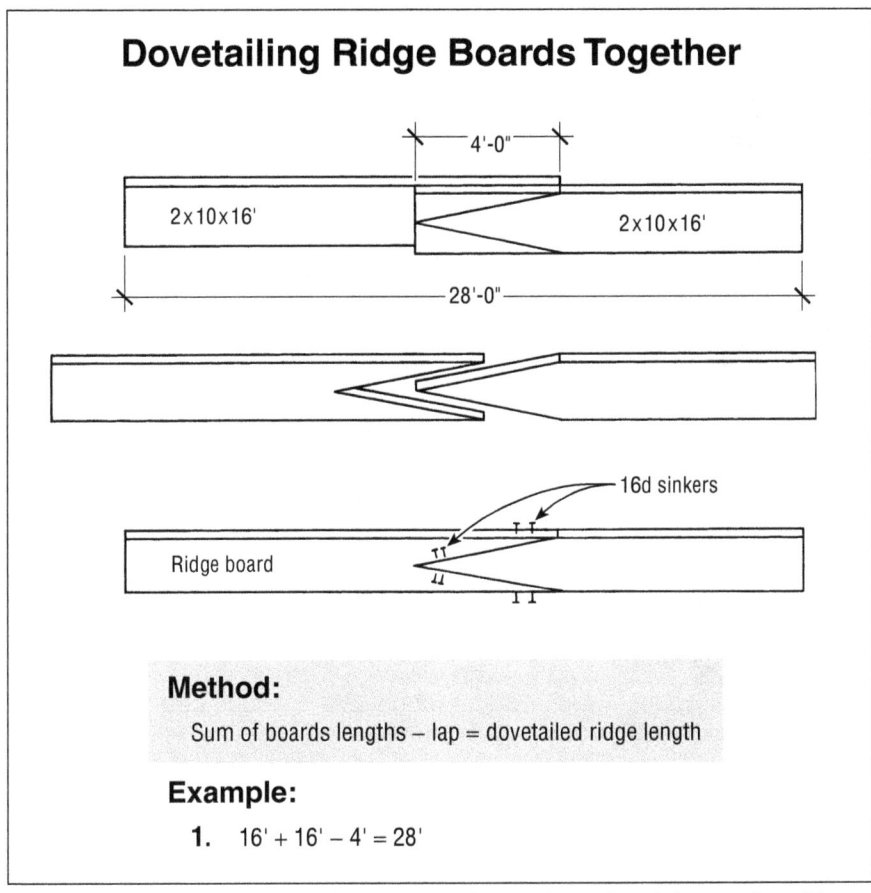

Figure 6-8. With a dovetail connection you can make two shorter boards into one long ridge.

To finish up the garage, run 2x4 vertical braces down from the ridge to hold up the center of each garage tie (refer back to Figure 2-14).

If a 2x ridge board is not long enough to run the full length, try dovetailing two pieces together as shown in ***Figure 6-8***. The best option for long, straight gable or hip roof runs is to install a segmented ridge. As an example, imagine stacking a gable roof on a 76-ft.-long building using 20-ft. ridge boards. Start by marking rafter layout on the first ridge board, and cut it to length on the center of the very last layout mark. Continue the rafter layout on the second ridge board, and again cut it on the center of the last layout mark. Do the same for as many ridge boards as needed, but leave the last ridge board long for the fascia.

Next, set up the two opposing gable-end rafters on the end of the building corresponding to the first ridge board, and tack one of them to the temporary sway-stick as before. Then, set up the two opposing rafters that are one layout mark short of the end of the first ridge board, and raise the ridge into position.

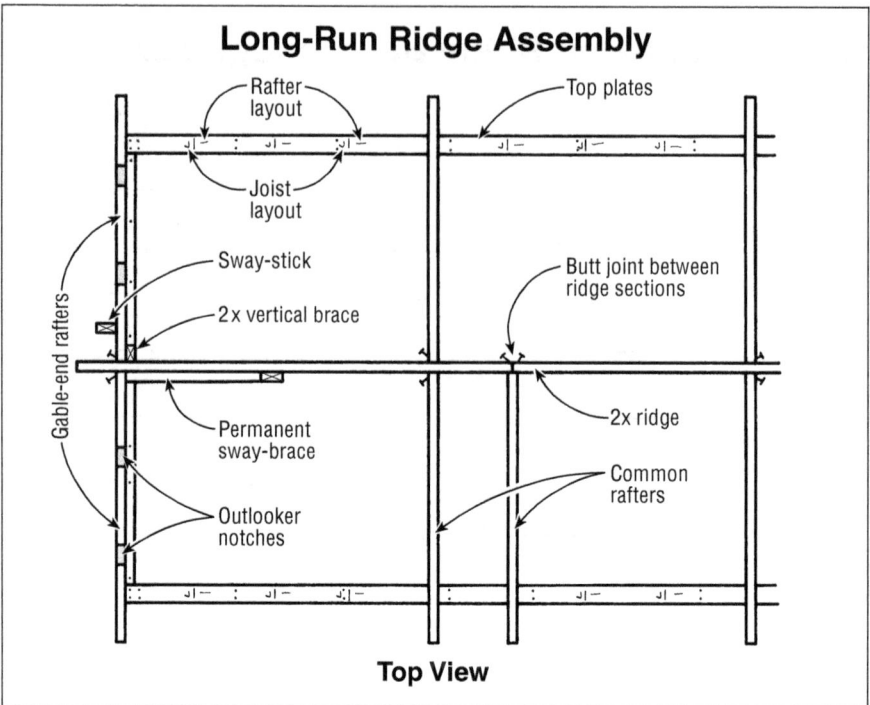

Figure 6-9. Lay out the ridge sections on a long gable so they splice in the center of a common rafter.

When the rafters are properly nailed and a sway-brace run, install one rafter of the pair that splits the end of the ridge board, and nail it off. There should be one-half of the rafter's ridge-cut still exposed. Now, set up the two rafters one layout short of the end of the second ridge board. Raise this board, and nail one end onto the rafter that splits the first ridge board and the other end at the pair of rafters. Continue this method through to the other end of the building *(Figure 6-9)*.

COLLAR TIES

Some roofs may require collar ties in the absence of a supporting ridge beam or inadequate ceiling-joist connections. Always install them as low as possible for the best tension tie. When a roof is designed with adequate ceiling-joist ties at the plate line, single 2x ties installed at half the roof rise can help resist rafter deflection on spans up to 20 ft. without the need of a stiffener. *(Figure 6-10)*. Collar tie lengths for a particular drop are calculated by dividing the drop by the RR ratio, multiplying by 2, and adding the thickness of the ridge *(Figure 6-11)*. For raised ceiling joists, use the same formula, but first subtract the height that the ceiling is to be raised from the total rise to the top of the

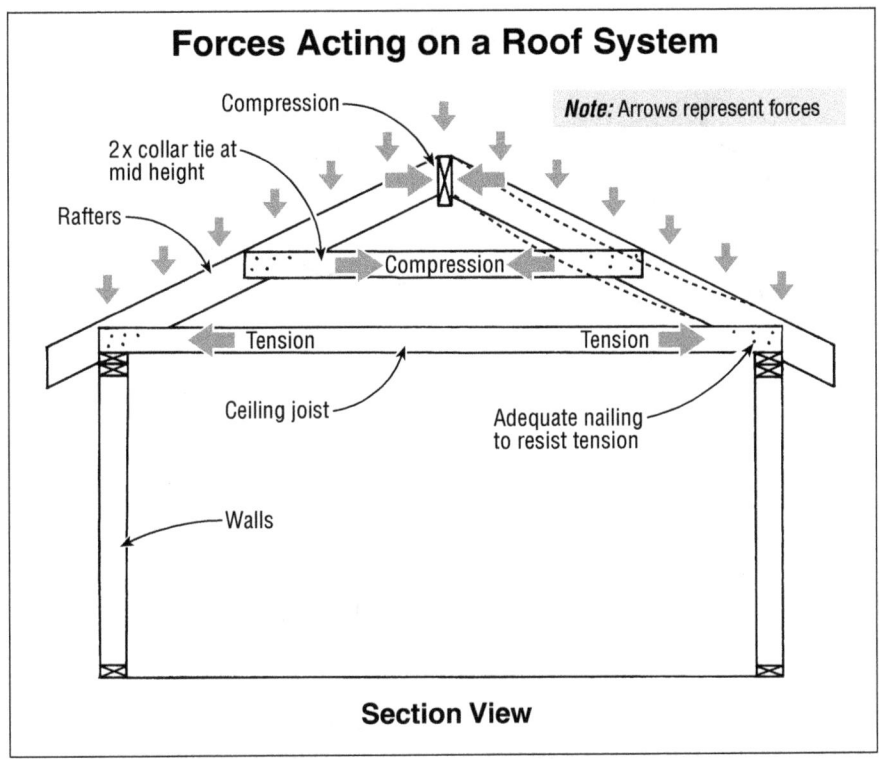

Figure 6-10. Mid-height 2x collar ties can help oppose rafter deflection when added above "stand-alone" ceiling-joist ties. Always verify that the ceiling-joist-to-rafter connection has the proper number of nails to resist the tension force.

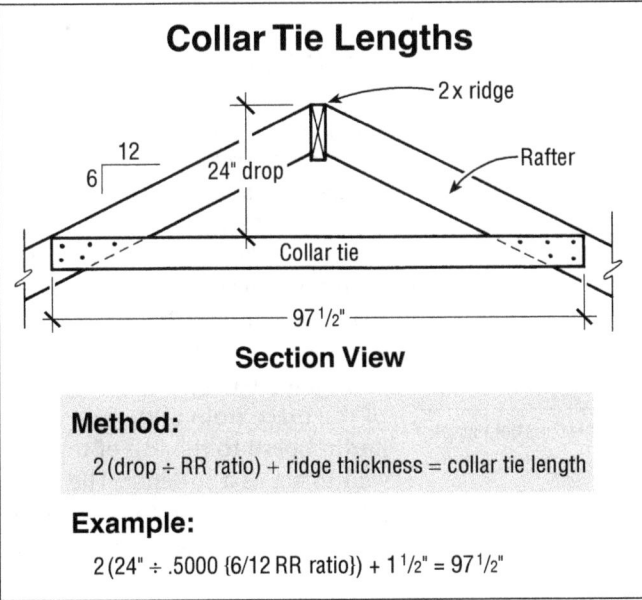

Figure 6-11. Calculate collar tie lengths by taking the desired drop and dividing by the RR ratio, multiplying by 2 and adding the thickness of the ridge.

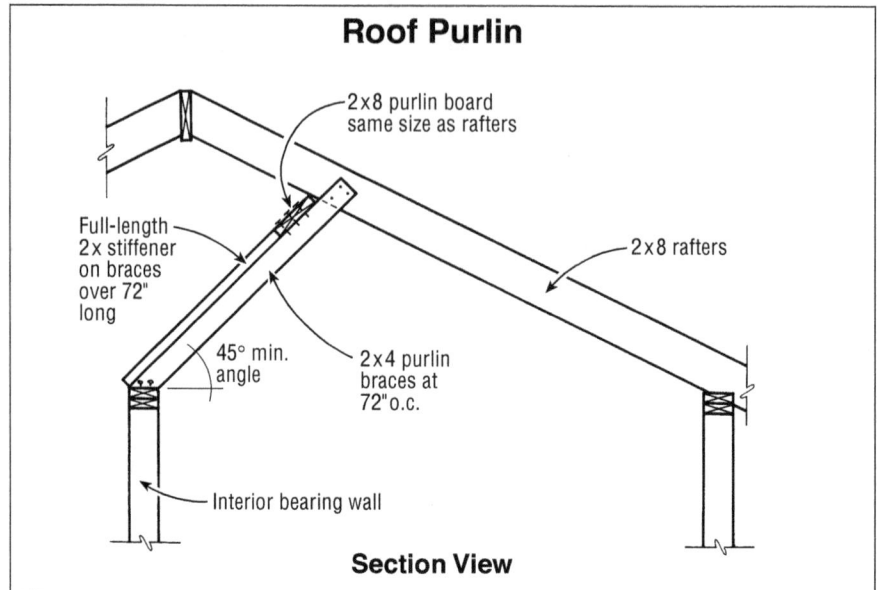

Figure 6-12. Purlins cut down the effective rafter span. Although the purlin braces can be run up to 45° off vertical, the closer to plumb the better.

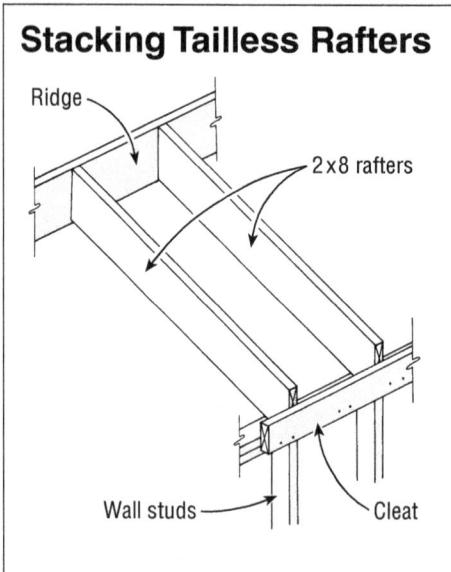

Figure 6-13. Use a temporary cleat to help stack tailless rafters.

ridge to find the actual drop, and then continue as shown. The result will be a measurement along the bottom of the board instead of the top (as shown).

PURLINS

Purlins reduce the effective rafter span, allowing a longer run for a given rafter size. Purlin braces can be installed at up to 45° off vertical *(Figure 6-12)*. These braces should be placed at 72 in. on-center (maximum) for normal roof loading. Standard 2x4 braces 6 ft. and longer should have a second 2x4 nailed flat against the inside of the brace from under the purlin board to the top of the wall to act as a stiffener. The purlin board should be at least the same size stock as the rafters.

Precut the bottom end of all the purlin braces with the desired

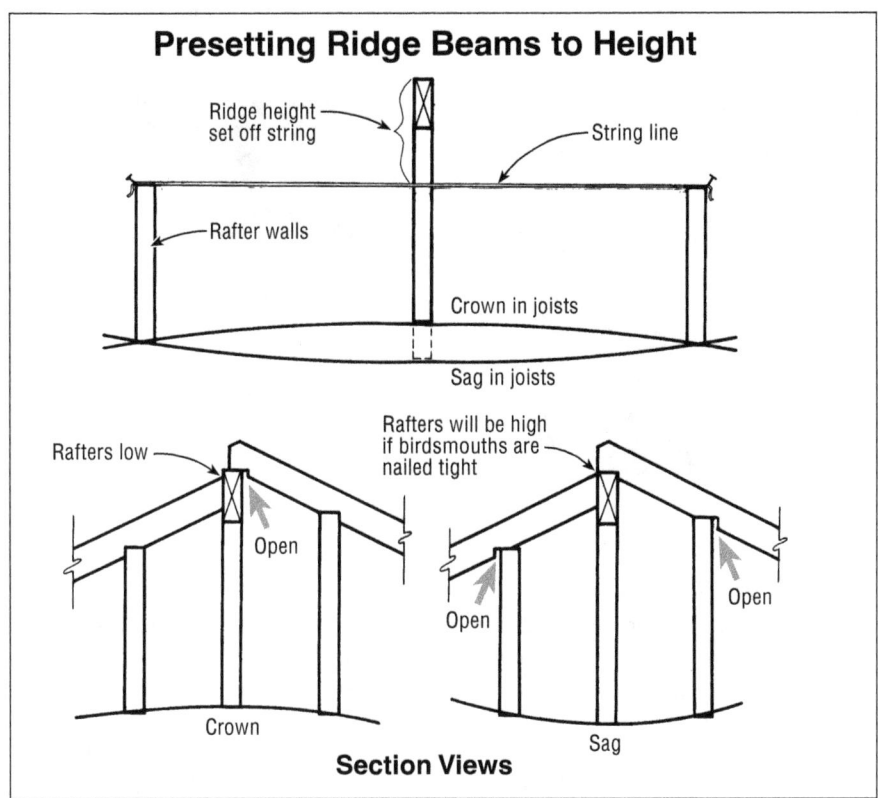

Figure 6-14. The most accurate way to set ridge beam heights is with a string from outside bearing wall to outside bearing wall. Setting beam heights off the floor when the joists have a crown leaves the top birdsmouths open or the ridge-cut low at the ridge. Likewise, sagging floor joists leave the lower birdsmouths open or the ridge-cuts high at the ridge if the birdsmouth heel-cuts were nailed tight against the building.

angle and nail them in place. Then, take the purlin and jam it up under the rafters before nailing it to the brace. The purlin brace can also be notched to receive the purlin board (similar to the vertical brace shown in Figure 6-6) or an 18-in.-long scrap of 2x4 installed lengthwise and flat on the inside of the brace under the purlin board for extra shear strength nailing.

To set the purlin exactly at a right angle to the rafters, cut the bottom of the purlin braces with the rafter ridge-cut angle.

TAILLESS RAFTERS

To help stack tailless rafters, put a cleat on the outside of the wall as shown in *Figure 6-13*.

Photo 6-15. This prefabricated steel ridge supports four converging hip beams.

RIDGE HEIGHT

Instead of using rafters to determine ridge height (as explained in the earlier section of this chapter, "Stacking a Gable Roof"), it is sometimes necessary to set the ridge beforehand and run the rafters to it. This is common practice when using large heavy ridge boards or beams. To calculate this height, use the following method: Subtract the ridge thickness from the span, divide by 2, multiply by the RR ratio, and add the heel-stand of a common rafter. The result is the vertical measurement to the top of the ridge above the horizontal plane defined by the outside walls. To avoid errors caused by measuring from an uneven floor, stretch a string from outside rafter wall to outside rafter wall, and measure up from this to set the ridge height *(Figure 6-14)*. A self-leveling laser tool set on the wall plates can also be used to verify correct ridge height, but only if it shows the far matching rafter wall to be dead-on level.

Always make a full-scale plan view drawing when figuring the height and size for prefabricated steel ridges. The special situation shown in **Photo 6-15** required careful attention to the theoretical centerlines of the four hips. The ridge height was set using the effective run of the two end commons, which were 6 3/4 in. short of the theoretical ridge center, while the two side commons flushed out above the steel ridge because they were only 2 3/4 in. short of the theoretical centerline.

STACKING A SIMPLE HIP ROOF

This section explains the proper stacking procedures for a 16 x 21-ft. full hip (shown in *Figure 6-16*). Begin by centering a rafter layout on each end-wall **(e, f)**. From each corner, measure along the long walls the same distance it was to the center of the two end-walls and lay out a rafter centered on each measurement **(a, b, c, d)**. Mark the layout for these six king commons in

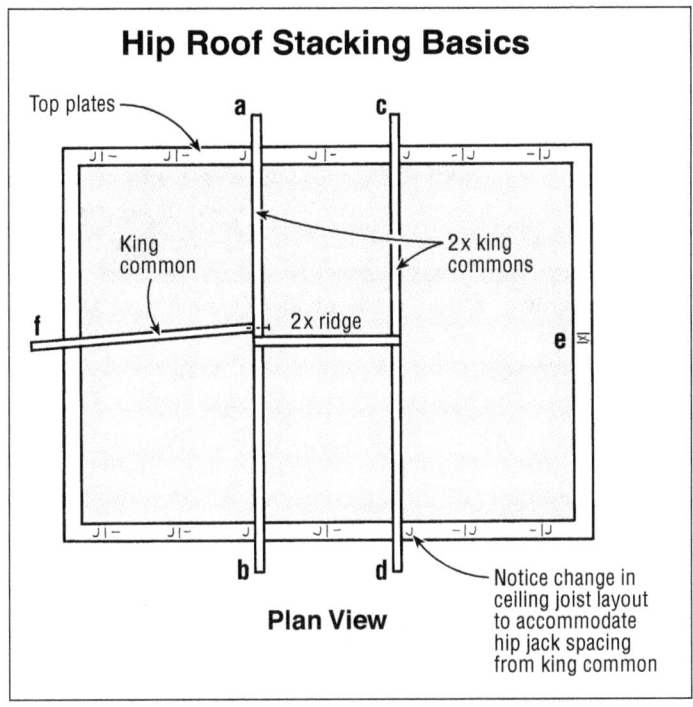

Figure 6-16. The king common rafters are used to set up the hip roof skeleton. Rafter **f** is initially tacked off-center until the ridge is raised and nailed.

keel so they can be spotted quickly when stacking. Pull layout for the remaining commons and jacks towards the corner from each of those six setup rafters. (Generally, the rafters are laid out in conjunction with installing ceiling joists, so marks for the rafters should already be on the plates.)

Lean all the common rafters around the building and pull them up top. Lay out and cut the ridge board to length (as discussed in the Chapter 4 section, "Hip Roof Ridge Lengths," page 63), and lean up one hip at each corner. At this point, set a toenail at the cheek-cut end of the hip jacks, and hang them from that nail along the exterior wall near the corners so they can easily be pulled up when needed.

Up top, with a helper holding the ridge-cut ends, set up the opposing king commons **a** and **b** by toenailing their birdsmouth on the plate-line keel marks. Let their ridge-cuts butt head to head. Next, set up the end-of-ridge king common **f** and tack it to rafter **a** so both tops are at the same height. It will act as a temporary sway-brace. After setting up the pair of king commons at the other end of the ridge **(c, d)**, raise the ridge and nail off both sets of king commons. Set up king common **e** and nail it to the end of the ridge board and reposition rafter **f** to center on the end of the ridge. Since rafters **e** and **f** act as sway-braces, no others are usually needed. In the absence of adequate ceiling-joist ties, vertical braces should be installed at each end of the ridge and every 72 in. on-center to a bearing wall below. Occasionally house ties run from hip-end to hip-end at 90° to

ROOF STACKING **121**

the span directly above the regular ceiling joists may be required at 48 in. on-center (see Photo 5-7).

The hips are next. When installing these, have your helper hold them slightly high at the ridge between the king commons so you can toenail the birdsmouth tight against the building. Rest the hip head-cuts in their slots, but don't nail the tops until all four hips are in place to avoid pushing things out of whack. Proper position of the hip is shown in *Figure 6-17*. If the building diagonals are so bad that they could not be corrected for during the plumb and line stage, it may be necessary to shorten the two opposing hips that are going the same direction as the smaller diagonal and add shims to the two opposing hips that are going the same direction as the larger diagonal.

Before running the hip fill, straighten the hip by setting up two opposing hip jacks in the middle, and vertically brace the hip if necessary (and possible). Hip-jack head-cuts are self-positioned at the hip when placed on their wall layout marks. Pull the hip-jack birdsmouth tight and nail the head-cut where it lines up with the top corner edge of the hip. If possible, leave the hip-jack birdsmouths unnailed (except for any opposing pairs used to straighten the hip) until running frieze blocks. When all the jacks are installed, nail the remaining commons to the ridge and block the exterior wall. In the process, toenail all the rafter birdsmouth notches previously left floating.

STACKING A VALLEY

Regular valley. Stacking a regular valley is not much different from stacking a hip. Pull the valley tight in the building corner and toenail the birdsmouth. The top is nailed to the ridge (as shown in Figure 6-17) with the centerpoint tangent to the top corner edge of the ridge. Paired valleys will nail to the ridge directly across from each other as shown in Figure 5-5. To verify the valley tie-in position at the ridge, plumb up from where the intersected roof's outside wall line carries through the intersecting house section. Mark the ridge at **e** (Figure 5-5). From **e**, measure the effective run of the intersecting roof ($95^1/4$") along the ridge towards the intersected roof to mark point **f** where the center of the valleys will attach.

Unless the valley has been backed, nail the cheek-cut end of the jacks high so they plane into the center of the valley rafter's top edge *(Figure 6-18)*. Also, it is a good practice to straighten the valley by setting up two opposing jacks near the middle first. The valley jack bottoms are self-positioned when nailed on a proper layout at the ridge. Valley jacks which were stepped shorter beginning from the common rafter LL actually begin layout $1/2$ 45° thk. of the valley away from the inside building corner where the sides of the valley cross the plate line, so remember to mark the ridge accordingly.

California valley. To stack a California valley (CV), all the common rafters for both the intersected and intersecting roofs should be up and the roof sheathed on the side of the intersected roof. Snap two valley reference lines by eyeballing down the intersecting ridge and commons (or running a string) to mark where the intersecting roof will die onto the plywood. A

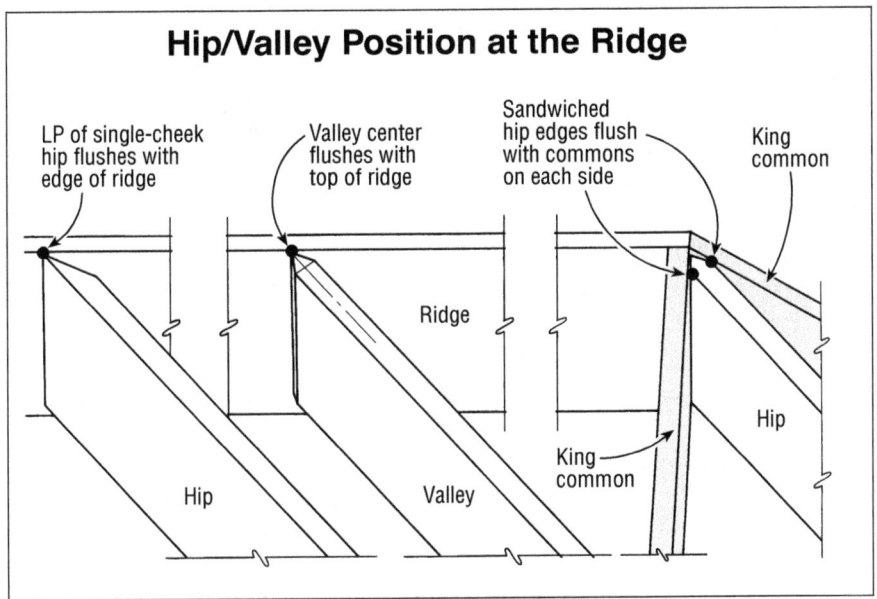

Figure 6-17. The center of the valley flushes with the top edge of the ridge, while the two top edges of a standard hip flush with the king common to each side. A single-cheek hip run to an extended ridge flushes with the ridge at the LP top edge.

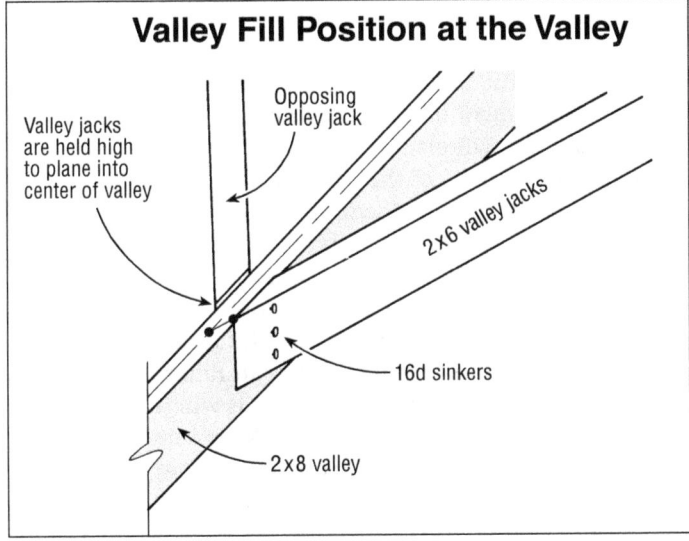

Figure 6-18. Unless the top edge of the valley is backed, valley jacks are held high to plane into the center of the valley.

board thrown across the top of the intersecting roof rafters at the outside wall line is a quick way to get the lower end of the CV snap-line. Extend the intersecting ridge to sit on the plywood (or a 2x valley sleeper as described in the following paragraph). The actual ridge length for a regular-pitch CV section — when the heel-stands for both roofs are equal — is the effective

■ Ridge Lengths for Regular Roof Intersections

The theoretical ridge length for a regular pitch roof intersection is equal to the intersect*ING* roof's effective run when the heel-stands are the same for both roofs. In other words, plumb up and mark the center of the ridge where the intersect*ED* roof's outside wall line carries through (or would carry through) the intersect*ING* building section. From there, measure along the ridge towards the intersect*ED* roof a distance equal to the effective run of the intersect*ING* roof, and place a second mark. This mark designates the location where the two valleys' centerlines will butt to the ridge board from each side (Figure 5-5, **e** to **f**).

I always run a ridge board or beam for a valley intersection long unless the situation dictates otherwise. For example, I would precut the ridge for a hip roof dormer that's locked in between the end king common and the upper headout as discussed in the Chapter 9 section, "Gable and Hip Dormers," page 189.

---

run of the intersecting roof (**e-f** in Figure 5-5) shortened for the thickness of the roof sheathing (or thickness of sheathing plus sleeper, if used). Cut the CV ridge board to sit on the supporting roof using the same cut pattern shown in Figure 5-9 except the saw angle is set square. Start layout for the CV jacks from where the tip of the California ridge-cut dies onto the plywood (or sleeper, if used). The jacks are placed on the uphill side of the layout marks (short side of the on-center mark) if they were cut with the method shown in Chapter 5. With the jacks nailed to the ridge, slide the bottom bevel-cut end to the snap-line (or 2x sleeper edge) and nail.

Unless the CV jacks will bear directly on a common rafter below, it's a good practice to run a 2x valley sleeper or toe-board over the roof sheathing on which to set the end of the ridge and the bottom beveled ends of the jacks. Position the sleeper downhill from the line so the bottom side of the intersecting roof's sheathing will plane in at the CV snap-line. In addition to eyeballing the correct position of the valley sleeper in relation to the snap-line, the location of the sleeper downhill from the snap-line can be calculated mathematically by inserting the thickness of the valley sleeper into a rise/run equation and solving for the run value. For example: A 2x valley sleeper used at a 6/12 equal-pitch CV intersection would be set downhill 3 in. from the snap-line ($1^{1}/2$" ÷ .5000 {6/12 RR ratio} = 3"). This downhill dimension is marked parallel to the main span rafters NOT perpendicular to the snap-line. An easy place to mark this is where the snap-line crosses the butt joint of the plywood sheathing. (*Note:* Set-back dimensions for a 2x valley sleeper measured perpendicular to the snap-line at various pitches are included in Chart 8, Appendix A, as the computation process is too lengthy for our purposes.)

STACKING A COMPLEX HIP ROOF

As a final exercise to sharpen your stacking skills, I will describe a way to stack the complex hip roof shown in ***Figure 6-19***. This illustration has examples of almost all the variations possible for a regular hip roof. Consider all ridges and rafters in this example to be 2x material.

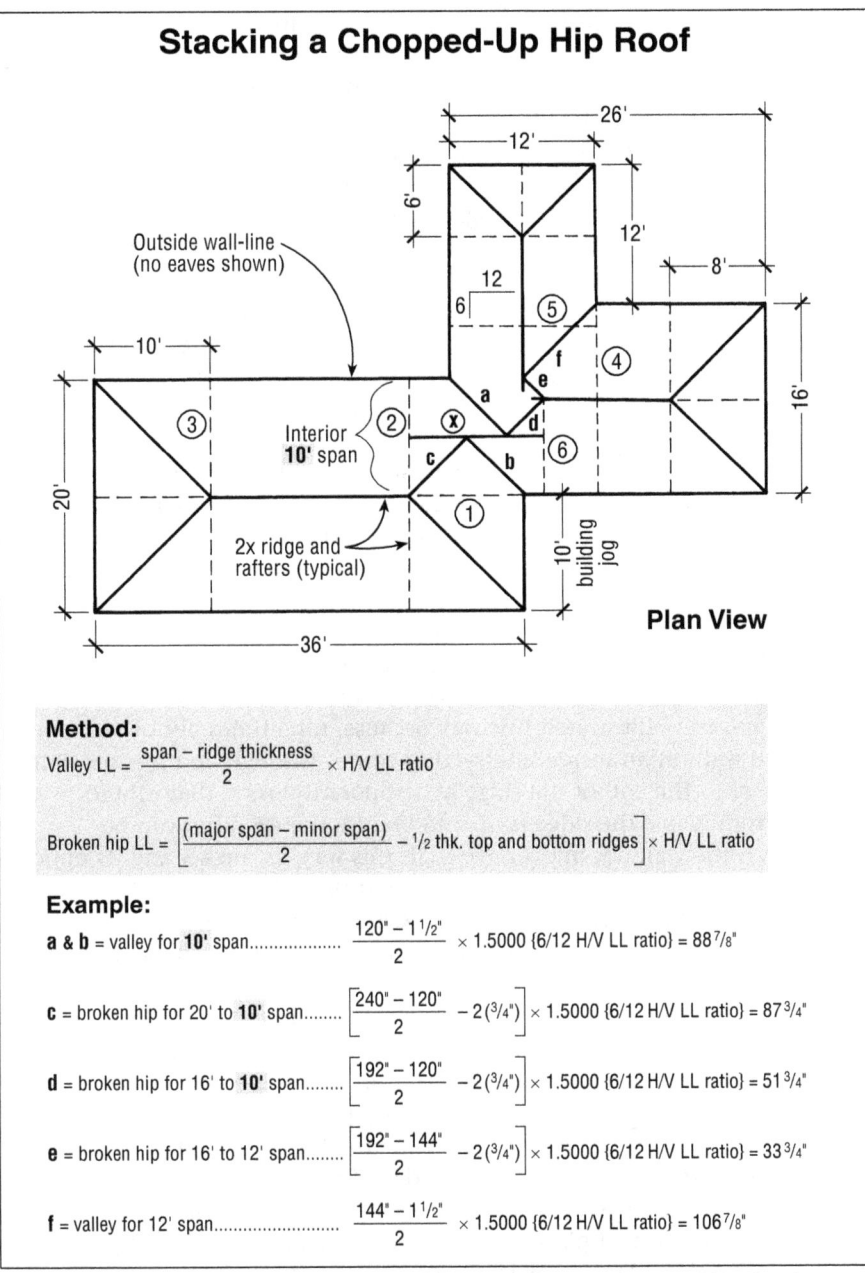

Stacking a Chopped-Up Hip Roof

Plan View

Method:

Valley LL = $\dfrac{\text{span} - \text{ridge thickness}}{2} \times$ H/V LL ratio

Broken hip LL = $\left[\dfrac{(\text{major span} - \text{minor span})}{2} - \tfrac{1}{2} \text{ thk. top and bottom ridges}\right] \times$ H/V LL ratio

Example:

a & b = valley for **10'** span.................. $\dfrac{120" - 1\tfrac{1}{2}"}{2} \times 1.5000$ {6/12 H/V LL ratio} = $88\tfrac{7}{8}"$

c = broken hip for 20' to **10'** span........ $\left[\dfrac{240" - 120"}{2} - 2(\tfrac{3}{4}")\right] \times 1.5000$ {6/12 H/V LL ratio} = $87\tfrac{3}{4}"$

d = broken hip for 16' to **10'** span........ $\left[\dfrac{192" - 120"}{2} - 2(\tfrac{3}{4}")\right] \times 1.5000$ {6/12 H/V LL ratio} = $51\tfrac{3}{4}"$

e = broken hip for 16' to 12' span........ $\left[\dfrac{192" - 144"}{2} - 2(\tfrac{3}{4}")\right] \times 1.5000$ {6/12 H/V LL ratio} = $33\tfrac{3}{4}"$

f = valley for 12' span........................ $\dfrac{144" - 1\tfrac{1}{2}"}{2} \times 1.5000$ {6/12 H/V LL ratio} = $106\tfrac{7}{8}"$

Figure 6-19. To stack this roof, set up the roof skeleton using commons positioned at the dashed line locations. The interior **10-ft.** span is found by subtracting the 10-ft. building jog at the lower right-hand corner from the 20-ft. span: (20' − 10'= **10'**).

The 20-ft.-span roof section is set up exactly as in Figure 6-16 by erecting the six king commons (shown as dashed lines). Since rafter **#1** splits the inside wall corner, it either must be cut tailless at 45° to allow for valley **b**, or square-cut tailless and nailed off layout towards the outside to stay out of the way of valley **b**. The location of rafter **#2** is found by measuring over from rafter **#3** the same dimension as was calculated for the ridge length. This ridge would be 193$^{1}/_{2}$ in. long, using the method shown previously in Figure 4-1 for 2x material (36' − 20' + 1$^{1}/_{2}$"). Vertically brace the ridge and put up the three full hips.

Next, move to the 16-ft.-span roof section and set up the king commons at each dashed line. It just so happens that a 16-in. on-center layout puts rafter **#4** right on the inside corner, so it must be cut tailless like rafter **#1**, or moved away from the valley one layout mark. (I prefer to set up commons as close to the end of the ridge as possible; therefore, I would stack it as shown). The ridge for the 16-ft. span should extend past the point where broken hips **e** and **d** connect and be cut later as shown in ***Figure 6-20***. (*Note*: This ridge length can also be figured mathematically as explained in Chapter 4, but whenever there isn't a full-length common rafter running directly off the end of the ridge, it is easier to run it long.) With the ridge up and braced, install the two full hips.

The 12-ft.-span roof section is set up exactly like the 16-ft.-span roof section. Notice the exception: rafter **#5** lands inside the corner of the house. It has been illustrated this way because, nine times out of ten, one of the two walls at an inside intersection carries through and it is possible to get closer to the end of the ridge by temporarily using that interior wall to stack from. Once the ridge is up and braced, the **#5** rafter can be removed. If the wall doesn't run through this way, set up **#5** and its opposing partner on layout outside the valley. Run the ridge for the 12-ft.-span roof section well past where broken hip **e** and valley **f** will connect and cut it later to nail to the closest hip-valley jack rafter. With the ridge up and braced, install the two full hips.

Next, put up valley **f** and, using a spacer block as shown in Figure 6-20, install the lower end of broken hip **e** so the top corner edge adjacent to the 12-ft.-span roof surface (opposite the letter **e**) will plane in with the far edge of the ridge on the 12-ft.-span roof section (opposite side of the ridge from where it is nailed). At the upper end, plane the top corner edge of broken hip **e** adjacent to the letter **e** into the ridge of the 16-ft.-span roof section. This can be done by eye or with a pattern as shown in Figure 6-20.

With broken hip **e** in place, mark the top location of broken hip **d** on the far side of the ridge by squaring over the top from broken hip **e**. Use this mark to locate rafter **#6** so that broken hip **d** will have a corner to run into while providing support for one end of ridge **x**. If rafter **#6** can be substituted for a regular rafter within a few inches, run the tail out. Otherwise, cut it tailless so the tail bays will stay uniform.

The span of the roof section where ridge **x** is located is found by subtracting the 10-ft. building jog from the main roof span (20' − 10' = **10'**). Using this span, calculate and cut one common rafter to use as a pattern to

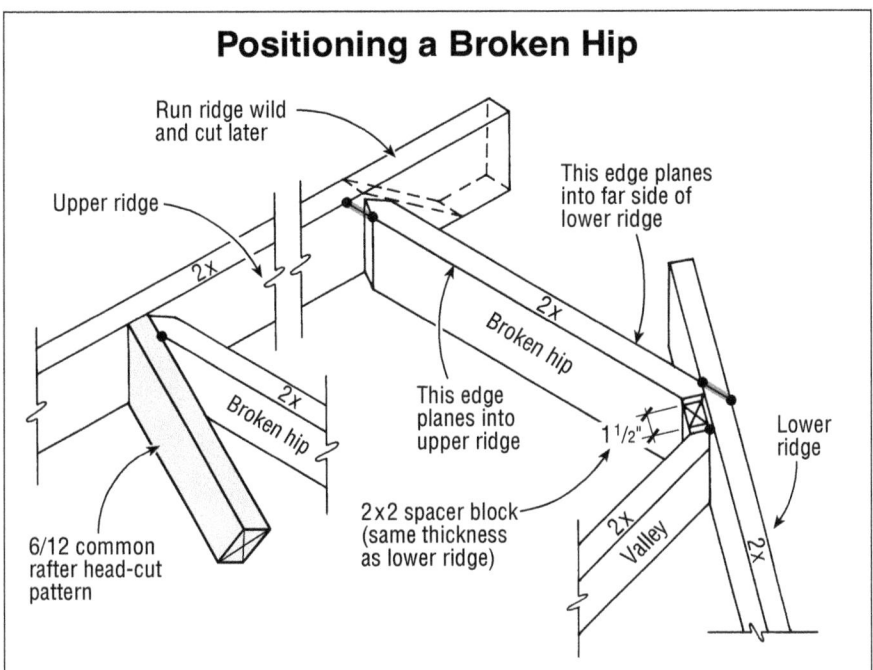

Figure 6-20. Positioning the upper end of a broken hip with a double 45° cheek-cut to a ridge is made easier by using a common rafter head-cut pattern. Use a small piece of wood the same thickness as the abutted ridge to correctly position the lower end of a broken hip.

set the height of ridge **x**. Place this pattern up against rafters **#2** and **#6** on the side towards where ridge **x** will be nailed, and scribe the ridge-cut. Cut a ridge to fit between and nail it to rafters **#2** and **#6** on the uphill side of the two scribe-lines.

Install valleys **a** and **b** and broken hips **c** and **d**. Don't forget the spacer blocks (Figure 6-20). Lastly, run the fill and remaining commons, and block the exterior walls.

Figure 6-19 shows the calculations used to solve the LL of the valleys and broken hips. Refer to the corresponding chapters if a review is needed. The theoretical ridge lengths for the hip roof shown in Figure 6-19 would be 16' for the 20' span (36' − 20' = 16'); 10' for the 16' span (26' − 16' = 10'), and 12' for the 12' span (building extension = 12'). While only the ridge for the 20-ft.-span roof section will be precut (add thickness of ridge to net actual length), knowing the theoretical ridge lengths for the other two spans will help verify correct tie-in position of the various broken hips and valley.

Chapter 7

Eaves and Plywood

Fascia Methods

Figure 7-1 illustrates the two common ways of hanging fascia. Running the fascia plumb makes constructing the joints at the inside and outside corners much easier. Either way, the rafter tails must be cut to length. For closed eaves, gang-cut all the tails on the cutting racks to save time. For open eaves, however, snapping and cutting them in the air will produce a straighter fascia line. At each end of an eave run, mark the last rafter with the desired overhang and snap a line between the two points. Carry the line all the way through to mark any hips or valleys. Square-cut tails can be marked with a fixed rafter square, while plumb-cut ends must be marked with an adjustable Quick Square® set to the pitch of the roof. Cutting 2x hip tails for plumb-hung fascia is easily done in the air by first making a 45° saw pass on the appropriate side of the tail (depending on the direction of your saw-table's tilt) and then resetting the saw bevel to square for a second saw pass straight down the center of the 45° cheek-cut. Don't try this with square-hung fascia, though; the angles are different. (*Note:* Beam hip and valley tails should always be pre-cut on the ground, and any intermediate 2x tails cut in the air by snapping a line from corner to corner.)

A taller fascia board is sometimes needed on steep pitches when the fascia is run plumb unless the bottom corners of the rafters are clipped. This horizontal clip can be gang-cut while the rafters are still on the rack. Make a level cut using a large swing-table saw exactly like the seat-cut for a birdsmouth without cutting the tails to length; if the tails are gang-cut to length, use a regular Skilsaw® set square and run it horizontally along the cut tail surface

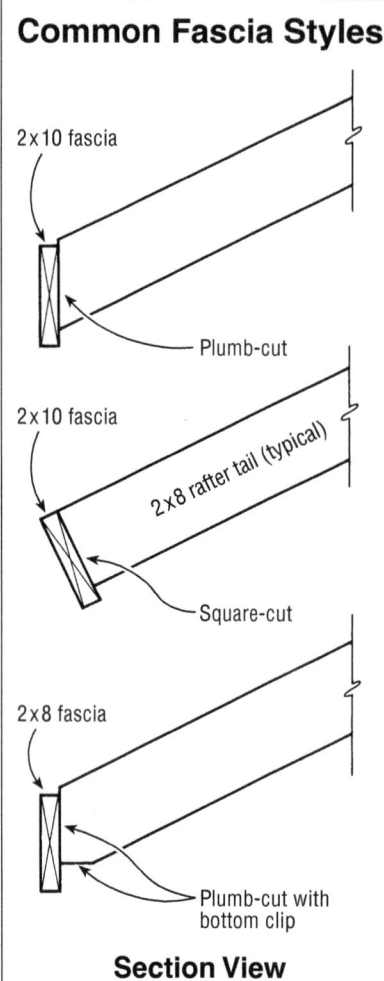

Figure 7-1. Plumb-hung fascia make the inside and outside corners much easier to cut, but due to the increased tail-end dimension on steep pitches, this method usually requires either the use of a taller fascia board or the bottom of the rafter tails to be clipped.

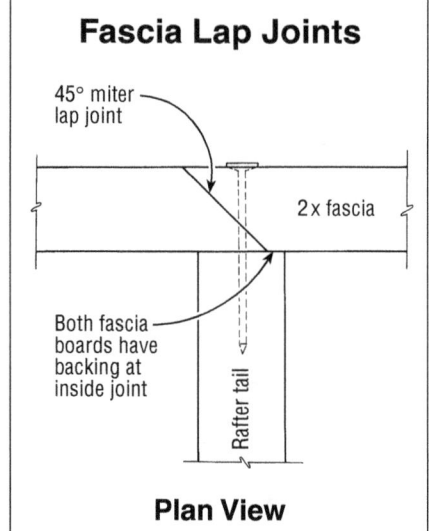

Figure 7-2. Center the fascia miter lap joint on the rafter tail so both boards will have some backing and not tend to slide apart when nailed.

of the pile to make the clip.

A 45° miter lap joint on 2x fascia is illustrated in ***Figure 7-2***. By centering the miter lap joint on the rafter, both fascia boards will have some backing and not tend to slide apart when nailed. (*Note:* Some carpenters use angles other than 45° for a 2x miter lap joint, but I prefer 45° for a multitude of reasons. First, using 45° keeps all bevels the same on both the corners and the laps. Second, the saw bevel can accurately be set time after time at 45° since it rests on the stop at the upper end of the saw adjustment. Third, fascia nails through a 45° lap joint prevent the splice from pulling apart much better than one with a lesser angle.)

When hanging fascia plumb, the outside corners at the hips are mitered at 45°, while the inside corners at the valleys are square-cut and butted.

The inside and outside corners for square-hung fascia can be quite a challenge. To mark the face-cut on the fascia, set up a framing square as shown in **A** of ***Figure 7-3***, with the unit of roof rise (6") on the tongue and the

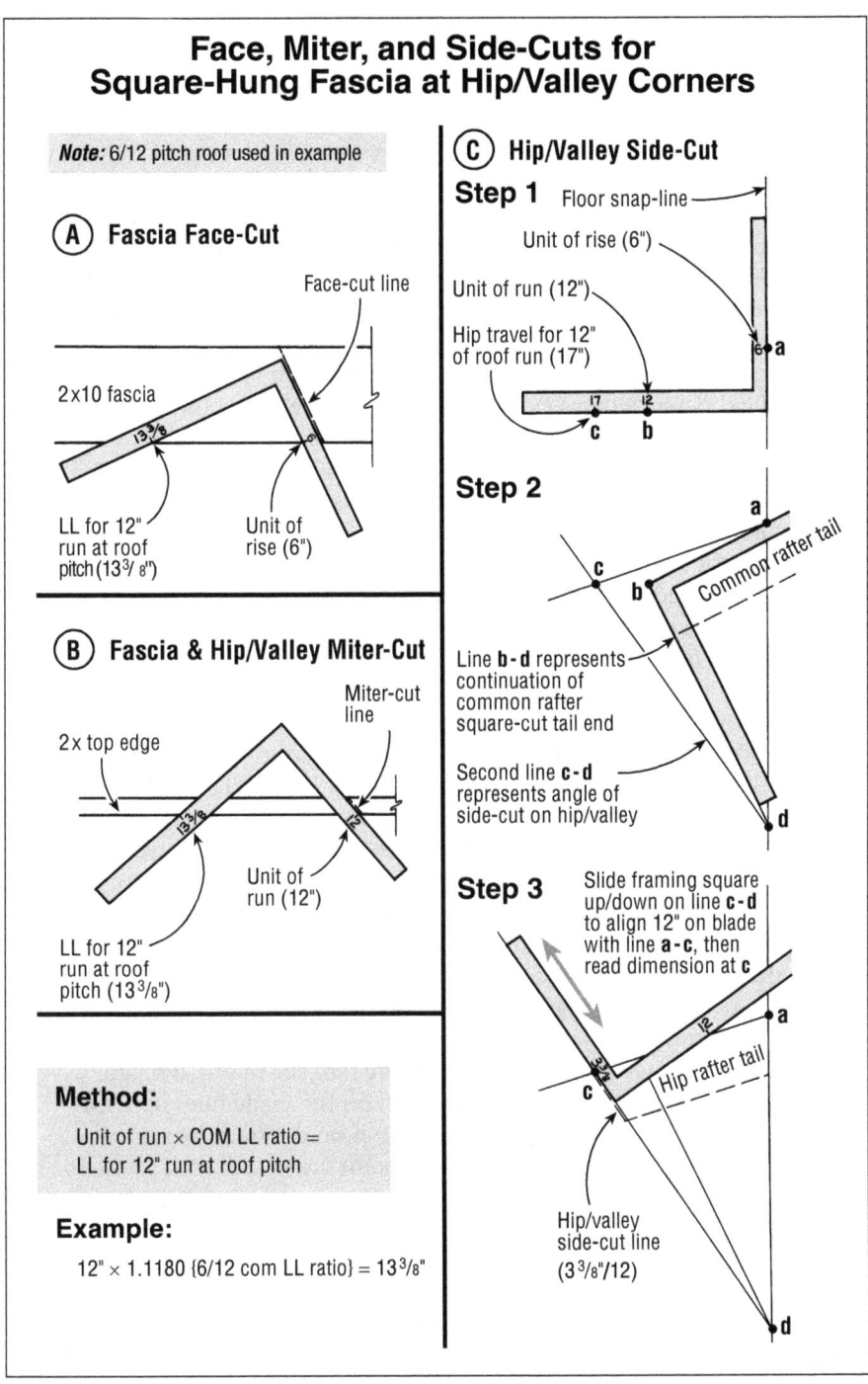

Figure 7-3. To lay out inside/outside corners for square-hung fascia, place a framing square as shown: in **A**, to mark the fascia face-cut; in **B**, to mark the top edge miter-cut line for both the fascia and the hip; and in Step 3 of **C**, to mark the side-cut on the hip/valley.

LL for 12 in. of roof run (12"×1.1180 {6/12 COM LL ratio} = 13 3/8") on the blade, and scribe a line along the tongue.

To mark the cut-line for the miter angle on the top edge of the fascia board, position a framing square as shown in **B** of Figure 7-3. Set the unit of run (12") on the tongue and the LL for 12 in. of roof run (13 3/8") on the blade, and once again scribe a line along the tongue. When adjusting a Skilsaw® to make the miter-cut, **do not** set the saw's bevel to the angle formed by the framing square on the edge. Rather, adjust the saw's bevel by eye so that while following the face-cut line on the fascia, the blade tracks through the top-edge cut-line. Once this angle has been found, note it for future reference since it will also be used to make the bevel on the end of the hip/valley tail. The butted inside corner joint at the valley is not mitered but still has a slight angle. This angle is the difference between 45° and the saw-bevel angle found in Figure 7-3. (For example: 45° − 40° = 5°.) Use this slight angle on both boards so the LP is always on the outside surface. *Note:* The method shown in ***Figure 7-3 (A and B)*** also applies to square-hung frieze blocks at the hip/valley.

Using a framing square to mark the side-cut on a hip/valley requires snapping out on the floor a full-size section view of the eave situation at both the common rafter and the hip rafter superimposed on each other to find the correct setting. This requires several steps shown in **C** of Figure 7-3:

1. Place a framing square on a floor snap-line with the outside edge of the tongue set along to this line. From the framing square "elbow," measure along the tongue the roof's unit of rise (6"), and place a mark **(a)** on the snap-line. Then measure out from the "elbow" along the blade and place marks (**b** and **c**) at both the unit of roof run (12") and the hip's diagonal travel dimension per unit of roof run (17"). Snap lines through both these points back to the unit of rise mark (**a–b** and **a–c**).
2. Draw a perpendicular line representing the extension of a square-cut common rafter tail from the unit of run mark **(b)** to intersect the original snap-line at **d**, and snap a long line from there back through the hip diagonal travel mark **(c)**.
3. Place a framing square on the section view drawing as shown with the tongue of the framing square tangent to line **d-c**, and slide it up until the 12-in. dimension on the blade lines up with the **a-c** line. Use the 3 3/8-in. dimension on the framing square adjacent to the hip diagonal travel point **c** together with 12 in. to lay out the side-cut on a hip/valley for square-hung fascia.

The technique shown in Figure 7-3 will also work to lay out and cut the square-hung fascia connection at bastard hip/valleys that divide the building corner angle. (See "Dog-Leg Bastard Hips and Valleys" in Chapter 8, page 151, and "Hexagons", "Octagons", and "Other Polygons" in Chapter 10, pages 205-215.)

With these situations, the face-cut on the fascia board would be laid out similar to what is shown in **A** of Figure 7-3, except substitute a corresponding hypothetical 12-in. on-center bastard jack-step measurement on the blade in place of the 13 3/8 in. depicted. (Refer ahead to Figure 8-5 for details on calculating the bastard jack rafter "step.") If this number will overextend the length of the framing square blade, divide both the tongue and blade measurements in half to shorten proportionally. For example, when applying this technique to the outside 45° dog-leg corner shown in Figure 8-2, **6 in.** would be set on the tongue, and **32³/₈ in.** (12" {hypothetical o.c. spacing} ÷ .4142 {from Chart 5, the tangent of half the building jog, or 22¹/₂°} = 29" run; then 29" {run} × 1.1180 {6/12 LL ratio} = 32³/₈" step) would be set on the blade. Since 32³/₈ in. is too large a number to be found on the framing square blade, divide both numbers in half. Therefore, **3 in.** is now set on the tongue, **16¹/₄ in.** is set on the blade, and the face-cut line is scribed as shown in **A** of Figure 7-3.

For the bevel-angle cut-line along the top edge of the fascia, substitute the result from the multiplication of the tangent of half the building jog angle with the unit of roof run in place of the 12-in. measurement depicted on the framing square tongue in **B** of Figure 7-3, and continue as before. Applying this technique to the fascia at the dog-leg hip corner in Figure 8-2, the framing square would be set up with **5 in.** on the tongue (.4142 {tangent of 22¹/₂° from Chart 5} × 12" {unit of roof run} = 5"), and **13³/₈ in.** would be set on the blade. (*Note:* Remember, once again, that the line along the top edge of the fascia is a cut-line. **Do not** set the saw's bevel adjustment to the angle formed by the framing square on the edge. Rather, set the saw angle so that while following the face cut-line on the fascia, the saw blade tracks through the cut-line. When found, this same angle is also used to make the miter-cut on the hip tail.)

To lay out the side-cut line on the hip/valley, substitute the pitch of the bastard hip for that of the regular hip shown in **C** of Figure 7-3 when snapping the superimposed section view on the floor. It will be necessary to convert the pitch/12 to a common rise numerator in order to find the corresponding hip travel. Once again, applying this procedure to the dog-leg hip in Figure 8-2, the 5¹/₂/12 dog-leg hip pitch is converted to 6/13 to plot it on the section view drawing. Therefore, point **c** would be at 13 in. rather than the 17 in. depicted. The remainder of the procedure continues as before. (We have Nick Ridge and his diligence to thank for resurrecting the framing square method to lay out various cuts shown in this section.)

David McIntire (author of *The Rafter Book*) and Barry Mussell (author of *The Roof Framer's Bible*) both calculated all the angles required to lay out and cut square-hung fascia at regular hip/valley corners. The angles for each pitch are listed in their rafter table style books. David has allowed me to reprint the angles for the most common pitches at the back of this book. (See Chart 7, Appendix A.)

OUTRIGGERS AND BARGE FASCIA

Figure 7-4 illustrates a cut-in outrigger (or lookout) used to hang barge fascia on a gable end. Gang-cut all the notches while the rafters are on the rack instead of cutting them one at a time in the air. Typically only the gable-end rafters are notched for a standard overhang. Be sure the gable-end rafters are straight before you nail off the outriggers.

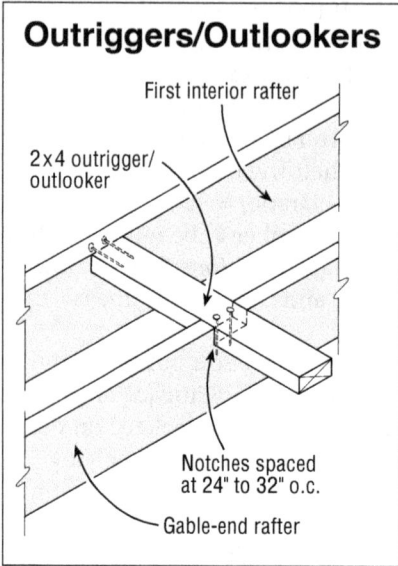

Figure 7-4. Gang-cut all the outrigger notches while the rafters are on the rack. Generally only the gable-end rafters are notched for a standard overhang.

While there are many different methods to hang barge fascia, I prefer to precut the bottom corner miter and run the top end long on the first barge fascia board. Once in place, nail the bottom corner miter joint and one outrigger down from the ridge. Draw a plumb-line on the fascia at the center of the ridge, and cut it in the place. Measure the actual length for the second barge fascia, and precut both ends adding $1/8$ in. to the overall dimension. Once in place, nail off the bottom corner miter joint, and rest the head-cut against the installed barge fascia's head-cut. It should sit slightly high at the ridge. Make one pass down the joint between the two boards to clean up any discrepancies, and nail off.

FAKE VALLEY TAILS

Often with a California Valley intersection, a fake valley tail or a "flying valley" must be installed. For low-pitch roofs use the same size lumber as the rafters, and for steeper pitches use the next size up. To determine where to cut the adjacent common rafter tails so a fake valley tail will slide down between them, measure to the inside building corner from the inside edge of each intersecting rafter and subtract $1/2$ 45° thk. of the valley *(Figure 7-5)*. Multiply this result by the COM LL ratio to find the measurement down the top inside edge of the rafter from a point plumb with the outside wall line to where the valley rafter will intersect. This is an SP measurement. Draw a plumb-line down the side of the tail from this mark, and cut the tails with the saw set at 45°. Cut a fake valley tail with an appropriate birdsmouth and slide it between the cut commons. Position the fake valley so the bevel-cut common rafter tails plane into the center as shown in Figure 6-18.

MISCELLANEOUS FASCIA TECHNIQUES

Figure 7-6 illustrates a butted valley corner. When running fascia from up top, cut the valley with a single bevel-cut according to the way your saw table tilts instead of a V-groove where half of the cut must be made from the bottom.

In the Southern California tracts, fascia guys developed many methods to help them hang fascia solo from up top. In addition to being blessed with great balance and agility, they employed several helper-nail techniques similar to the ones shown in *Figure 7-7*. Michael Stary wrote a super article on

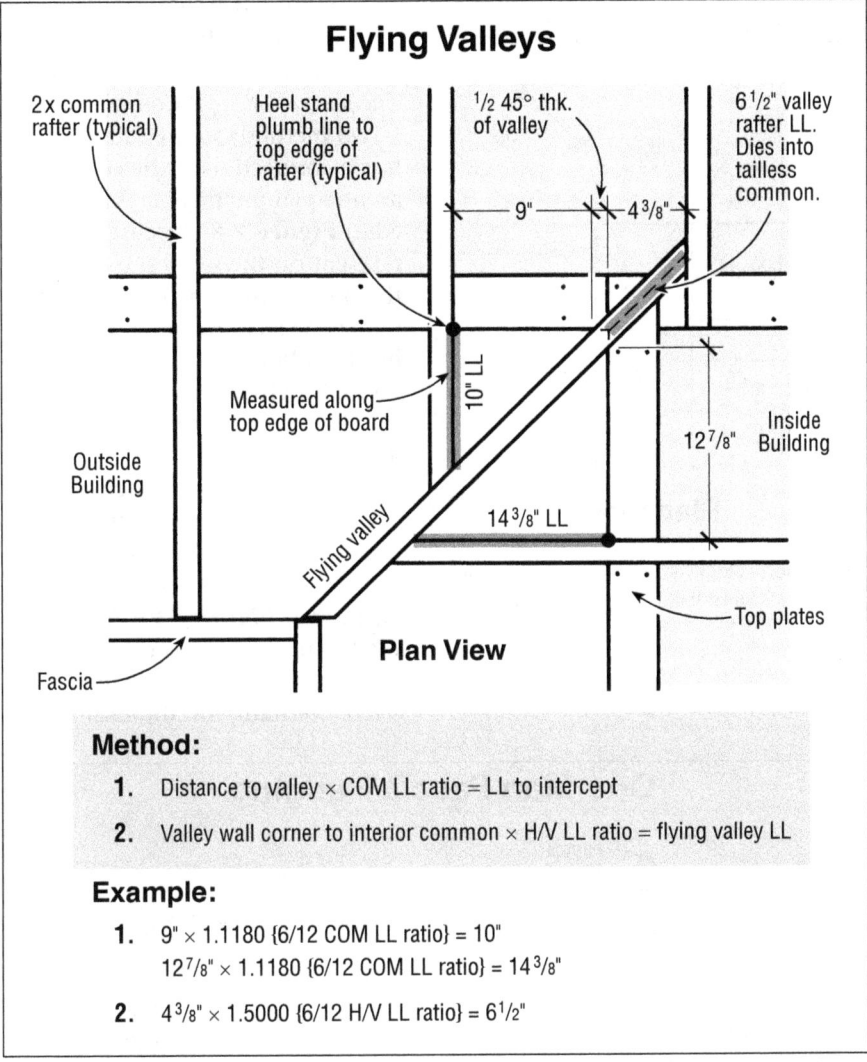

Figure 7-5. When an intersection is framed California-style, a fake or "flying valley" must be installed from the building corner to the fascia. To determine where to cut the existing common rafter tails so the "flying valley" will slide down between them, measure from the inside edge of each common over to the corner, subtract 1/2 45° thk. of the valley, and multiply by the COM LL ratio.

EAVES AND PLYWOOD   **135**

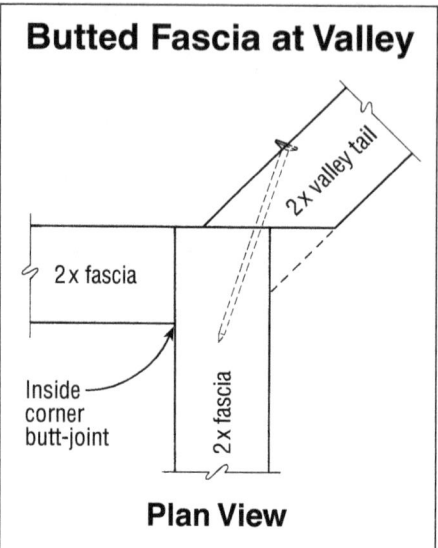

Figure 7-6. A single 45° cheek-cut is made on a 2x valley tail when hanging fascia from up top.

one-man fascia hanging which was reprinted in the book, *Residential Structure and Framing*, published by *The Journal of Light Construction*.

Two methods for handling the fascia connection at the ridge of an unequal-pitch gable is illustrated in **Figure 7-8**. Because the rake-cut on the steep side is longer, the bottom must be notched up under the shallow pitch, or the head-cut butt-joint must be skewed slightly off vertical towards the shallow pitch to equal up the dimensions.

When two unequal-pitch roofs with equal heel-stands intersect, the overhangs will be different lengths to keep the fascia the same height (see **Figure 7-9**). To calculate the unknown overhang for a consistent fascia height, divide the given overhang run dimension

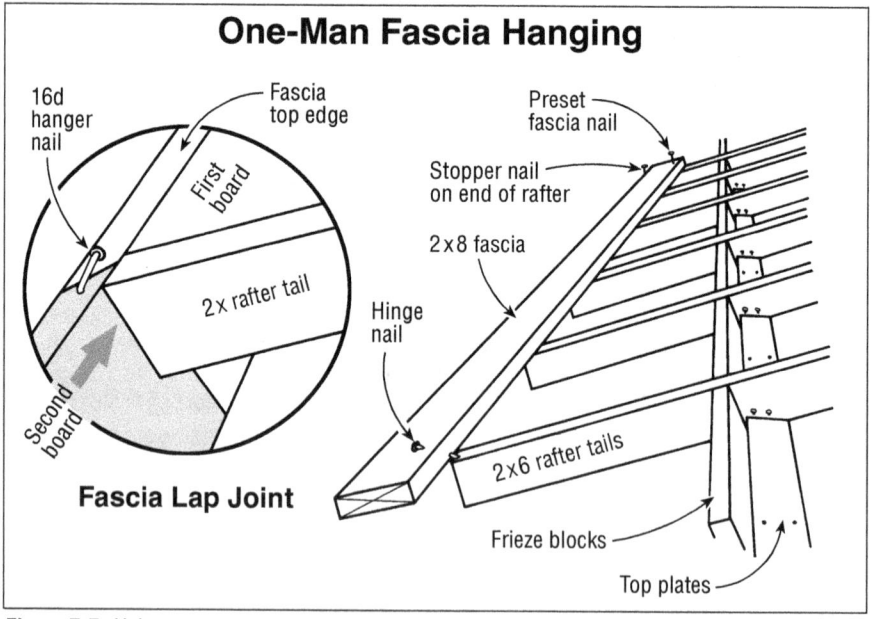

Figure 7-7. Using a toenail driven at an angle into the rafter tail takes the place of a helper when hanging fascia solo from up top. The nail acts like a hinge as the board is lowered into place from the far end. Tract board hangers cut the miter lap joint with the LP of the bevel on the outside face so the adjoining bevel will slide in behind, held up by a bent hanger nail.

(24") by its corresponding RR ratio (.5000) to calculate the rafters' vertical fall (rise) from the outside wall to the fascia-line. Next, take the result (12") and divide it by the opposing roof's (7 1/2 /12) rise ratio (.6250) to find the run of its overhang (19 1/4"). With unequal heel-stands, either snap out a full-scale section view of the two eaves superimposed on each other *(Figure 7-10)*, or add/subtract the difference between the two pitches' heel-stands to the amount of vertical fall (12" + 1/2"), and divide the result by the opposing roof's RR ratio.

False purlin/ridge beams can be held in position using vertical 2x4 cleats or collar ties *(Figure 7-11)*.

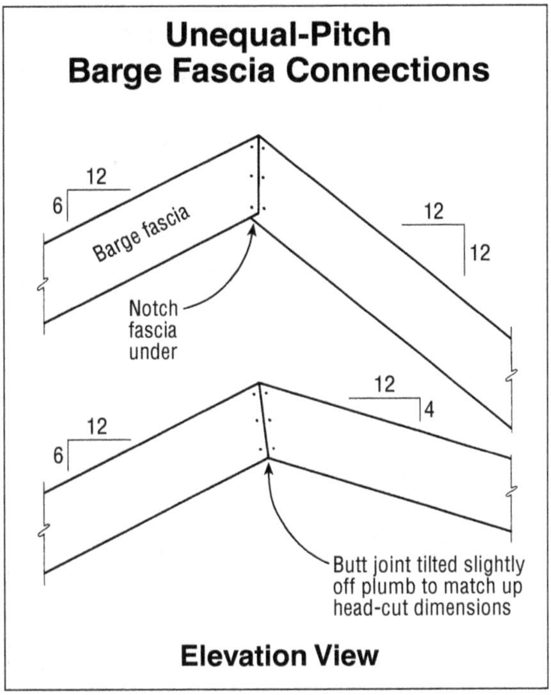

Figure 7-8. To handle the barge-fascia butt-joint connection at the ridge of an unequal-pitch gable, notch the steeper pitch fascia up under the shallow pitch or skew the head-cuts slightly off vertical to equal up the dimensions.

ROOF SHEATHING

The trickiest part to roof sheathing is the valley-cut. This can be simplified by making a plywood valley-cut pattern *(Figure 7-12)*. When using this pattern, only a bottom measurement to the valley from the last sheet is needed. Place the pattern as shown, and draw a cut-line down the diagonal edge. The pattern for each pitch is made with one leg as the width of the ply (48"), and the other leg as the width divided by the COM LL ratio (48" ÷ 1.1180 {6/12 COM LL ratio} = 42 7/8"). The pattern will only work one way, so you can't get confused. Some guys just calculate the top dimension of the pattern and add/subtract it as needed.

To save time marking a square-cut end on sheathing (roof of wall), try using a large drywall T-square rather than marking both edges and connecting the two points with a snap-line.

Use the triangular plywood cutoffs from one side of a hip as starter pieces on another side as shown in *Figure 7-13*. When the rafter on-center spacing is varied, overlap the ends of adjoining plywood sheets across an errant

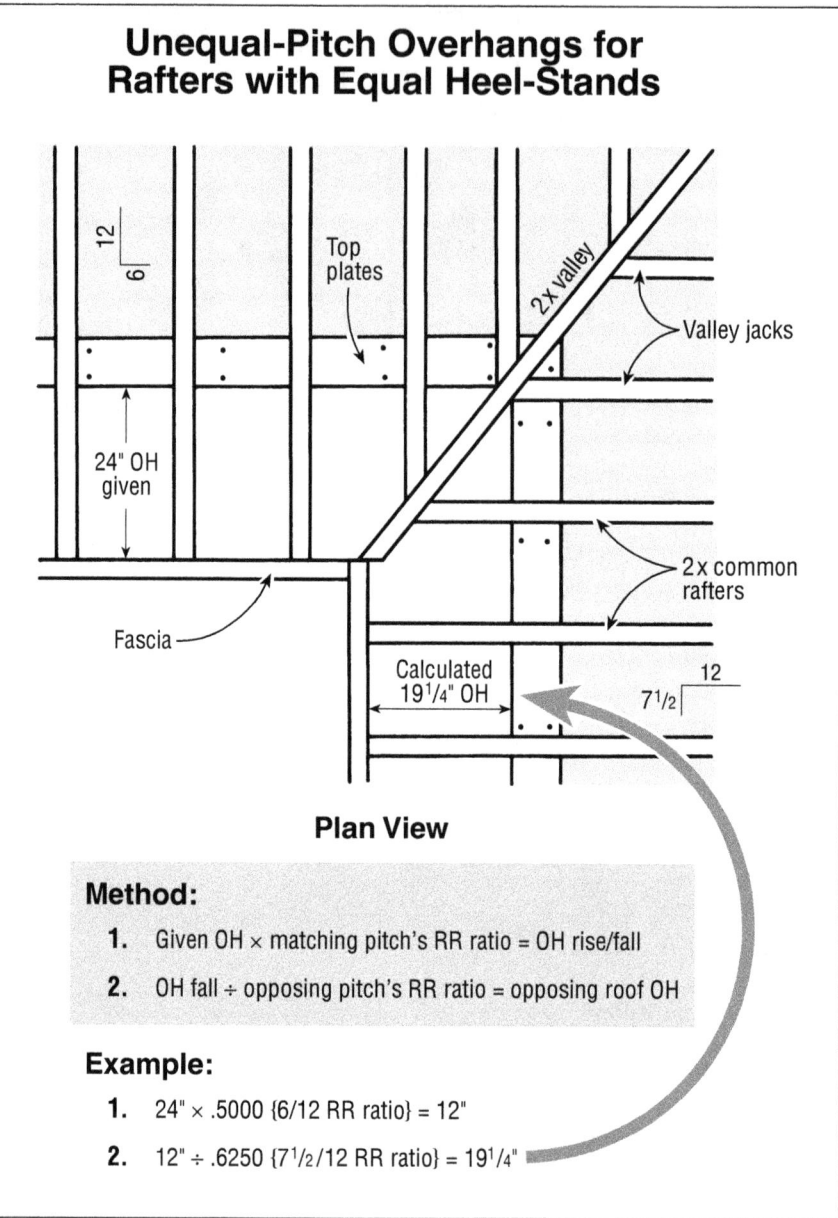

Figure 7-9. An intersection of two unequal-pitch roofs with the same heel-stand will have different length overhangs to keep the fascia at a common height.

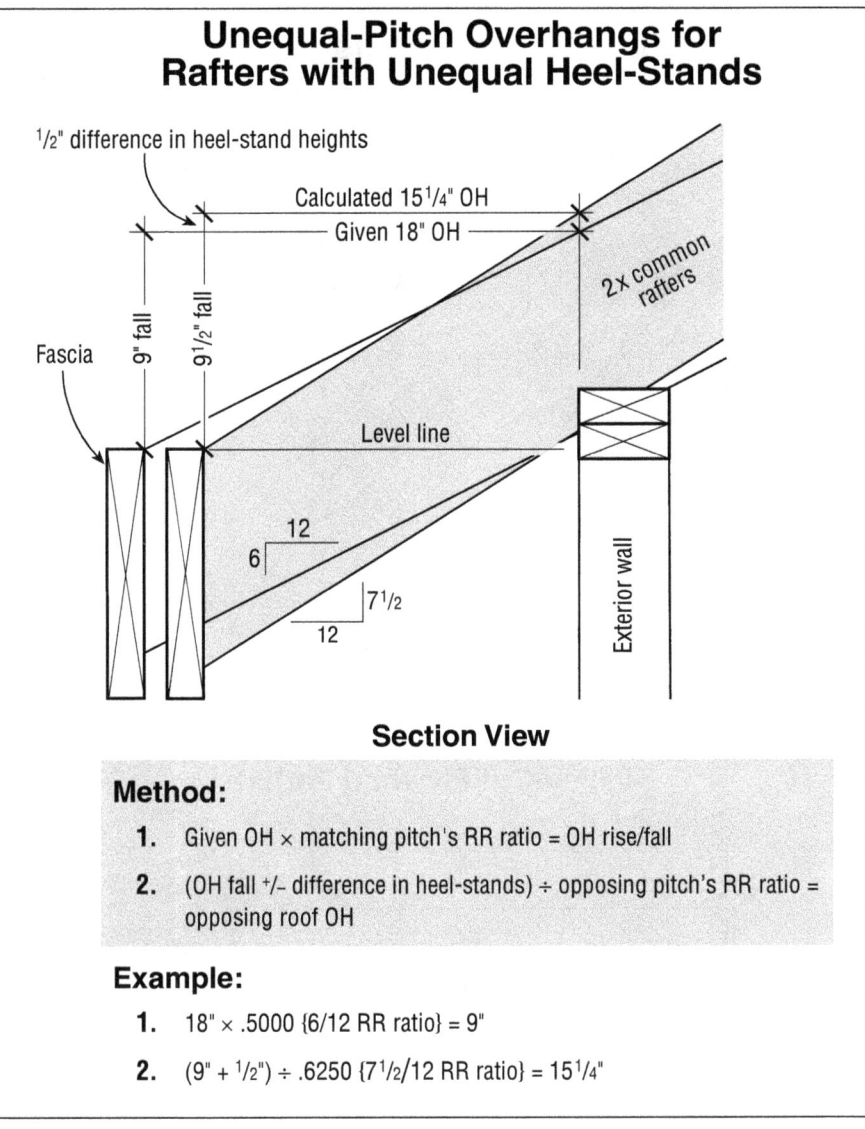

Figure 7-10. Determining a common fascia height for the intersection of two unequal-pitch roofs requires that adjustments be made not only for the pitch difference, but also for any difference in heel-stands.

rafter, and make one cut through both sheets centered on the rafter. Often with a change in on-center spacing, only one sheet is affected. In this instance, put the sheet that needs to be cut on the bottom, and overlap it with the successive sheet that fits on layout. Since the edge of the top sheet will be centered on the rafter, use it as a cutting guide for the lower sheet instead of a snap-line.

EAVES AND PLYWOOD   **139**

False Purlin/Ridge Beams

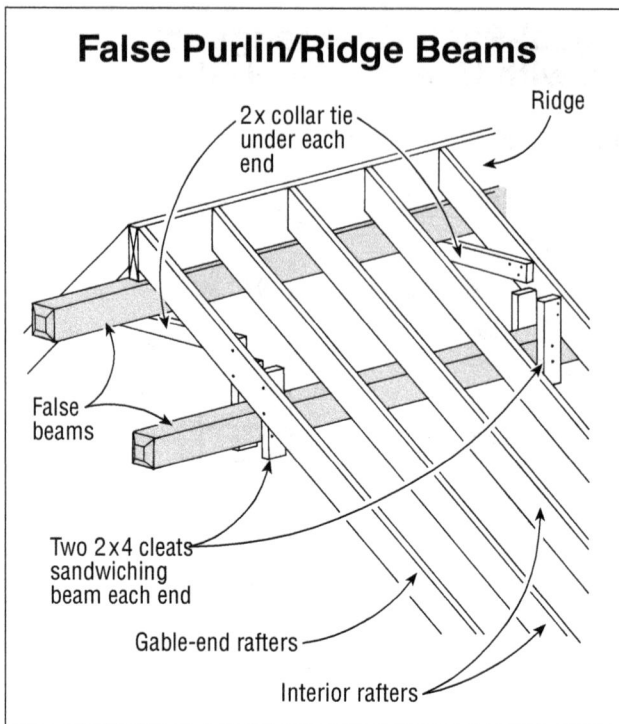

◀ **Figure 7-11.** False purlin/ridge beams can be held in place using vertical 2x4 cleats or collar ties.

Figure 7-12. When installing roof sheathing, use a valley-cut pattern so only a bottom measurement to the valley is needed. ▼

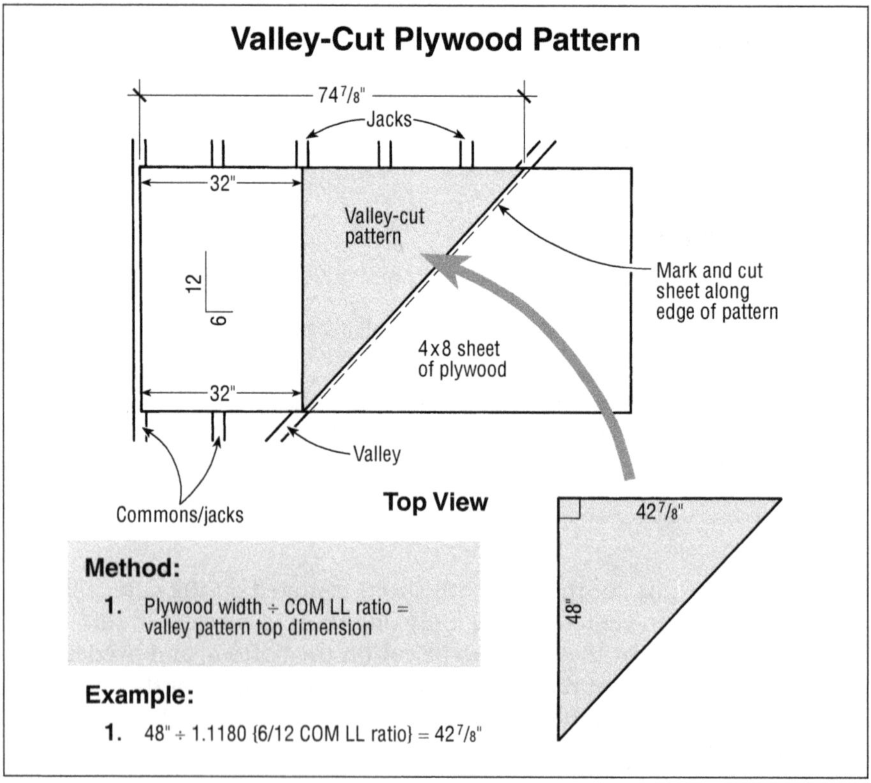

Valley-Cut Plywood Pattern

Method:

1. Plywood width ÷ COM LL ratio = valley pattern top dimension

Example:

1. 48" ÷ 1.1180 {6/12 COM LL ratio} = 42⁷⁄₈"

140 CHAPTER 7

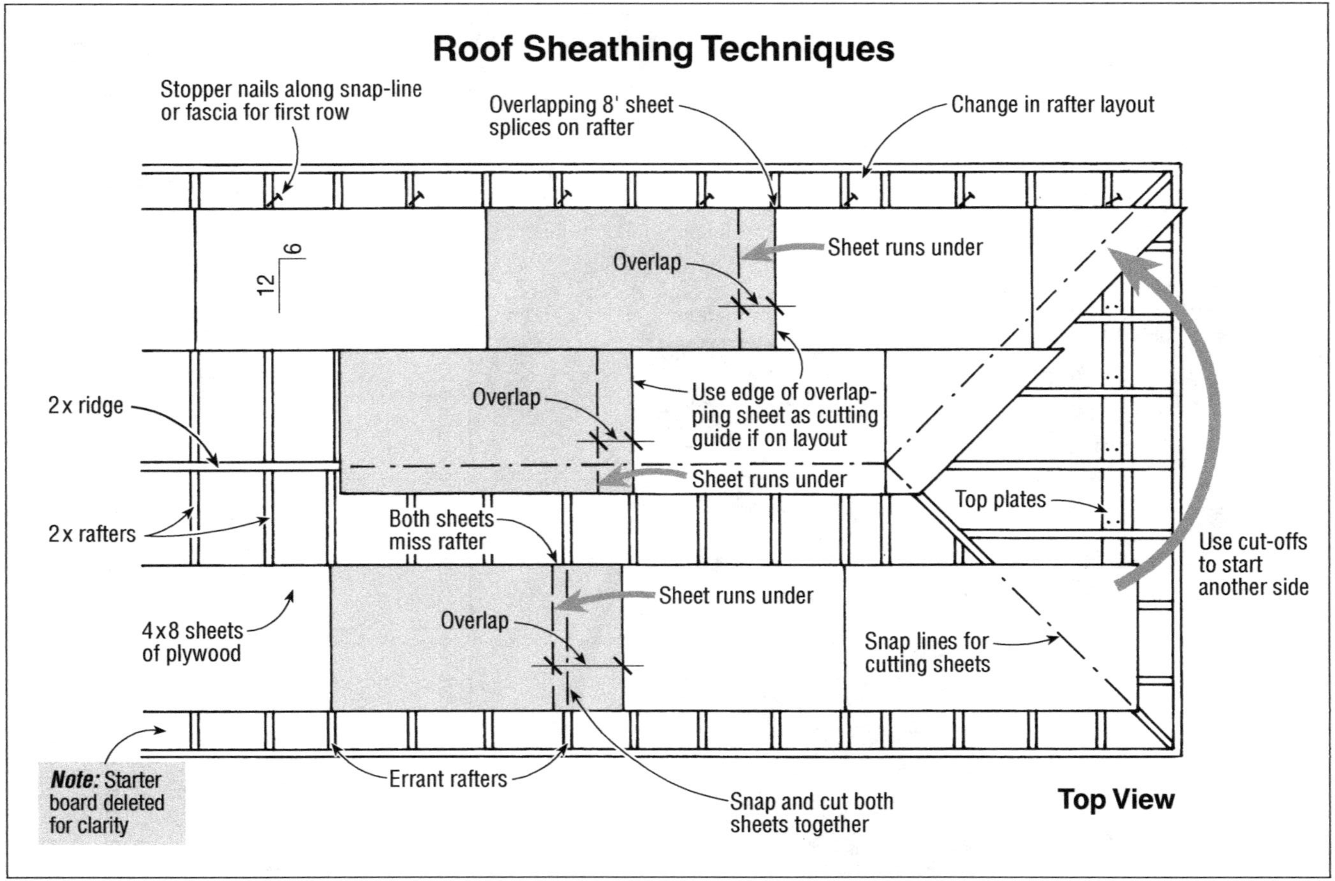

Figure 7-13. Use the plywood cutoffs from one side of a hip as starters for another side. Overlap two plywood sheets that miss a rafter, and cut both sheets at once (or use one edge as a guide when only one needs to be trimmed to splice on a rafter). Use stopper nails along the fascia (or a starter snap-line) to position the first row of roof plywood.

Photo 7-14. This roof is ready for 1¹/₂-in. rigid insulation. The flat 2x4s provide edge nailing for the plywood sheathing.

Photo 7-15. Install five rows of boards at a time with a homemade tongue-and-groove clamping tool.

RIGID INSULATION

The proper method for running 1¹/₂-in. rigid insulation on a 2x decked roof is to install 2x4 flat nailers for the roof sheathing around the perimeter and across the middle at 48 in. on-center. (Use ripped 2x4s on edge or double-stack 2x4s flat for 3-in. rigid insulation.) Stop the insulation at the outside wall line and block the eaves with scraps of 2x wood at 24 in. on-center to support the plywood. Cut 3¹/₂ in. off the long edge of the rigid insulation so the panels will fit between the 2x4s (see **Photo 7-14**). A homemade

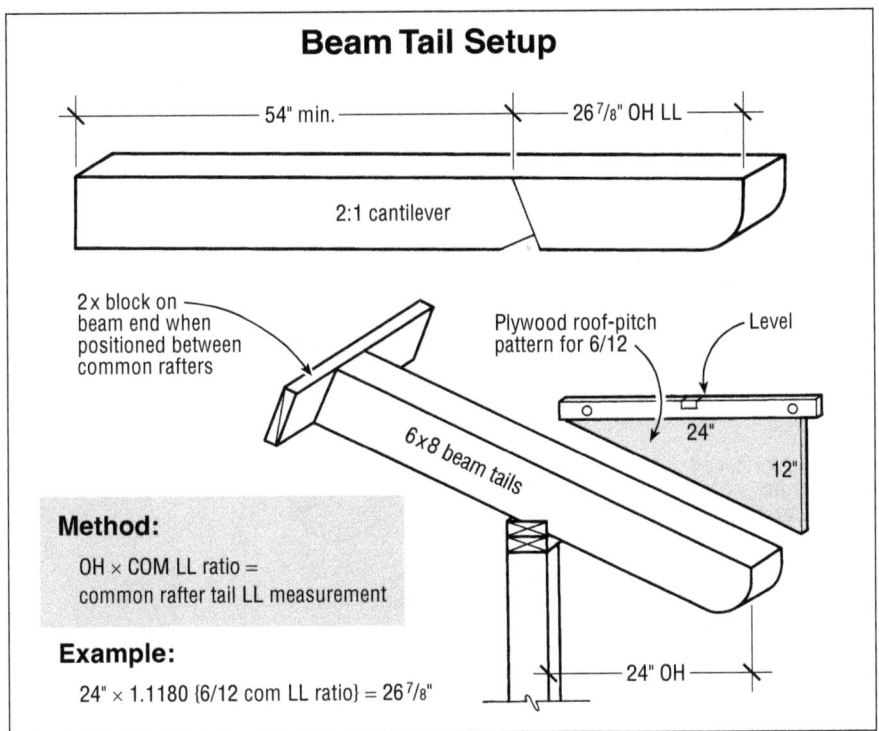

Figure 7-16. Use a level and a roof-pitch pattern to set the false tails at each end of a long eave run, and string the tails in between.

clamping tool like the one shown in **Photo 7-15** is a great way to install 2x tongue-and-groove decking over large areas.

BEAM TAILS

Many Tudor and Spanish style homes use false beam tails in conjunction with tailless rafters. If the beam spacing is 32 in. on-center and the rafters are 16 in. on-center, the beam tails can be placed up against every other rafter. The beams should extend inside the building at approximately a 2:1 ratio. Use a level and a roof-pitch pattern (as shown in **Figure 7-16**) to set the tails at each end of an eave run, and string the tails in between. This corrects for any problems with rafter crowns or variations in the plate height. Beams not located against a rafter can be held in place by blocking the end of the beam between the rafters. (*Note:* The roof-pitch pattern with a level technique comes in handy for other situations like setting up flying hips/valleys and some blind roof sections that do not originate from a wall but over-frame another roof at odd angles.)

Figure 7-17 illustrates one method of running a self-supporting split-pitch kick-up. If the cantilever ratio is less than 2:1, the tailless common

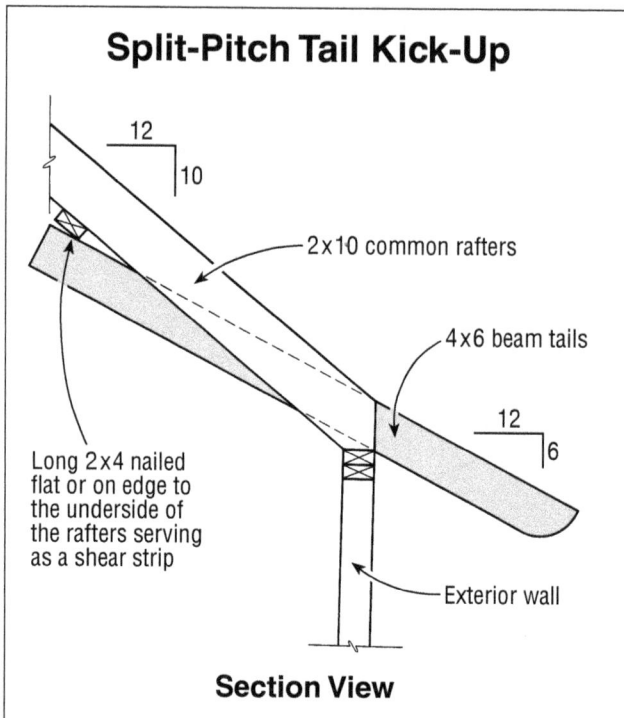

Figure 7-17. Installing a 2x4 shear strip is one way to support a split-pitch tail kick-up.

rafters should be securely connected to the plate; otherwise, weight on the beam tail may pry them up due to leverage.

Figure 7-18 illustrates the proper length for exposed hip and valley beam tails with no fascia. Notice particularly the point from which each tail is measured: the hip from the outside edge at the building line and the valley from the inside corner. The outside edge of the starter board will follow the eave line shown. Run exposed hip and valley beam tails full-length to the ridge and back the top edge unless rain gutters or a small fascia will hide the sheathing gap at the ends of the tails. In that case, only the valley beams will need to be backed to eliminate the sheathing gap along the side top edges (refer back to Photo 5-4).

If you don't have a band saw on the job-site, a radius beam tail can be cut using a Makita 16-in. beam saw. Make multiple saw passes on the side of the beam following a radius line, and smooth the cuts with a belt sander (see **Photo 7-19**).

SWALED TAILS AROUND A CORNER

Curved tail kick-ups or swaled tails get tricky at the building corners where a special swale kick-up must be created for the hip or valley rafters. Use a superimposed or side-by-side view of a common rafter as compared to a hip/valley rafter to match all the horizontal lines as shown in *Figure 7-20*.

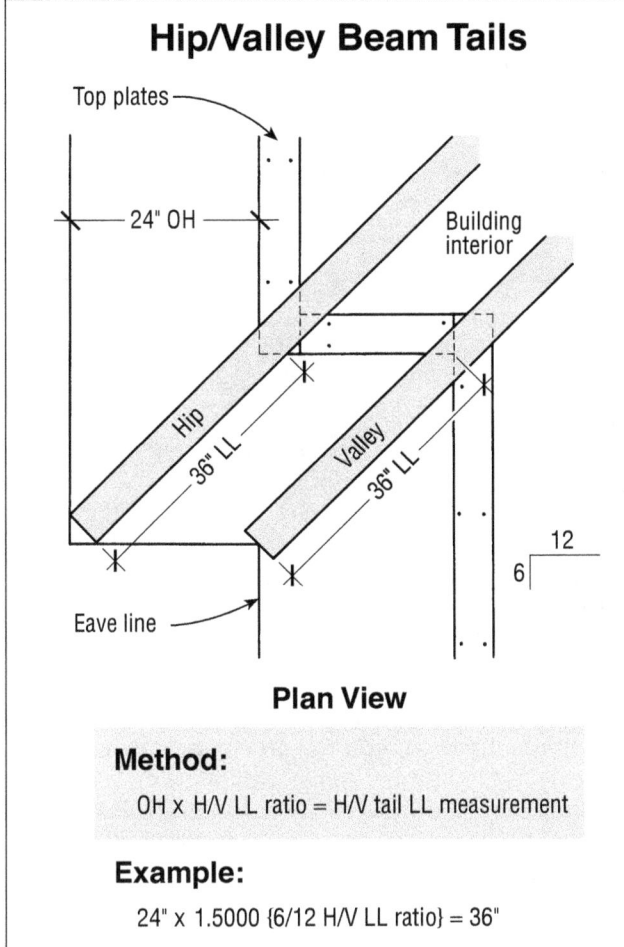

Figure 7-18. A radius-cut exposed hip tail should be marked with the appropriate tail LL measurement from where the side crosses the plate line. An exposed valley tail is measured from its center.

Horizontal measurements from the common rafter are converted to matching dimensions on a regular hip or valley by multiplying by the secant of 45° or 1.4142. Dog-leg bastard hip/valleys are done similarly, but substitute the secant value of the angle representing half the building's corner jog to convert. For example, on an octagon with a corner jog of 45°, use 1.0824 (secant of $22^{1}/_{2}$° from Chart 5, Appendix A). To correctly lay out the hip/valley side-cut, the converted horizontal dimensions must be plotted from a plumb-line that denotes where the edge of the rafter crosses the building's exterior wall line. On a regular hip, this would be from a plumbline drawn $^{1}/_{2}$ thk. of the regular valley measured uphill from the LL plumb-line at the birdsmouth. On a regular valley, the horizontal dimensions are plotted from a plumb-line drawn $^{1}/_{2}$ thk. of the rafter measured downhill from the LL plumb-line at the birdsmouth.

To save time on closed eaves, square-cut the ends of the hip/valley tails without bevels as shown in Figure 7-18. On open eaves where the bevels on

Photo 7-19. Rafter beam tails rounded using a 16-in. beam saw prior to finish sanding.

the ends of the tails are exposed, install all the rafters in place, and use a chalk line to carry a top cut-line through onto the hip/valley rafters from the common rafters.

If the fascia is square-hung in relation to the common rafter kick-up pitch, the procedures outlined in Figure 7-3 may be applied by substituting the pitch of the kick-up where appropriate.

The swale's radius for the common rafter is determined by solving the shaded triangle in Figure 7-20 for it's hypotenuse and using that dimension as **y** together with the maximum arc dip as **x** in the equation found in Figure 15-4. Use the method illustrated in Figure 15-9 if the curve is not a circular arc.

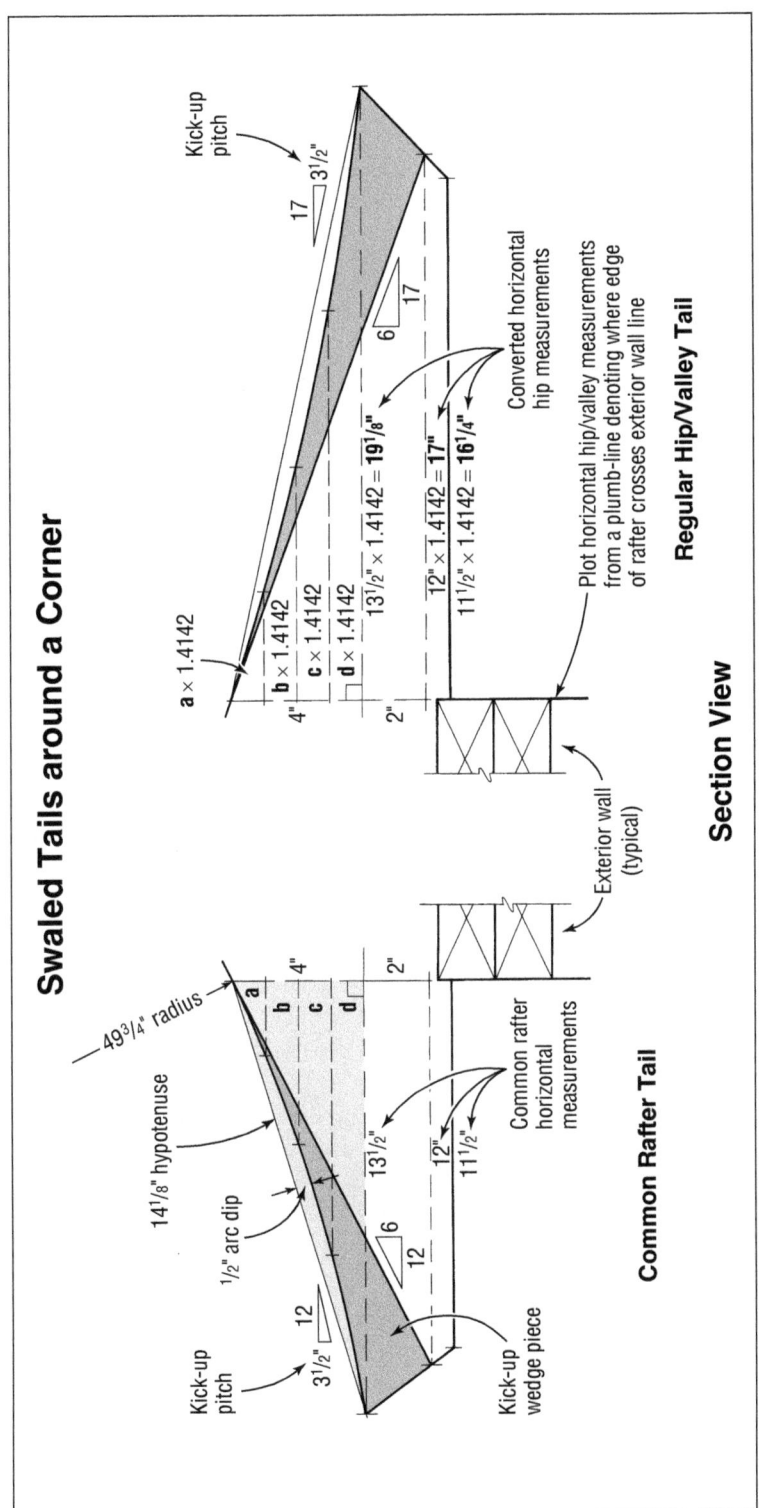

Figure 7-20. Multiply the horizontal measurements from a common rafter swaled tail by **1.4142** to calculate the corresponding dimensions on a regular hip or valley swaled tail. For the common rafter, solve the shaded right triangle for it's hypotenuse, and use that length as **y** together with the maximum arc dip as **x** in the equation found in Figure 15-4 to find the radii.

EAVES AND PLYWOOD   **147**

Chapter 8

Bastard Hips and Valleys

Anytime two different pitches intersect at an inside/outside corner or when a building makes a jog other than 90°, bastard hips and valleys are required *(Photo 8-1)*. While the method of snapping a full-size plan view of the bastard roof sections on the floor and measuring the hip/valley travel, jack runs, cut-lines, cut-angles, etc., works well for these situations (and while this technique alone is sufficient), the addition of a few trigonometric functions to your bag of resources will make cutting some bastard intersections a little easier.

Photo 8-1. In this addition there were six dog-leg bastard hips, seven bastard valleys (one is almost invisible), two bastard broken hips, four regular hips, one regular valley, two California valleys (framed after roof sheathing), one regular broken hip, and one hip-end California-framed onto a conical tower. Talk about fun.

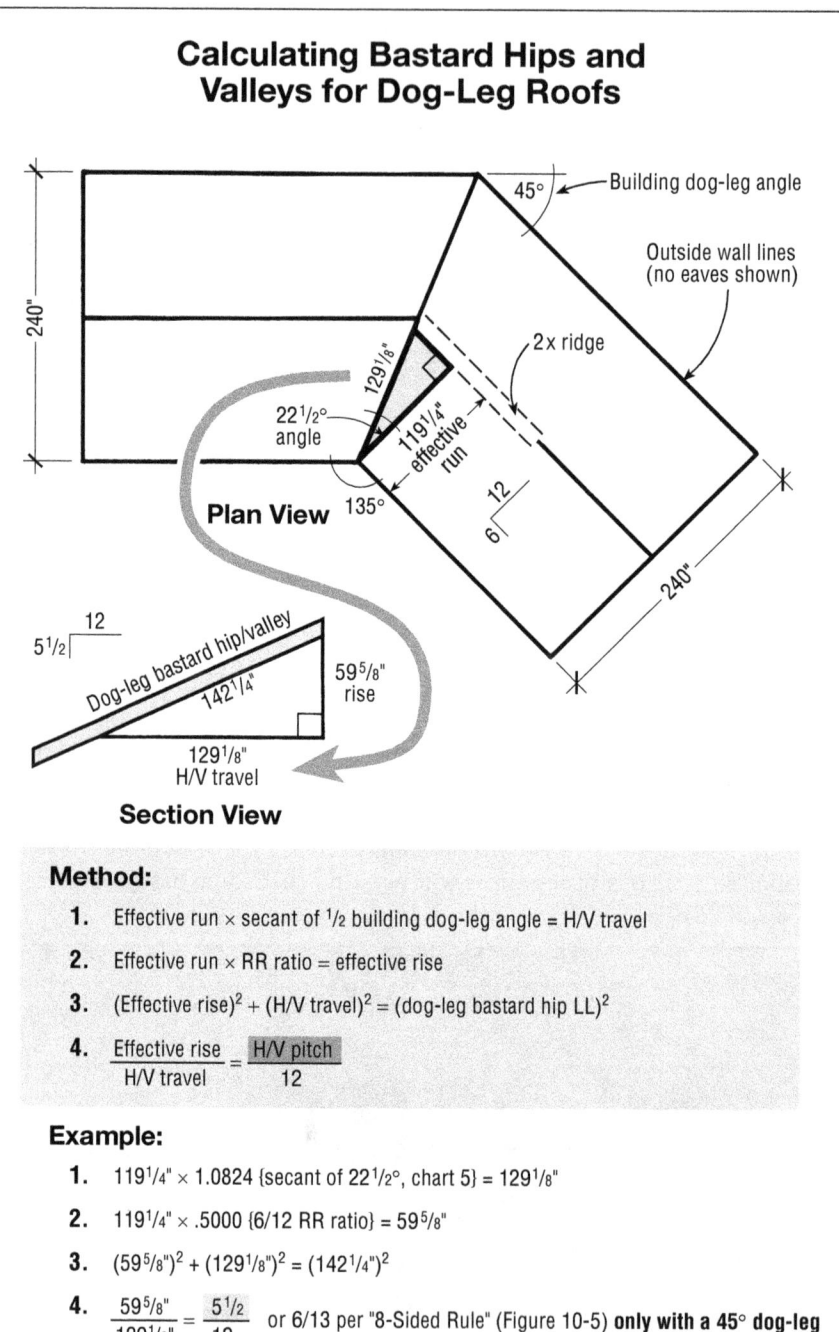

Calculating Bastard Hips and Valleys for Dog-Leg Roofs

Method:

1. Effective run × secant of ½ building dog-leg angle = H/V travel
2. Effective run × RR ratio = effective rise
3. (Effective rise)² + (H/V travel)² = (dog-leg bastard hip LL)²
4. $\dfrac{\text{Effective rise}}{\text{H/V travel}} = \dfrac{\text{H/V pitch}}{12}$

Example:

1. 119¼" × 1.0824 (secant of 22½°, chart 5) = 129⅛"
2. 119¼" × .5000 (6/12 RR ratio) = 59⅝"
3. (59⅝")² + (129⅛")² = (142¼")²
4. $\dfrac{59\tfrac{5}{8}"}{129\tfrac{1}{8}"} = \dfrac{5\tfrac{1}{2}}{12}$ or 6/13 per "8-Sided Rule" (Figure 10-5) **only with a 45° dog-leg**

Figure 8-2. A full-size plan view of a bastard situation snapped on the floor will minimize the amount of math required to find the various rafter runs or travel distances. See Appendix B

Book Guideline: Throughout this and other sections of the book that deal with unequal-pitch intersections or dog-leg-type corners, you will notice that I always convert unknown hip or valley pitches to **x/12** so I can use an adjustable rafter square for layout.

DOG-LEG BASTARD HIPS/VALLEYS

The example in **Figure 8-2** illustrates a single-span gable roof that makes a 45° dog-leg from a straight line. Think of any building jog other than 90° as a corner from some polygon. The 45° jog in this example is one corner from an octagon, and the trig functions shown in Figure 10-5 and Figure 10-9 can be applied to calculate various lengths.

Solve for the effective hip/valley travel (hypotenuse of the horizontal $22^1/_2$° right triangle in Figure 8-2) by multiplying the common rafter effective run with the secant of $22^1/_2$°. (See Chart 5, Appendix A. Interpolate between 22° and 23° by adding both their secant values together and dividing by 2.) Next, use the Pythagorean theorem to solve for the hypotenuse of the vertical right triangle formed by the effective rise at the ridge ($119^1/_4$" × .5000 {6/12 RR ratio} = $59^5/_8$") and the effective hip/valley travel. The bastard hip/valley rafter pitch is calculated using a proportion as shown, or — for the specific case of a 45° dog-leg — the pitch would be the unit of main roof rise/13 per Figure 10-5.

The easiest way to find the cut-lines and cut-angles is to work from a full-scale plan view of the bastard roof section snapped on the floor. **Figure 8-3** illustrates layout of the bastard hip and valley using cheek-cut measurements taken from the snapped-out plan view and transferred to the side of the rafter. The various required saw angles are taken from the snapped-out plan view using a protractor or Speed® Square.

When a dog-leg bastard hip/valley is an exposed beam **(Photo 8-4)** and must be backed on the top edge, use the method shown in Figure 8-27 to find the rip-cut line and rip-angle. In this situation, mark the birdsmouth seat-cut line prior to backing the top edges by positioning a common rafter heel-stand measurement on the lower LL plumb-line (**b** in Figure 8-3) for a hip and downhill from the lower LL plumb-line where the outside edge of the rafter crosses the wall (**c** in Figure 8-3) for a valley.

The jack rafter step can be determined by finding the difference between the run dimensions of two adjacent jacks from the snapped-out plan view and multiplying by the COM LL ratio or by using a trig function. **Figure 8-5**

■ **Floor Drawing Angles vs. Saw Bevel Adjustment**

Remember, a standard circular saw's bevel is adjusted from vertical (90°) and not from the surface of the board (0°). Therefore, be very careful when deciding whether to use the angle taken from the snapped-out plan view of the roof or its complement when setting the bevel adjustment on the saw to make the bastard rafter's various angle-cuts. For hip/valleys that bisect any building corner, set the saw's bevel adjustment at one-half the building's inside corner angle to make the jack cheek-cuts. For example, in Figure 8-2 or Figure 10-4, the inside corner angle is 135° (90° + 45°), so the swing-table saw is set at $67^1/_2$° for the jack cheek-cuts.

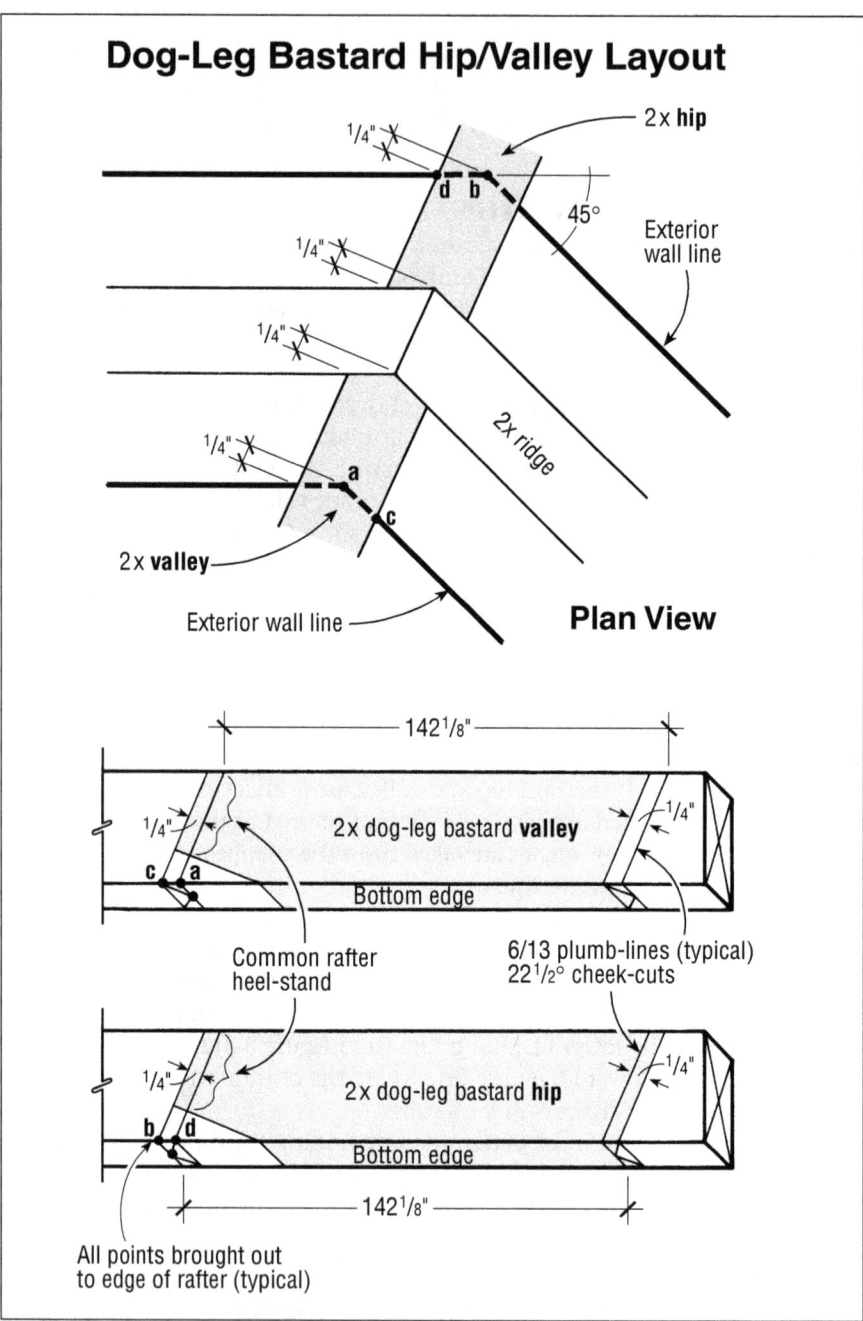

Figure 8-3. Use a snapped-out full-size plan view to find the various cheek-cut layout lines and angles on the bastard hips/valleys.

Photo 8-4. The underside of a 22½° dog-leg bastard hip and valley ridge connection. The hip is on the left, the valley on the right.

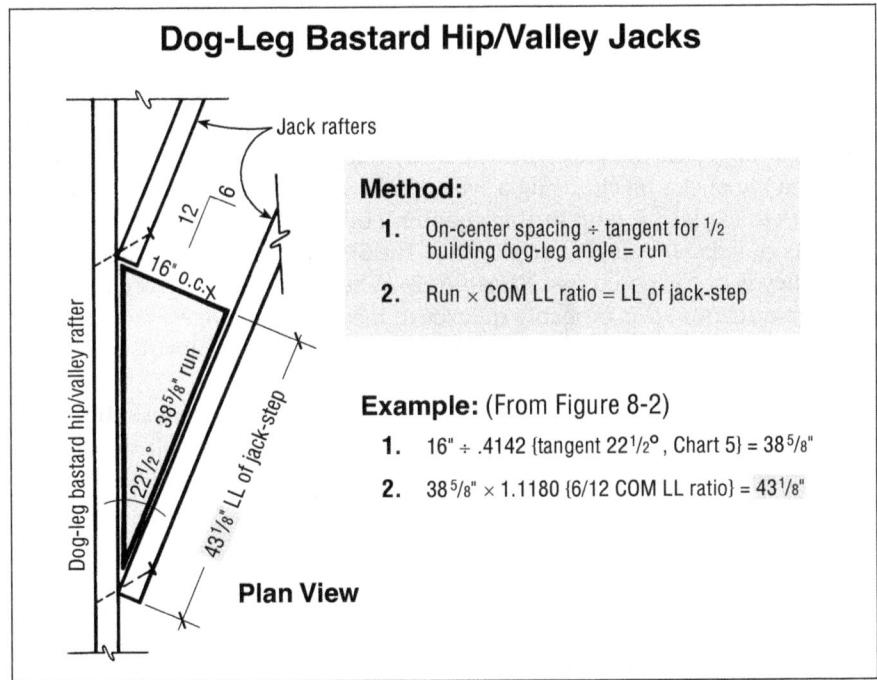

Figure 8-5. The jack-rafter-step measurement for dog-leg bastard hip (or valley) jacks can be calculated by using a trig function in combination with a COM LL ratio or by measuring the difference in run lengths from the snapped-out plan view on the floor and multiplying this by the COM LL ratio.

See Appendix B

Photo 8-6. A 22^1/$_2$° dog-leg bastard valley and square-cut jack rafters.

(applied to Figure 8-2) demonstrates using the tangent of 22^1/$_2$° to calculate the run difference for jacks spaced 16 in. on-center. This run difference is then multiplied by the COM LL ratio to find the jack-step length. The steep cheek-cut angle on the jacks (measured with a protractor off the snapped-out plan view) can be cut using a swing-table saw, a chainsaw, or a regular Skilsaw® as explained later in this chapter. The steep-angled cheek-cuts on 2x jacks can also be square-cut plumb at the SP if the connection to the hip/valley is not exposed (see **Photo 8-6**). When very few jacks are involved in an intersection, it is probably quicker to measure the longest jack in the air and step down from there rather than snapping out a full-size plan view of the bastard section to get a "starter" jack run.

For dog-leg angles other than the 45° used in this example, use the appropriate secant or tangent values from the trig tables for half the angle of the building jog.

DOG-LEG BASTARD BROKEN HIPS

When a dog-leg bastard roof has two different spans, a bastard broken hip must be installed to connect the roof sections (see **Figure 8-7**). This unusual rafter is a segment from the line bisecting the acute angle formed when the two outside wall lines are run out to intersect at a common corner point **(a)**. In effect, this bastard broken-hip rafter is a piece of the longer imaginary bastard hip that would run from the angle's apex at **a**. Points **b** and **c** are located by drawing lines bisecting the inside and outside building corner angles to intersect with the imaginary acute angle's centerline originat-

Dog-Leg Bastard Broken Hips

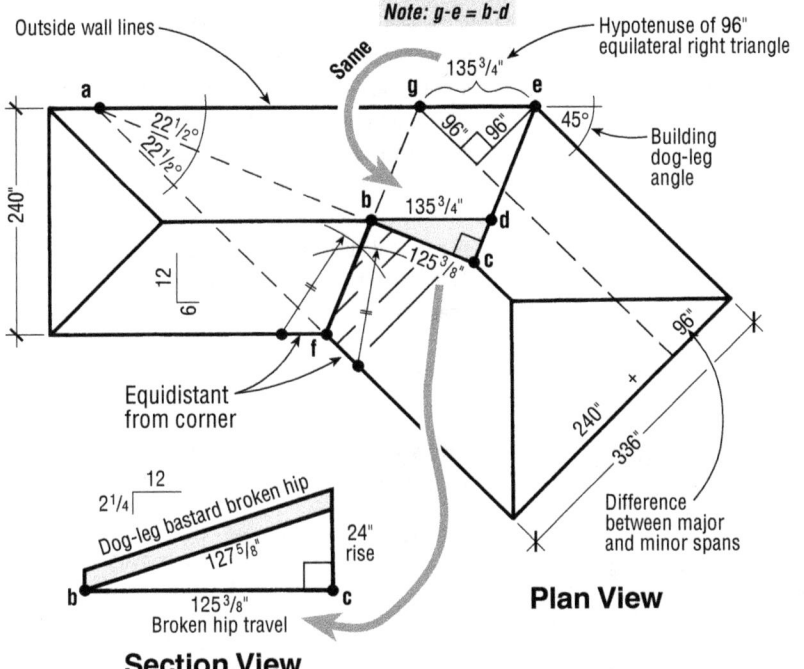

Method:

1. $\dfrac{\text{(Large span – small span)}}{2} \times \text{RR ratio} = \text{rise difference}$

2. Wall length **g-e** ÷ secant of ½ building dog-leg angle = dog-leg broken hip travel **b-c**

3. (Rise difference)² + (dog-leg broken hip travel **b-c**)² = (dog-leg broken hip LL)²

4. $\dfrac{\text{Rise difference}}{\text{Dog-leg broken hip travel } \textbf{b-c}} = \dfrac{\text{Dog-leg broken hip pitch}}{12}$

Example:

1. $\dfrac{(336" - 240")}{2} \times .5000 \; \{6/12 \text{ RR ratio}\} = 24"$

2. 135 3/4" ÷ 1.0824 {secant 22½°, Chart 5} = 125 3/8"

3. (24")² + (125 3/8")² = (127 5/8")²

4. $\dfrac{24"}{125 \, 3/8"} = \dfrac{2\,1/4}{12}$

Figure 8-7. A dog-leg bastard broken hip is a segment from the line which bisects the acute angle between two diverging rafter walls. See Appendix B

BASTARD HIPS AND VALLEYS **155**

■ Cutting Steep Cheek-Cuts on 2x Material

A simple method to make a cheek-cuts greater than 45° on 2x material with a regular Skilsaw® can be accomplished using two saw-cuts that are less than 45°. The first cut is made at the LP cheek-cut plumb-line with the saw angle set to the complement of the steep angle (90° − steep angle = complementary angle). This cut creates a surface perpendicular to the steep cheek-cut. (In other words, it should angle away from the steep cheek-cut.) Now, resting the saw foot on the previous cut, make a second pass with the saw set square (0° on the angle tilt) following the complementary angle's SP edge (which corresponds to the LP of the steep cheek-cut).

With very steep cheek-cuts, the maximum depth of the saw may not be enough to reach all the way through to the other side of the board, and the cut must be finished off with a handsaw. If the cut is not exposed, make only a partial cheek-cut. To do this, position the complementary angle-cut short of the LP by an amount that will enable the blade to reach through to the other side of the board on the second saw pass with the saw set square. Head-cuts for unequal-pitch hips and valleys can also be made using this technique as illustrated in *Photo 8-8*.

Photo 8-8(a-e).
This photo sequence demonstrates making a steep-angled cheek-cut on 2x material using only a regular Skilsaw.®
Caution: The lower blade guard was removed in this demonstration for visual clarity .

A

B

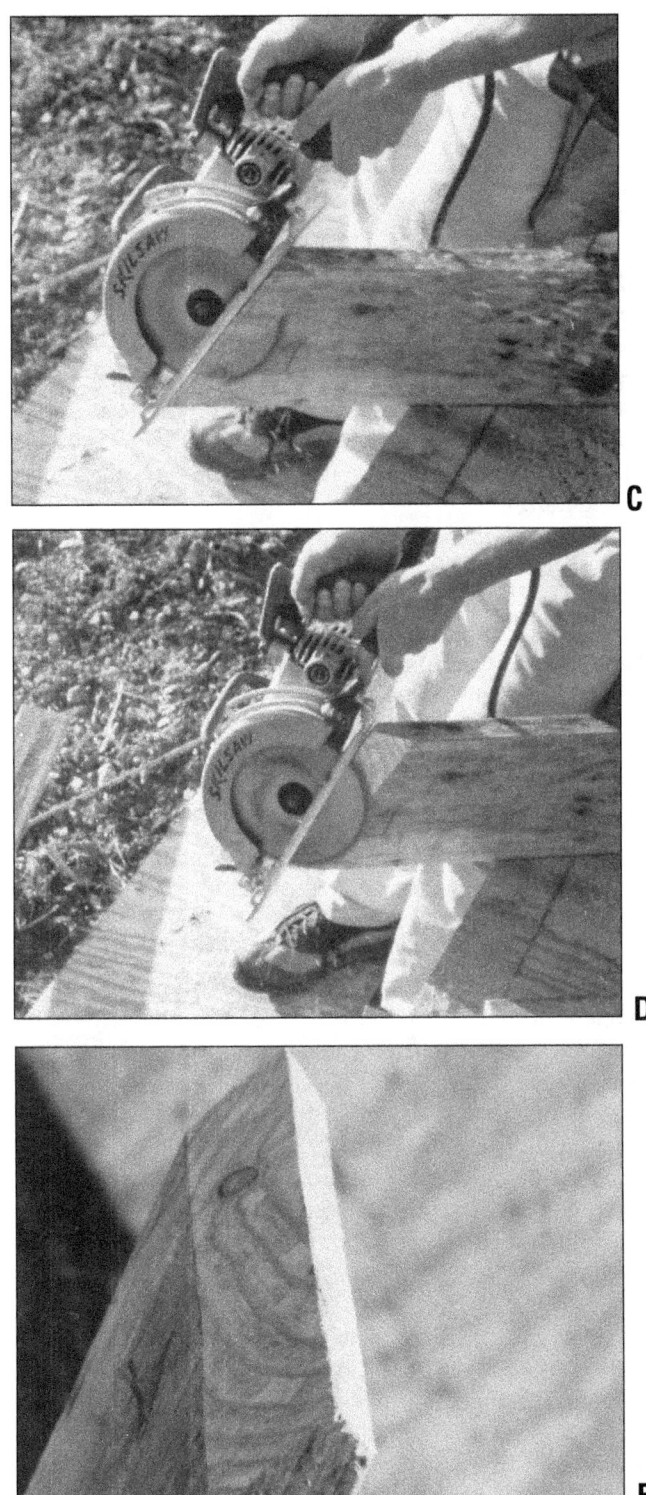

■ **Solving proportions:** A proportion is solved by a procedure known as cross-multiplication.

Method:	Example:
1. Given the proportion rise/run = unknown/12	1. $\left(\dfrac{\text{Rise}}{\text{Run}}\right) \dfrac{96}{192} = \dfrac{\text{unknown}}{12}$
2. Multiply diagonally across the = sign (rise × 12 = run × unknown)	2. $96 \times 12 = 192 \times \text{unknown}$
3. Divide both sides by the run to segregate the unknown value (rise × 12 /run = unknown)	3. $\dfrac{1152}{192} = \text{unknown}$
4. Reduce the resulting fraction by dividing the denominator into the numerator.	4. $6 = \text{unknown}$

ing from **a**. (To bisect any angle, make marks that are equidistant from the corner in each direction. From these points, swing two equal-length arcs to intersect, and draw a line from the corner through the intersection point. See Figure 11-7 for more detail.)

Use the difference in ridge heights between points **b** and **c** together with the bastard hip travel (measured off a snapped-out full-size plan view or by applying trig as shown) as legs of a vertical right triangle, and solve for the hypotenuse (bastard broken-hip centerline LL) using the Pythagorean theorem. The bastard broken-hip pitch is found by solving a proportion where the bastard broken-hip rise divided by the travel is set to equal an unknown pitch/12. The snapped-out plan view can be used to find the appropriate cheek-cut angle at the ridge butt joints. Otherwise, divide the building jog in fourths, and cut everything with this bevel angle ($45° \div 4 = 11^{1}/_{4}°$).

The bastard valley at **b-f** is identical to the one calculated in Figure 8-2 for the 240-in. span, whereas the bastard hip **e-c** must be calculated for the larger effective run ($167^{1}/_{4}"$).

The cheek-cut angles at the head of the bastard broken hip jacks can be taken off the snapped-out plan view or by dividing the building jog angle in half ($45° \div 2 = 22^{1}/_{2}°$). Now, either take a measurement from the snapped-out plan view or use the tangent of half the building jog angle multiplied by the on-center spacing to find the jack-step run for the rafters that frame from the bastard broken hip to the outside wall ($16" \times .4142$ {tangent $22^{1}/_{2}°$} = $6^{5}/_{8}"$). Multiply this run by the COM LL ratio to calculate the bastard broken hip jack-step LL ($6^{5}/_{8}" \times 1.1180$ {6/12 COM LL ratio} = $7^{3}/_{8}"$). The jack-step length for the rafters that frame from the bastard broken hip to the bastard valley is the sum of this bastard broken hip jack-step LL and the dog-leg hip/valley jack-step LL calculated in Figure 8-5 ($7^{3}/_{8}" + 43^{1}/_{8}" = 50^{1}/_{2}"$).

DOVETAIL HIPS

In a dovetail hip *(Figure 8-9)*, the corner of the building is clipped at a 45° angle, and the regular hip forks into a slice from an octagonal pie (see the upcoming Chapter 10 section "Octagons," page 208).

Always snap a full-scale plan view of difficult roof areas on the floor to help find or check various runs, hip/valley travels, cut-angles, and shortening amounts. To calculate the dovetail hips, begin by using the Pythagorean

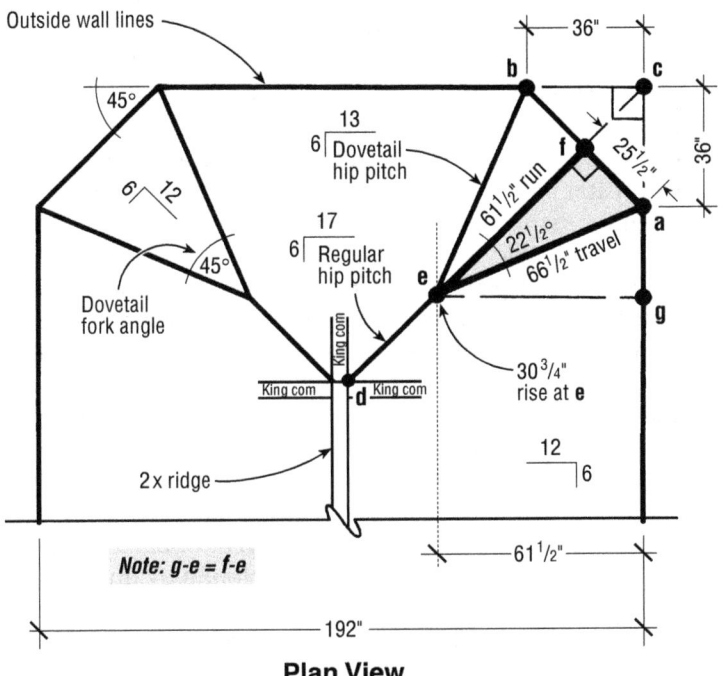

Dovetail Hip Calculations

Plan View

Method:

1. (Corner setback **a-c**)² + (corner setback **b-c**)² = (corner wall **a-b**)²
2. Corner wall **a-b** ÷ 2 = corner half wall **a-f**
3. Corner half wall **a-f** ÷ tangent of ½ dovetail fork angle = run **e-f**
4. Run **e-f** × secant of ½ dovetail fork angle = dovetail hip travel **a-e**
5. Run **e-f** × RR ratio = rise at **e**
6. (Rise at **e**)² + (hip travel **a-e**)² = (dovetail hip theoretical LL)²

Example:

1. (36")² + (36")² = (50⁷⁄₈")²
2. 50⁷⁄₈" ÷ 2 = 25½"
3. 25½" ÷ .4142 {tangent 22½°, Chart 5} = 61½"
4. 61½" × 1.0824 {secant 22½°, Chart 5} = 66½"
5. 61½" × .5000 {6/12 RR ratio} = 30¾"
6. (30¾")² + (66½")² = (73¼")²

 See Appendix B

Figure 8-9. To solve the dovetail hip mathematically requires the Pythagorean theorem, tangent/secant values (from the trig tables in Chart 5, Appendix A), and the RR ratio.

theorem to find the length of corner wall **a-b** ($50^7/_8"$). Bisect this corner face, and divide the result **(a-f)** by the tangent of one-half the dovetail fork angle (tangent of $22^1/_2° = .4142$ from Chart 5, Appendix A) to find **e-f**. Now use either the Pythagorean theorem with legs **a-f** and **e-f** to find the bastard hip travel **a-e** (hypotenuse of the horizontal triangle), or multiply **e-f** by the secant of $22^1/_2°$ (1.0824 from Chart 5, Appendix A). Finally, transform the bastard hip-travel dimension into an LL measurement by using the Pythagorean theorem with the bastard hip-travel **a-e** and the roof rise at **e** as legs of a vertical right triangle and solving for the hypotenuse. The bastard hip pitch for marking plumb-lines during rafter layout would be 6/13 per the "Eight-Sided Rule" (see Figure 10-5).

Use the snapped-out plan view to find the shortening amount (2") and the positions for both the SP and LP of the acute angled cheek-cut by measuring along the centerline of the dovetail hip from the theoretical hip intersection point **(e)** and squaring out to each specific point on the edge. Transfer these dimensions to the side of the rafter board perpendicular to the LL plumb-line at the head-cut end *(Figure 8-10)*. Square-cut the rafter at the SP plumb-line if the rafters are not exposed. Mathematically, the horizontal distance **i-j** between the SP and LP is calculated by dividing the thickness of the rafter board ($1^1/_2"$) by the tangent of $22^1/_2°$ ($1^1/_2" \div .4142 = 3^5/_8"$). The shortening amount can likewise be found by dividing $1/_2$ thk. of the ridge ($3/_4"$) by the sine of $22^1/_2°$ ($.75" \div .3827 = 2"$).

To find the depth of the seat-cut, mark the heel-stand of a common rafter at **h**, where the edge of the dovetail hip crosses the plate line (Figure 8-10). The distance point **h** is located uphill from **a** which can be taken from the snapped-out plan view or calculated by multiplying $1/_2$ thk. of the dovetail hip ($3/_4"$) by the tangent of $22^1/_2°$ ($.75" \times .4142 = 1/_4"$). Always remember: The measurements taken from the snapped-out plan view and any calculated shortening solutions are horizontal dimensions and must be measured perpendicular from one plumb-line over to a second plumb-line unless converted to an LL measurement.

If the loose end of the partial hip section **d-e** (Figure 8-9) can be permanently supported, run the lower end long and nip the top edge to stay below the dovetail roof plane *(Photo 8-11)*. When there isn't a bearing wall or support beam below onto which this partial hip can be braced, cut a common rafter **(e-f)** to run directly off the end of partial hip **d-e** and plywood gusset the two boards together at the correct change of rafter pitch (6/12 to 6/17). Snap section-view lines on the floor to aid in assembly of this "hunchback" combo rafter *(Figure 8-12)*. Hold the plywood gussets below the top edge of the hips so they will not interfere with the roof sheathing, and don't forget to shorten the dovetail hips for the gusset material.

Referring to Figure 8-9, multiply the horizontal travel distance **e-f** ($61^1/_2"$) by the COM LL ratio to calculate the dovetail center common-rafter length. The LL for partial-hip **d-e** is found by subtracting the run **e-g** (**e-g** equals **e-f** by design) from the effective run of the main span and multiplying by the H/V LL ratio.

Stack the dovetail hips so the top outside edge planes into the adjacent top edge of the partial hip to which it is nailed.

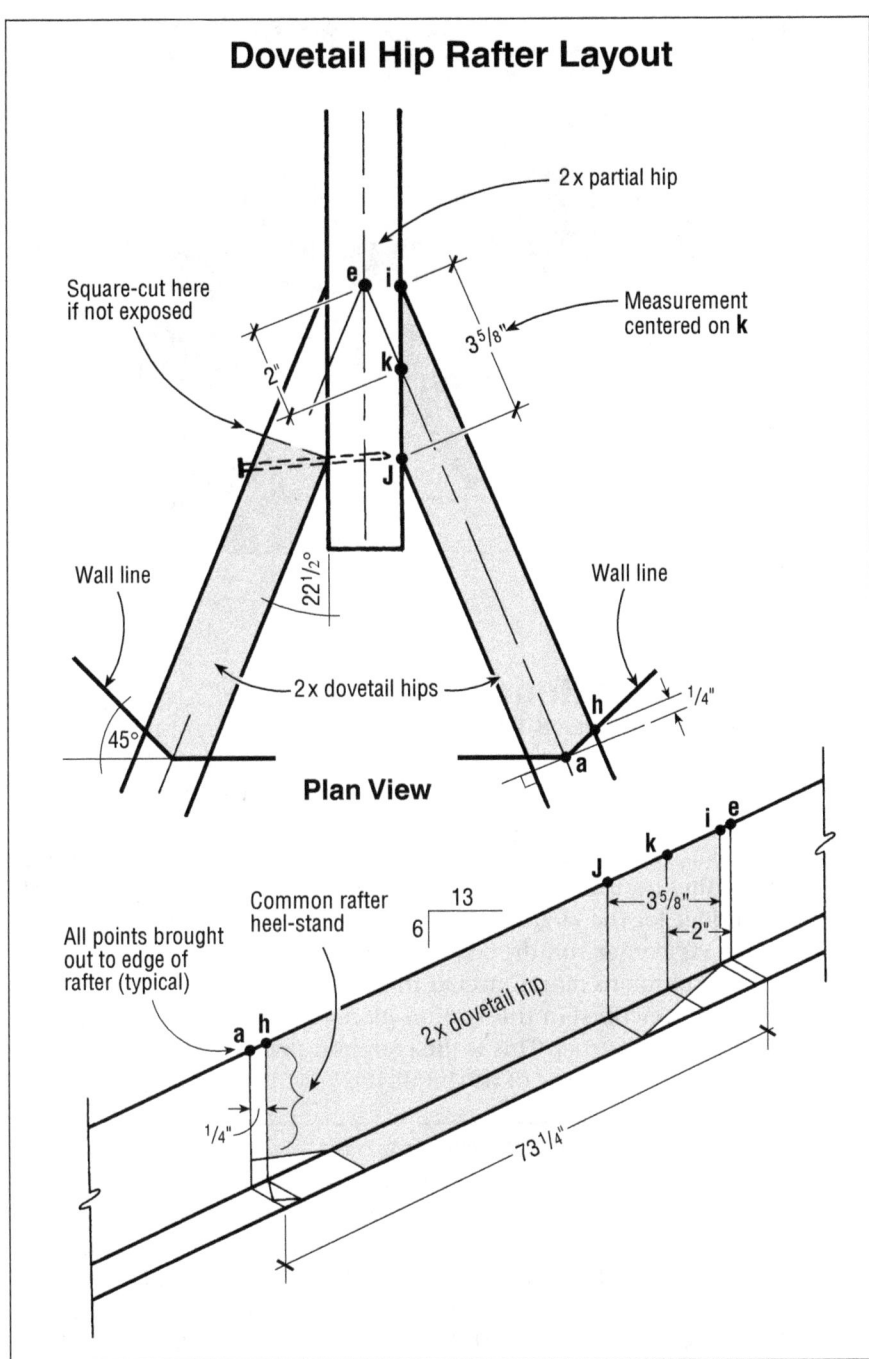

Figure 8-10. Always remember that measurements taken from the snapped-out full-scale plan view and the mathematical solutions described for shortening, etc., are horizontal dimensions and must be measured perpendicular from one plumb-line to a second plumb-line when laying out the rafter unless they are converted to an LL measurement.

Photo 8-11. A dovetail hip end.

A Diamond Hip Roof

A diamond hip roof *(Figure 8-13)* is an unequal-pitch hip roof that comes to a peak from a rectangle instead of from a square as does a regular hip. Although a diamond-hip roof is rare, it best illustrates the principles involved in solving an unequal-pitch intersection without clouding the illustration with intermediate rafters (which can be run in either direction by elongating the building either horizontally to create a ridge for the 6/12 pitch or vertically to create a ridge for the $7^1/_2/12$ pitch). With all unequal-pitch hip roofs framed from a 90° corner, run the centerlines of each hip to the inside corner where the king commons rafters meet at the ridge.

The procedure described in this section places the unequal-pitch hip rafter on the building corner. This is the common practice with open eaves. Many prefer this style because of its simplicity, but the overhangs will end

---

■ **The Top Framing Point on Unequal-Pitch Roofs**

The method I use on unequal-pitch hips and valleys framed from a 90° corner is a departure from the age-old method of using the building's theoretical centerpoint as the top framing point. I choose to treat the small square block of material darkened in *Figure 8-14* as if it were a square ridge peg. Remember back in the earlier chapters where the ridge-board thickness is subtracted from the span to find the effective run, thereby eliminating the need for any shortening. The same holds true here. The two shallow-pitched king commons which butt head to head act as the ridge thickness for the steep-pitched roof, while the two steeper-pitched king commons could act as the ridge thickness for the shallower-pitched roof. So by using the inside intersection between the two different-pitched king commons as our framing point (point **f** in Figure 8-14), everything is simplified. The same holds true for unequal-pitch valleys as signified by point **f** in upcoming Figure 8-23.

---

162   CHAPTER 8

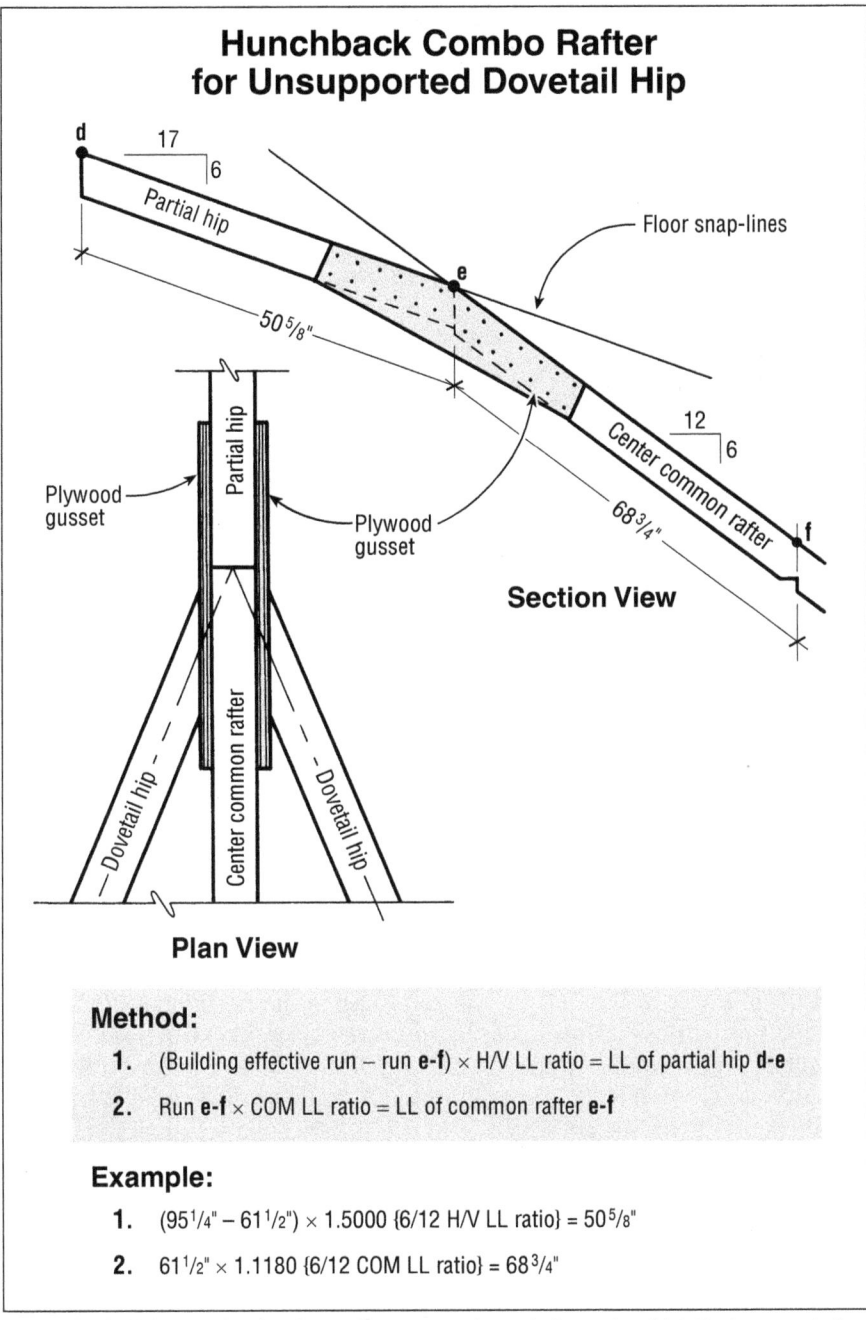

Figure 8-12. If there isn't a bearing wall or support beam below onto which the loose end of the partial hip can be braced, cut a common rafter to butt directly off the end of the partial hip, and use plywood to gusset the two boards together.

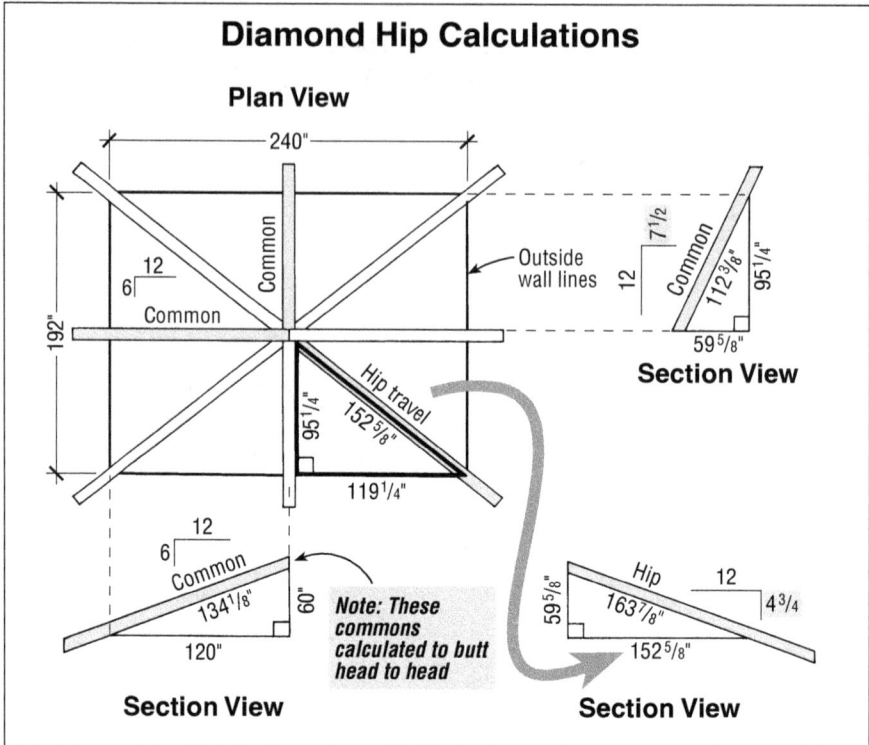

Figure 8-13a. Use the COM LL ratio to calculate the rafter length for standard pitches and the Pythagorean theorem to solve for the hip's horizontal travel and rafter length. Rise/run proportions are used to calculate unknown pitches.
See Appendix B

up different lengths (between the two pitches) to achieve a common fascia height. An unequal-pitch hip with equal-length overhangs is covered in full detail later in this chapter.

In the example in Figure 8-13, the 240-in. span has been set at 6/12 pitch. The 192-in. span has the same rise but a shorter span, so it is steeper. To find this pitch, set up a proportion as shown, with the effective rise from the 240-in. span (119$^{1}/_{4}$" {6/12 effective run} × .5000 {6/12 RR ratio} = 59$^{5}/_{8}$" {effective rise}) over the effective run of the 192-in. span set equal to an unknown/12. If the pitch is standard use the appropriate COM LL ratio (Chart 2, Appendix A); if not, use the Pythagorean theorem ($a^2 + b^2 = c^2$) to solve for the common rafter LL.

The two common rafters for the 240-in. span are chosen to run full length and butt head to head, while the two common rafters for the 192-in. span are calculated to nail to them and are shortened accordingly.

Finding the hip rafter LL involves two steps. First, determine the hip travel (hypotenuse of the horizontal triangle) by either snapping out a full-scale plan view on the floor or by using the Pythagorean theorem with the effective run for each pitch as the legs of the right triangle ([119$^{1}/_{4}$"]^2 + [95$^{1}/_{4}$"]^2 = [152$^{5}/_{8}$"]^2). Next, solve for the hip LL (hypotenuse of the vertical triangle) by using the

Method:

1. COM LL ratio or Pythagorean theorem to calculate rafter LL
2. Rise/run proportion to solve for unknown roof or rafter pitch

Note: "Effective run" abbreviated "run" in following equations

Example:

120" effective run commons (standard pitch 6/12)

1. 120" run × 1.1180 {6/12 COM LL ratio} = $134\frac{1}{8}$" LL (to butt head to head)
2. Pitch : given
   Calculate rise: $119\frac{1}{4}$" run to inside top corner × .5000 {6/12 RR ratio} = $59\frac{5}{8}$" rise

$95\frac{1}{4}$" effective run commons (unknown pitch)

1. $(59\frac{5}{8}\text{" rise})^2 + (95\frac{1}{4}\text{" run})^2 = (112\frac{3}{8}\text{" LL})^2$
2. $\dfrac{59\frac{5}{8}\text{" rise}}{95\frac{1}{4}\text{" run}} = \dfrac{7\frac{1}{2}}{12}$ roof pitch

Bastard hip

1a. $(119\frac{1}{4}\text{" run})^2 + (95\frac{1}{4}\text{" run})^2 = (152\frac{5}{8}\text{" hip travel})^2$

1b. $(59\frac{5}{8}\text{" rise})^2 + (152\frac{5}{8}\text{" hip travel})^2 = (163\frac{7}{8}\text{" LL})^2$

2. $\dfrac{59\frac{5}{8}\text{" rise}}{152\frac{5}{8}\text{" hip travel}} = \dfrac{4\frac{3}{4}}{12}$ hip pitch

Figure 8-13b.  See Appendix B

Pythagorean theorem with the total effective rise ($59\frac{5}{8}$") as one leg, and the hip travel ($152\frac{5}{8}$") as the other. The pitch for the hip rafter is found by setting up a proportion using these same two numbers as shown in Figure 8-13.

The best way to find the cheek-cut lines and cheek-cut angles for the hips is to snap a full-size plan view of one hip corner. Without the necessity of an all-encompassing full-scale plan view, only the various connections need to be drawn to scale on plywood to get the cut-lines, cut-angles, etc. (see **Photo 8-15**). Angles are taken from these drawings using a rafter square or protractor. The cheek-cut lines are transferred to the sides of the hips by measuring perpendicular to the LL plumb-lines uphill/downhill as shown in Figure 8-14. Angles steeper than 45° can be cut with a swing-table saw, a chainsaw, or a regular Skilsaw® as shown in Figure 8-8. Remember, the opposing hip is a mirror image of the one snapped on the floor, so all the cut-lines, cut-angles, etc., are reversed.

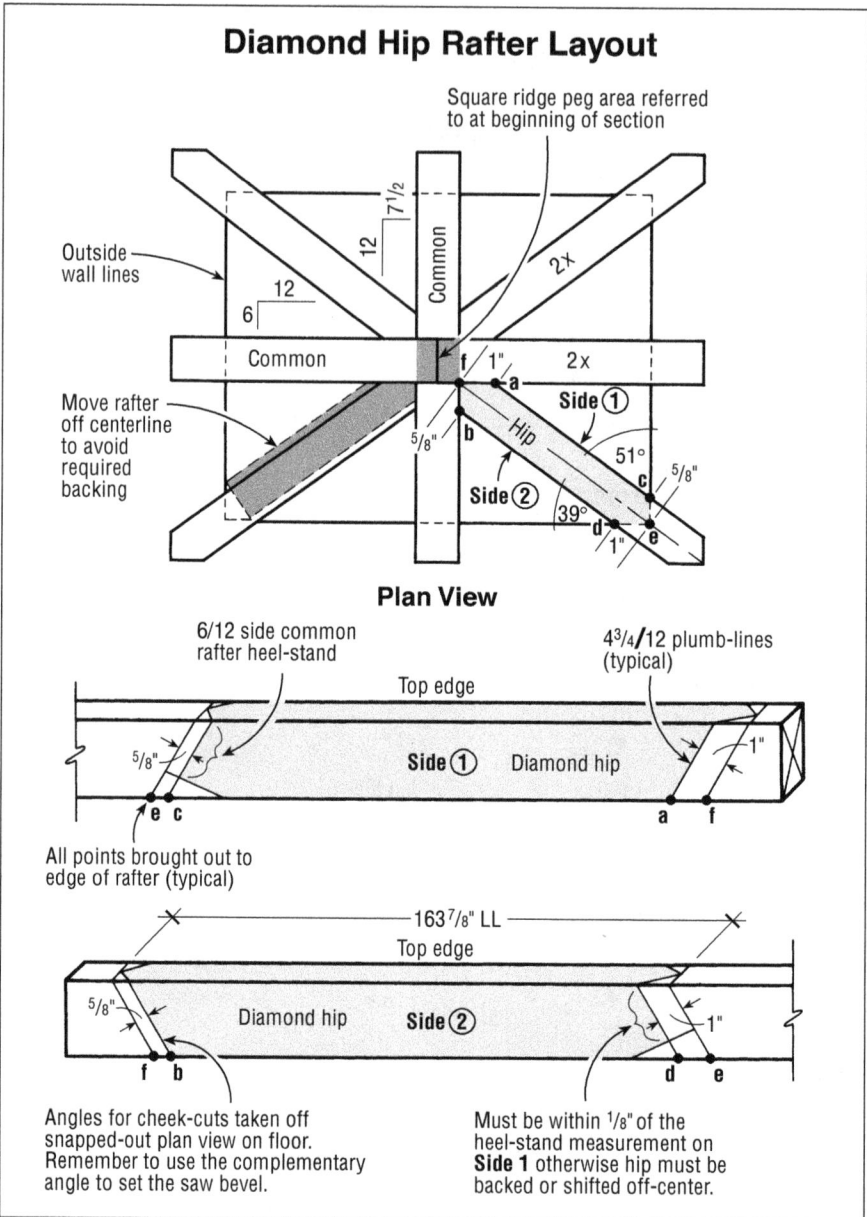

Figure 8-14. If the heel-stand dimensions at **c** and **d** vary by more than 1/8 in., back the rafter or slide the whole board off the theoretical centerline so the tail of a square-cut hip board will fit on the building corner.

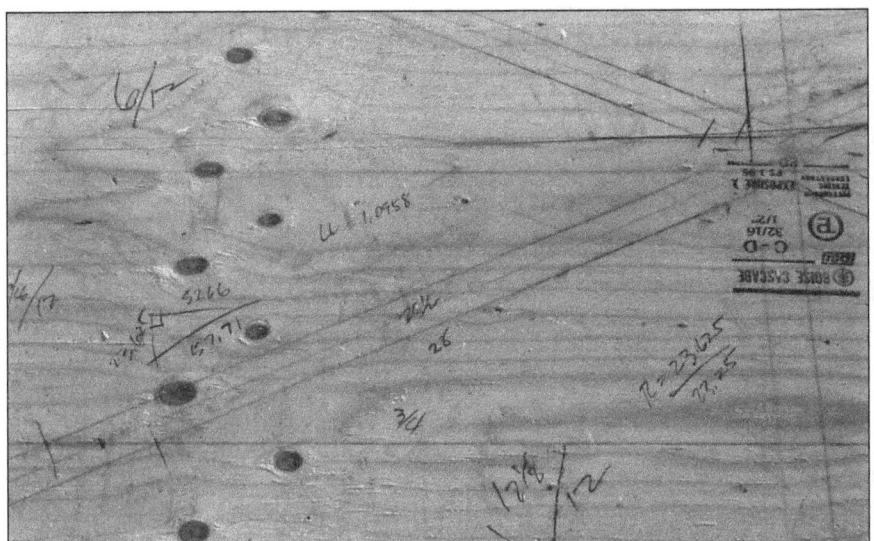

Photo 8-15. Always snap a full-size plan view of the bastard roof section to get the cut-angles, cut-lines, dimensions, etc.

Mark the heel-stand of a common rafter for the 6/12 side at **c** and draw the level seat-cut line through this point. If the heel-stand dimensions at **c** and **d** vary more than 1/8-in., back the top edge of the hip or reposition it by sliding the whole board off the theoretical centerline so the tail of a square-cut hip board will fit on the building corner as shown in Figure 8-14. (Use the snapped-out plan view and a square-cut scrap of the same size material as a pattern to find the offset position.) By doing this, the heel-stands on both sides of the bastard hip automatically become equal, and the top corner edges of the offset bastard hip plane in with the adjacent roof surface as a regular hip does. Resnap the bastard hips in their offset position, and readjust the cheek-cut and heel-cut lines accordingly. If the top edge of the hip will be backed, mark the heel-stand of a common rafter at **e** to lay out the birdsmouth. Do this prior to ripping the top edges. (Refer to the upcoming section, "Backing Bastard Rafters," for a discussion of how to find the rip-angle and rip-cut lines for this or any similar situation.

By applying the method for calculating unequal-pitch overhangs shown in the Chapter 7 section, "Miscellaneous Fascia Techniques," (page 138) the overhang on the 7 1/2 /12 side of the roof will be 19 1/4 in. if the overhang on the 6/12 side on the roof has been set for 24 in.

DIAMOND ROOF HIP JACKS

To lay out hip fill for a diamond roof, special jack-rafter steps must be found for both roof pitches. To determine the length of each step, divide one pitch's effective run by the rafter's on-center spacing to find the number of

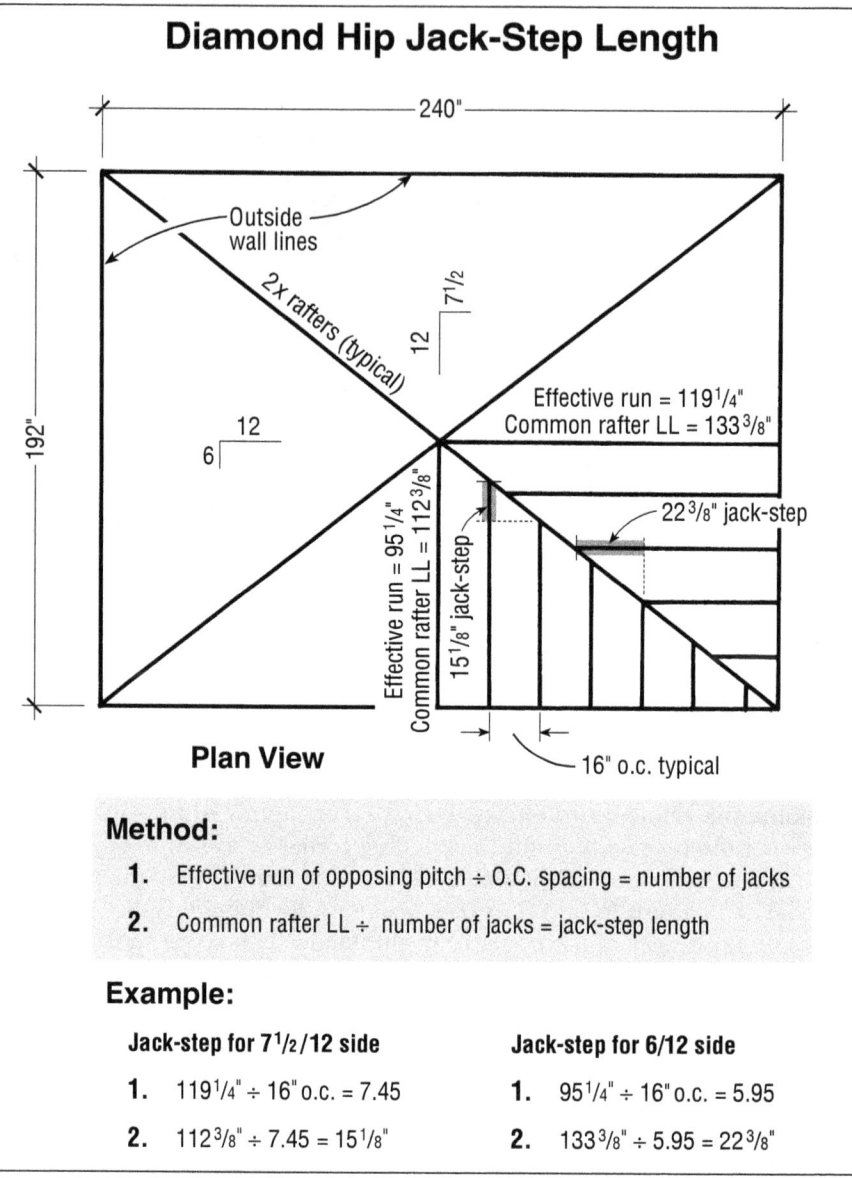

Figure 8-16. The jack-step length for a diamond hip or unequal-pitch hip can be calculated by dividing one pitch's effective run by the on-center spacing to find the number of jacks required, and then dividing that number into the other pitch's common rafter length. See Appendix B

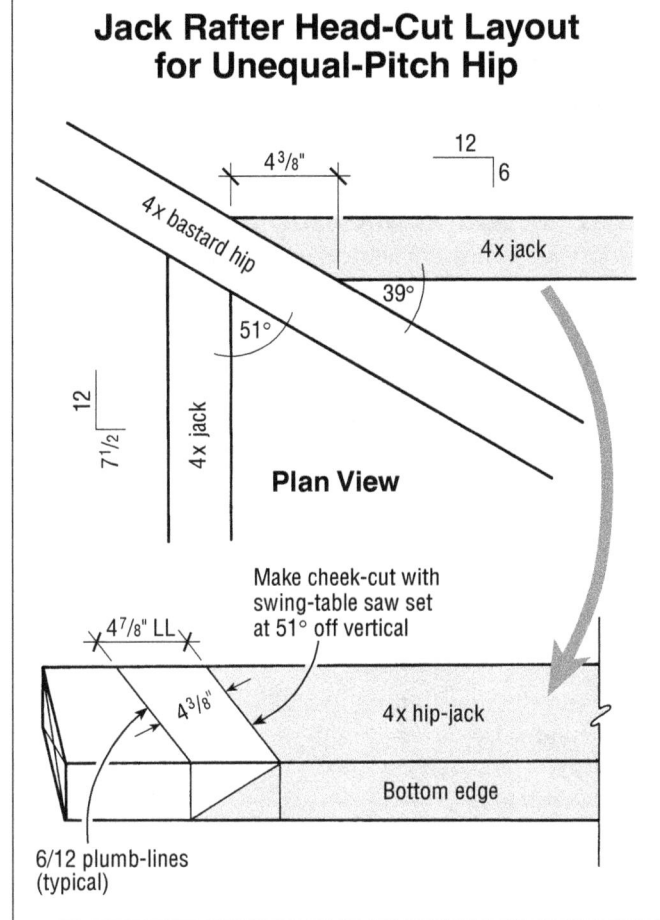

Figure 8-17. Use the snapped-out plan view to find the cut-lines for steep-angled cheek-cuts. Square over from the SP to the outside edge and measuring to the LP. Transfer this measurement to the side of the beam perpendicular to the SP LL plumb-line.

See Appendix B

jacks required. Then divide this number into the other pitch's common rafter LL to calculate the jack-step dimension *(Figure 8-16)*.

The LL of the longest jack (spaced from the king common) to the SP can be calculated by measuring the run from a full-size snapped-out plan view of the roof and multiplying it by the appropriate COM LL ratio; or by subtracting the appropriate step measurement from the corresponding king common and shortening for the hip connection per the snapped-out plan view. (The king common must be calculated for the effective run.) The rest of the jacks are found by stepping down progressively.

The cheek-cut angles for the fill are taken from the snapped-out plan-view by using a Speed® Square or protractor. In Figure 8-14, the 7 1/2 /12 side cheek-cuts will be cut at 39° and the 6/12 side at 51°. When the angle goes over 45° and the cut is not exposed, square-cut the cheek-cut at the SP plumb-line, and nail it to the hip flush on the inside edge. If the jacks are beams, transfer the head-cut lines from the snapped-out plan view to the beam as shown in *Figure 8-17*. Use a swing-table saw to make the cuts on both sides and a Skilsaw® to make the cuts on the edges. Finish the cuts with a handsaw if necessary.

Note: Since the bastard hip jacks layout will not line up across the bastard hip rafter, the hip should be vertically braced or of sufficient size to allow it to serve as a beam and carry half the roof load acting upon the jack rafters.

THE UNEQUAL-PITCH RELATIONSHIP

The unequal-pitch relationship defined: The runs for the two different pitches on an unequal-pitch roof with standard 90° corners are inversely related to the unit rise for each pitch.

In the example in **Figure 8-18**, the unequal-pitch relationship is used to find the unknown effective run leg of the right triangles that define the bastard rafter travel for every intersection shown: the full hip, the valley, and the broken hip. Use the effective run dimensions to snap out a full-size plan view of one hip corner (as shown in the previous section) and super-impose the smaller two rectangles for the valley and the broken hip inside to help visualize the various cut-lines, cut-angles, etc.

The broken-hip steep-side effective run was calculated by subtracting the effective run of the building wing extension (47$1/4$") and the full thickness of the ridge (1$1/2$") from the main roof's steep-side effective run (71$1/2$" − 47$1/4$" − 1$1/2$" = 22$3/4$").

The 2$1/2$-in. space between the upper end of the valley and the lower end of the broken hip was calculated by subtracting the shallow-side effective run of both the broken hip (37$7/8$") and the valley (78$3/4$") from the main roof's shallow-side effective run (119$1/4$" − 37$7/8$" − 78$3/4$" = 2$5/8$").

The LL for the full-length bastard hip is calculated as shown in the previous section using the Pythagorean theorem. First, solve for the hip-travel (hypotenuse of the horizontal triangle) using both the steep- and shallow-side effective runs as legs of a right triangle. Then solve for the hip LL (hypotenuse of the vertical triangle) using the rise and hip-travel as legs of another right triangle. The LL of the bastard broken hip and bastard valley are calculated using a proportion as shown in the "method" segment of Figure 8-18. Set the LL of the primary span's bastard hip (151$1/4$") divided by its corresponding steep-side effective run (71$1/2$") set equal to a yet-to-be-determined (unknown) value divided by the appropriate steep-side effective run (22$3/4$" for the broken hip, or 47$1/4$" for the valley, as the case may be). Solving for the unknown value nets the bastard rafter LL. Using the proportion to find the rafter length is, in effect, making an unequal-pitch hip/valley LL ratio for when those two specific roof pitches (6/12 and 10/12) meet at 90°. This ratio can be used in any other similar situation if the effective-run measurement is pulled parallel to the steep-pitch direction as in this example.

The unequal-pitch relationship can also be applied to the creation of valley-cut patterns to be used when sheathing an unequal-pitch intersection. Simply multiply the appropriate number in the relationship (depending on which pitch is to be sheathed) by the opposing pitch's COM LL ratio, and upsize the modified relationship to fit a plywood sheet. For example, in

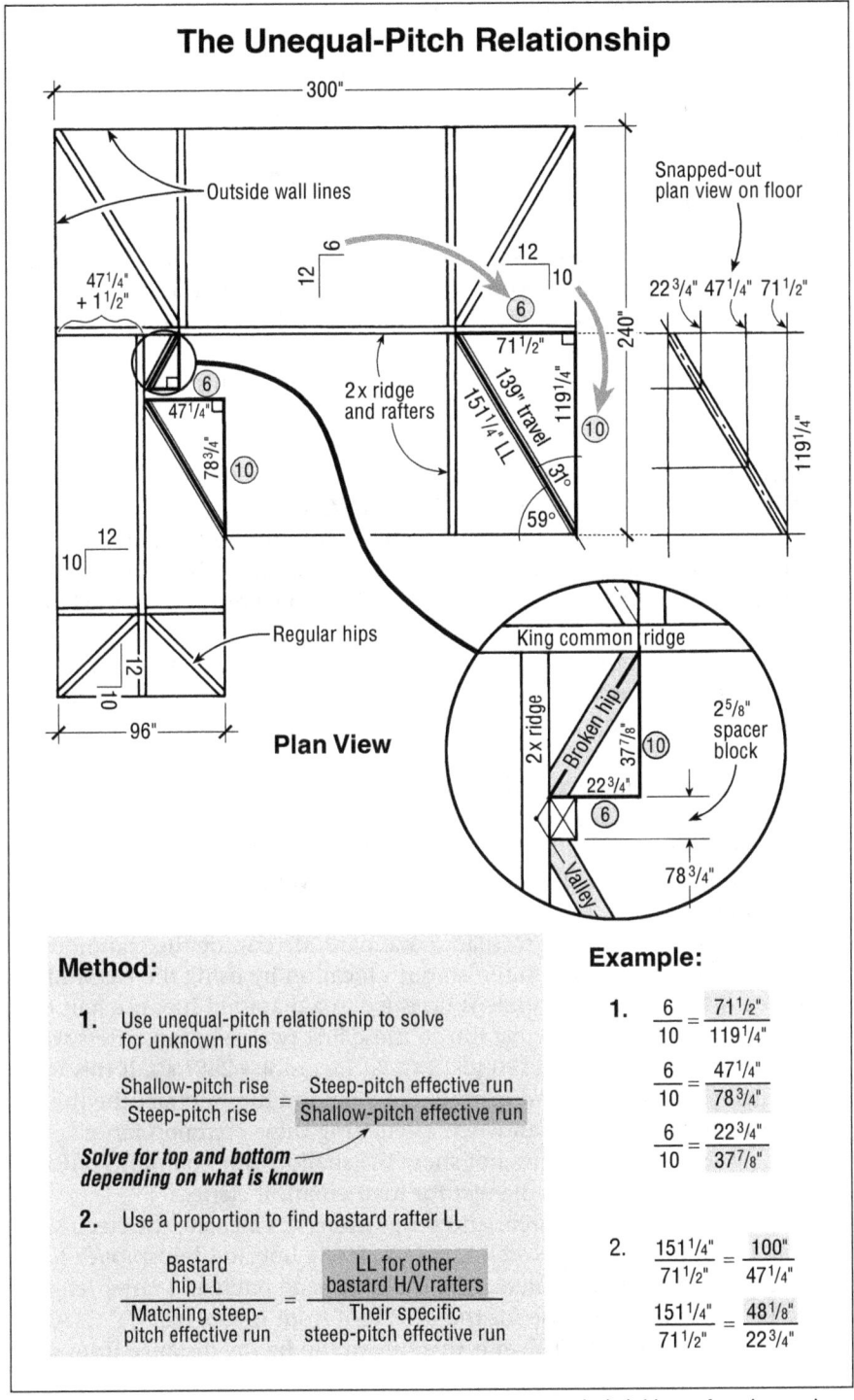

Figure 8-18. The runs for the two different pitches on an unequal-pitch hip roof are inversely related to the unit rise for each pitch. See Appendix B

Figure 8-18, the major span would have a valley-cut pattern top dimension of 25³/₄ in. (replacing the 42⁷/₈-in. dimension shown in Figure 7-12), while the minor span would have a top dimension of 61¹/₂ in.

Math: $\dfrac{6}{10 \times 1.1180 \ \{6/12 \ \text{COM LL ratio}\}} = \dfrac{\text{unknown}}{48"}$ answer = 25³/₄"

$\dfrac{10}{6 \times 1.3017 \ \{10/12 \ \text{COM LL ratio}\}} = \dfrac{\text{unknown}}{48"}$ answer = 61¹/₂"

In his rafter table style book, *The Roof Framer's Bible*, author Barry Mussell has done much of the homework you will need to calculate and lay out hip/valley rafters, jacks, etc., for the unequal-pitch intersection between all the common roof pitches.

(Thanks to Bill Saar and Bill Miller for their input in this section.)

AN UNEQUAL-PITCH HIP ROOF WITH EQUAL-LENGTH OVERHANGS

Things get a bit more difficult when the overhangs for both pitches must be the same. All the rafters are figured from the fascia line rather than the building's outside wall line. This causes the hips to be offset from the building corners toward the steeper-pitched side.

As always, snap a full-size plan view of the roof on the floor to get the cheek-cut angles, cheek-cut lines, dimensions, etc. (unless you are good with your Construction Master® calculator). If space is limited, you may have to keep the snapped-out plan view to one hip corner as shown in **Figure 8-19**; but remember, the opposing hip is a mirror image of the corner snapped on the floor and the cut-lines, cut-angles, etc., are reversed.

Figure 8-19 illustrates a diamond hip corner for a 18 x 38-ft. building with a 12-in. overhang on all four sides (or for layout purposes, a 20 x 40-ft. roof rectangle).

Since the pitch for the 40-ft. span is standard, determine the common rafter LL to the fascia line and birdsmouth location by using the COM LL ratio for a 6/12 pitch. Since there is no ridge in a diamond hip, use half the actual 40-ft. span as the effective run so these first two common rafters will butt head to head (240" × 1.1180 {6/12 COM LL ratio} = 268³/₈"). If this were an unequal-pitch hip roof-end instead of a diamond hip, subtract the thickness of the ridge from the span when calculating these common rafter's lengths. (*Note:* Figure 8-19 does not show the shallow-side commons butting at the head as mentioned in the text for mathematical clarity.)

Use the Pythagorean theorem and proportions to calculate the steep-side roof pitch, common rafter overall LL to the fascia line and birdsmouth location. The rise to use when calculating the steep-side pitch and rafter length would be the same as the rise for the 6/12 roof from **h** to **z** (239¹/₄" × .5000 {6/12 RR ratio} = 119⁵/₈"). The effective run would be the distance from **g** to **z** (119¹/₄").

Find the hip-rafter pitch and overall length in a similar fashion. Use the **z-g** (119¹/₄") and **z-h** (239¹/₄") measurements to solve for the **z-i** (267³/₈") diagonal by applying the Pythagorean theorem, or pull a measurement from the snapped-out plan view on the floor. Then solve a vertical right triangle with this diagonal distance (**z-i**) as the base leg and the roof rise (119$^5/_8$") as the other leg. The resulting hypotenuse (292$^7/_8$") is the hip-rafter LL. Hip-rafter pitch and birdsmouth location at **x** are found by solving the proportions as shown.

When dealing with unequal-pitch hip situations, the steep-pitch outside wall height must often be padded up if the rise differences between the two pitches cannot be compensated for by adjusting the depth of the birdsmouth. In the example in Figure 8-19, the 6/12 roof plane rises 6 in. in the 12-in. overhang and the 12+/12 pitch side rises 12 in. creating a difference of 6 in. at the wall line. Therefore, with the heel-stand dimensions set the same for both pitches, the wall on the 12+/12 pitch side must be padded up 6 in. to correct for the difference.

The next step is to determine the various birdsmouth depths. Calculate or measure the plumb dimension of a common rafter for both pitches. Using 2x8 material, the 6/12 rafter plumb dimension is 8$^3/_8$ in. (7$^1/_2$" × 1.1180 {6/12 COM LL ratio}= 8$^3/_8$") and 10$^5/_8$ in. (7$^1/_2$" × 1.4161 {12+/12 COM LL ratio} = 10$^5/_8$") for the 12+/12 pitch. A 1$^1/_4$-in.-deep birdsmouth on the 6/12 side gives a heel-stand of 7 in. (8$^3/_8$" − 1$^1/_4$" = 7$^1/_8$"). The same heel-stand on the 12+/12 side (wall padded up 6") would result in a 3$^5/_8$-in.-deep birdsmouth (10$^5/_8$" − 7$^1/_8$" = 3$^1/_2$"). To vary this depth up or down, simply adjust the wall padding to compensate. For example, because 3$^1/_2$ in. is too deep per the maximum birdsmouth notch penetration rule, we decide to cut a 2$^1/_2$-in.-deep birdsmouth (1" less) and compensate by lowering the wall padding from 6 in. to 5 in. Likewise, to cut a deeper birdsmouth, raise the wall padding.

Note: Plate height padding and birdsmouth depths can also be determined by snapping out a section view of the two different-pitched eaves superimposed on one another originating from the fascia line, similar to the upcoming Figure 12-11.

One way to find the location of the hip on the outside wall is by using a proportion as shown. In this proportion, the effective run of the shallow-side pitch is set over the effective run of the steep side pitch as equal to the unknown distance **k-x** set over the overhang of the steep side (**l-x**). Cross-multiplying and subtracting the 12-in. overhang (**u-k**) from the resultant, the hip offset from the corner is found (**k-x** less **u-k** equals **x-u**, or 24" − 12" = 12"). An alternate, and perhaps simpler method of figuring the hip offset is to take the rise difference between the two roof pitches at the outside wall line (6" in Figure 8-19) and divide by the shallower roof pitch's RR ratio. (Example: 6" ÷ .5000 {6/12 RR ratio} = 12")

Since the hip-rafter birdsmouth sits on the built-up 12+/12 walls, its birdsmouth depth will be marked using the same heel-stand as on the 12+/12 commons (7 in. if you kept both pitches heel-stands the same, or 8 in. if you lowered the built-up wall height 1 in. for a 2$^1/_2$-in.-deep birdsmouth as previously discussed). Because the hip rafter must be backed on the top edge (unless it is slid off centerline to fit square in the fascia corner similar to what

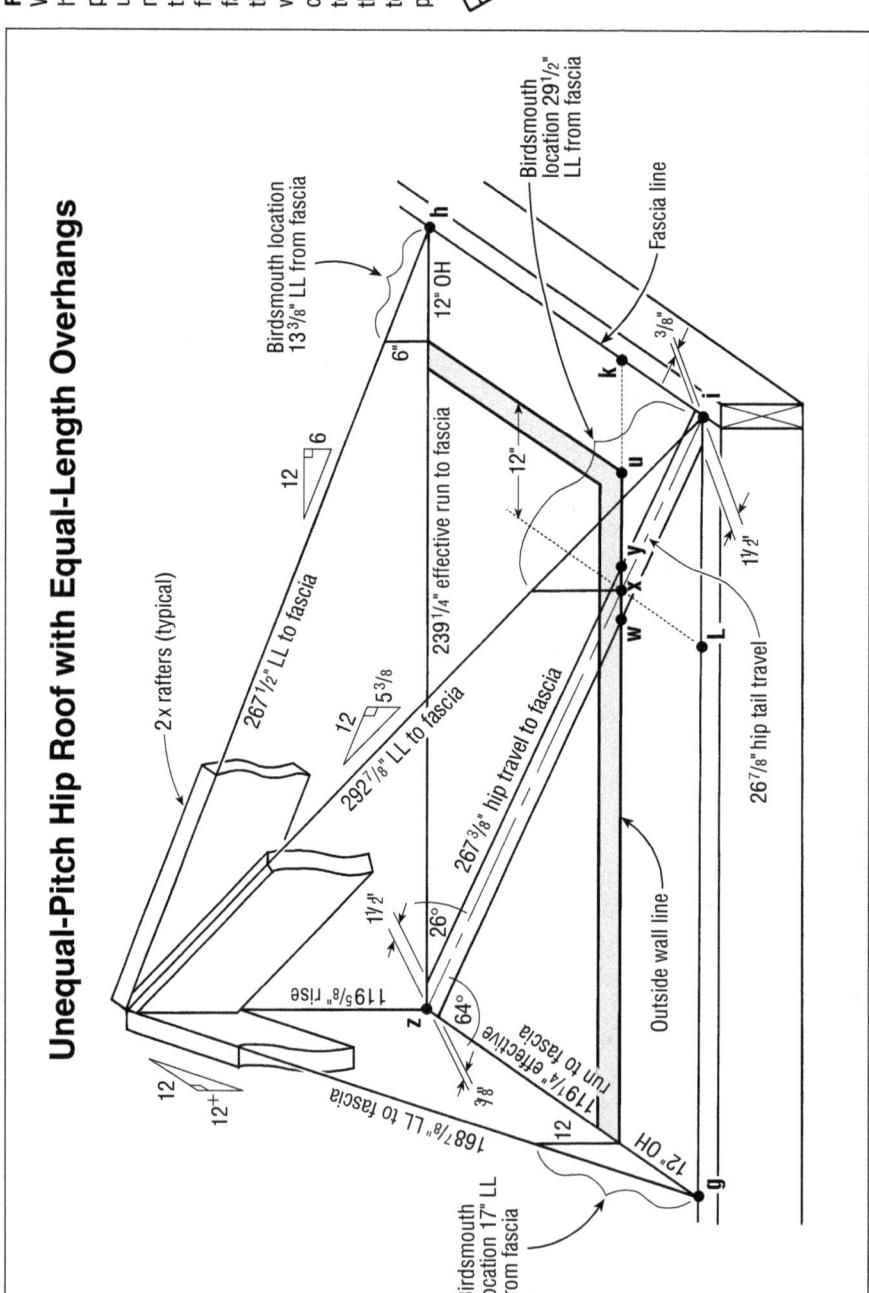

Figure 8-19a. When the overhangs for both pitches on an unequal-pitch hip must be the same, the rafters are figured from the fascia line rather than the outside wall line. This causes the hips to be offset from the building corner toward the steeper-pitch side.

See Appendix B

Unequal-Pitch Hip Roof with Equal-Length Overhangs

Method:

1. COM LL ratio or Pythagorean theorem to calculate rafter LL
2. COM LL ratio or proportion to calculate birdsmouth LL from fascia
3. Rise/run proportion to solve for unknown roof or rafter pitch
4. Run/run proportion to solve for hip offset

Note: "Effective run" abbreviated "run" in following equations

Example:

$239^{1}/_{4}$" effective run commons (standard pitch 6/12)

1. $239^{1}/_{4}$" run × 1.1180 {6/12 COM LL ratio} = $267^{1}/_{2}$" LL
2. 12" OH × 1.1180 {6/12 COM LL ratio} = $13^{3}/_{8}$" birdsmouth location LL
3. Pitch : given
   Calculate rise: $239^{1}/_{4}$" run × .5000 {6/12 RR ratio} = $119^{5}/_{8}$" rise

$119^{1}/_{4}$" effective run commons (unknown pitch)

1. $(119^{5}/_{8}\text{" rise})^2 + (119^{1}/_{4}\text{" run})^2 = (168^{7}/_{8}\text{" LL})^2$
2. $\dfrac{168^{7}/_{8}\text{" LL}}{119^{1}/_{4}\text{" run}} = \dfrac{17\text{" birdsmouth location LL}}{12\text{" OH}}$
3. $\dfrac{119^{5}/_{8}\text{" rise}}{119^{1}/_{4}\text{" run}} = \dfrac{12^{+}}{12}$ roof pitch

Bastard hip

1a. $(119^{1}/_{4}\text{" run})^2 + (239^{1}/_{4}\text{" run})^2 = (267^{3}/_{8}\text{" hip travel})^2$

1b. $(119^{5}/_{8}\text{" rise})^2 + (267^{3}/_{8}\text{" hip travel})^2 = (292^{7}/_{8}\text{" LL})^2$

2. $\dfrac{292^{7}/_{8}\text{" LL}}{119^{1}/_{4}\text{" run}} = \dfrac{29^{1}/_{2}\text{" birdsmouth location LL}}{12\text{" OH}}$

3. $\dfrac{119^{5}/_{8}\text{" rise}}{267^{3}/_{8}\text{" hip travel}} = \dfrac{5^{3}/_{8}}{12}$ hip pitch

4. $\dfrac{239^{1}/_{4}\text{" run}}{119^{1}/_{4}\text{" run}} = \dfrac{24\text{" \textbf{k-x} setback}}{12\text{" \textbf{L-x} OH}}$

Figure 8-19b.  See Appendix B

Photo 8-20. A scale model corner mockup of the unequal-pitch hip with equal-length overhangs illustrated in Figure 8-19. The hip has been moved off centerline so a square-cut tail will fit in the fascia corner. This eliminates the need to back the top edge of the hip. Note the additional 2x4 plate added to the steep-pitch side for wall padding.

is shown in **Photo 8-20** and explained in Figure 8-14), mark the heel-stand at position **x** on the hip rafter prior to backing the top edges *(Figure 8-21)*. The greater the difference between the two adjoining roof pitches and the longer the overhang, the taller the built-up wall plates become. When the built-up wall plate height becomes taller than the hip rafter heel-cut, stop the plates at **x** (Figure 8-19), and square-cut the hip rafter's heel-cut at the same location. This works well with 2x material where the exterior wall covering will hide the gap. On beam hips you must cut the V-notch. Refer to Figure 8-21 for a diagram of the various types of unequal-hip birdsmouths.

The cut-lines and associated angles for both the head- and tail-cuts are taken from the snapped-out plan view and transferred to the side of the rafter perpendicular to the LL plumb-line as shown earlier in Figure 8-14.

Jacks are found as previously discussed in the "Diamond Hip Jacks" section, but substitute the overall effective run to the fascia line for calculating the steps instead of the effective run to the exterior wall shown in that section. The jack rafter birdsmouth location and depths are identical to the corresponding common rafters.

Not all unequal-pitched hips with equal overhangs are as extreme as the example illustrated here. Often the hip is located just slightly off the building corner and the birdsmouth depths can be adjusted accordingly rather than raising or lowering the wall heights.

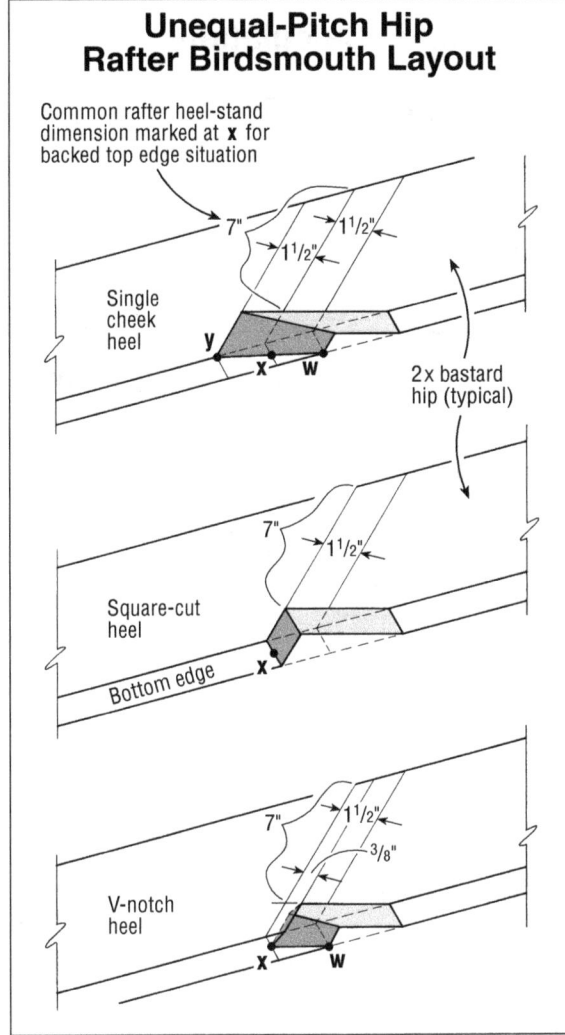

Figure 8-21. Which type of unequal-pitch hip birdsmouth to use depends on the specific situation, but in all cases, the heel-stand is marked at **x** in preparation for backing the top edge.

UNEQUAL-PITCH VALLEYS

Described in this section is an unequal-pitch valley stacked to the center of a building corner. The overhangs for each pitch will be different dimensions to achieve a common fascia height. If equal-length overhangs are desired, the valley is run to the inside corner of the fascia line and its birdsmouth moves off the building inside corner. Follow similar procedures outlined in the previous section on unequal-pitch hips with equal-length overhangs.

In **Figure 8-22**, the ridges of both the main and secondary span are framed to the same height, but only the main span's roof pitch is given. Calculate the secondary span's roof pitch by setting up a proportion as shown using the effective rise of the main span (119 1/4" {main-span effective run} × .5000 {6/12 RR ratio} = 59 5/8") divided by the effective run of the secondary span set equal to an unknown value/12. The secondary span common rafter LL is calculated using the Pythagorean theorem or a COM LL ratio depending on whether or not it is a standard pitch (with a ratio available in Chart 2, Appendix A). Since heel-stands for both pitches will be the same, the birdsmouth depth for the secondary span will be deeper than the main roof's birdsmouth depth by the difference between their plumb dimensions.

The LL for the valley is calculated by solving two right triangles in succession for their hypotenuses: the first, a horizontal right triangle, to get the

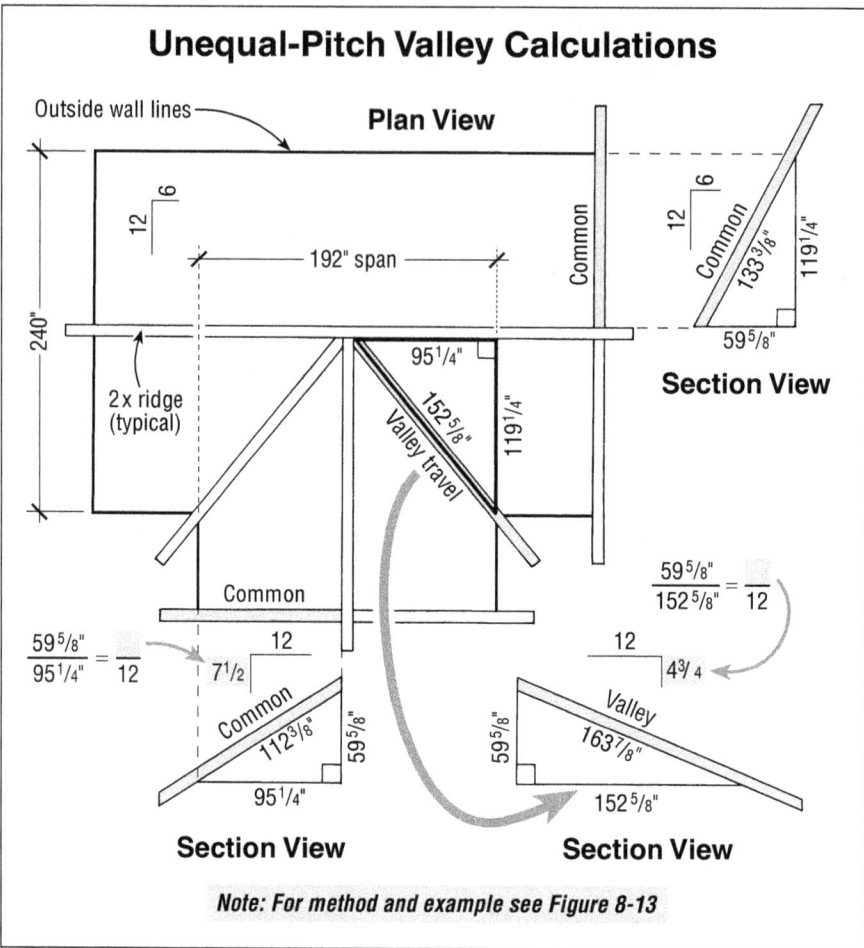

Figure 8-22. This unequal-pitch valley is stacked to the center of the building corner. The overhangs for each pitch must be different to achieve a common fascia height. See Appendix B

valley travel using each span's effective run as a leg; the second, a vertical right triangle, to get the valley LL using the effective rise and valley travel as legs. Calculate the pitch of the valley rafter using a proportion as before. To find the cut-lines and angles for the cheek-cuts at the head, and the heel-cut lines and angles for the birdsmouth, snap a full-size plan view of the valley section on the floor as shown in **Figure 8-23**. Transfer the corresponding measurements to each side of the rafter as previously shown.

To lay out the bastard-valley birdsmouth depth, mark the heel-stand of the main roof's common rafters at the valley's lower LL plumb-line and draw the level seat-cut line through this point.

When required, backing the unequal-pitch valley rafter is accomplished as shown in the upcoming section, "Backing Bastard Rafters."

To lay out the fill, determine the special step for each pitch by dividing the

178   CHAPTER 8

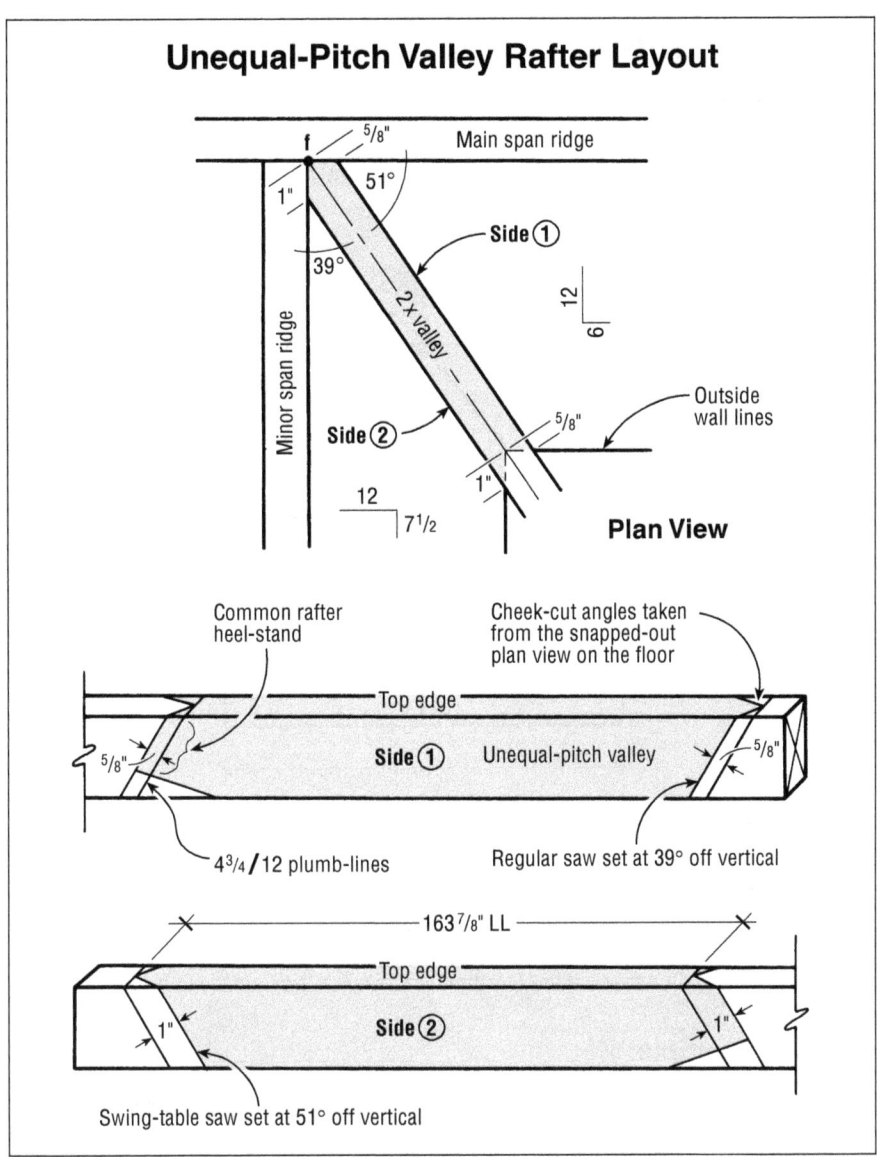

Figure 8-23. Transfer the corresponding head- and heel-cut line measurements from the full-size snapped-out plan view on the floor to the corresponding side of the rafter. Mark the heel-stand of a common rafter at the lower LL plumb-line.

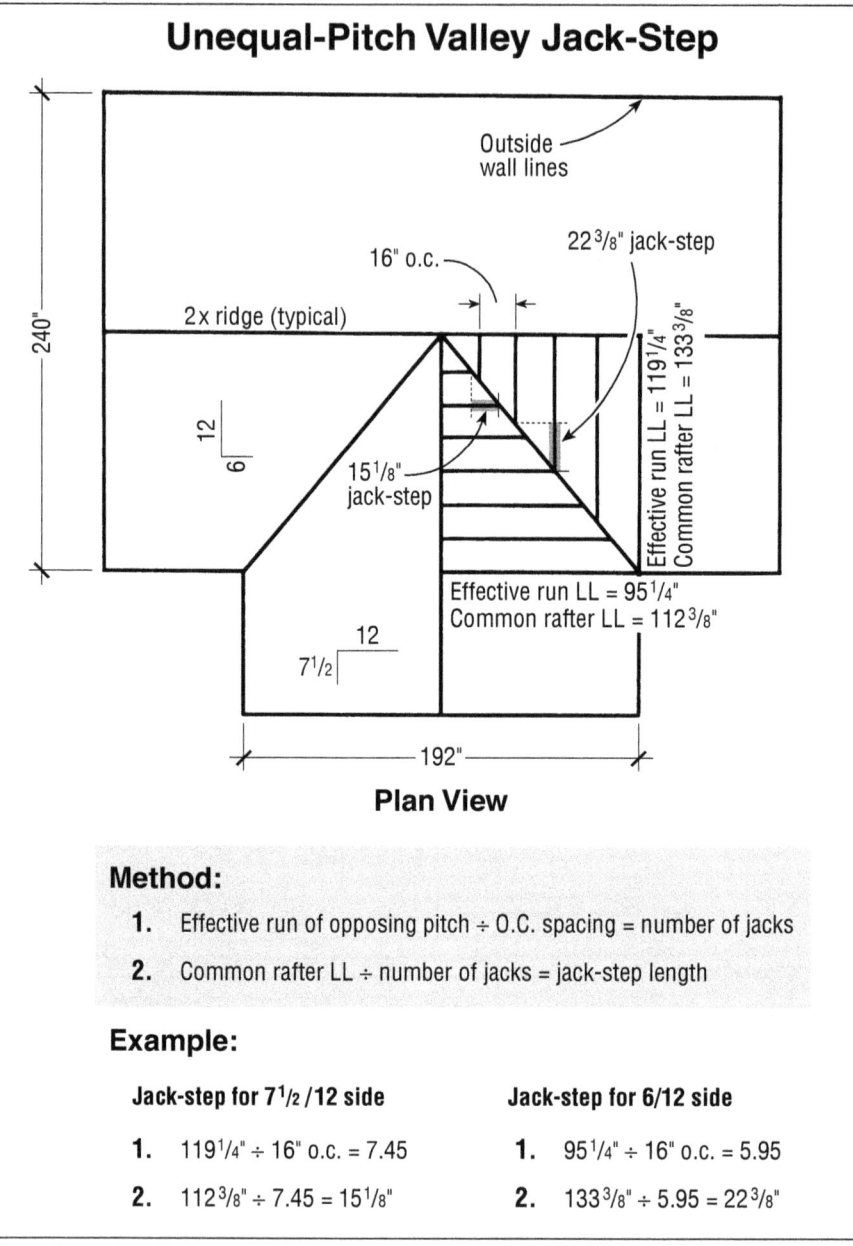

Figure 8-24. As with the unequal-pitch hip, the jack-step for an unequal-pitch valley can be calculated by dividing one pitch's effective run by the on-center spacing to find the number of jacks required, and then dividing that number into the other pitch's common rafter length.

180 CHAPTER 8

common rafter LL for each span by the number of on-center spaces found in the opposite pitch's effective run *(Figure 8-24)*. These steps are then subtracted progressively from the common rafter LLs to get the jack LP measurements.

The angle for the cheek-cuts is taken from the snapped-out plan view on the floor. Cheek-cuts greater than 45° which are not exposed can be square-cut at the SP plumb-line, and nailed to plane into the center of the valley. For steep cheek-cuts on exposed beams, transfer the SP and LP from the snapped-out plan view to the side of the jack rafters perpendicular to the LL plumb-line as shown in Figure 8-17.

Actually, the easiest way of framing an unequal-pitch valley connection is to make a California valley (or overlay) intersection. Mark the bottoms of the jacks with a level line corresponding to the intersect*ING* pitch and set the saw bevel to the degree of the intersect*ED* roof. The California end of the intersect*ING* ridge is cut with the intersect*ED* roof's roof-pitch angle. The sleeper for a bastard valley can be calculated using a modified version of the standard sleeper calculation procedure shown in Chapter 5 for regular roof intersections (see page 94). Step **1** of the Chapter 5 procedure is modified so that the thickness of the sheathing plus sleeper is changed into a plumb dimension by multiplying by the intersect*ED* roof's COM LL ratio. Step **2** of the Chapter 5 procedure is modified so that the run value is calculated by dividing the sheathing plus sleeper plumb dimension by the intersect*ING* roof's RR ratio. And lastly in Step **4** of the Chapter 5 procedure, the sleeper's effective run is multiplied by a case-specific unequal-pitch H/V LL ratio. That ratio can be found using the method described towards the end of the earlier "Unequal-Pitch Relationship" section where a bastard valley's (or hip's) actual rafter length is divided by the intersect*ING* pitch's effective run. In other words, although the intersection will be framed California-style, the length of an actual bastard valley rafter must be calculated in order to determine the case-specific pitch-to-pitch H/V LL ratio. For example, the unique unequal-pitch H/V LL ratio for Figure 8-22 would be 1.7205 when applied to the secondary span's run ($163^7/_8$" {bastard valley LL} ÷ $95^1/_4$" {secondary span's effective run} = 1.7205).

To mark cut-lines at the head and tail of an unequal-pitch valley sleeper, set up a framing square with the intersect*ED* pitch on one leg and the intersect*ING* pitch multiplied by the intersec*ED* pitch's COM LL ratio on the other leg. If a hypothetical minor-to-major-span overlay intersection was applied to Figure 8-22, the framing square would be set at **6 in.** and **$8^3/_8$ in.** ($7^1/_2$ {intersecting pitch} × 1.1180 {6/12 COM LL ratio: intersected pitch} = $8^3/_8$"). Mark head-cuts along the $8^3/_8$-in. leg and tail-cuts along the 6-in. leg. The head-cut is made with the saw set square, while the tail-cut is made with the saw's bevel set at the pitch of the intersect*ED* roof's pitch in degrees.

Use the unequal-pitch relationship (shown in Figure 8-18) to help find the jack-step runs when the ridges do not plane in at the same level and the method shown in Figure 8-24 cannot as easily be applied. Referring to Figure 8-18, create a proportion with the shallow-side pitch divided by the steep-side pitch set equal to an unknown jack-step run divided by the desired on-center spacing to calculate the jack-step run for the steep-side

Photo 8-25. On the far side: an off-angled California valley intersection. On the near side: jack rafters across an angled wall.

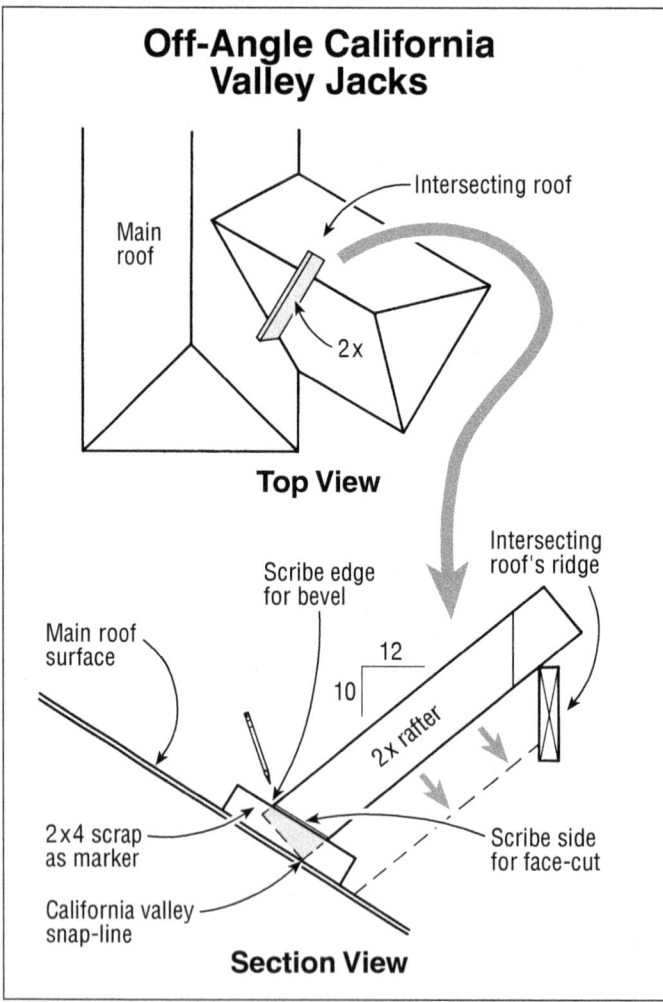

Figure 8-26. Use a block of wood as a guide to find the face- and bevel-cut for the lower end of off-angle California valley jacks.

pitch. Then, multiply this run by the appropriate LL ratio to determine the jack-step length.

Example: $\dfrac{6}{7^{1}/_{2}} = \dfrac{\text{unknown run}}{16" \text{ o.c.}}$ Answer = $12^{3}/_{4}"$ run

($12^{3}/_{4}"$ run × 1.1792 {$7^{1}/_{2}/12$ COM LL ratio} = $15^{1}/_{8}"$ jack-step). Flip-flop the proportion to calculate the jack-step run for the shallow-side pitch.

OFF-ANGLE CALIFORNIA JACKS

When California valley jacks meet another roof at an angle other than 90° *(Photo 8-25)*, the side-cut angle and cheek-cut angles can be found most judiciously by the "scribe to fit" method shown in *Figure 8-26*. Start with an eyeballed side-cut on a board so the heel of that cut will sit on the CV snap-line while the other end of the board extends beyond the ridge. Take a 2x4 scrap either on-edge or flat (depending on how close your eyeball cut was to the actual CV-cut), place it against the rafter on both sides, and scribe the face- and cheek-cut angles. With this as a pattern for the bottom ends, tape-measure a few starter jacks in the air to find a common step measurement, and finish cutting the rest on the ground.

BACKING BASTARD RAFTERS

When a bastard rafter bisects the corner of a building that makes a jog other than 90° (dog-leg bastards or polygon beams), the rip-angle and rip-cut lines for backing the tops can be found most easily using a level-cut pattern block simulating the bastard rafter to mock-up the corner and scribe the crossing edges. For this procedure, start by making a level-cut at the bastard-rafter pitch on a scrap of hip or valley material.

For a hip, place this pattern block so the point of the tapered end is tangent to and bisects the dog-leg or polygon corner. The pattern block's angle will open towards the inside of the building just like the actual bastard hip will do when installed (View **A** in *Figure 8-27*). Square down from the top edge of the pattern block to mark the intersection of the beam and the outside edge of the top plates (View **B** in Figure 8-27, point **p**). Scribe rip-cut lines along both sides parallel to the top edge originating from point **p**. Find the rip-angle using the measurement from the top edge of the pattern block to the rip-cut line (distance "**x**") together with $1/2$ thk. of the beam as legs of a right triangle, and note the angle formed with a Speed® Square or protractor. If required, the underside of a hip can be backed with the same angle to form a concave V-notch.

The backing rip-angles for a dog-leg bastard valley are identical to those for its paired bastard hip, except the cuts are reversed; the concave V-notch is on top, and the convex shoulder is on the bottom. To figure them separately if so desired, use a modified version of the upcoming unequal-pitch valley backing layout technique, but rather than placing the pattern block askew as shown in View **E** of *Figure 8-28*, bisect the inside wall corner angle with the pattern block so both edges of the tapered end are tangent to

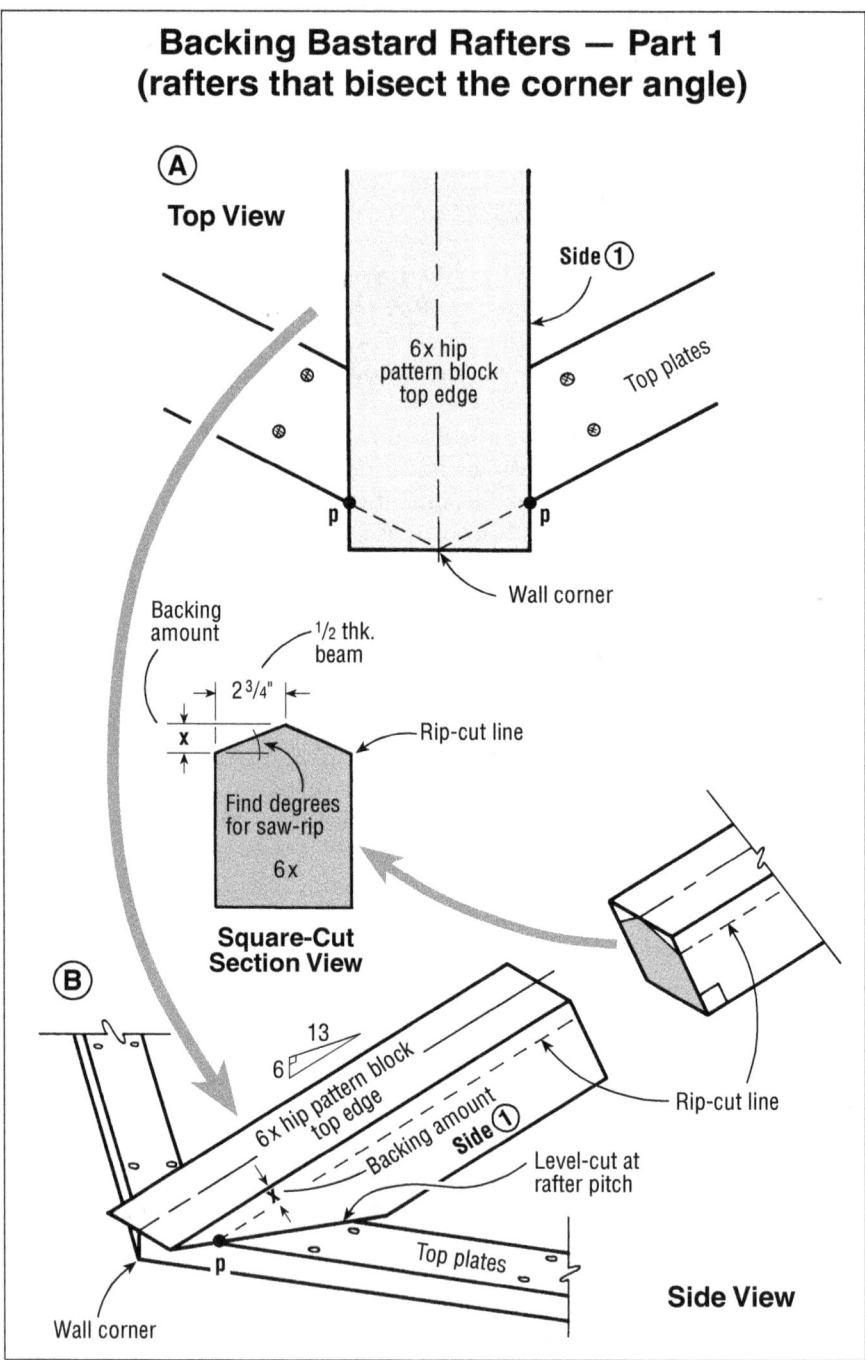

Figure 8-27. Both backing rips are made with the same angle when a beam bisects the corner angle.

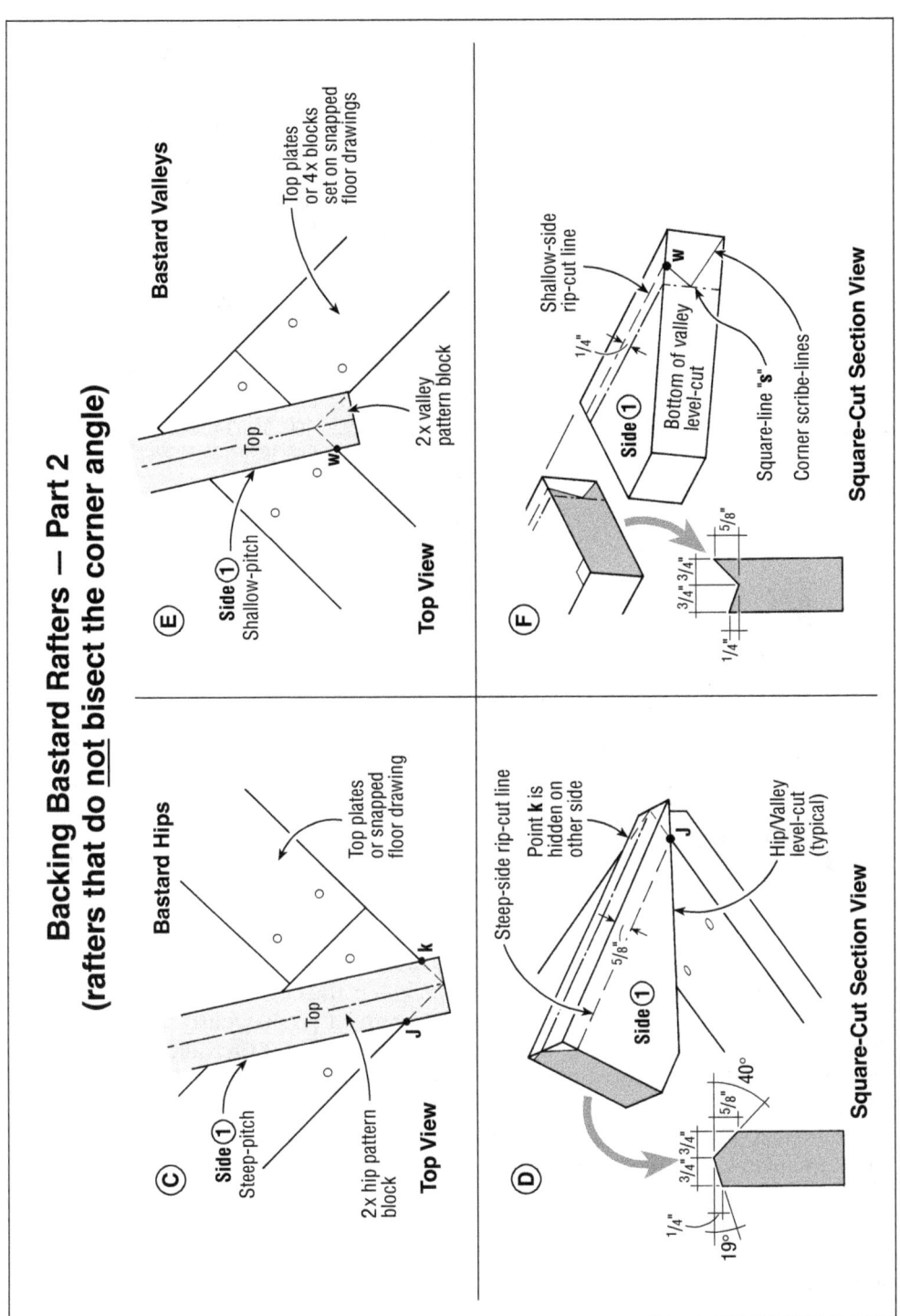

Figure 8-28. In situations where the rafter does not bisect the angle formed by the corner, the rip-cut lines and rip-angles will be different and must be found separately.

Photo 8-29. Top: Place a level-cut scrap of wood the same size and relative position as the bastard rafter tangent to the corner at the center of the tip. Mark the backing rip-cut lines where the sides cross the outside edge of the plate. Bottom: Use the perpendicular distance down from the top edge to the rip-cut line together with the 1/2 thk. of the rafter dimension as legs of a right triangle for determining the rip-angle.

the wall plates and mark the bottom edge to find line "**s**." Line "**s**" — when brought around to the side of the pattern block — is the depth of the backing-cut at the rafter's centerline. Use this measurement (as previously shown with the dog-leg bastard hip) together with 1/2 thk. of the valley to find the rip-angle, and back the top edge with the saw blade following the upper outside corner edges.

For unequal-pitch rafters that do not bisect the angle formed by the corner of the plates, the rip-cut lines and rip-angles for each side of the rafter are different and must be figured separately.

In these situations, place the pattern block level-cut for the rafter pitch over the unequal-pitch hip snap-lines on the full-size floor plan view at the outside corner (wall or fascia depending on equal or unequal overhangs), and mark each side as before (points **j** and **k** in Views **C** and **D** of Figure 8-28). The distance down to each rip-cut line will be different, as will the rip-angles for each side, so each must be figured individually *(Photo 8-29)*.

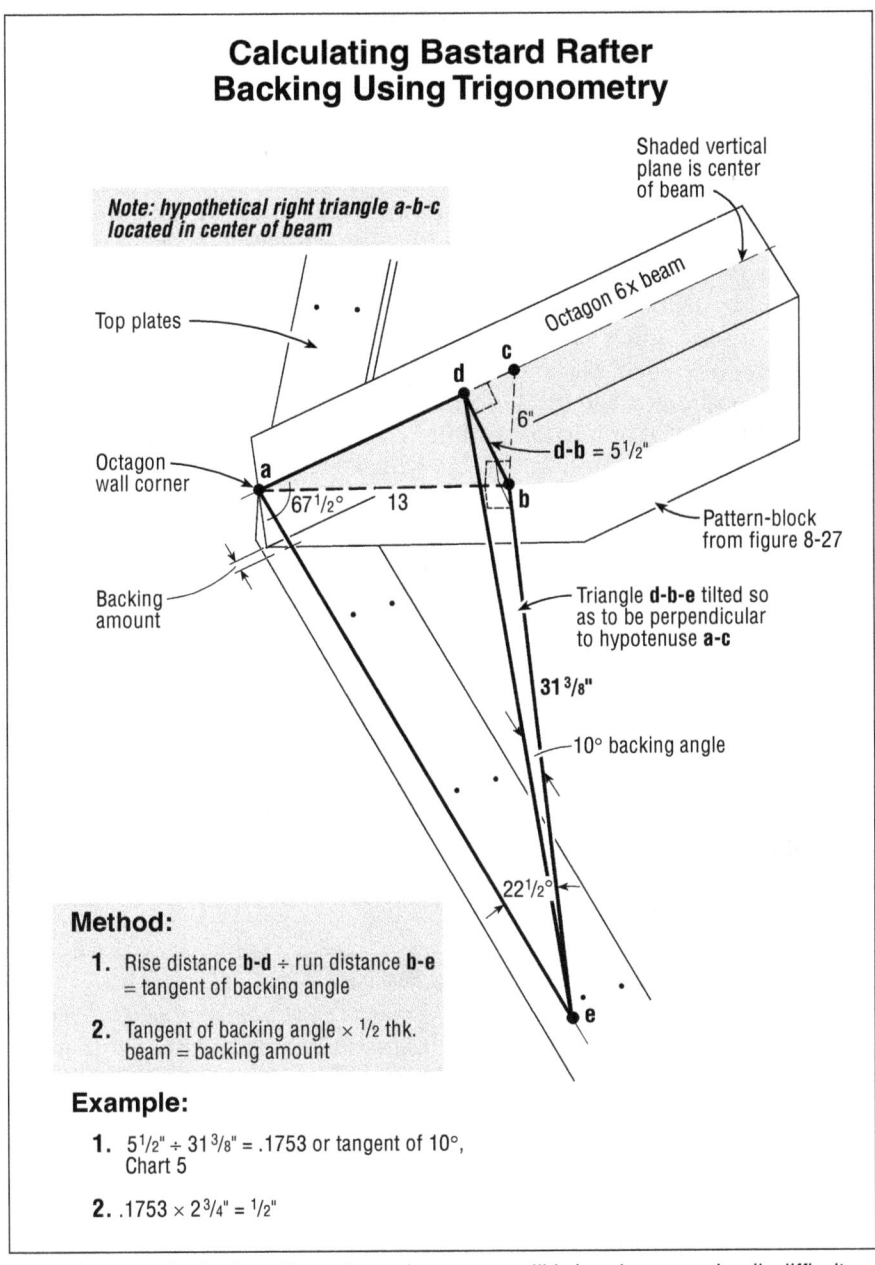

Figure 8-30: Applied in three dimensions, trigonometry will help solve some visually difficult situations like calculating the backing rip-angles and cut-lines for bastard rafters.

When laying out the backing on these hips, make sure that the correct rip-angle is facing the appropriate pitched roof plane.

As opposed to making a scale drawing and using a protractor or rafter square to find the rip-angles, the Trig tables in Chart 5 (Appendix A) can be applied. For example, with 5/8 in. down to the mark and 2x material used for the bastard hip, the .625 in./.750 in. (rise/run) ratio equals .8333, the tangent for 40°. Likewise, with 1/4 in. down to the mark, the .250 in./.750 in. ratio equals .3333, the tangent for 19° (Figure 8-28). Remember that the saw tilts from square (90°), so always verify if the saw bevel should be set to the calculated angle or its complement.

For an unequal-pitch valley, follow a similar procedure. On the full-size snapped-out plan view, place the level-cut pattern block at the correct bastard valley position at the inside corner (wall or fascia, depending on whether it has equal or unequal overhangs) and line up the edge of the tapered end facing the steep-pitch roof with the corresponding wall or fascia line. Scribe the bottom of the level-cut pattern block with the inside corner (use two blocks of 4x material set on the snapped-out plan view simulating the corner so a pencil will fit underneath). Also mark the shallow-side rip-cut line "**w**" where the plate line intersects near the tip (View **E** in Figure 8-28). Next, on the bottom of the level-cut pattern block, draw line "**s**" square across the thickness at the very inside point of the valley corner scribe-line and bring it around to the sides parallel to the top edge (View **F** in Figure 8-28). Measure down perpendicular from the top edge of the pattern block to line "**s**" on the steep-pitch side and from the rip-cut line to line "**s**" on the shallow-pitch side to find the backing amounts. Use these two measurements (1/4", 5/8") together with 1/2 thk. of the valley as the legs of a right triangle to find the rip-angles as previously explained. The steep side of the valley is ripped following the top edge while the shallow side follows the rip-cut line at **w**.

■ Using Trigonometry to Find Bastard Rafter Backing

The mathematical procedure for determining backing angles on bastard hip/valleys is a bit arcane. For example, to calculate the backing angle for the octagon bastard hip shown in *Figure 8-30*, you must solve the slightly off-vertical right triangle defined by points **d**, **b**, and **e** for both leg dimensions, and convert their ratio to a degree-equivalent by applying the tangent table (found in Chart 5, Appendix A) or by using a Construction Master® calculator.

This procedure actually involves solving several right triangles to get the required dimensions. The first, a vertical right triangle (**a-b-c**) is embedded on the beam centerline. The second, a horizontal right triangle (**a-b-e**) is defined by the beam centerline and the wall plates. The third (**c-d-b**), is a portion of the vertical triangle **a-b-c**.

This procedure will apply to any dog-leg or unequal-pitch situation if the principles are applied correctly. The **a** to **b** leg could be any length as long as the height can be determined at point **b**. For example, in Figure 8-19, the total hip travel (267 3/8") and total rise (119 5/8") could be used along with the 64° or 26° angle at the outside fascia corner to create a similar situation to the one illustrated in Figure 8-30.

Chapter 9

Dormers

GABLE AND HIP DORMERS

The example in *Figure 9-1* illustrates a 48-in.-wide gable dormer with a 40-in.-tall front window wall. The two sets of double rafters along the sides are placed flush with the inside of the dormer walls. Since 2x4 walls are shown, the inside dimension is 41 in. (48" − 3^1/$_2$" − 3^1/$_2$" = 41").

With the main roof's lower rafter headout set and the dormer's front window wall and side rake walls built, locate the upper rafter headout in Figure 9-1 by the following steps:
  1. Calculate the height to the top of the dormer ridge above the dormer's side walls (refer to the Chapter 6 section "Ridge Height," page 120).
  2. Divide that rise by the RR ratio to determine the run.
  3. Multiply that run by the COM LL ratio to find the LL distance up the main roof from the uphill end of the dormer walls to the upper headout.

Once the upper headout is in place, run the ridge and commons.

As an option, it is also acceptable to use the total height at the front of the dormer (56^3/$_4$") and follow the same procedures to find **a-b**. This technique has the added benefit in that the determined run in Step **2** is also the length of the ridge from the upper headout to the dormer's front wall in a gable dormer.

The length of the dormer valleys are calculated by subtracting the ridge thickness from the inside dormer dimension, dividing by 2, and multiplying by the H/V LL ratio (Steps **1** and **2**, *Figure 9-2*). This length is measured from the tip of the double 45° cheek-cut at the head to the center of

Locating the Dormer Ridge Headout

Method:

1. $\dfrac{(\text{Span} - \text{ridge thickness})}{2} \times \text{RR ratio} = \text{rise}$

2. (Rise + heel-stand) ÷ RR ratio = run

3. Run × COM LL ratio = LL distance up main roof to upper headout

Example:

1. $\dfrac{(48" - 1\,^{1}/_{2}")}{2} \times .5000 \ \{6/12 \text{ RR ratio}\} = 11\,^{5}/_{8}"$

2. $(11\,^{5}/_{8}" + 5\,^{1}/_{8}") \div .5000 \ \{6/12 \text{ RR ratio}\} = 33\,^{1}/_{2}"$

3. $33\,^{1}/_{2}" \times 1.1180 \ \{6/12 \text{ COM LL ratio}\} = 37\,^{1}/_{2}"$

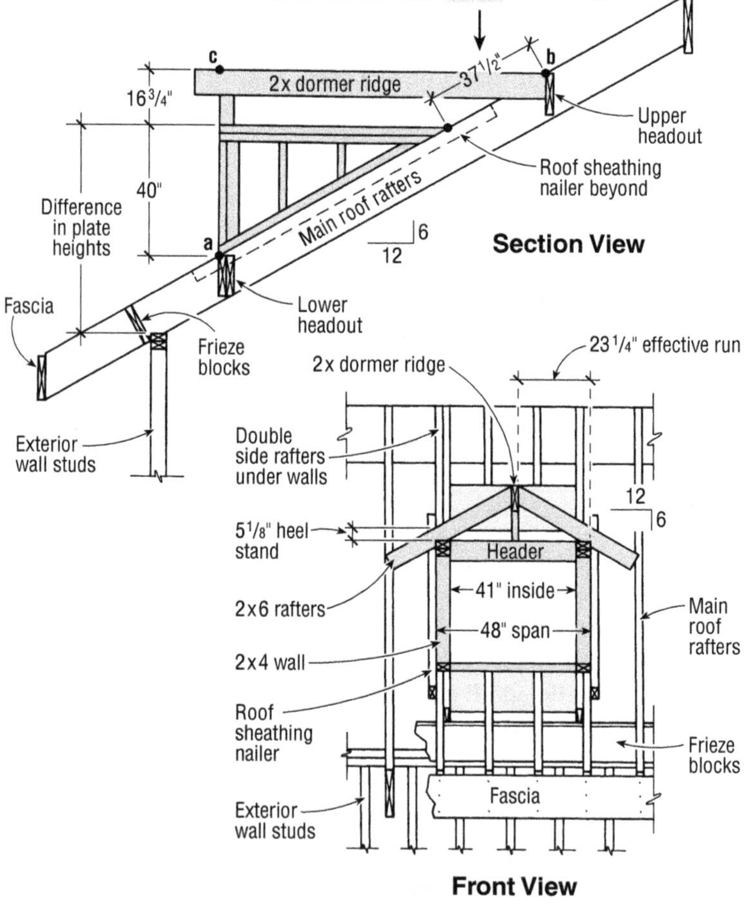

Figure 9-1. To locate the main roof upper headout, change the height to the top of the dormer ridge above the sidewalls into an LL dimension and use it to measure up the main roof line from the uphill end of the dormer walls.

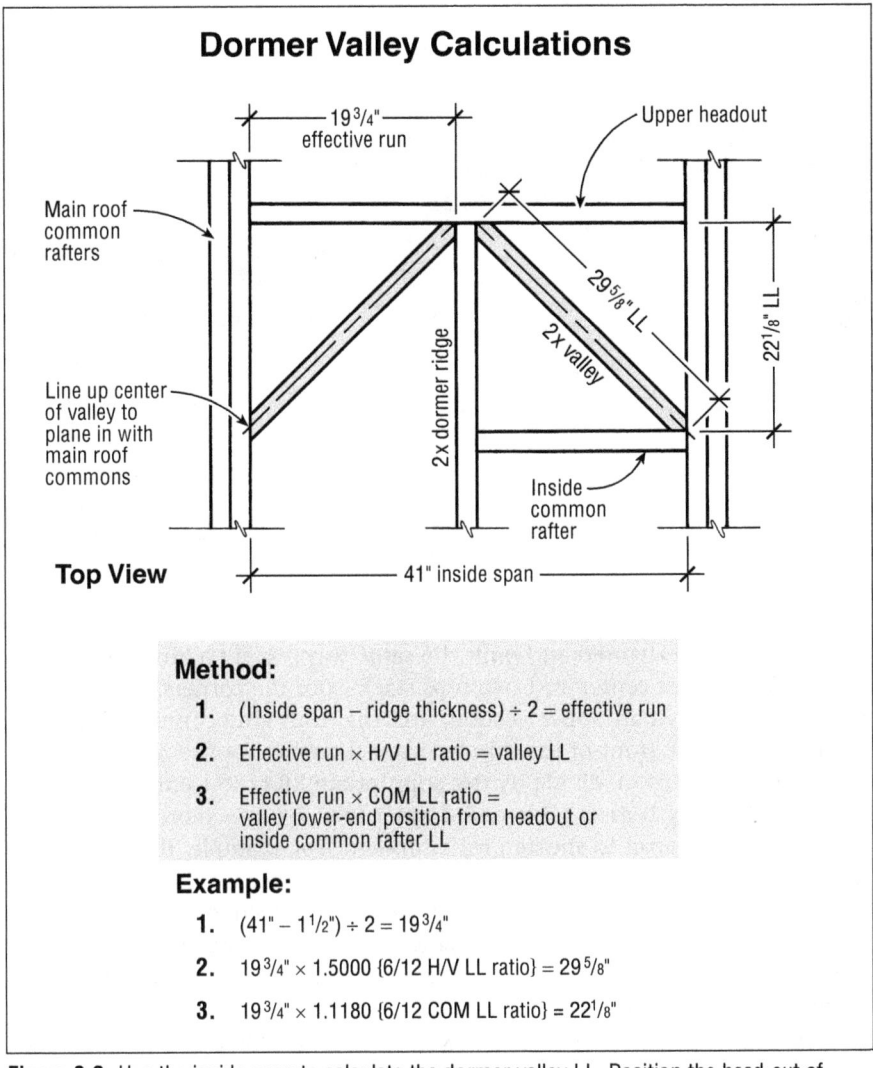

Figure 9-2. Use the inside span to calculate the dormer valley LL. Position the head-cut of the valley so the center tip lines up with the top of the ridge-to-upper-headout corner. Nail the lower end where the center planes in with the main roof's common rafters.

the single cheek-cut at the tail. (Remember to set your rafter square to H/V for layout purposes.) Nail the head of the valley in the corner so the top center of the tip lines up with the top edge of the ridge and the upper headout (Figure 6-17). Nail the lower end of the valley where the center of the top edge planes in with the top edge of the main roof commons. Verify position by measuring down the main gable roof from the headout the common rafter LL distance for the effective run of the valley (Step **3**, Figure 9-2). To finish, measure and cut any required valley jacks.

Photo 9-3. A shed dormer originating from the main roof's ridgeline.

A hip dormer is figured and built the same way, except a king common stacks off the front center and two hips stack from the corners. To precut a ridge to fit between an upper headout and the front king common, take the total height at the front of the dormer from the main roof to the top of the dormer's ridge (**a** to **c**), divide by the appropriate RR ratio to find the hypothetical ridge length for a gable-end dormer (**c** to **b**), and subtract the dormer's effective run to shorten for a hip-end. For example, the ridge length for Figure 9-1 when modified into a hip dormer would be 90$^{1}/_{4}$ in. ([56$^{3}/_{4}$" ÷ .5000 {6/12 RR ratio}] − 23$^{1}/_{4}$" {dormer's effective run} = 90$^{1}/_{4}$").

Occasionally, a dormer may be designed to use a support*ING* valley reaching from inside one of the dormer's side double rafters to the main-span ridge rather than valleys run to an upper headout as shown in Figure 9-2.

To find the length of the support*ING* valley when the main-span rafters and the dormer rafters are of the **same-size** material, convert the difference in plate heights between the main span and the dormer into a run dimension by dividing by the RR ratio as shown in Figure 5-10. To this run dimension add the thickness of one of the dormer's side walls (to adjust for an inside valley connection) and subtract the sum total from the effective run of the main-span common rafters. Multiply the result by the H/V LL ratio to calculate the support*ING* valley LL.

When the main-span rafters and the dormer rafters are of a **different size**, subtract the difference in heel-stands (if the dormer's rafters are the smaller-sized material) from the difference in plate heights, and continue as before.

The support*ED* valley is calculated using the full inside span and shortened $^{1}/_{2}$ thk. of the support*ING* valley. (Refer to the Chapter 5 section "Supported Valley Situations," page 100, for more detail and the proper stacking position of these valleys and the intersecting ridge.)

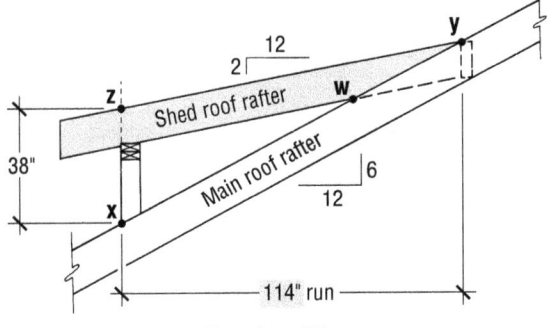

Figure 9-4. The point of intersection between the shed roof and the main roof is located by finding the converging pitch (angle of closure), and using that pitch to calculate the shed dormer's effective run. This effective run dimension is then used to calculate the upper headout/ridge position and the dormer rafter length.

Method:

1. Main roof pitch − shed roof pitch = converging pitch

2. Total height of dormer (**x-z**: dormer front wall + heel stand) ÷ converging pitch RR ratio = run

3. Run × main roof COM LL ratio = LL up main roof from front wall to upper headout (**x-y**)

4. Run × shed dormer COM LL ratio = shed rafter LL (**y-z**)

Example:

1. 6/12 − 2/12 = 4/12

2. 38" ÷ .3333 {4/12 RR ratio} = 114"

3. 114" × 1.1180 {6/12 COM LL ratio} = 127 1/2"

4. 114" × 1.0137 {2/12 COM LL ratio} = 115 1/2"

SHED DORMERS

A shed roof dormer can be framed to intersect at the main roof ridge (**Photo 9-3**) or somewhere lower as shown in **Figure 9-4.** The point of intersection between the two roofs is found in three steps:

1. Subtract the unit of rise for the shed roof from the unit of rise for the main roof to calculate the converging pitch.

2. Divide the height of the front dormer face, including dormer rafter heel-stand (**x-z**), by the RR ratio of the converging pitch to determine the total run of the shed dormer's rafters.

3. Multiply that run distance by the main roof's COM LL ratio to calculate the distance up the main roof pitch from the dormer's front wall (**x-y**) to position the headout/ridge, and multiply that same run by the shed roof's COM LL ratio to calculate the shed roof's rafter length (**y-z**).

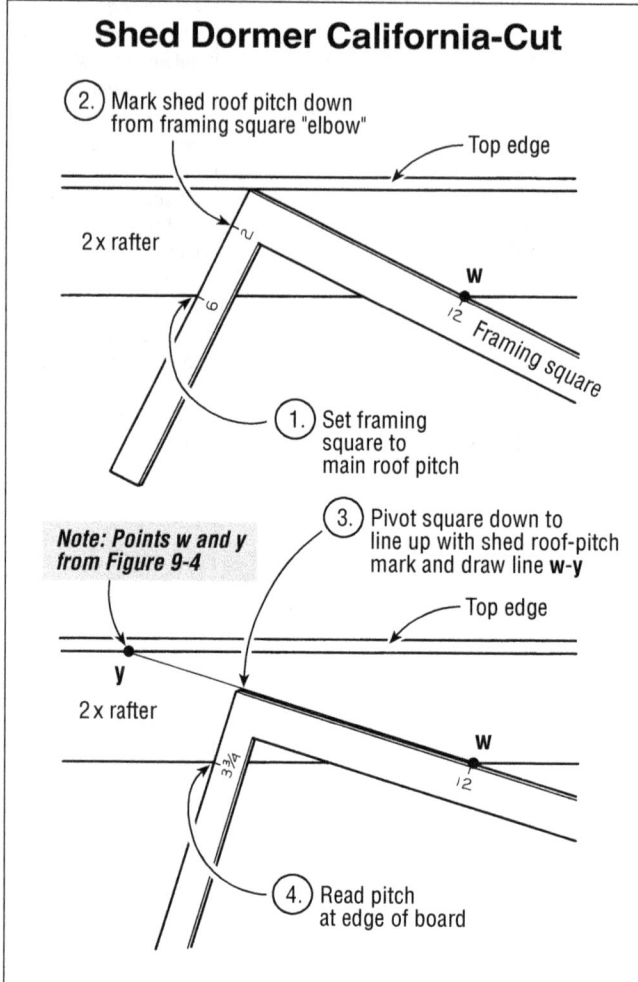

Figure 9-5. When the shed dormer is framed to sit on an existing roof, the California-cut at the head is laid out by using a framing square set to the pitch of the main roof, then marking the shed roof pitch on the tongue and pivoting the square down to the mark.

SHED DORMER CALIFORNIA-CUTS

If the shed dormer in Figure 9-4 were framed to overlay on an existing roof rather than butt to an upper headout ridge, the **y-w** California-cut can be found as shown in *Figure 9-5*. Place a framing square on the side of a rafter with the legs set to the pitch of the main roof (6/12), and make a mark down from the corner of the framing square corresponding to the pitch of the shed roof (2/12). Pivot the square to line up with this mark, and draw line **y-w**. Note the "new" pitch at the edge of the board for future reference.

EYEBROW DORMERS

This section describes the construction of a 20-ft.-wide structural eyebrow dormer (with a finished inside radius ceiling) using fabricated ribs that span the gap between two bastard valleys, as opposed to a more common method

Photo 9-6. The most common method used to frame an eyebrow dormer has regular rafters radiating from an upper main-roof headout and bearing on a circular crown-shaped front wall or header. (Photo courtesy of Joe Wood.)

of construction which uses regular rafters radiating from an upper main-roof headout and bearing on an arch-shaped front wall or header (see **Photo 9-6**).

While a rib-style dormer is rare, it provides a good platform to demonstrate the technique of combining the cross-section, front, and plan views to lay out, cut, and stack difficult roof situations. The method shown will focus on the eyebrow dormer's main structural design (a cylinder intersecting a sloping flat plane), while the small curved returns at the sides on the front end are bypassed for now to be applied California-style after the sheathing (see **Photo 9-7**).

Begin by snapping a full-scale section view and front elevation on the floor as

Photo 9-7. The eyebrow dormer's upward returns are applied California-style. (Photo courtesy of Dan Daley.)

■ Roof-Surface Bell-Shaped Curves

A roof-surface "bell-shaped" curve (as opposed to the horizontal plan-view illustrated in Figure 9-9) can also be created by laying out each rib's span dimension along a length equal to the main roof's intersection with the eyebrow dormer. (The LL distance **ab** to **s** shown in the cross-section view of Figure 9-8 would be substituted for the 208$^1/_2$" run distance.)

A roof-surface bell-shaped curve is not only helpful for marking out the valley-cut along the eyebrow dormer when sheathing the supporting roof, but it is essential when building a nonfunctional eyebrow dormer California- or layover-style. (I prefer to frame a layover eyebrow dormer on the ground and set it in place with a crane or a Lull.) Use the roof-surface view to cut a bell-shaped plywood roof sleeper, and run parallel-positioned horizontal "rafter-joists" between it and a vertical eyebrow-shaped plywood front face. Run each rafter-joist plumb (as opposed to perpendicular to the curve), and bevel the top edge of the board to match the curve at each location. Before assembly, position the plywood sleeper downhill slightly to negate its thickness as was done in Chapter 5 with 2x valley sleepers.

Another use for the roof-surface bell-shaped curve is when building an open or functional eyebrow dormer using parallel-positioned horizontal rafter-joists. For this situation, create a ceiling-surface view denoting the transition from radial to flat by plotting the span dimensions from the front view where the inside radius intersects the underside of the supporting roof's rafters. Cut an inside bell-shaped curve (like a horseshoe) and temporarily attach it to the underside of the supporting roof's rafters straddling the rectangular hole in the main roof defining the eyebrow dormer's rough opening. Using this plywood curve as a guide for locating the curved-to-flat ceiling transition, "close-frame" the opening using several layers of plumb-oriented corner blocks (similar to those shown in the top view of Figure 15-9). Run the horizontal rafter-joists to these corner blocks, and install filler pieces where required to finish outlining the transition. (Thanks to Jim Rouvalis for his input in this section.)

---

shown in ***Figure 9-8.*** (Use the formula shown in Figure 15-4 if the eyebrow radius is unknown.) Next, draw in the ribs at 24 in. on-center on the section view, and measure the height of each rib above the main roof's surface or subtract the difference between the dormer roof's rise and the main roof's rise in the rib's spacing to find the amount they "step" up (11$^1/_4$" {main roof rise in 24" o.c.} – 4" {dormer roof rise in 24" o.c.} = 7$^1/_4$"). Transfer these measurements to the front-elevation view, and snap horizontal lines through each vertical rise mark to find the span of each rib at the roof surface. Or use the Pythagorean theorem to find the missing leg of the right triangle at each level as shown, and then double the result to calculate the span. Using the span measurements of each rib, lay out on the floor a full-scale plan view of the eyebrow dormer's intersection with the main roof ***(Figure 9-9)***.

Next, locate the dormer's bastard valleys. Using the front-elevation view, locate the transition from the inside rib radius to the underside of the main roof's rafters (ceiling plane) by placing a second horizontal line, the plumb dimension of the main roof's rafters below each rib's main-roof intersection line. From this transition, each rib must turn and run horizontally a short distance in the main roof plane to create a "tail" for beam hangers (see ***Photo 9-10***). Extend these "tails" 4 in. horizontally, then carry that distance back to the upper surface of the roof and mark the appropriate rib

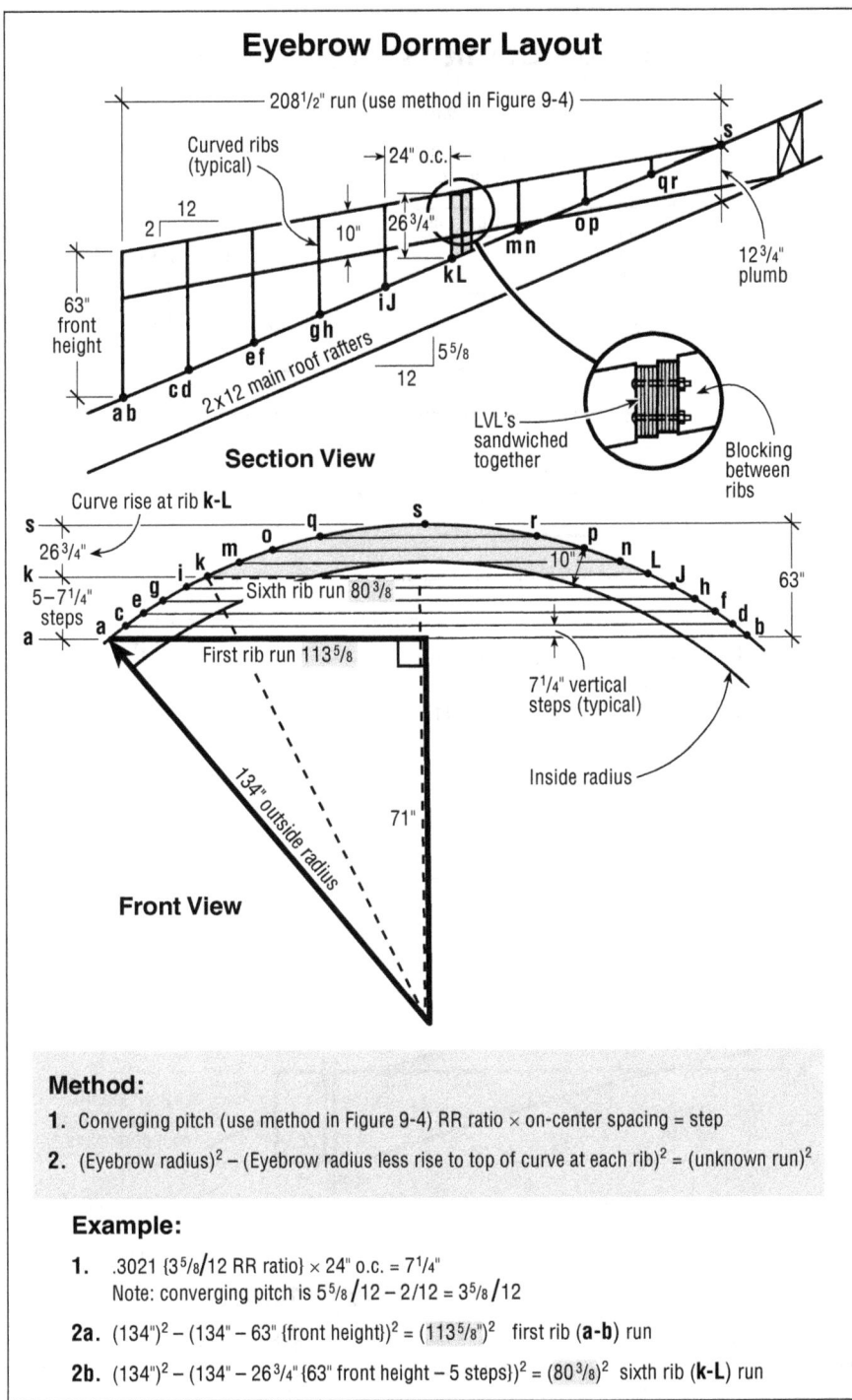

Figure 9-8. A full-scale snapped-out section view is used to measure the height of each rib above the main roof plane, which is then transferred to the front view in the form of a horizontal line to get the actual span of the roof's arc at that location.

DORMERS 197

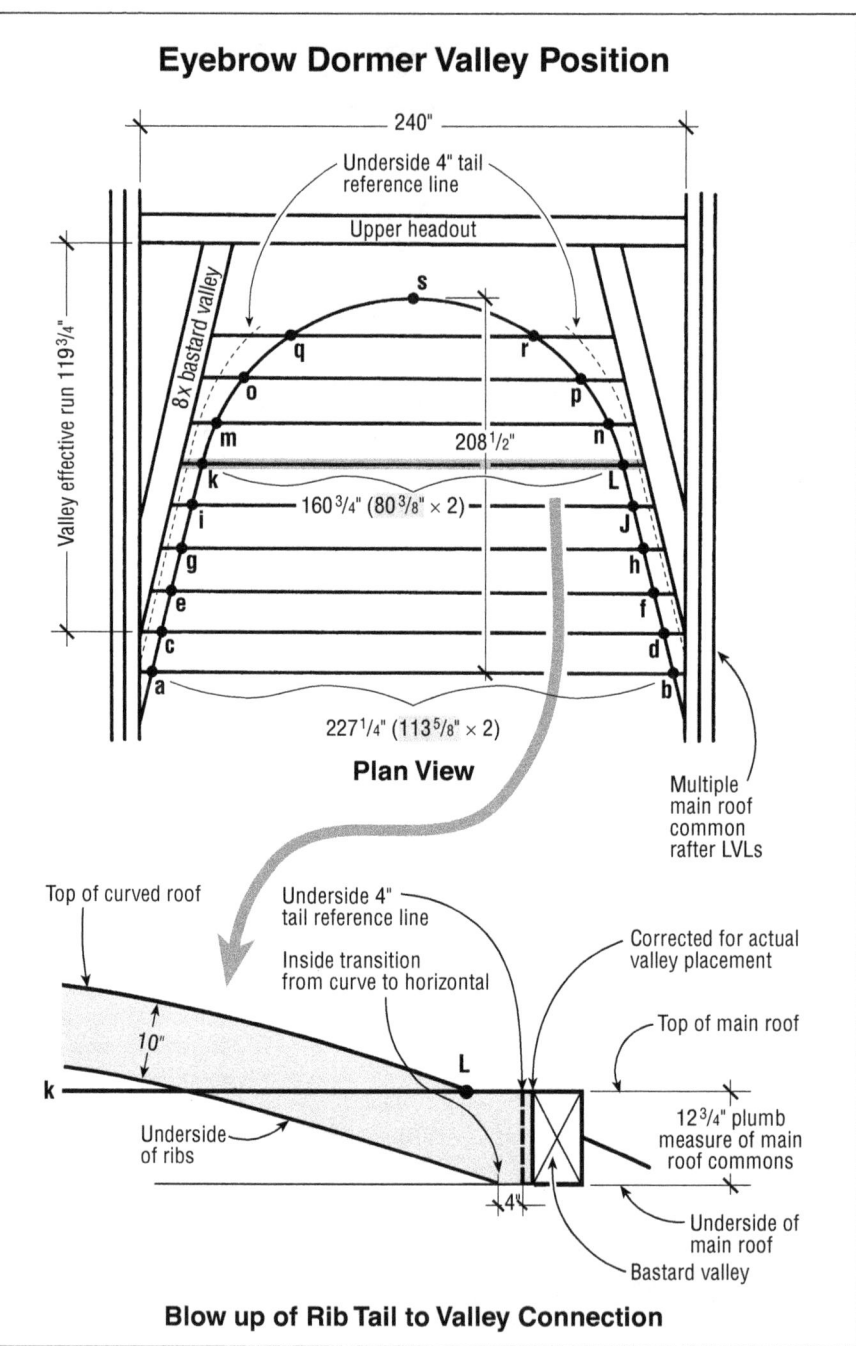

Figure 9-9. Use the span measurements of each rib taken from the front view to snap out a full-size plan view. Then, using the front view again, lay out 4-in. "tails" reaching back into the main roof for each rib. These 4-in. tails are measured starting at the inside transition from the curve shape to the horizontal underside of the main roof rafters. Finally, bring the 4-in. tail marks back up to the surface of the main roof where they are plotted on the plan view to help locate the best position for the eyebrow dormer valley.

Photo 9-10. The ribs run a short distance back into the main roof plane to allow for beam hangers.

line on the plan view to create a second set of points outside the original bell-shaped curve (dashed line in Figure 9-9). These marks will serve as a guide to help position the inside of the structural bastard valley. Stretch a string on the plan view to find the best average of all the hypothetical 4-in. tail reference marks, and snap an inside valley edge line. Note the corrected distance from this valley snap-line to the original bell curve (point **L** to the bastard valley in Figure 9-9). This is the amount needed to extend each of the rib-tails to meet the valley. Transfer these measurements to the front-elevation drawing to get the actual shape of each rib's transition to horizontal, and make a plywood pattern for each tail (see **Photo 9-11**).

Cut the ribs out of wide $1^{3}/_{4}$-in. laminated veneer lumber (LVL), and sandwich several layers together with construction adhesive, screws, and bolts. Depending on the span, make the ribs either two or three layers thick. Swing the curves with a pencil and a tape measure using both the inside/outside radii. The width of the LVLs will dictate the maximum length you can get out of each piece. Mark the outside ends of the ribs with the appropriate "tail" pattern. A regular Skil® 77 with a thin-kerf carbide blade will cut most gradual curves. Place the curved pieces directly over the snapped-out front-elevation view to piece together each rib and to maximize the amount of overlap between layers. Because the illustrated eyebrow dormer has a shed-roof pitch of 2/12, each lamination layer must step up $1/4$ in. to keep the inside and outside radii in the plane of the dormer roof (Figure 9-8). Use a stepped jig nailed to the floor to assemble the pieces (see **Photo 9-12**).

Finally, with the layers laminated together, bevel-cut the bottom of each rib-tail to follow the underside of the main roof as it rises using measurements taken from the section view. Similarly, use the plan view to make a cheek-cut to the end of each rib so it will butt properly into the bastard valley. Position the upper headout in the main roof to start where the top of the eyebrow dormer's inside radius planes into the underside of the main roof's rafters. Find this location on the section-view drawing, and transfer it to the plan view.

Determine the bastard valley length along the inside edge using the Pythagorean theorem with the actual valley diagonal taken from the plan view and the appropriate main roof rise for the valley run as legs of a

Photo 9-11. Each rib has a different tail pattern for the transition to horizontal.

vertical right triangle. The top and bottom valley cheek-cut lines are taken from the snapped-out plan view and measured perpendicular to the LL plumb lines. A proportion is used to find the valley rafter pitch (rise/valley diagonal = $x/12$). Back the top and bottom of the dormer valley so it will fit in the roof plane. To do this, make a level-cut at the valley pitch on a scrap of the valley rafter material and place it over the valley snaplines on the full-size plan view with the outside leading edge tangent to a line parallel to the main roof's front bearing wall (see *Figure 9-13*). Where the inside of the beam scrap intersects with this line, square down from the top edge and note the dimension. Use this measurement to mark a rip-line along the upper edge of the valley nearest the dormer for top edge backing. The rip-angle is found by using this same measurement together with

Photo 9-12. A graduated floor jig is used to laminate layers of microlams into curved roof ribs.

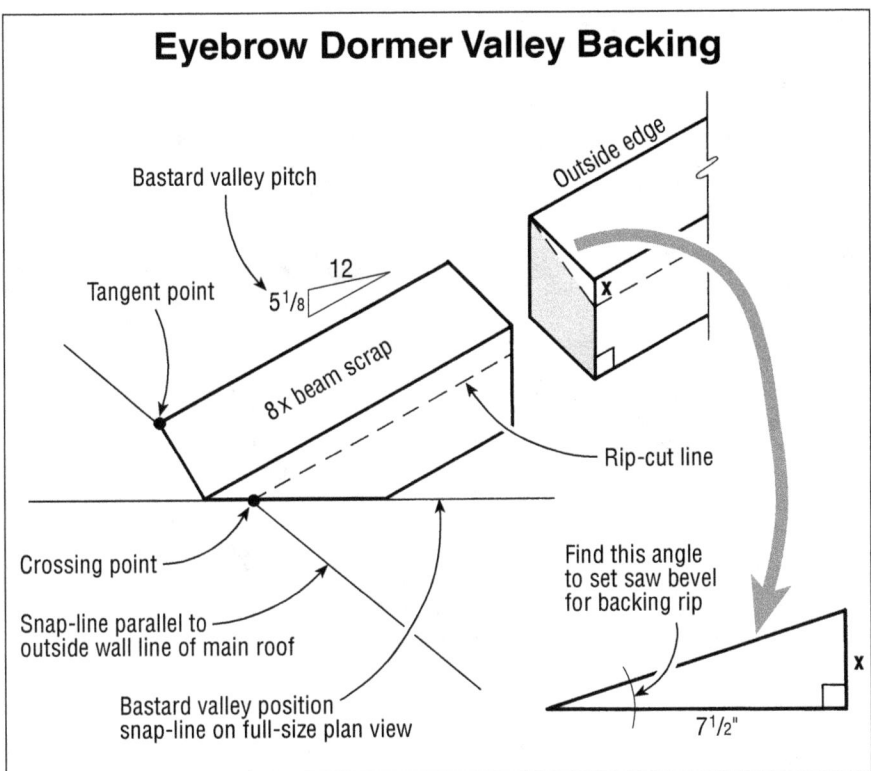

Figure 9-13. Back the top (and bottom if necessary) of the dormer valley so it will fit into the main roof plane by making a level-cut for the valley pitch on a scrap of valley material and placing it over the valley snap-lines, tangent on the outside with a line parallel to the main roof plate line. Mark the rip-cut line on the inside where it crosses this same line. The full thickness of the beam together with the perpendicular measurement from the top edge to the rip-cut line is used to draw a right triangle (as shown) from which the rip-angle is taken using a rafter square or protractor.

the thickness of the beam as legs of a right triangle and noting the angle formed with a Speed® Square or protractor (similar to Figure 8-27). If the underside must be backed, the outside of the valley is marked with a rip-cut line corresponding to the plumb dimension of the main roof's rafters and cut with the same rip-angle used on the top.

Stack the ribs using a temporary support ridge tilted at 2/12 with the top set to the height of the inside radius *(Photo 9-14)*. Use hangers where the rib tails connect to the bastard valley, and run a row of blocks centered on the top of the curve. Sheathe the top with 1x6s similar to an old barrel *(Photo 9-15)*, and install the small, curved upward returns at the sides on the front end California-style (refer back to Photo 9-7).

Run 6x blocks at the upper end of the bell shape along the transition from the curve to the underside of the main rafters, and use a long straightedge together with a chainsaw to fine-tune the transition from radial to flat.

Photo 9-14. Stack the ribs using a temporary support ridge set to the height of the inside radius.

Photo 9-15. Sheathe the top of the eyebrow dormer with 1x6s like an old wood barrel.

Note: When framing an eyebrow dormer using the method where rafters (framed plumb on edge) radiate from an upper headout and bear on an arch-shaped front wall or header, snap out a full-size front view to find each rafter's rise together with a full-size top view to find each rafter's travel. Use these numbers to calculate their LL and pitch. For rafters that attach to the upper headout at an angle other than 90°, the head-cut bevel angle is taken from the snapped-out plan view using a protractor or rafter square.

Chapter 10

Towers and Polygons

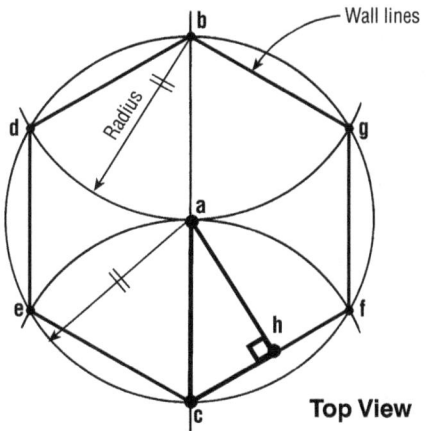

Laying out a Hexagon Tower Roof on the Floor

Top View

Method:

1. Snap an extended line (**b-c**).
2. Swing a circle using a given radius and any point on the line (**a**) as the center.
3. Swing two half-circle arcs with the same radius using the line intersects (**b** and **c**) as centerpoints.
4. Connect all circle intersects.

HEXAGONS

For a hexagon-shaped beam roof tower, snap out a full-scale plan view on the floor to find the cut-lines and cheek-cut angles. Start with a single snap-line and pick a centerpoint (**a** in *Figure 10-1*). From this point, swing a given radius to draw a full circle. From the two points where the circle intersects the line (**b** and **c**), swing two semicircles of the same radius to intersect the main circle at four points (**d**, **e**, **f**, and **g**).

Figure 10-1. Use a snap-line, a centerpoint, and a given radius to mark out the six-sided hexagon geometrically.

Connect the hexagon sides as shown. Snap lines from the opposing corners through point **a** to locate the centerlines of the hip beams. Using these centerlines as a reference, measure out and snap the sides of the hip beams. Next, connect the centerpoint **a** with the intersection of the beam edges. When finished, it should look like ***Figure 10-2***.

The pitch of a polygon roof is normally assigned to the pie-shaped roof plane between the corners, and the hips are actually some variation of the dog-leg bastard hip shown in Figure 8-2. Calculate the hexagon hips in Figure 10-2 as follows:

1. Begin by measuring run **a-h** from the snapped-out plan view, or determine it mathematically by dividing the hip travel (radius) by the secant of half the angle formed between the hip beams (360° circle ÷ 6 sides = 60° per side, secant 30° = 1.1547 from Chart 5, Appendix A, or the upcoming Figure 10-9).
2. Use that run dimension to find the total rise at centerpoint **a** by multiplying it by the appropriate RR ratio (10/12 in the example).
3. Calculate the hip LL using the Pythagorean theorem with the total rise and the hip travel (radius) as legs of a vertical right triangle.
4. Determine the hip-rafter pitch by solving a proportion with total rise divided by the hip travel set equal to an unknown value/12.

If run (**a-h**) is the given dimension and the hip travel (radius **a-c**) is unknown, multiply the run by the secant value for half the angle formed between the hip beams to find the radius length.

Note: Think of the right triangle **a-h-c** in Figure 10-2 as you would for any roof pitch right triangle where **a-h** is the "horizontal" measurement and is converted into a "rake" or LL dimension by multiplying by the COM LL ratio (secant). Conversely, to find the "horizontal" measurement given the "rake" dimension, divide the "rake" by the COM LL ratio (secant).

To mark the top cheek-cuts, measure the distance along the centerline from **a** to **k**, and transfer this measurement to the side of the hip beam perpendicular to the LL plumb-line as shown in Figure 10-2. Point **k** is found by squaring out from the centerline to the beam edge intersection at **m**. Using trig, you can check the **a** to **k** distance by multiplying the cotangent of half the angle formed between the hip beams (Chart 5, Appendix A) with 1/2 thk. of the beam.

The cut-angle for **a-p** and **a-m** is taken from the snapped-out plan view with a protractor or calculated mathematically by dividing 360° by the number of polygon sides and using half the result as the angle. Since this angle is measured off the centerline or edge of the beam, it will be 90° out of phase from how a standard circular saw's bevel is adjusted. Therefore, set the saw bevel to the complementary angle (90° − 30° = 60°) when making the cheek-cuts on the side of the rafter.)

With any polygon beam connection, make a trial ridge-cut on a scrap of the same-size material to set the correct saw-bevel angles. A swing-table saw is used to make the face-cut from **p** to **q** and the corresponding cut on the other side, while a Skilsaw® can be used to cut **a** to **p** and **a** to **m** along the top and bottom edges of the board. Once the angles have been found on the practice

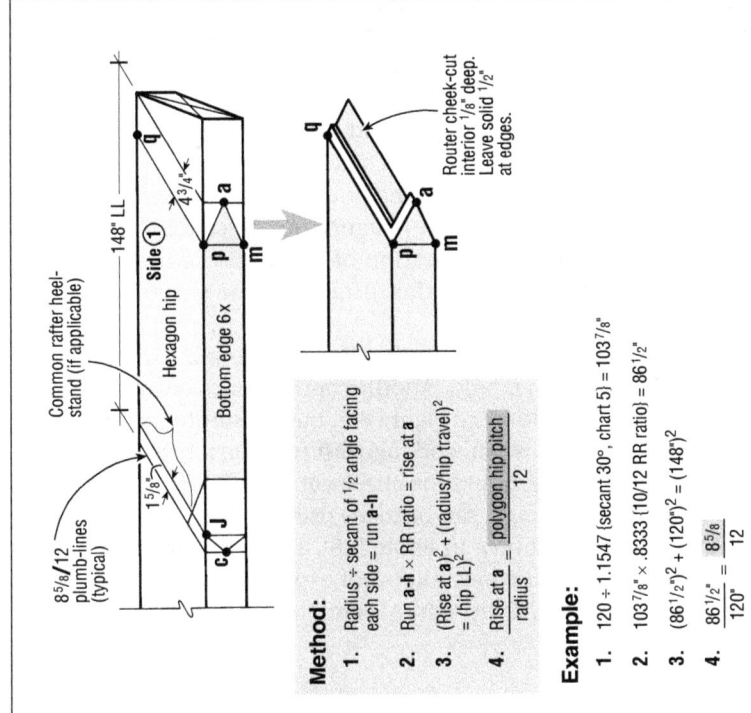

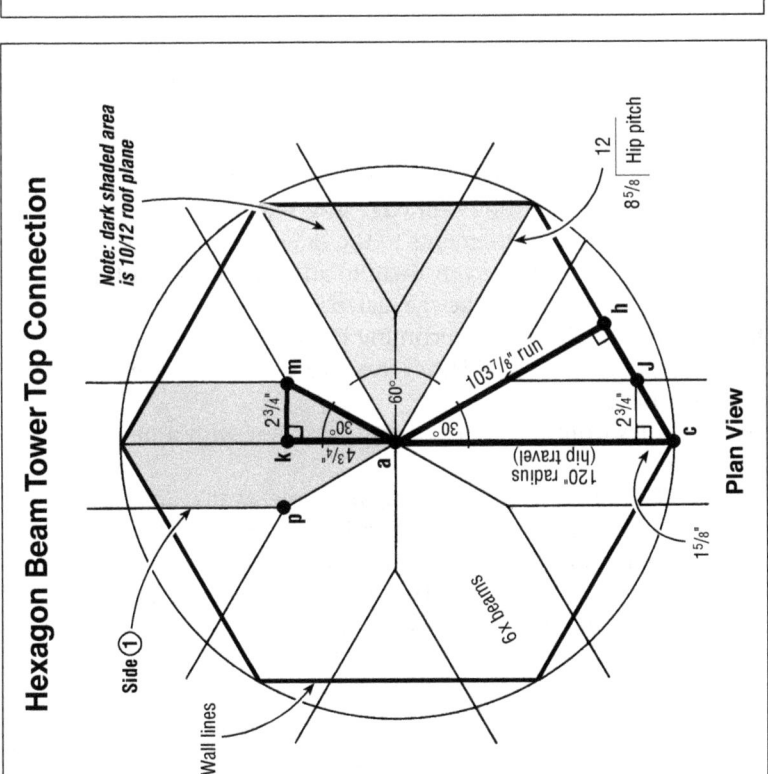

Figure 10-2. Use trig as shown to calculate the common rafter run or measure the run off a snapped-out full-size plan view. Multiply the run by the RR ratio to calculate the rise at the centerpoint. Then use the Pythagorean theorem to calculate the hip LL and a proportion to calculate the hip pitch. Head/heel-cut lines and angles are taken from the snapped-out plan view.

TOWERS AND POLYGONS   207

piece, the bevel settings on the saws are not changed until all the beams are cut. Cut all four sides as deep as possible, and finish them off with a handsaw.

Use a router to take 1/8 in. off the center of the cheek-cut, leaving 1/2 in. of solid wood around the sides and bottom edges (Figure 10-2). This allows a tighter fit when all the beams are together and makes for a much easier time closing a gap with a handsaw pass when stacking.

The heel-cut lines and the cut-angle for the birdsmouth are found the same way as for the head-cut. Measure the distance up the centerline to a line drawn perpendicular from the intersection of the outside edge of the hip beam with the wall line (**J**). Transfer this distance to the side of the rafter as shown in Figure 10-2.

Snap the jacks on the floor at their proper location to determine the run, and multiply by the 10/12 COM LL ratio. Another option for calculating jack lengths is to use the procedure shown in Figure 8-5, but substitute the tangent for half the angle facing any side when working with polygons. Use the snapped-out floor drawing or trig to find the cheek-cut angle for the jacks. On 2x material, the steep cheek-cut angle can be made using a swing-table saw, a chainsaw, or a regular Skilsaw® (shown in Photo 8-8). The jacks can also be square-cut plumb at the SP if the connection is not exposed. When the jacks are cut from beam stock, follow the procedure found in Figure 8-17 to lay out the jack head-cut.

OCTAGONS

The octagon roof, or any other polygon-shaped roof, is solved using the same procedures found in the hexagon section. Remember that whatever you draw on the ground will work in the air, as long as you:

1. Find the cheek-cut lines by measuring along the centerline from the theoretical centerpoint (or wall corner for the birdsmouth heel-cut) to a point perpendicular from the beam edge intersections.
2. Transfer these centerline measurements to the side of the beam perpendicular to the LL plumb-line or convert them to an LL measurement. (*Note:* A special LL conversion ratio can be calculated by dividing the rafter's LL by the travel. For example, in the upcoming Figure 10-4, divide the octagon hip LL [151 3/8"] by the travel [120"] to arrive at the hip-travel-to-LL conversion ratio of 1.2615.)
3. Take the saw angles from the snapped-out plan view with a protractor or rafter square.

Refer to ***Figure 10-3*** to draw out an octagon geometrically. Snap a single straight line on the floor, and swing a circle with a given radius from any point located on the snap-line (centerpoint **a**). From the two points where the circle intersects the snap-line (**c** and **b**), swing equal-radius arcs to locate the perpendicular line **d-e** that bisects line **c-b**. Next, swing equal-radius arcs from **c** and **d** to bisect the difference between them at **f**. Do the same between points **d** and **b** to find **g**. Snap long lines from **f** and **g** though the centerpoint to intersect the far side of the circle. Connect all the line-to-circle intersections to form an octagon.

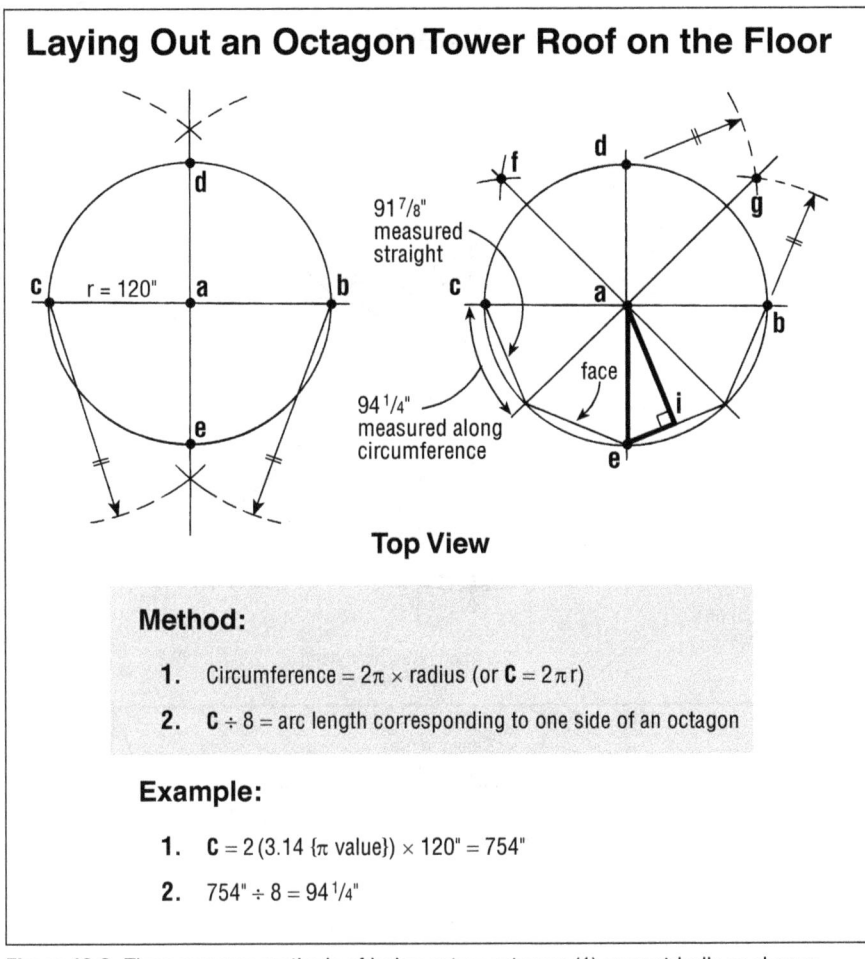

Figure 10-3. Three common methods of laying out an octagon: (1) geometrically as shown; (2) mathematically by calculating the circumference and dividing by eight to find the length of each arc segment; or (3) with trig by multiplying the radius by the sine of half the angle opposing each side and doubling the result to find the length of each octagon face. Example: 2 × (120" × .3827 {sine 22 1/2°}) = 91 7/8"

The following procedure outlines the method used in **Figure 10-4** to calculate the hips:

1. Measure run **a-i** from the snapped-out plan view, or calculate it mathematically by dividing the hip travel (radius) by the secant of half the angle formed between the hip beams (secant 22 1/2° = 1.0824, Chart 5, Appendix A).
2. Use that run dimension to find the total rise at centerpoint **a** by multiplying by the appropriate RR ratio (10/12 in example).
3. Calculate the hip LL using the Pythagorean theorem with the total rise and the hip travel as legs of a vertical right triangle.
4. Hip rafter pitch is 10/13 per **Figure 10-5**.

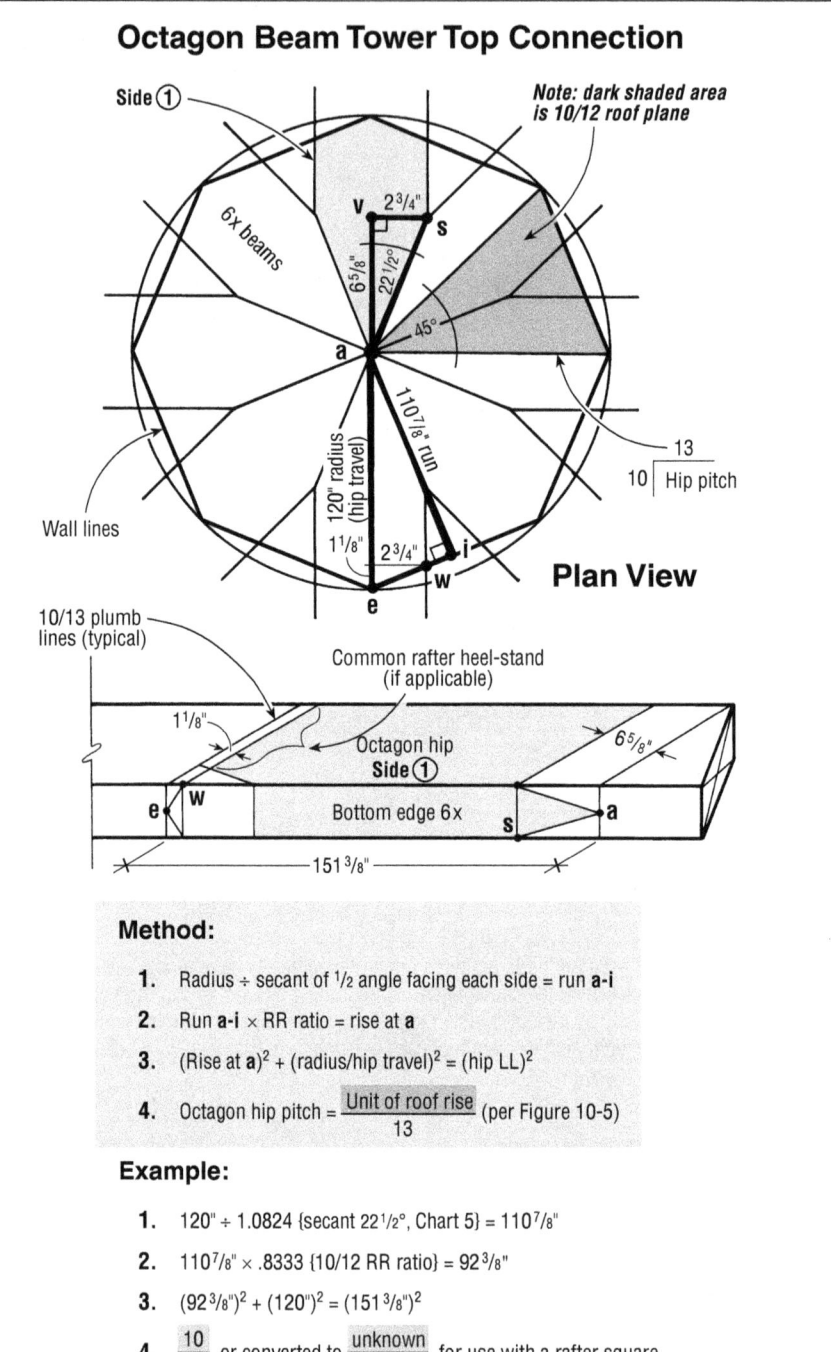

Figure 10-4. Use trig as shown to calculate the common rafter run, or measure the run off a snapped-out full-size plan view. Multiply the run by the RR ratio to calculate the rise at the centerpoint. Use the Pythagorean theorem to calculate the hip LL. In an octagon, hip rafter pitch is unit of roof rise/13. Head/heel-cut lines and angles are taken from the snapped-out plan view.

See Appendix B

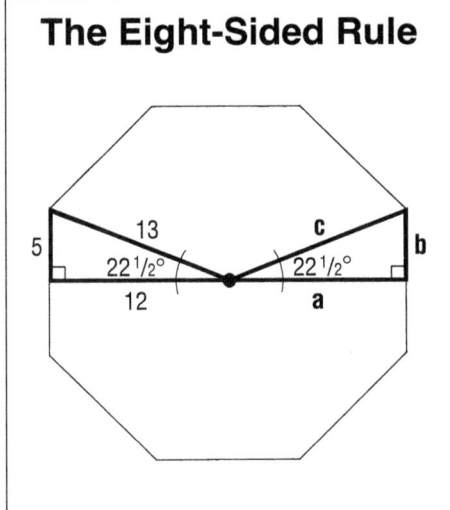

Figure 10-5. With 45° facing each of the eight sides, the octagon is unique among the polygon family. Bisecting one of the octagon sides with a line drawn to the centerpoint creates a 22½° right triangle, which for most practical purposes is identical to the right triangle formed by the roof pitch 5/12 where the hypotenuse is a whole number (13). Those skilled at rafter layout with a framing square can mark off the octagon hips by setting 13 in. on the framing square blade rather than the 17 in. used for regular hip travel.

After snapping the rafter beam width centered on the four lines, the top head-cuts and the bottom heel-cuts are found exactly as they were in the hexagon section. Measure from points **a** and **e** along the centerline to a point perpendicular to the beam-edge intersects, and transfer this dimension to the side of the beam to find the cut-lines (see Figure 10-4).

The most common method for making an eight-beam connection is illustrated in ***Figure 10-6***. It is simple to cut and stack, but the finished product doesn't look nearly as nice from below as beams radiating from a centerpoint.

Another common technique, especially when using small 4x beam rafters, is to bring all the beams together into a short vertical section of a large-diameter pipe. Weld tangs at the top through which lag bolts can be run into each beam. The diameter of the pipe should be sized so all the beams can be square-cut at the ridge end and fit around. Eight 4x beams create a 9-in.-diameter circle (8 beams × 3½" = 28"; 28" ÷ 3.14 {π} = 9").

The method shown in ***Figure 10-7*** is similar to the pipe technique but uses a shaped, long, vertical 10x10 king pin (see ***Photo 10-8***). Since eight beams with full-width square-cut heads will not fit around the king pin, four beams have their head-cut side edges clipped with small 45° cheek-cuts so they fit between the others. Notice in Figure 10-7 the different amounts each type of rafter beam must be shortened (4¾" vs. 5¼"). Locate the 45° cheek-cuts by measuring down the centerline to a point square over from the beam-edge joint and marking as shown.

Note: Hip jacks for all polygons are calculated as shown in the hexagon section.

OTHER POLYGONS

By applying trig functions from the right triangle formed by bisecting any side of a polygon to the centerpoint, the unknown sides can be calculated.

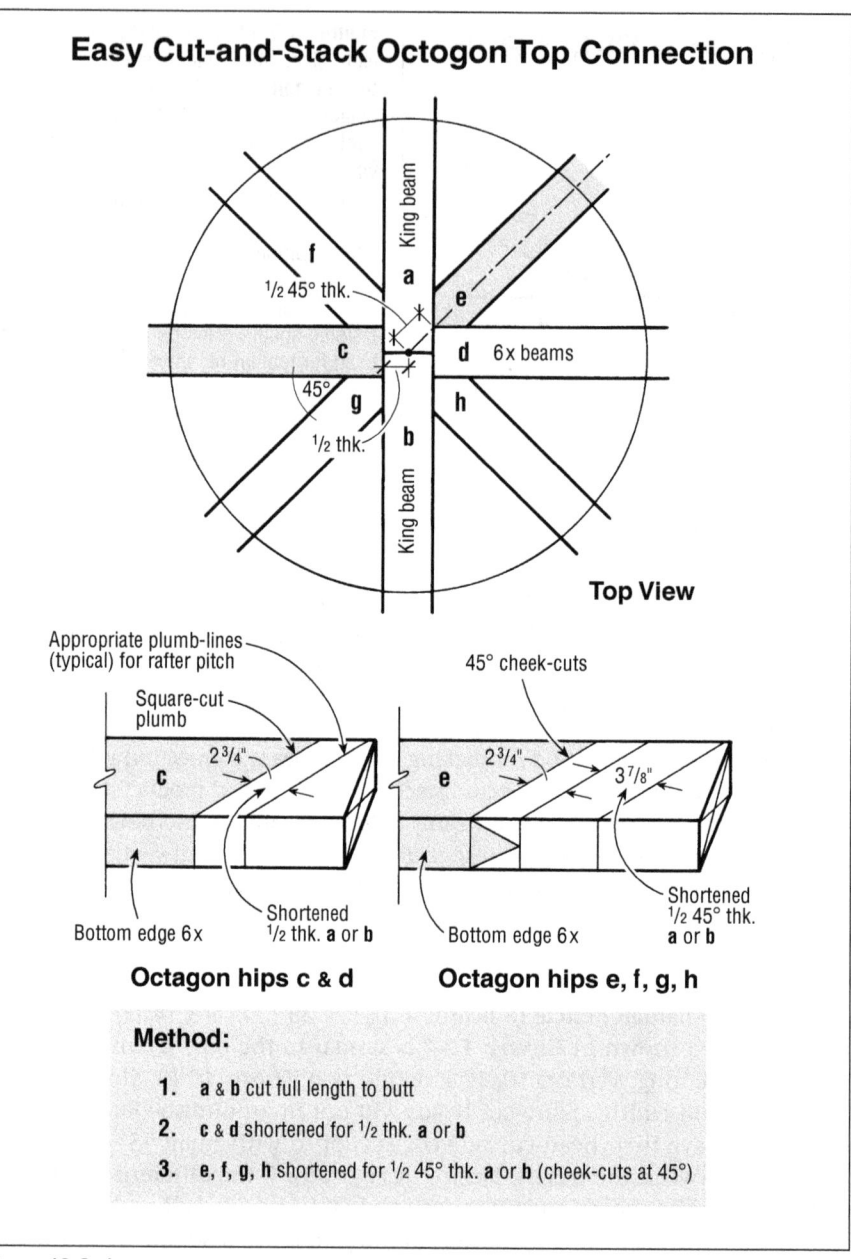

Figure 10-6. A very common method of framing an octagon top beam connection is to run two king beams full length to butt head to head, then run two beams off them at 90°, and finally run four beams off the inside corners at 45°.

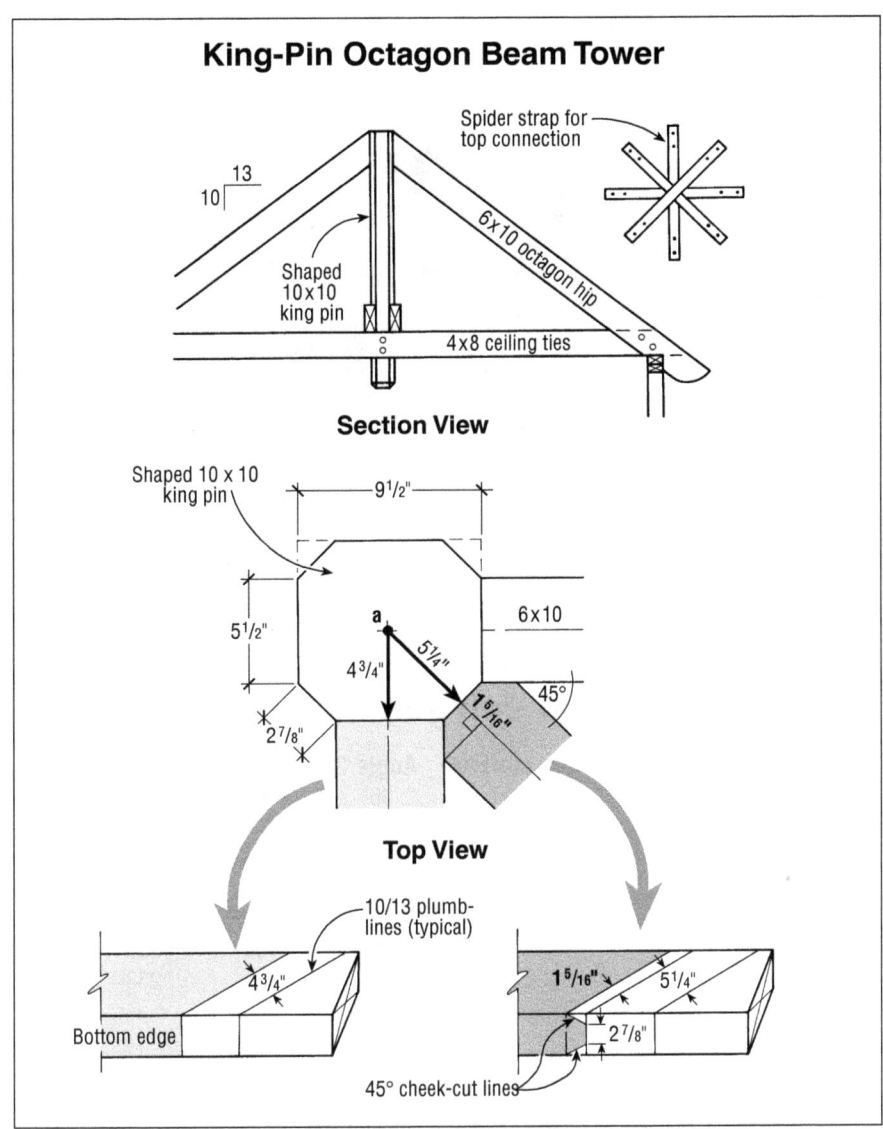

Figure 10-7. An octagon with a center king pin requires careful attention to the shortening amounts and cheek-cut lines if the faces of the king pin have different dimensions.

Photo 10-8. Stick-framing an octagon tower with a center 10x10 king pin and 4x8 cross-ties.

Common Polygon Functions

Name	# Sides	Angle per Face	Angle/2	Tangent	Secant	Sine
Pentagon	5	72°	36°	.7265	1.2361	.5878
Hexagon	6	60°	30°	.5774	1.1547	.5000
Octagon	8	45°	22½°	.4142	1.0824	.3827
Nonagon	9	40°	20°	.3640	1.0642	.3420
Decagon	10	36°	18°	.3249	1.0515	.3090
Dodecagon	12	30°	15°	.2680	1.0353	.2588
Hexadecagon	16	22½°	12¼°	.2171	1.0233	.2122

Method:
Using octagon functions in Figure 10-5:
1. Find **a** given **b**   **b** ÷ tangent of angle/2 = **a**
2. Find **b** given **a**   **a** × tangent of angle/2 = **b**
3. Find **c** given **a**   **a** × secant of angle/2 = **c**
4. Find **b** given **c**   **c** × sine of angle/2 = **b**

Example:
1. 5 ÷ .4142 {tangent of 22½°} = 12.07, round to 12
2. 12 × .4142 {tangent of 22½°} = 4.95, round to 5
3. 12 × 1.0824 {secant of 22½°} = 12.99, round to 13
4. 13 × .3827 {sine of 22½°} = 4.98, round to 5

Figure 10-9. By applying trig functions from the right triangle formed by bisecting any side of polygon to the centerpoint, the unknown sides can be calculated.

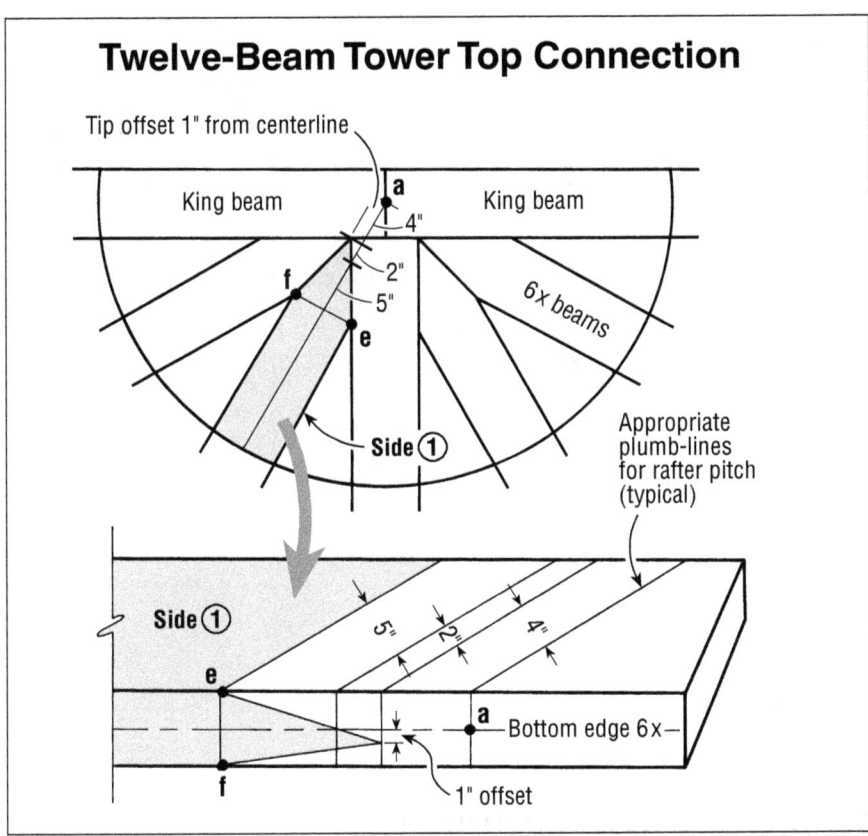

Figure 10-10. When a tower is stacked in the air piece by piece (rather than preframed on the ground and lifted into place as a completed unit by crane), it is often easier to square-cut as many head-cuts as possible to facilitate assembly.

The octagon shown in Figure 10-5 is used as the example in ***Figure 10-9*** for applying trig functions. Also included is a list of the most frequently used trig values for common polygons.

Figure 10-10 shows one way of doing a twelve-sided roof or a six-sided end to a straight gable roof. Instead of cutting all the pieces radiating from the center as shown in the hexagon and octagon examples, several beams are square-cut plumb to make the roof easier to stack. This is especially helpful if the roof is stacked in the air rather than built on the ground and lifted into place with a crane.

Notice that the tips of the four angle-cut beams are off-center. By using a full-scale snapped-out plan view on the floor, the various distances from point **a** can be found. The offset is measured over from the centerline. By transferring the measurements to the beam as shown, even the most odd-ball connection can easily be done.

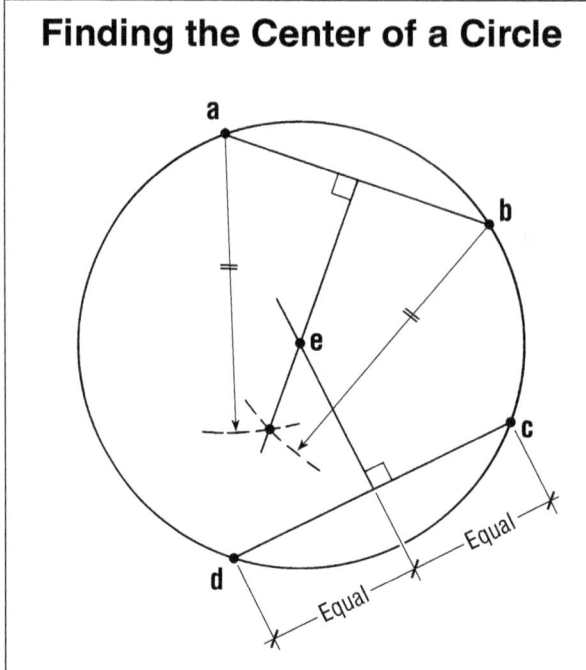

Figure 10-11. Snap two random lines across the circle, and bisect the interior line segments with perpendicular lines. The intersection of these perpendicular lines (point **e**) is the centerpoint of the circle.

CONICAL TOWER CONSTRUCTION

Towers are a special challenge. Usually, the first problem that must be solved is how to find the center of the circular floor area where the tower is to be framed. Start by snapping two random lines across a portion of the circle (*Figure 10-11*, lines **a-b** and **c-d**). Bisect their two interior line segments with perpendicular lines by swinging equal-radius arcs from the circumference intersects similar to Figure 10-3. The intersection of the two perpendicular lines from the midpoint of each interior line segment is the centerpoint of the circle.

Once the centerpoint of the circle has been located, use either a piece of 1x4 with clamp-on compass points (available from several tool manufacturers) or a pencil held against a tape measure stretched from a "centerpoint nail" to swing the circular wall position lines on the floor and mark the cut-lines on plywood sheets for the curved plates *(Figure 10-12)*.

Cut the top and bottom plates from $1^{1}/_{8}$-in. plywood (use a layer of treated plywood as the sill plate when on a concrete slab). Depending on how tight the curve is, a Skilsaw® may be used for the radius cuts. The latest thin-kerf carbide blades work well. If the radius is really tight, use a fast-cutting jigsaw or buy/make your own special three-sided circle-cutting circular saw blade *Figure 10-13)*. Another tool some folks use for mass-producing curves is a homemade radius cutter. This is nothing more than a long 2x4 with a trammel point on one end and a metal plate on the other for attaching a Skilsaw® or router.

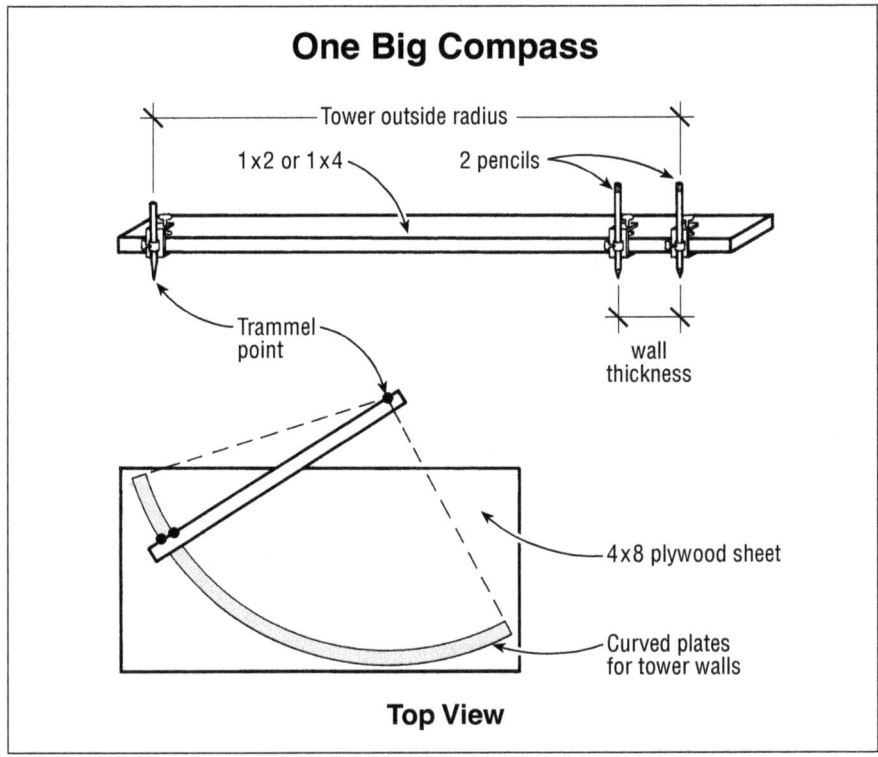

Figure 10-12. A 1x4 with clamp-on compass points makes an excellent oversized compass, or use a centerpoint nail, a tape measure, and a pencil.

The ends of each curved piece must be cut at the angle formed by a straight line from the centerpoint to the radial position (shown in Figure 10-12 by the dashed lines). Plate and frame the wall in sections *(Figure 10-14)*.

Studs are laid out on **both** edges of the circumference plates with only a center mark. Use a line stretched from the centerpoint to position these layout marks.

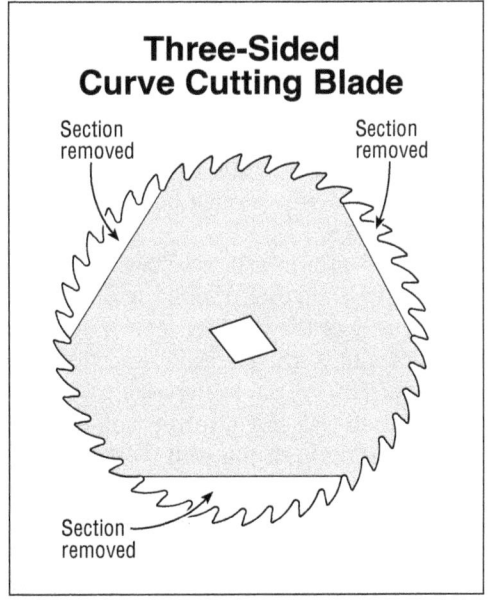

Figure 10-13. Chop off three equal sections from an old steel circular saw blade to make a tighter-turning model.

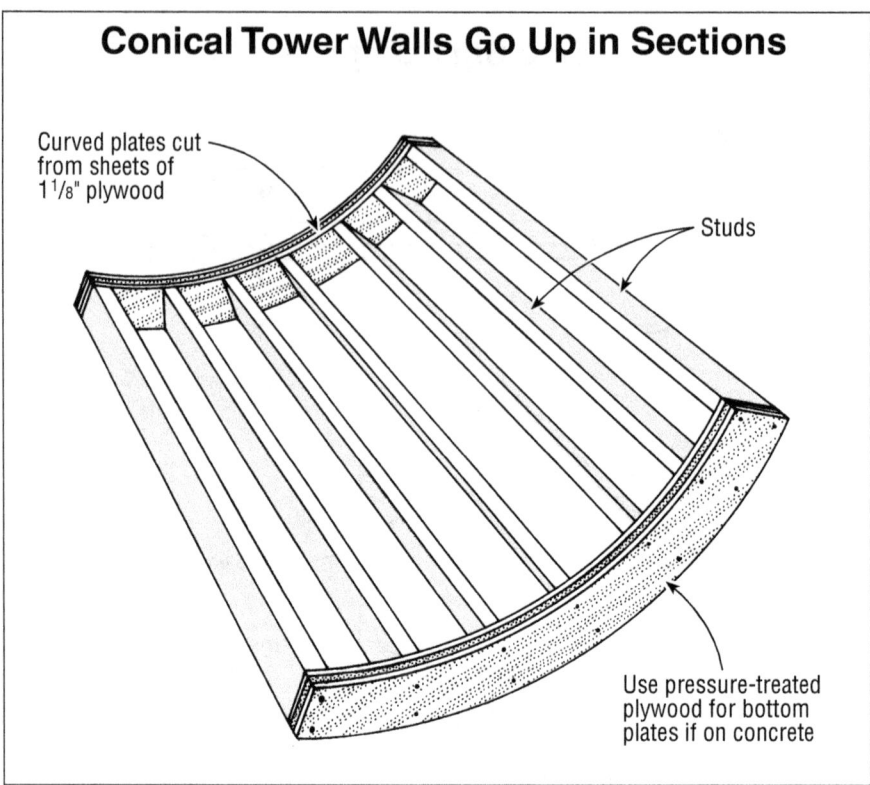

Figure 10-14. Plate and frame the circular tower wall in sections. After they are stood, tie all the sections together with a second layer of 1¹/₈-in. plywood as a doubler.

Since many towers have circular stairs, now is the time to coordinate the stud layout to hold up the stair risers (see Figure 14-8).

Curved headers can be band-sawed out of 6x16 beam stock, Parallams, or Microlams, etc., laid flat or fabricated out of metal, depending on the span. Unless the outside door and windows are custom made with the tower's radius, the openings must be recessed to create a flat surface as shown in **Figure 10-15**.

Once all the wall sections are framed and stood, run a second layer of 1¹/₈-in. plywood as a doubler to tie everything together (³/₄-in. plywood can be used as the doubler if the tower roof will be preframed on the ground). Check the circumference measurement to make sure you haven't gained anything (circumference = 6.28 {2π} × radius).

To plumb and line a tower, you must first lock in the diameter measurements at the top of the wall by installing interior temporary horizontal ties from side to side. If the wall is thick, the plywood plates will keep the diameter correct without the need for any ties. Next, tack a 2x4 across the top plates from side to side, and measure the radius from various spots along the outside circumference to locate the exact center on the 2x4. Drive a nail

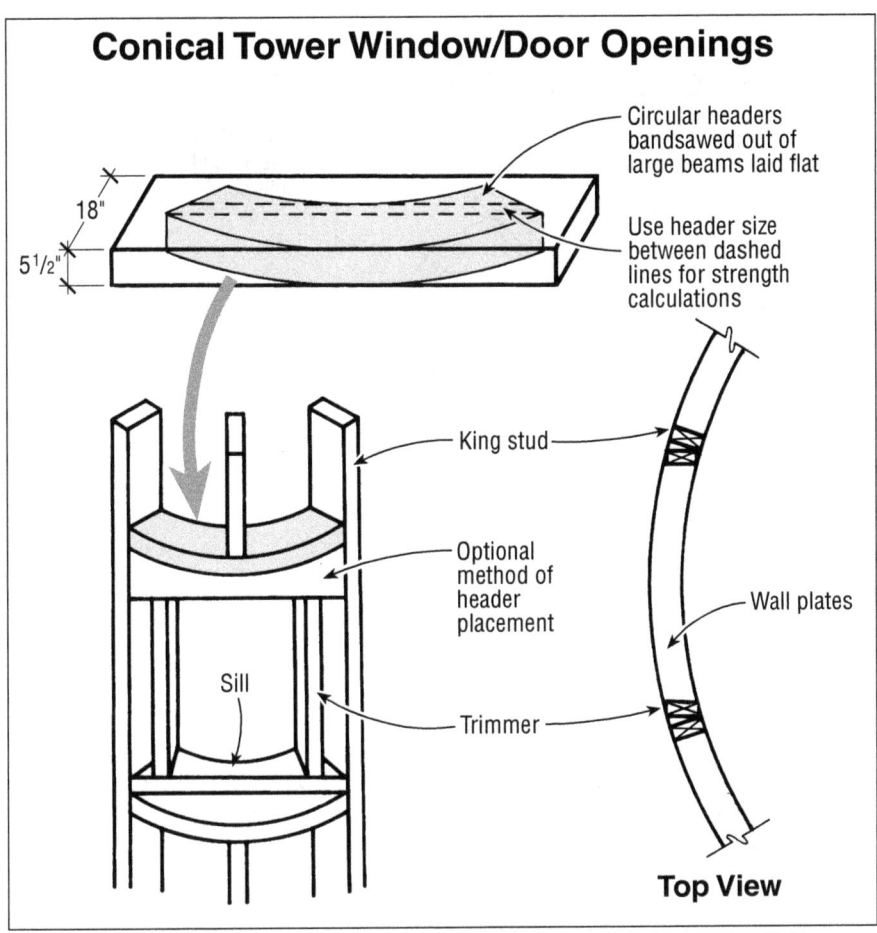

Figure 10-15. In a round tower, unless the doors and windows are custom-made with the tower's radius, the openings must be recessed to create a flat square.

straight down through the mark, and attach a plumb-bob to the point. Rack the tower around until the bob is directly over the circle's centerpoint mark on the floor (or use a laser shooting up from the centerpoint on the floor to the nail), and nail up temporary sway-braces on the inside *(Figure 10-16)*. Shear the outside with one or two layers of ³/8-in. plywood.

The quickest and easiest way to construct a tower roof is to build it on the ground and lift it into place with a crane (see **Photo 10-17**). To set up for this method, sandwich two layers of precut 1¹/8-in. curved plywood plates together to form a circular plate the same diameter as the tower walls and run a metal strap (Simpson Strong-Tie® CS22R) around the outside circumference. Then build and level an octagon-shaped rack where the crane can reach, and place the circular tower plate on it. Raise the circular plate off the ground high enough to allow for any overhang drop *(Photo 10-18)*.

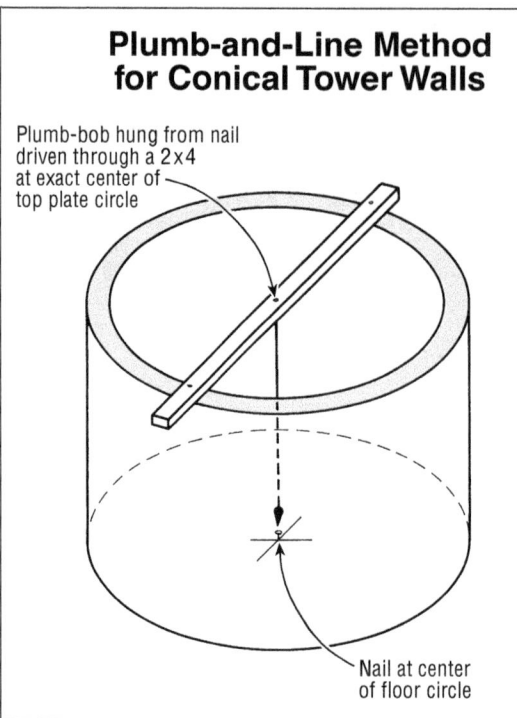

Figure 10-16. Plumb the cylindrical tower walls as a unit using a nail driven through a 2x4 at the centerpoint of the circular top plates, and rack the walls around until it matches the centerpoint mark on the floor.

Photo 10-17. Setting a completed conical tower roof with a crane.

Photo 10-18. Two roof cones ready for fascia and plywood.

Conical tower roofs are sometimes framed using exposed beams (with tongue-and-groove decking) in the shape of some polygon, and then rounded into a conical shape using 2x rafters framed above. When double-framed in this fashion, set the polygon hip beams at the given pitch of the tower cone rather than the roof plane between the corners as was shown earlier in the "Hexagons" and "Octagons" sections. Since there are no corners on a circle, all birdsmouth heel-cuts are square-cut.

Fasten the polygon beams at the plate line with countersunk lags or angle brackets to resist any spreading action. A long seat-cut on the tower beams will enable several lags to be installed up through the circular plate. A thick spider-type strap should be installed over the top of any polygon beam connection for strength, especially when lifting the tower roof with a crane.

Figure 10-19 illustrates a quick way to cut tongue-and-groove decking for a tower ceiling or any similar situation. On the floor, put together enough pieces to reach the peak, and snap lines corresponding to the center of the polygon hip beams. The tongues on the decking will face up on one set and down on the next, but that shouldn't matter; they look the same either way.

Polygon beam towers that are double-framed to bring the shape back out to a cone require short, curved walls between the beams at the outside plate line to raise the second roof high enough to clear the polygon hip beams and decking *(Figure 10-20)*.

To calculate the number of 2x rafters required around the circular tower wall plate, divide the circumference measurement by a multiple of eight to find the closest value to the desired on-center spacing. For example, there will be 48 rafters converging at the top of a 20-ft.-diameter tower with a $15^{3}/_{4}$-in.-on-center spacing at the plate line. (Working with a multiple of

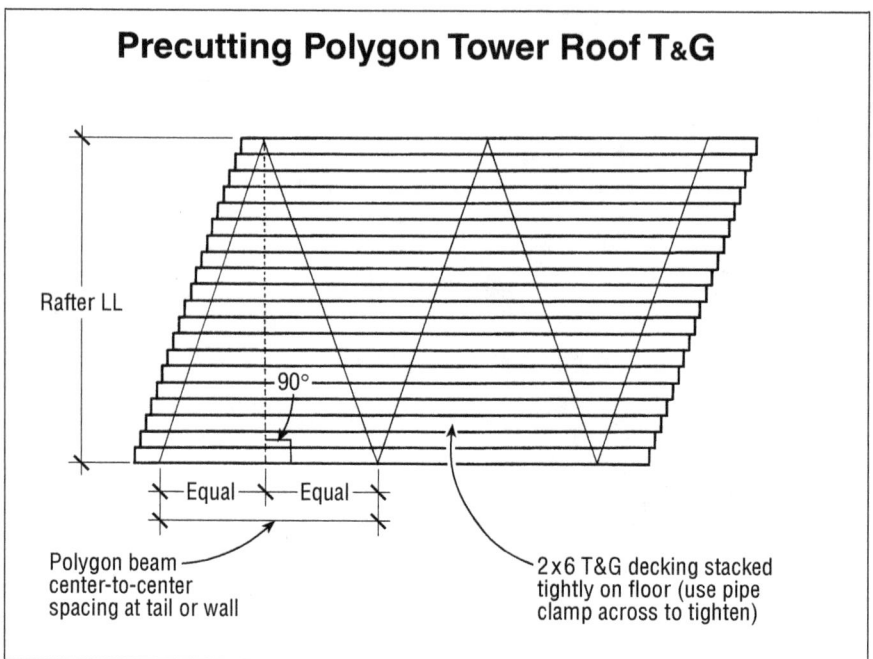

Figure 10-19. Rather than cut tongue-and-groove decking piece by piece, gang-cut several complete sides of the polygon roof.

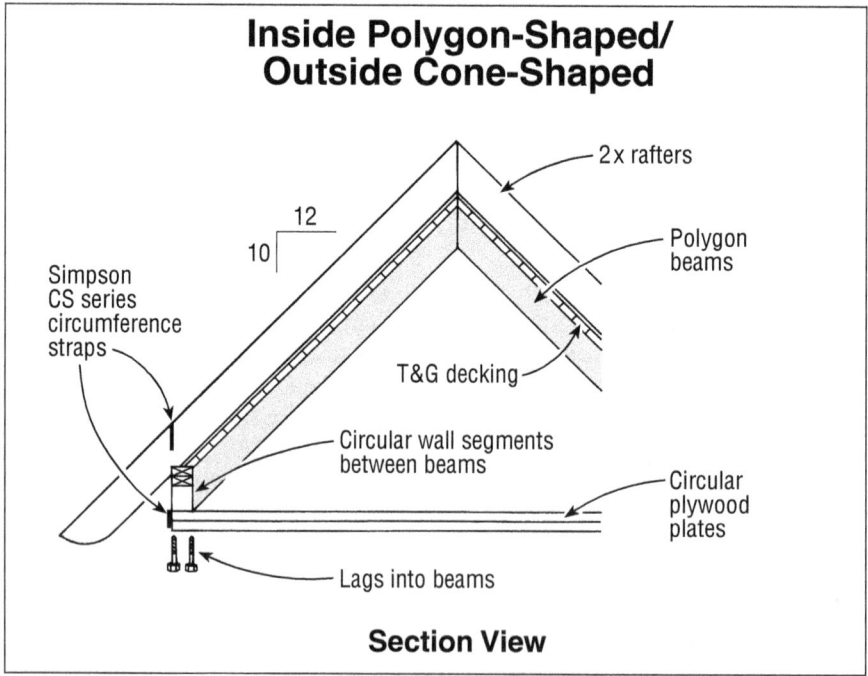

Figure 10-20. Install short, curved walls between the beams at the outside plate line to raise the conical double roof high enough to clear the polygon hip beams and decking.

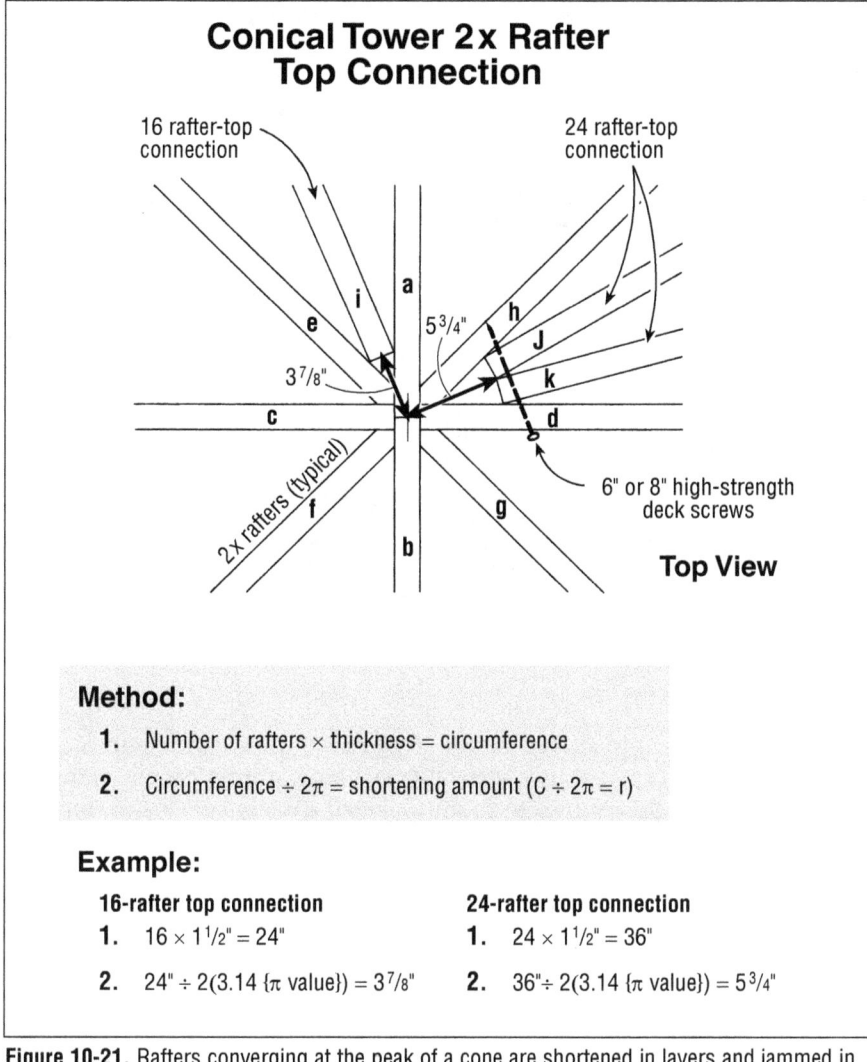

Figure 10-21. Rafters converging at the peak of a cone are shortened in layers and jammed in the gaps so the top edges line up with the rafter on each side.

eight makes stacking the rafters much easier.) A full-scale snapped-out plan view of the 2x rafter conical tower top connection can be used to find the shortening amounts, or use trig as illustrated in **Figure 10-21**. Rafters **a** and **b** are square-cut plumb at full length and butted together. Rafters **c** and **d** are shortened 1/2 thk. of **a** or **b**. Rafters **e**, **f**, **g**, and **h** are shortened 1/2 45° thk. of **a** or **b**, and given a double 45° cheek-cut. From this point on, stick one rafter between each pair of adjoining rafters (as in **i**) or two rafters (as in **J** and **k**) depending on what combination will achieve the desired number of rafters. Rafter **i** is shortened 3 7/8 in., square-cut plumb, and jammed in until the top edges line up with the rafter on each side. Rafters **J** and **k** are shortened 5 3/4 in., square-cut plumb, and jammed simultaneously between

Photo 10-22. A birds-eye view of the top connection in a 2x rafter conical tower.

two rafters as shown in **Photo 10-22**. If you need to run more rafters, go around again either one or two at a time. Working around the tower in one direction should allow sufficient room to install a couple 6- or 8-in. high-strength deck screws through the follow-up intermediary rafters.

Note: I do not recommend terminating intermediate rafters into blocks short of the peak, but if you choose to do so, they must be set to the correct height and lateral position with a string stretched from the peak centerpoint to the top edge at the end of the rafter tail.

Sometimes the 2x rafters on a conical tower roof are cut tailless, and fake beam tails run for the eaves. Always center these beam tails in the rafter bays both at the plate and where they head into a block. **Do not slap them next to a tailless rafter** as this will put their centerlines askew from running to the center of the cone's peak. It's also a good idea to make a 2-in. plumb-cut into the beam tails at the building line so a second circumference strap will run around the ends of the tailless rafters.

The top connection method shown in Figure 10-21 is also used for a 2x rafter conical tower that has no exposed beam work and is plastered smooth on the inside.

The trick to running plywood sheathing on a conical tower is to precut the plywood sheets into curved sections as shown in **Figure 10-23**. To lay out a marking jig, snap a long line on the floor, and locate the radius pivot point **(a)** towards one end. From **a**, measure the full LL of the tower rafters to the fascia, and mark **b**. Then place a mark at the midpoint of each of the plywood sheet's long edges, and position them perpendicular to snap-line

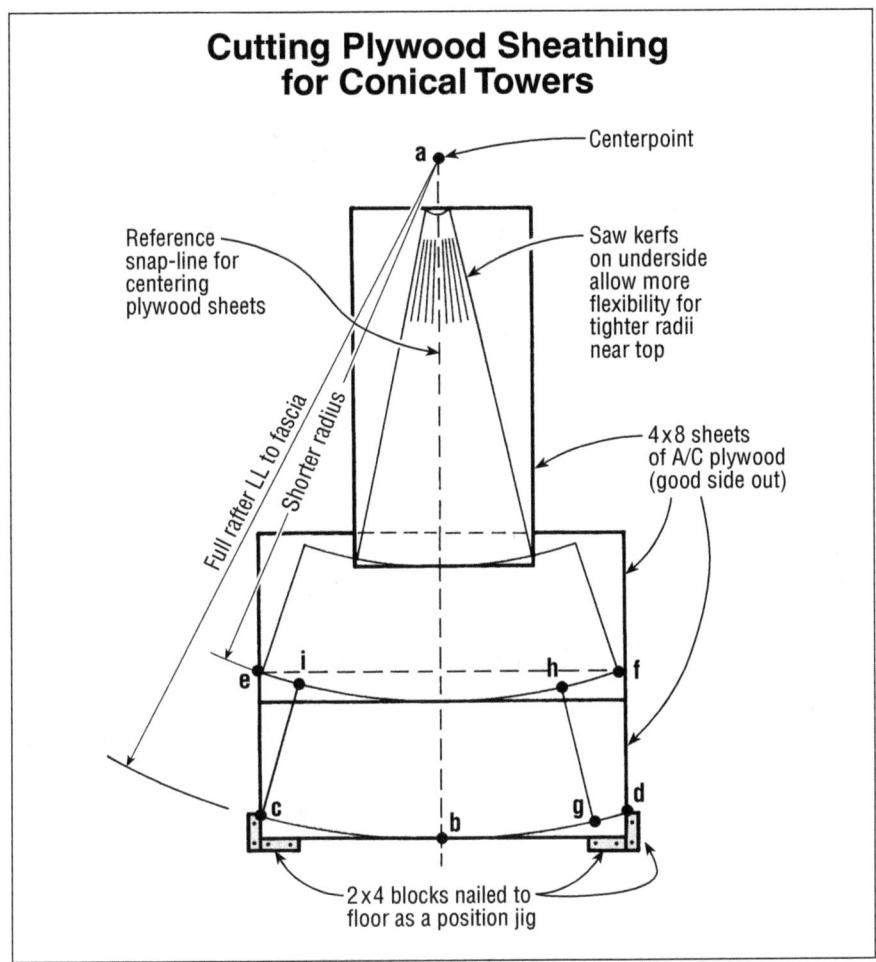

Figure 10-23. Always precut the roof plywood into curved sections on the floor prior to installation. Use the full conical tower rafter LL to the fascia as the radius for the lower edge of the first sheet with a shorter radius (rafter LL less **c-i**) for the upper edge of the first sheet, and so forth. Choose radii that make the best use of the 4x8 plywood sheets, and turn the sheets lengthwise near the peak.

a-b, with one midpoint edge mark tangent to point **b** and the other midpoint edge mark centered on the snap-line. Now nail some corner-positioning blocks to the floor for subsequent sheets. Use a compass set to the rafter LL to scribe arc **c-d**, and a shorter radius that makes the best use of the plywood sheet to mark the uphill arc (**e-f**). This same arc will be the bottom radius for the next sheet up. Cut the right and left sides of the pie-shaped plywood sheets (**i-c** and **h-g**) using the longest arc measurement possible between rafters at the lower edge (**c-g**).

To determine the on-center spacing at each layer of curved plywood sheathing, divide the LL measurement from the radius point to each layer

TOWERS AND POLYGONS 225

Photo 10-24. Plywood sheets can be turned lengthwise to make better use of the material.

by the appropriate COM LL ratio to determine the horizontal radius at that level. Then multiply that radius by 6.28 (2π) to calculate a circumference. Divide that circumference by the total number of rafters in the tower cone to yield the on-center spacing at that level. Use the most practical multiple of that on-center spacing measured along the curved bottom edge of the plywood sheathing for that level to locate the side edge cuts.

Towards the top, turn the plywood sheets lengthwise to make better use of the material *(Photo 10-24)*. Shallow kerf-cuts on the back of the plywood near the top will help make it flexible enough to nail down. Install 1x4s or 1x6s diagonally on convex towers like the one in **Photo 10-25**.

Note: Several layers of 3/8-in. bending Lauan hardwood plywood can be used to sheathe tight, unusual curved surfaces. It is imported by some of the larger lumber mills like Georgia Pacific, etc. For oddball shapes, trial-fit a piece of housewrap paper as a pattern.

When a conical tower has a kick-up eave projection, use the roof pitch of the kick-up to calculate the radii for the plywood sheathing on the eave. Consider the hypothetical situation of a 120-in.-radius conical tower at a 10/12 pitch together with a 24-in. kick-up eave projection at a 6/12 pitch

Photo 10-25. Intermediate plates are used to break up the long curved rafters in this beehive-shaped tower. Shaped horizontal blocking at 12 in. on-center will enable 1x6s to be run diagonally on the lower half. (Photo courtesy of Shone Freeman.)

(pitch-to-pitch change occurring at the plate line). In this case, the bottom radius for the conical tower's plywood sheathing (see Figure 10-23) is equal to the LL of the conical tower's radius at a 10/12 pitch (120" × 1.3017 {10/12 COM LL ratio} = 156 1/4"), while the abutting inside edge of the eave plywood would have a radius equal to the LL of the conical tower at a 6/12 pitch (120" × 1.1180 {6/12 COM LL ratio} = 134 1/8"). The eave's outside plywood sheathing radius would be the LL for the summation of the conical tower radius to the plate line and the 24-in. eave overhang at a 6/12 pitch (144" × 1.1180 {6/12 COM LL ratio} = 161").

Long, heavy-duty lags drilled through the plywood into the tower beams above the midpoint, or an eye-bolt attached to the spider strap, allow the crane to lift and place the tower roof.

CALIFORNIA VALLEYS AT A TOWER

Use the framing method shown in *Figure 10-26* when another roof plane intersects a tower. Double the last full-length common rafters on each side, and hang a purlin beam underneath from side to side to support the inter-

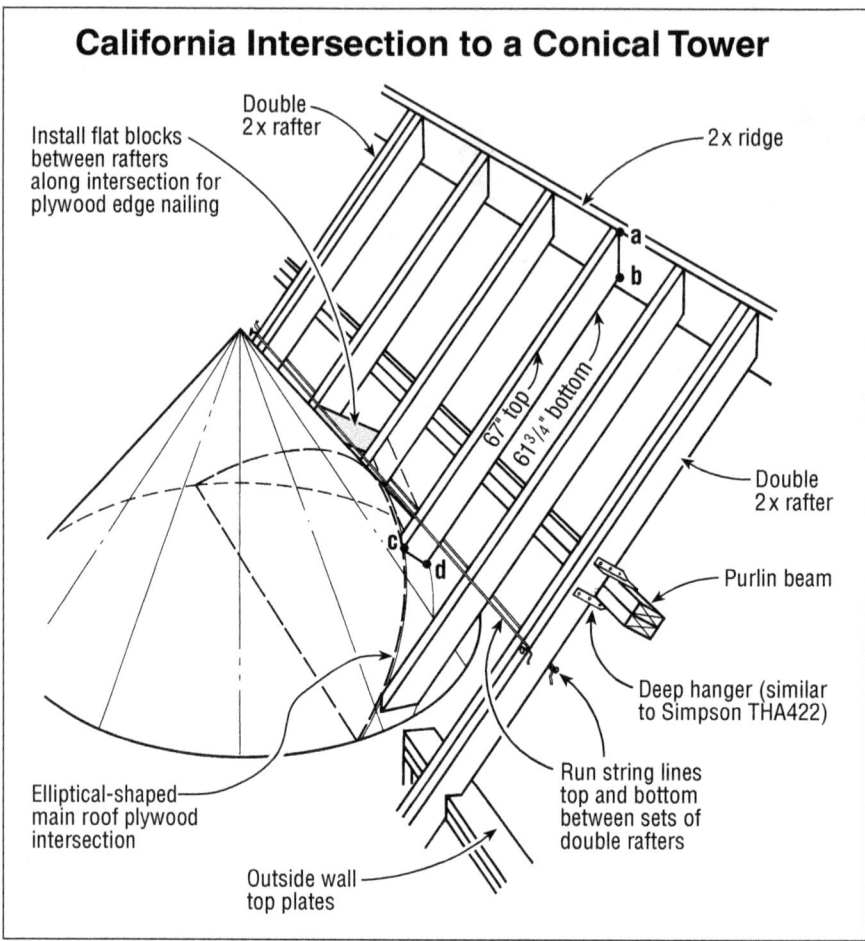

Figure 10-26. Run strings top and bottom stretched between the two sets of side doublers as a position guide to help find the upper- and lower-edge dimensions of the various California jacks. A purlin hung from side to side under the sets of doublers supports the loose ends of the jacks.

mediate California jacks. (A regular braced purlin can be used instead if bearing walls are nearby below.) Snap out the California intersection on the tower sheathing using the top edges of the last full-length common rafters on each side of the tower as a guide. From a variety of positions spanning from side to side, create a sufficient number of short snap-line segments to mark out the curved shape, and hand-measure jack lengths from that line. Another method is to run a string top-and-bottom between the two doublers as close to the tower roof as possible, and lay out the purlin, the string-lines, and ridge for the jacks. Measure down at each ridge mark the rafter plumb dimension to find the bottom of the head-cut (**b**). From points **a** and **b**, measure to the tower roof using the strings as a guide. Transfer the proper measurements to each jack. Leave a $1/4$-in. gap between the jack and the tower roof, and make the cut from **c** to **d** with the saw set square. If the cantilever from the purlin is too large, it will be necessary to find the bevel-cut angle so the tail end of the rafter will bear directly on the tower surface.

Note: The "scribe to fit" method illustrated in Figure 8-26, will **not** work at the intersection of a standard roof plane to a conical roof. To get the proper California-cut, it is necessary to place each jack rafter in its exact position.

If the tower is not sheathed, the jacks can be cut long to extend into the tower roof's rafter bays. This saves a lot of time cutting the California jacks, but requires more time for roof sheathing since now both the regular roof and the tower roof must have a curved cut made to the roof sheathing at the intersection.

Chapter 11

Bay Roofs

COMMON BAY ROOFS

Bay roofs come in all shapes and sizes. Although they could rightfully come under the heading of "Bastard Hips and Valleys," I decided to give them a chapter of their own and position it to follow "Towers and Polygons," since they are more or less related. The two most common styles are shown in ***Figure 11-1***. Both have a 45° angle of departure from the building. Style **A** has three equal-length sides and is solved like an octagon with each roof plane being the same pitch ***(Photo 11-2)***. Style **B** has two short, equal-length sides and a long front face which makes the side roof planes a shallower pitch than the front ***(Photo 11-3)***. In both styles, "flying valleys" are installed at the eaves (see **b-d** and **v-t**).

Note: All the examples shown in this chapter have the centerlines run through the building's framed corners. This will cause the overhangs to be of different dimensions to achieve a common fascia height. If equal-length overhangs are desired, snap out the hips on the floor drawing from the centerpoint through to the fascia corners, which are laid out equidistant. Determine birdsmouth depths and hip-rafter position off the corner as shown in the Chapter 8 section, "An Unequal-Pitch Hip Roof with Equal-Length Overhangs," page 172.

Standard operating procedure for any bay roof is to snap out a full-size plan view on the floor to get the various runs, hip travels, cut-angles, shortening amounts, etc. Locate the centerpoint (**a** or **u**) by measuring half the bay span from the front bay wall (120"/2). Style **A** has three regular commons — one off each side — while style **B** has only one off the front. **Rise/run** and **rise/hip-travel** equations are required to find the bastard hips and the off-pitch commons. The off-pitch commons in style **B** are

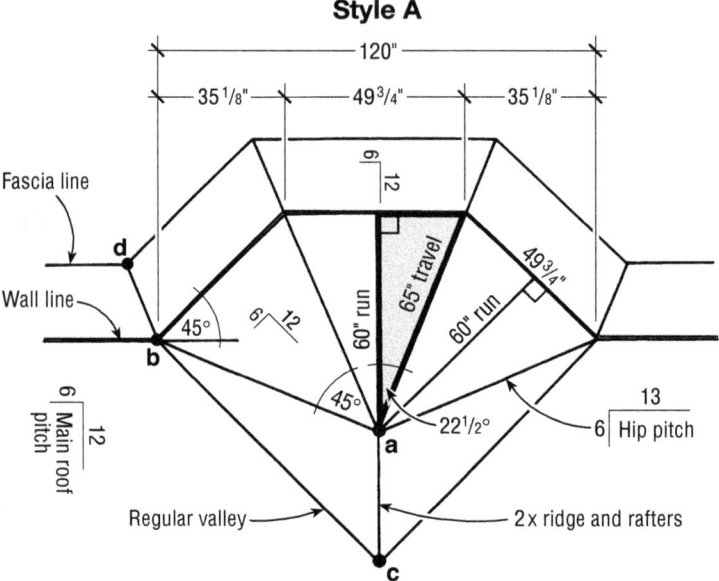

Bay Roof Hip Calculation
Style A

Method:

1. Run × secant of ½ angle facing each side = hip travel
2. Run × RR ratio = rise at **a**
3. (Rise at **a**)² + (hip travel)² = (hip theoretical LL)² shorten per snapped-out plan view
4. Octagon bay roof hip pitch = $\dfrac{\text{unit roof rise}}{13}$ (per Figure 10-5)
5. Run × COM LL ratio = side common **theoretical** LL shorten ½ 45° thk. of ridge

Example:

1. 60" × 1.0824 {secant 22½°, Chart 5} = 65"
2. 60" × .5000 {6/12 RR ratio} = 30"
3. (30")² + (65")² = (71½")², shortened 3⅞" to square-cut end per snapped-out plan view
4. $\dfrac{6}{13}$ or converted to $\dfrac{\text{unknown}}{12}$ for use with a rafter square
5. 60" × 1.1180 {6/12 COM LL ratio} = 67⅛" shortened 1 1/16" with double 45° cheek-cut

Figure 11-1a. Bay roofs come most often in two styles. Style **A** has three equal-length sides and is solved like an octagon with each roof plane being the same pitch. Style **B** has two equal sides and a longer front face, making the side roof planes a shallower pitch than the front.

See Appendix B

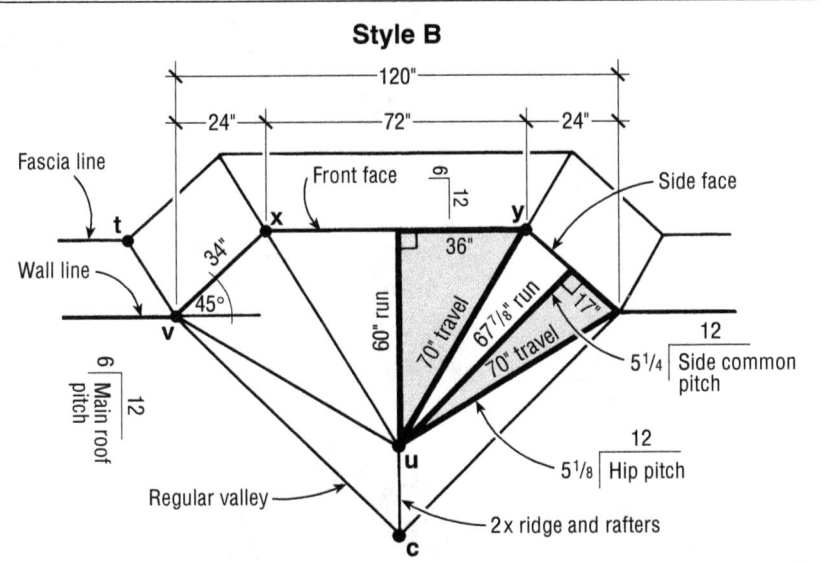

Method:

1. (Front common run)^2 + ($^1/_2$ front face)^2 = (hip travel)^2

2. Front common run × RR ratio = rise at **u**

3. (Rise at **u**)^2 + (hip travel)^2 = (hip **theoretical** LL)^2 shorten per snapped plan view

4. $\dfrac{\text{Rise at }\mathbf{u}}{\text{hip travel}} = \dfrac{\text{Hip pitch}}{12}$

5. (Hip travel)^2 − ($^1/_2$ side face)^2 = (side common run)^2

6. (Rise at **u**)^2 + (side common run)^2 = (side common **theoretical** LL)^2 shorten $^1/_2$ 45° thk. of ridge

7. $\dfrac{\text{Rise at }\mathbf{u}}{\text{side common run}} = \dfrac{\text{Side common pitch}}{12}$

Example:

1. (60")^2 + (36")^2 = (70")^2

2. 60" × .5000 {6/12 RR ratio} = 30"

3. (30")^2 + (70")^2 = (76 $^1/_8$")^2 shortened 6" to square-cut end per snapped-out plan view

4. $\dfrac{30"}{70"} = \dfrac{5 ^1/_8}{12}$

5. (70")^2 − (17")^2 = (67 $^7/_8$")^2

6. (30")^2 + (67 $^7/_8$")^2 = (74 $^1/_4$")^2 shortened 1 $^1/_{16}$" with double 45° cheek-cut

7. $\dfrac{30"}{67 ^7/_8"} = \dfrac{5 ^1/_4}{12}$

Figure 11-1b.   See Appendix B

Photo 11-2. A style **A** equilateral bay roof is three sides from an octagon.

Photo 11-3. This style **B** bay roof has a straight return on one side.

calculated to the theoretical centerpoint and shortened accordingly ($1/2$ 45° thk. of the ridge with a double 45° cheek-cut). Proportions are used to determine the unknown pitches. Jack rafter runs can be taken from the snapped floor drawing or a jack-step measurement can be calculated as described in Chapter 8. A COM LL ratio for a roof pitch not included in Chart 2, Appendix A, is found by dividing the total LL by the appropriate run. (Example: The COM LL ratio for the side commons in **B**: $74 1/4"$ {LL} ÷ $67 7/8"$ {run} = 1.0938.)

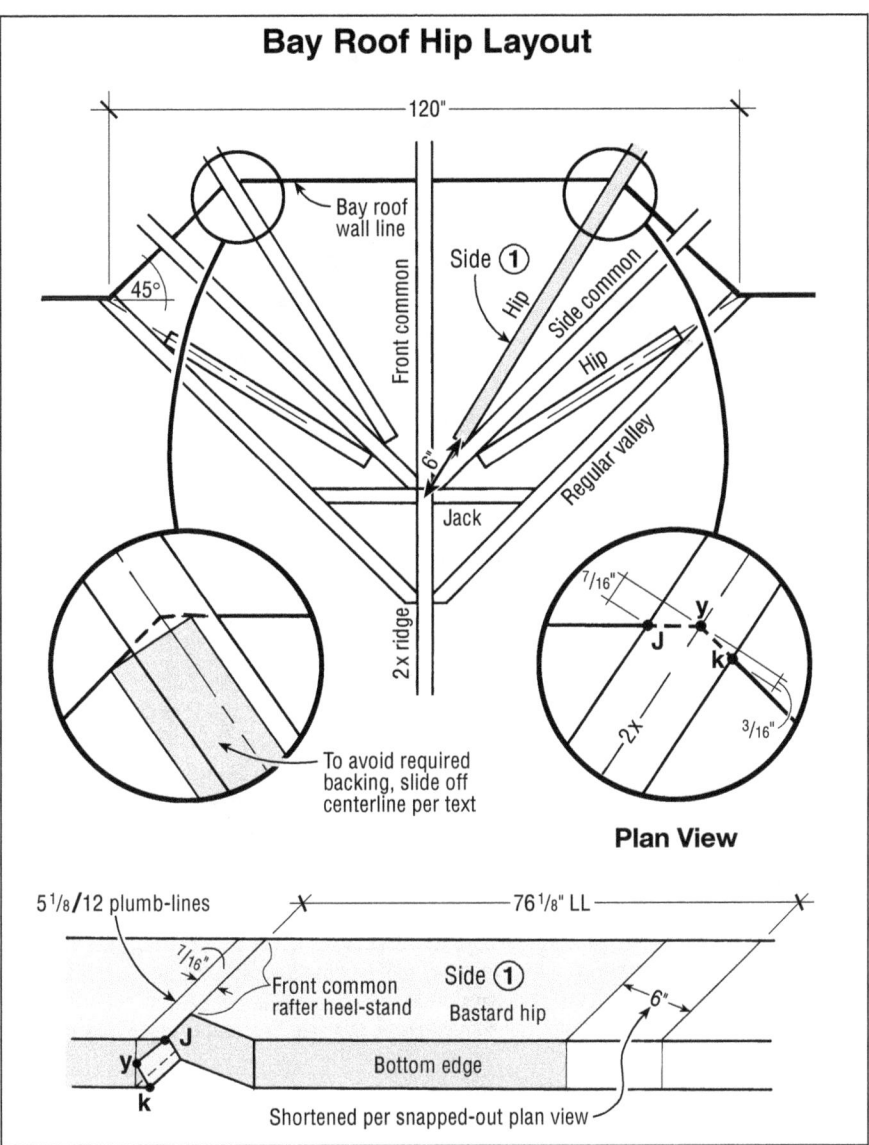

Figure 11-4. As with all bastard hip situations, the difference between the heel-stand at **j** and **k** must be 1/8 in. or less, otherwise the hips should be backed or slid off centerline. The bastard hips are shortened per the snapped-out plan view and square-cut plumb (unless exposed) to stack as shown.

In style **A**, the hips are shortened 3 7/8 in. per the snapped-out plan view and square-cut plumb to stack between the commons. Mathematically, the number of converging rafters multiplied by their width and divided by 6.28 (2π) equals the radius to shorten ([16 × 1 1/2"] ÷ 6.28 = 3 7/8"). In style **B**, the hips are shortened per the snapped-out plan view so a square-cut end (if not

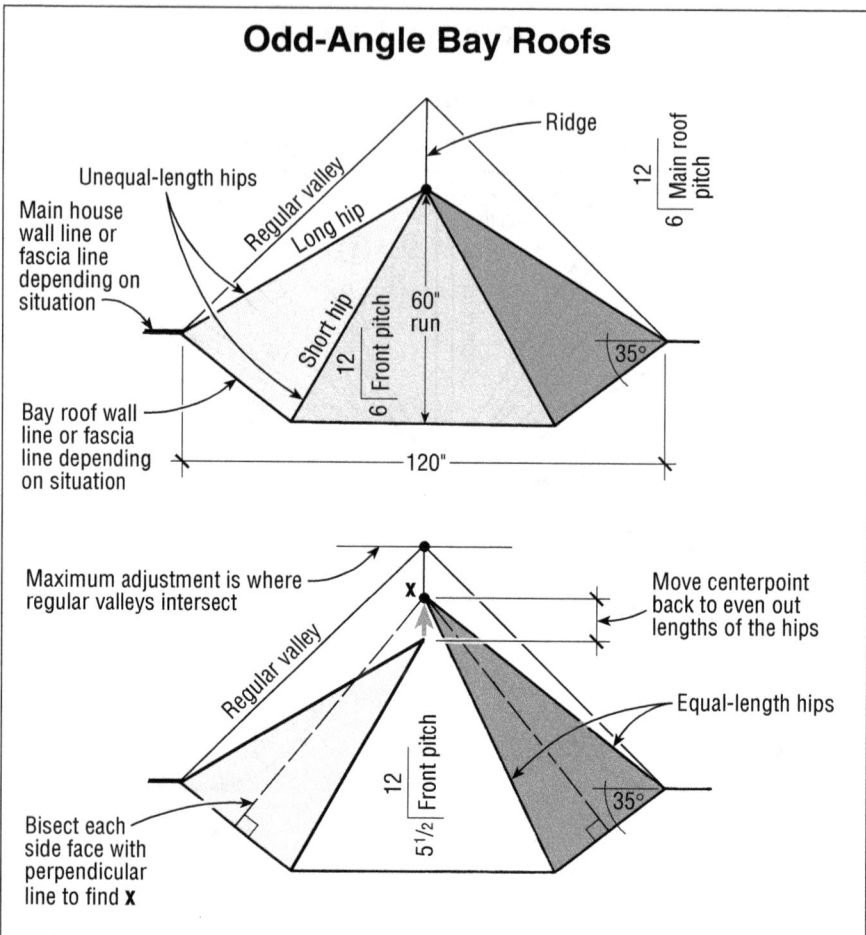

Figure 11-5. When the departure angle of the bay roof is other than 45°, the inside and outside hips will be different lengths to keep the bays' front roof pitch equal to the main roof pitch. If this isn't paramount, the centerpoint can sometimes be adjusted in or out to allow the hips to be of equal length.

exposed) will nail to the off-pitch common rafter originating from each side wall and will remain on its centerline as shown in ***Figure 11-4***. An optional construction method for both styles is to leave out the center king commons on each side, run the hip rafters full-length to the ridge, and use jack fill alone to complete each side (see Photo 11-2).

Lay out the hip birdsmouth by marking the heel-stand of the front common at **J** (Figure 11-4), and draw a level seat-cut line through this point. In style **A**, both heel-stands will be the same, while in style **B**, the heel-stand for the side off-pitch commons is taken from the plumb height at **k** on the hip birdsmouth. On most unequal bays of this type, the variation between the heel-stands at **J** and **k** is negligible, unless the pitch difference is extreme. If it is more than 1/8 in., the hips should be backed (or slid off-center as shown in Chapter 8). Square-cut the hip's heel-cut at the LL mark for 2x material. Larger stock may require a chisel or chainsaw to make the V-notch.

Whereas in 45° bay roofs the hips were all the same length, bay roofs with a departure angle other than 45° will have two different-length hips on each side to keep the bay's front roof pitch equal to the main roof's pitch. This all gets sorted out in the snapped-out plan view.

If matching the bay's front pitch to the main roof pitch is not paramount, the centerpoint can sometimes be adjusted in or out to allow all the hips to be of equal length. The "new" centerpoint is found by bisecting both departure sides with a perpendicular line and marking the intersection (**x**) as shown in *Figure 11-5*. To stay with regular valleys at the intersection to the main roof, the rise at the centerpoint is still found using half the bay roof span together with the main roof RR ratio. All the rafters including the commons must be calculated using rise/run and rise/hip-travel equations for LL, with proportions used to solve for roof pitch.

BAY WINDOW ROOFS AGAINST A WALL

Anytime a bay roof frames to a wall, think of it as a parallel slice from a polygon. Therefore, the common 45° bay to a wall shown in *Figure 11-6* is a parallel slice from an octagon and is solved accordingly using the relationships outlined in Figures 10-5 and 10-9. Although a snapped-out plan view may not always be necessary, it is nice to have one available for verification. Divide the obtuse angle geometrically as illustrated in *Figure 11-7* by marking points equidistant from the corner in each direction, then from these points swinging two equal-radius arcs to intersect, and finally drawing a line from the corner through their intersection.

As shown in Figure 11-6:
1. The common rafters off the front are calculated using the effective run to the ledger ridge (34 1/2").
2. The ledger-ridge length equals the front bay dimension less twice the result of the tangent of 22 1/2° multiplied by the effective run.
3. The ledger hips are actually regular hips (only in a 45° bay) and are calculated by multiplying the effective run by the appropriate H/V LL ratio. Mark the hip rafter LL on the side of the rafter from **a** to **c** as shown. The heel-stand dimension of the front common rafters is set at **c**, while the heel-cut angle opens from **c** at 45°. Square-cut the hips plumb at the head-cut to butt to the end of ledger ridge **a-b**.
4. Calculate the bastard hip's travel (**a-d**) by multiplying the effective run to the ledger ridge by the secant of 22 1/2°
5. Calculate the rise to the ledger ridge by multiplying the effective run by the appropriate RR ratio.
6. Using these two measurements (rise from #4 and hip travel from #5), solve for the bastard hip length using the Pythagorean theorem.

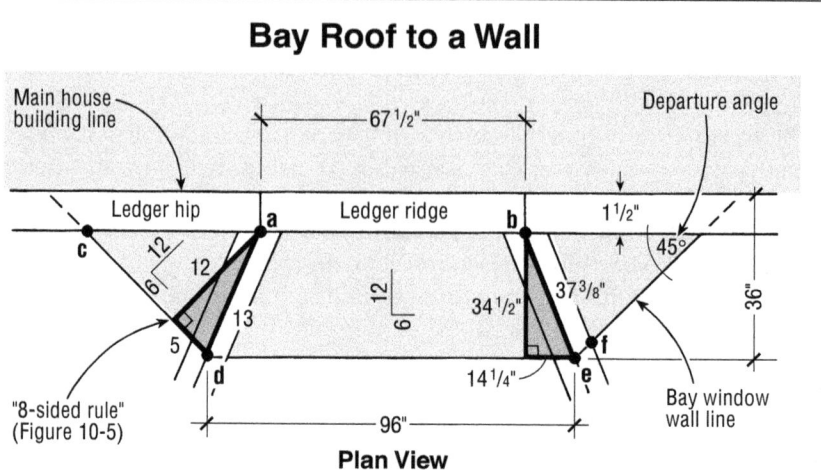

Bay Roof to a Wall

Plan View

Method:

1. Effective run × COM LL ratio = front common rafter LL
2. Front face **d-e** – 2 (effective run × tangent of ½ departure angle) = ledger ridge **a-b**
3. Effective run × H/V LL ratio = ledger hip **a-c** *45° bay only*
4. Effective run × secant of ½ departure angle = bastard hip travel **a-d**
5. Effective run × RR ratio = rise at **a**
6. (Rise at **a**)² + (bastard hip travel **a-d**)² = (bastard hip LL)²
7. ½ thk. bastard hip × tangent ½ departure angle = uphill heel-cut line
8. Octagon bay roof hip pitch = $\dfrac{\text{unit roof rise}}{13}$ (per Figure 10-5)

Example:

1. 34½" × 1.1180 {6/12 COM LL ratio} = 38½"
2. 96" – 2(34½" × .4142 {tangent of 22½°, Chart 5}) = 67½"
3. 34½" × 1.5000 {6/12 H/V LL ratio} = 51¾" *45° bay only*
4. 34½" × 1.0824 {secant 22½°, Chart 5} = 37⅜"
5. 34½" × .5000 {6/12 RR ratio} = 17¼"
6. (17¼")² + (37⅜")² = (41⅛")²
7. ¾" × .4142 {tangent 22½°, Chart 5} = ¼"
8. $\dfrac{6}{13}$ or converted to $\dfrac{\text{unknown}}{12}$ for use with a rafter square

Figure 11-6. A 45° bay window roof to a wall is a parallel slice from an octagon and can be solved with a full-size snapped-out plan view or the trigonometric relationships shown in Figures 10-5 and 10-9.

See Appendix B

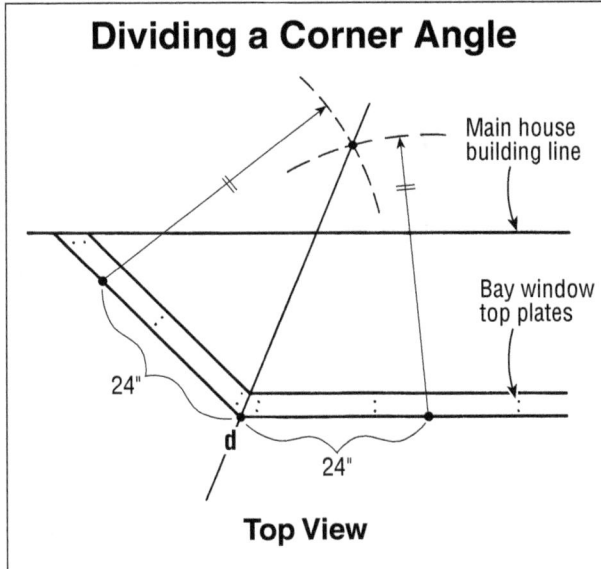

Figure 11-7. Divide the obtuse corner angle in a bay roof window by measuring the same distance from the corner along each wall and swinging two equidistant arcs to intersect.

7. The uphill plumb-lines for the bastard hip heel-cut lines are found by first multiplying 1/2 thk. of the bastard hip with the tangent of 22 1/2° and then marking this amount perpendicular to the lower rafter LL plumb-line. The heel-stand of the front commons is marked at **f** on the bastard hip. The bastard hip head-cut is made at 22 1/2° centered on the uphill LL line. Jack fill for the **c-d** side walls are regular hip jacks cut with a standard 45° cheek-cut to nail to the ledger hips.

Bays to a wall with other angles of departure are figured similarly, but usually require a snapped-out plan view. The ledger hips will always be bastards when the angle of departure is anything other than 45°. Therefore a **rise/hip-travel** equation must be used to calculate the LL with a proportion applied to find the hip's pitch.

Chapter 12

Other Miscellaneous Roofs

EQUAL-PITCH ROOFS FROM VARYING PLATE HEIGHTS

Figure 12-1 illustrates the method used to calculate rafter lengths for an equal-pitch roof that originates from opposing outside walls of different heights. Start by dividing the difference in wall heights (120"– 96" = 24") by the RR ratio to calculate how much run at the given roof pitch is attributable to that rise (24" ÷ .5000 {6/12 RR ratio} = 48" or 4').

Next, add this run dimension (4 ft.) to the 24-ft. span to create a "phantom" 8-ft. wall outside the 10-ft. wall, and calculate the left-side rafter lengths originating from the 8-ft. wall using the "new" 28-ft. span. For the right-side rafters originating from the 10-ft. wall, subtract the run dimension (4 ft.) from the 24-ft. span to create a "phantom" 10-ft. wall inside the 8-ft. wall and calculate the rafter lengths using the "new" 20-ft. span.

MATCHING RIDGE HEIGHTS

The difference in wall heights for equal-pitch roofs of varying spans framed to a common ridge height is calculated as shown in *Figure 12-2*. Take one-half the difference between the two spans and multiply by the appropriate RR ratio to find the wall height change.

In Figure 12-2, valleys for the smaller-span roof are cut tailless at **a** and **b** (45° single cheek-cut centered on the downhill LL mark) to sit on the taller walls where the walls carry through to the inside of the building. Otherwise, the connection is handled as shown in the Chapter 9 section, "Gable and Hip Dormers," page 189, by nailing the lower end of the valley where the

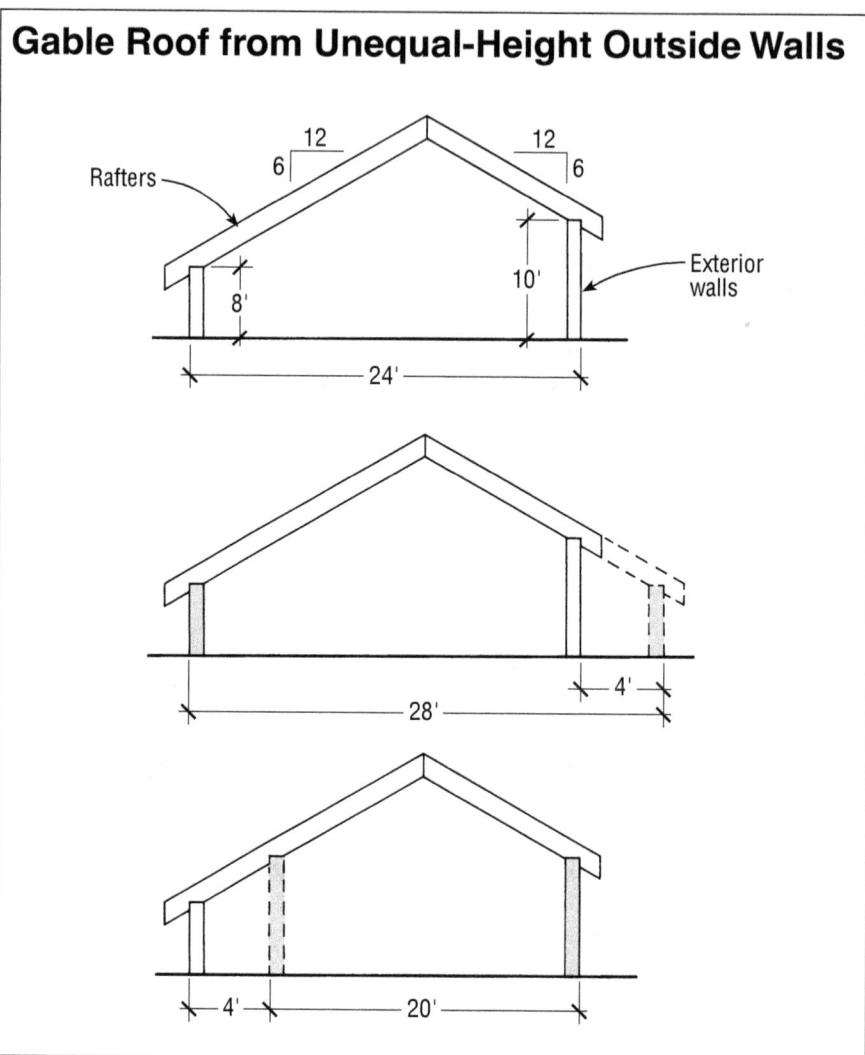

Figure 12-1. Rafter lengths for an equal-pitch gable roof from varying plate heights are calculated by creating two equal-height "phantom" wall situations to find the theoretical span for rafters on each side of the ridge. See Appendix B

center of the top edge planes into the last main roof common rafter nailed against the stepped-up walls (see Photo 5-11).

PARALLEL-ROOF CALIFORNIA-CUTS

Figure 12-3 demonstrates the method used to find the California-cut when one of two parallel equal-pitched roofs overlaps the other. Using a framing square, draw a level line for the given pitch across the board (**x-y**), bisect that

Matching Ridge Heights on Equal-Pitch Roofs

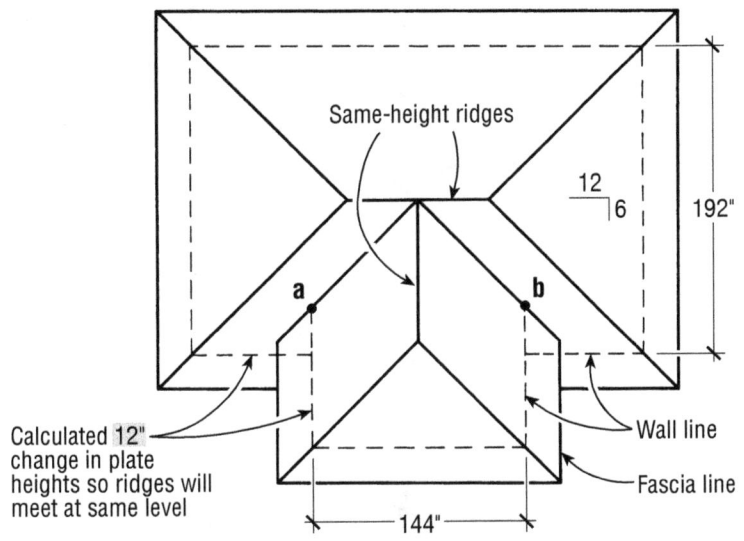

Method:

1. Major span – minor span = span difference
2. Span difference ÷ 2 = run
3. Run × RR ratio = change in plate height

Example:

1. 192" – 144" = 48"
2. 48" ÷ 2 = 24"
3. 24" × .5000 {6/12 RR ratio} = 12"

Figure 12-2. Match ridge heights for equal-pitch roofs of varying widths by dividing the span difference in half and multiplying by the RR ratio to calculate the difference in plate heights.

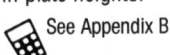 See Appendix B

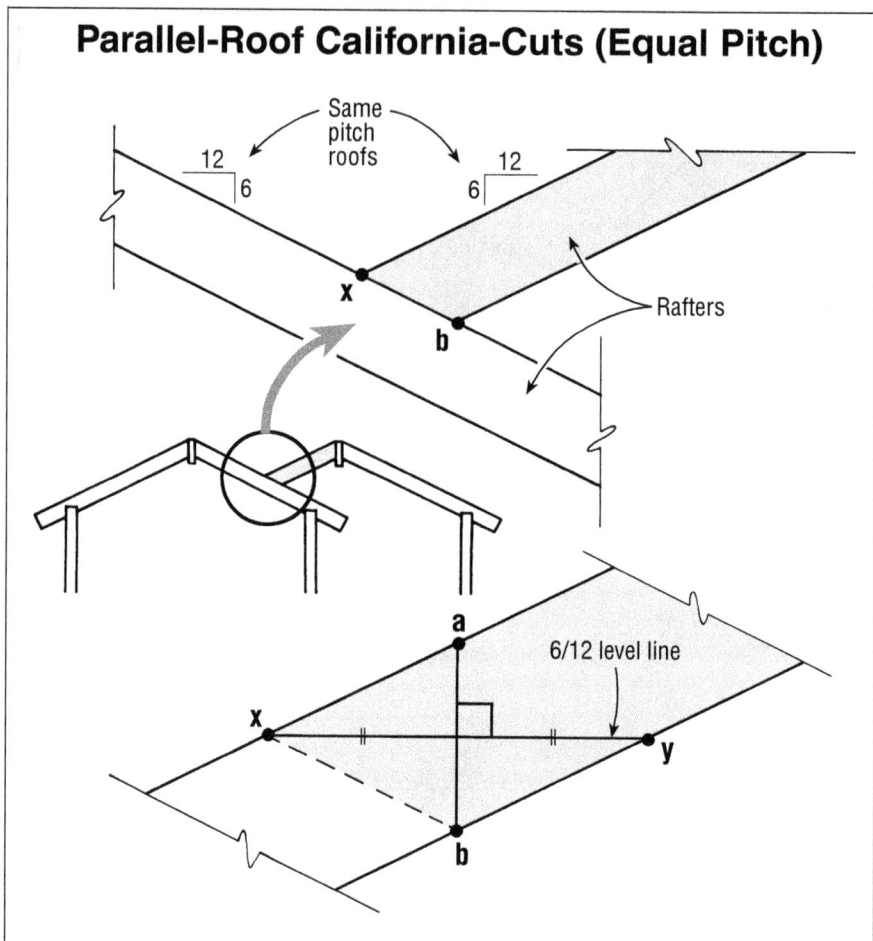

Figure 12-3. For a same-pitch parallel-roof California-cut: Bisect the roof's level line with a plumb-line, and connect the two ends across the board.

line with a plumb-line (**a-b**), and connect the ends of the two lines as shown (**x-b**). Make the cut with the saw set square.

Figure 12-4 illustrates the same type of intersection, but here the two parallel roofs have different pitches. Draw level line **x-y** at the pitch of the intersect*ING* roof, but instead of bisecting the line, measure over 12 in. from **x** and draw a plumb-line (**c-d**). On this line, measure down the pitch of the intersect*ED* roof and extend a line from **x** through this point to create line **x-e**.

If either of the above two situations involved a broken hip California-framed onto a parallel roof, the same procedure to lay out the California-

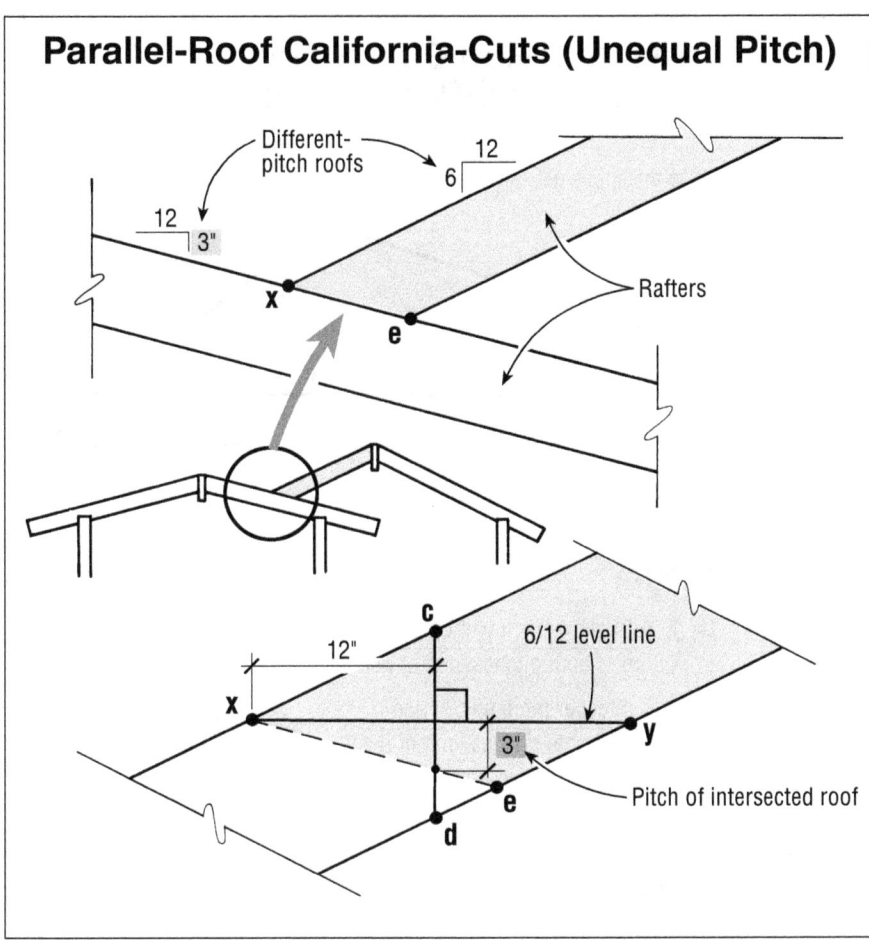

Figure 12-4. For a two-pitch parallel-roof California-cut: Draw a plumb-line 12 in. over on the intersecting roof level line, then measure down the intersected roof pitch and connect this point back to the start of the level line.

cut along the side of the rafter would apply as shown in Figure 12-3 and Figure 12-4, except the level line is made for the pitch of the hip rafter rather than for that of the common rafter. Also, the 3-in. rise measurement in Figure 12-4 would be placed at 17 in. (unit of hip travel) rather than the unit of roof run as illustrated. For the equal-pitch situation, cut the bevel angle along the bottom of the board to bear on the intersected roof's sheathing with the same angle that would be used to back a hip/valley for that pitch (Chart 6, Appendix A). When making the California-cut on a broken hip placed in the unequal-pitch situation of Figure 12-4, set the saw's bevel angle using the procedures outlined in Figure 8-28, or make a quick scribe as shown in Figure 8-26.

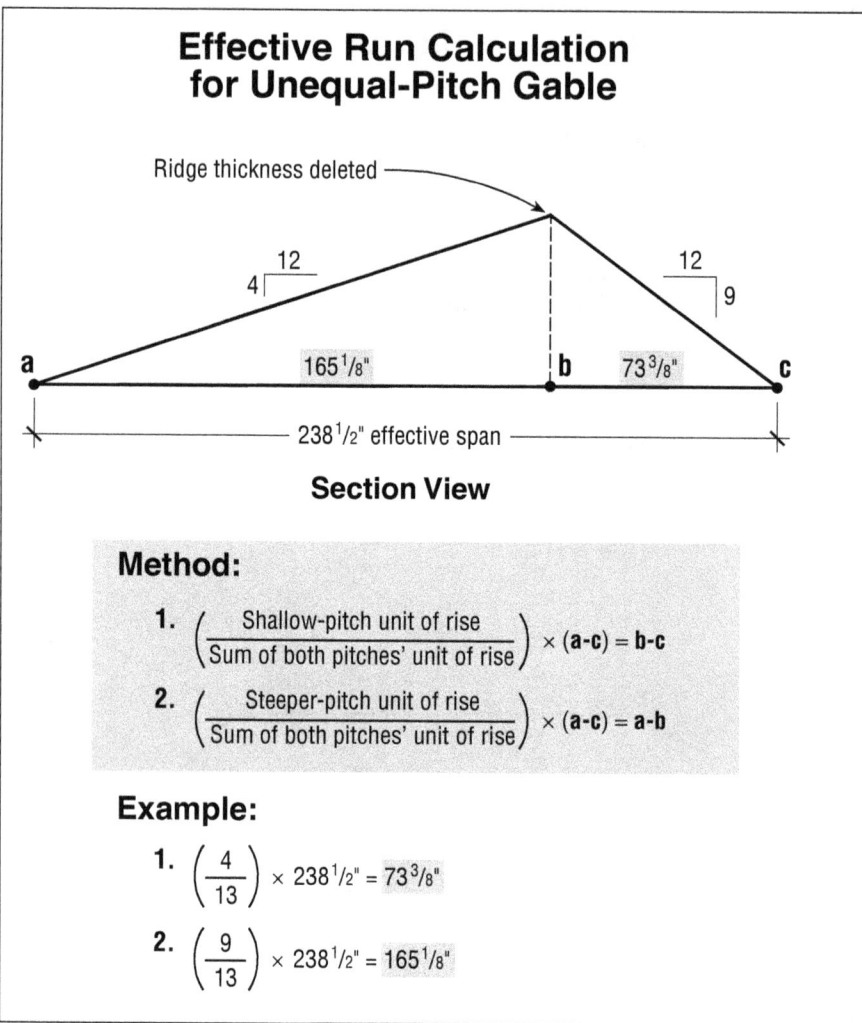

Figure 12-5. Use proportions representing the rise of each pitch set over the sum of both to calculate the effective run for each side of the unequal-pitch gable (or the common-rafter center section of the similar-style bastard hip roof).

UNEQUAL-PITCH GABLES

Unless you are given the centerpoint for an unequal-pitch gable, you must find the intersection of the two roof pitches at the ridge by snapping a section view on the floor or using the proportions shown in *Figure 12-5*. The "a-c" measurement is the effective span dimension (span less the thickness of the ridge). To use the proportions, the heel-stands and wall heights for both pitches must be the same, otherwise any difference must be transformed into a run measurement and added/subtracted to the effective span dimension for calculation purposes only. For example, in Figure 12-5, if the

246   CHAPTER 12

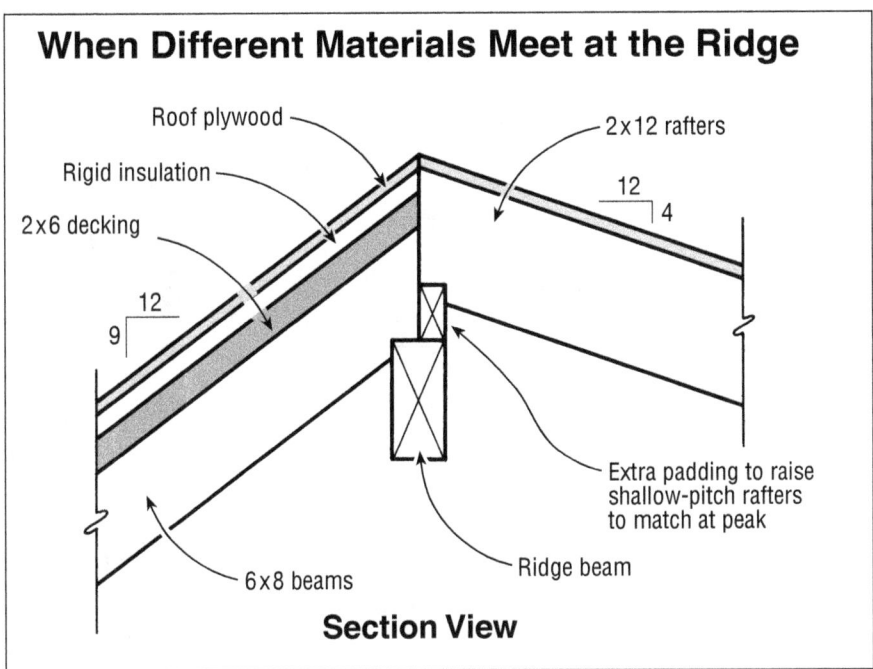

Figure 12-6. When confronted with an equal- or unequal-pitch ridge connection that joins many different materials, always draw it out to scale on plywood to determine how much to adjust the birdsmouths and/or the ridge beam height so everything will meet at the peak.

heel-stand or wall height on the 9/12 side is $1^{1}/_{2}$ in. taller, the effective span would be increased by 2 in. ($1^{1}/_{2}$" ÷ .7500 {9/12 RR ratio} = 2") so both roof planes generate from the same horizontal level (the top of the 4/12 heel-stand in this case). The proportion calculations would then be made using $240^{1}/_{2}$ in. instead of the $238^{1}/_{2}$ in. shown, and the 2-in. increase would be subtracted from the resulting steep-side run before converting it into an LL measurement. (For more detail, refer back to "An Equal-Pitch Roof from Varying Plate Heights" at the beginning of this chapter).

When confronted with a ridge connection similar to ***Figure 12-6***, either equal or unequal pitch, always draw a section view to scale on plywood to determine how much to adjust the birdsmouths and/or ridge beam height to allow the two different pitches and materials to meet at the peak.

CANTILEVER EAVES

Sometimes for various reasons it is necessary to turn and cantilever the rafters over the exterior rake wall ***(Figure 12-7)***. In this type of situation, the rake wall should be framed to the exact height without the $^{1}/_{4}$-in. play described in Chapter 1 (check the floor where the wall will be stood for any up-and-downs). The typical 2:1 cantilever ratio applies here unless metal connectors are used to counter the uplift force.

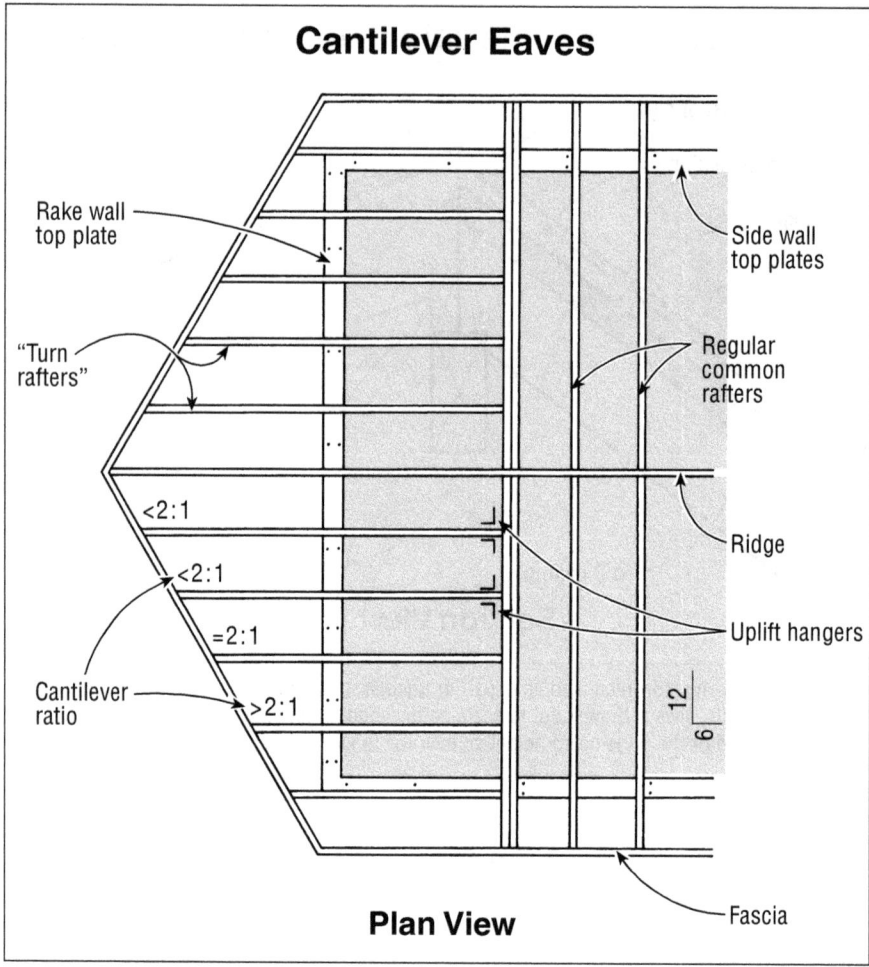

Figure 12-7. Sometimes it is necessary to turn and cantilever the rafters over the exterior rake wall. The typical 2:1 cantilever ratio applies here unless metal connectors are used to counter the uplift force.

"Turn-rafters" that connect to a regular valley inside the building and extend out over a gable end are cut with the same miter degree and side-cut angle as illustrated for square-hung fascia (Figure 7-3, **A** and **B**).

COMMON RAFTERS ACROSS AN ANGLED WALL

The odd-angle rake wall at the clipped corner of a gable end or any other similar situation is set up and framed like a rake wall (see Chapter 1), only the top plates are handled slightly differently. The wall should be framed to an exact height without allowing for any free-play. When the building corner is clipped at 45° as illustrated in **Figure 12-8**, it is identical to a hip/valley, and all calculations are greatly simplified. Substitute the degree

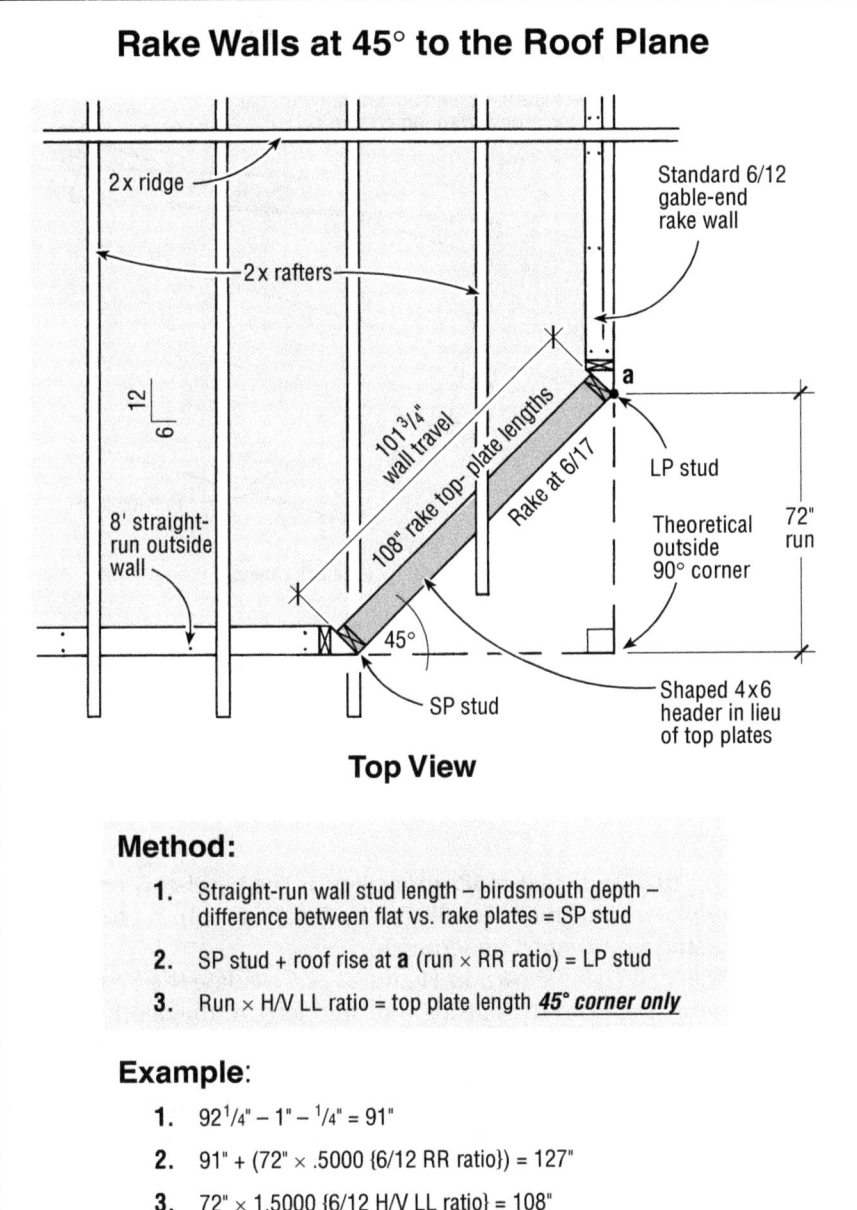

Rake Walls at 45° to the Roof Plane

Top View

Method:

1. Straight-run wall stud length − birdsmouth depth − difference between flat vs. rake plates = SP stud
2. SP stud + roof rise at **a** (run × RR ratio) = LP stud
3. Run × H/V LL ratio = top plate length **45° corner only**

Example:

1. $92\frac{1}{4}" - 1" - \frac{1}{4}" = 91"$
2. $91" + (72" \times .5000 \{6/12 \text{ RR ratio}\}) = 127"$
3. $72" \times 1.5000 \{6/12 \text{ H/V LL ratio}\} = 108"$

Figure 12-8. When a building corner is clipped on a gable roof at a departure angle of 45°, the resulting rake wall is similar to a hip/valley. Use the degree equivalent for that particular roof's hip/valley as the bevel-cut on studs and the ends of the top plates. Multiply the wall's run (not diagonal length) by the H/V LL ratio to find the length of the top plates.

OTHER MISCELLANEOUS ROOFS

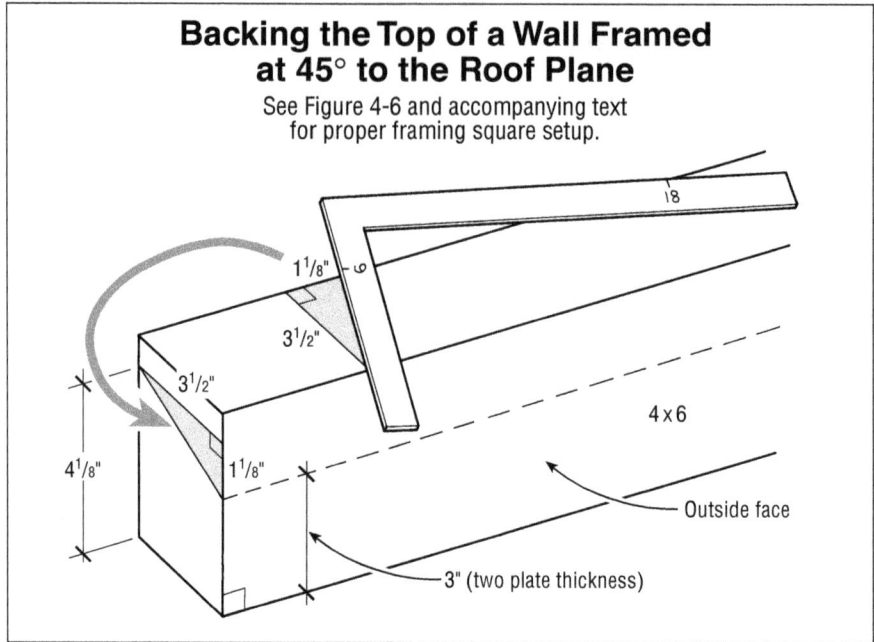

Figure 12-9. Substitute a backed 4x6 for the two top plates on an angled wall. The rip-cut line for the outside face on the 4x6 would be 3 in. (thickness of two plates) up from the bottom edge measured square, while the rip-cut line for the inside face would be 4 1/8 in. up (the front 3" + 1 1/8" from 6/18 across the header width). The rip-angle would be 18 1/2° for a 6/12 roof from Chart 6, Appendix A.

equivalence for that particular roof's hip/valley as the bevel-cuts on the studs and top plates (imagine this wall as a backed beam hip set below the rafters with a stud wall framed underneath).

Plate the wall exactly as shown in Figure 12-8. Calculate the SP stud length by subtracting from the outside wall stud length: the depth of the common rafter birdsmouth and the difference between the thickness of the straight-wall top plates versus the plumb thickness of the angled-wall top plates. The LP stud is found by multiplying the run of the angled wall (horizontal distance from the outside theoretical 90° corner = 72") with the appropriate RR ratio and adding the result to the SP stud. Top plate length is calculated by multiplying the wall run by the H/V LL ratio. Studs are bevel-cut at the pitch of the hip/valley or 19 1/2° for a 6/12 pitch roof (bevel angle taken from a rafter square set to H/V, or use trig).

Now instead of installing the two top plates, substitute a full-length 4x6 header that has been backed on the top edge (4x6 for a 2x4 wall, 6x6 for a 2x6 wall). To make this bevel-cut, scribe a rip-cut line along the outside surface, two plate thickness up from the bottom edge, and rip the header with a beam saw set to the backing pitch of a hip/valley (18 1/2° for a 6/12 pitch roof, Chart 6, Appendix A). ***Figure 12-9*** illustrates how to find the rip-line for the backside of the header when it is necessary to make a finishing cut

Figure 12-10. Double-frame the gable-end kick-ups California-style when drywall will be installed to the underside of the main rafters in a Swiss Chalet style roof.

due to insufficient blade depth on the front pass. (For more detail, see the Chapter 4 section, "Backing a Hip," page 67.) This bevel-cut creates a surface for the rafters to sit on similar to installing a wedge-shaped filler piece to the top of a wall when running wood I-joist rafters with no birdsmouth notches. To keep the rafters from sliding downhill, metal framing clips installed from the rafter to the wall are a good idea—especially on steeper pitches. Vertical blocks that are run between the rafters on top of the angled wall are marked with H/V plumb-lines and cut at 45°.

When a clipped building corner has a departure angle other than 45°, the pitch of the rake walls must be determined with a rise/wall-travel-to unknown-roof-pitch/12 proportion as shown throughout Chapter 8. Additionally, the rip-angle for the 4x6 top plate header must be found by making a level cut at the wall pitch on a scrap of 4x beam and placing it along the angled wall snap-lines so the inside leading edge aligns with the front wall snap-line. Mark the opposite side of the beam scrap where the front wall snap-line carries through (see Figure 9-13). Use the perpendicular measurement from the top edge of the beam scrap down to the "mark" together with the beam scrap thickness as legs of a right triangle. Then find the angle shown using a Speed® Square or protractor.

Another way to frame this type of wall is to stick-frame it after the rafters are up, using a temporary purlin to support the rafters across the angled section until completed.

SWISS CHALET-STYLE ROOFS

Swiss Chalet roofs sometimes have a kick-up on each end of the gable. This can be framed in two ways. In *Figure 12-10*, the kick-ups have been

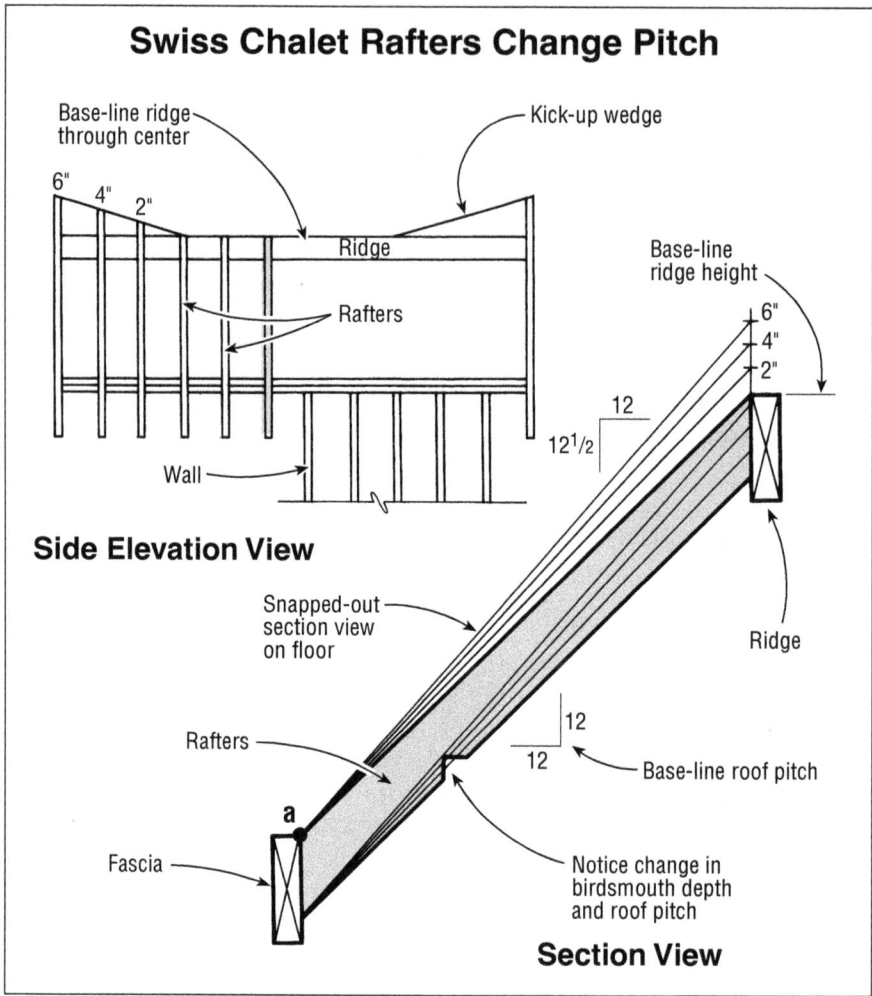

Figure 12-11. A Swiss Chalet roof that frames to a kick-up wedge is snapped out on the ground in the section view. Snap the affected rafters from the fascia line through to their raised position at the ridge, noting the changes in birdsmouth depth, LL, and pitch.

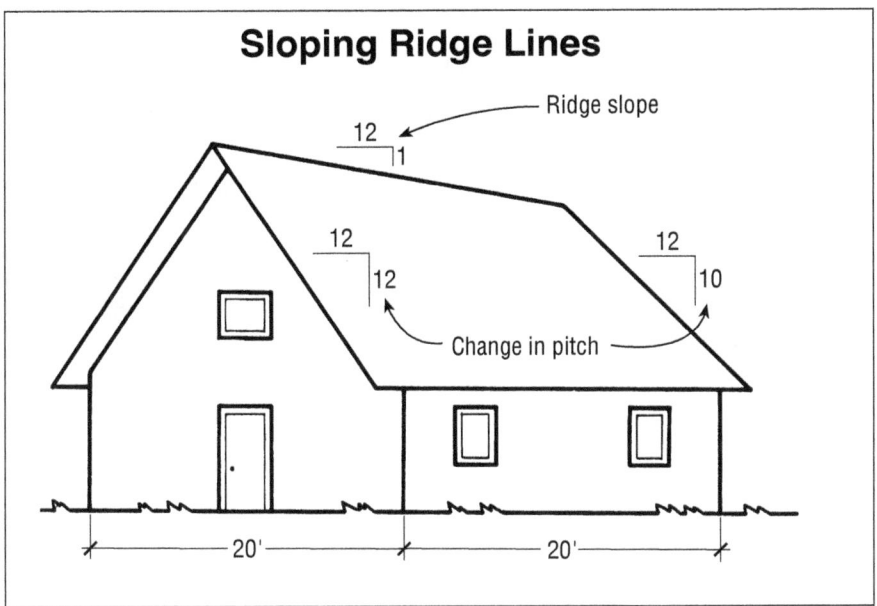

Figure 12-12. Each pair of opposing rafters will be a slightly different length and pitch from the adjacent pair on a roof that has a sloping ridge due to a change in roof pitch from one end of the building to the other. Snap out a section view on the floor with all rafters generating from the fascia line.

California-framed on top of the main roof. This allows drywall to be installed on the underside of the rafters for a straight-through cathedral-type ceiling. In *Figure 12-11*, the roof ends actually slope up. Kick-up wedges are attached to the main ridge, and special rafters are cut to accommodate the change in height and pitch. On the floor, snap out a full-size section view showing each rafter located in the kick-up section to find the new LL, pitch, and birdsmouth depth. The snap-lines should all generate from the fascia line.

This same method can be used to frame a roof with a ridge designed to slope uphill (slightly) due to a change in roof pitch from one end of the building to the other (as illustrated in *Figure 12-12*). Another option is to "turn" the rafters to span from one outside rake wall to the other and run them like floor joists similar to what's shown in Figure 12-7.

GAMBREL ROOFS

Different methods for framing a Gambrel roof are illustrated in *Figure 12-13*. Method **A** uses fabricated bent rafters, **B** uses ridge and purlin beams, **C** uses a mid-height ridge and collar ties, **D** uses angled walls and ceiling joists, **E** and **F** use cantilever floor joists, and **G** uses an inset pony wall.

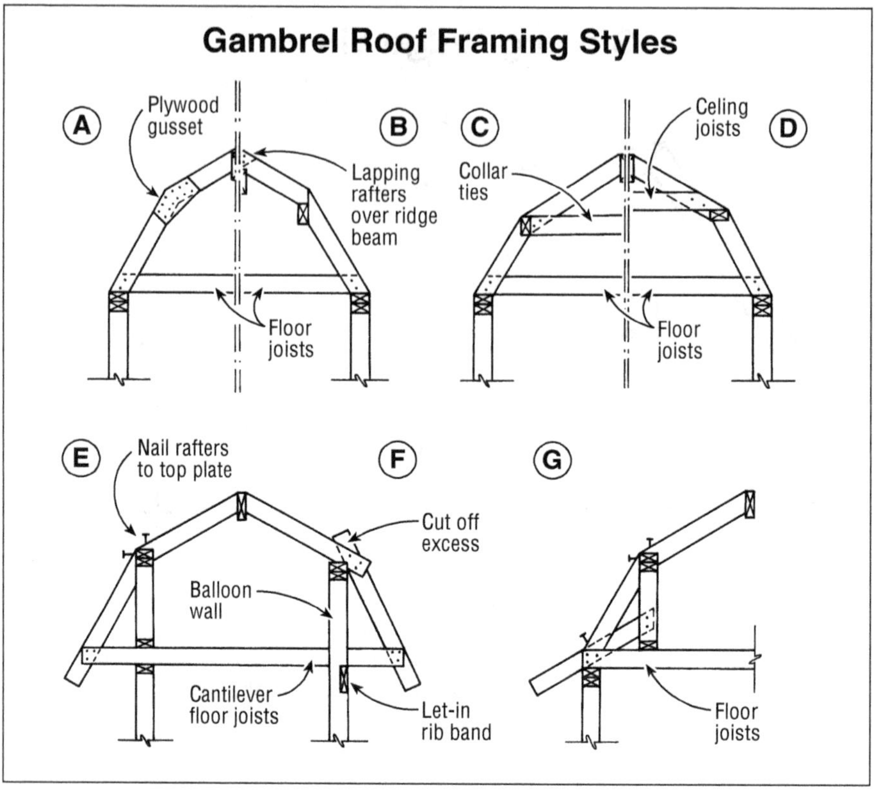

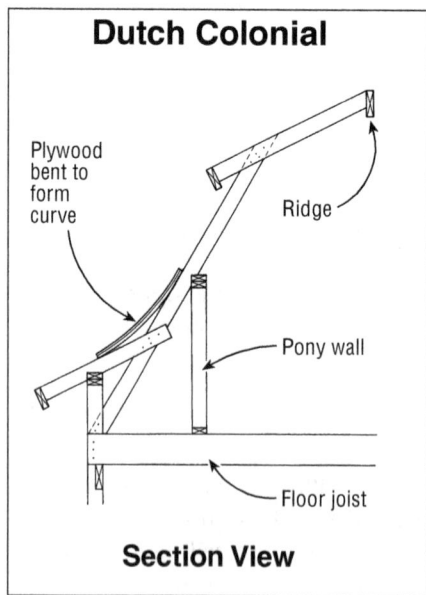

Figure 12-13. The Gambrel roof can be framed in many different ways: **A** uses fabricated bent rafters; **B** uses ridge and purlin beams; **C** uses a mid-height ridge and collar ties; **D** uses angled walls and ceiling joists; **E** and **F** use cantilevered floor joists; and **G** uses an inset pony wall.

Figure 12-14. The Dutch Colonial is basically a variation of the Gambrel design.

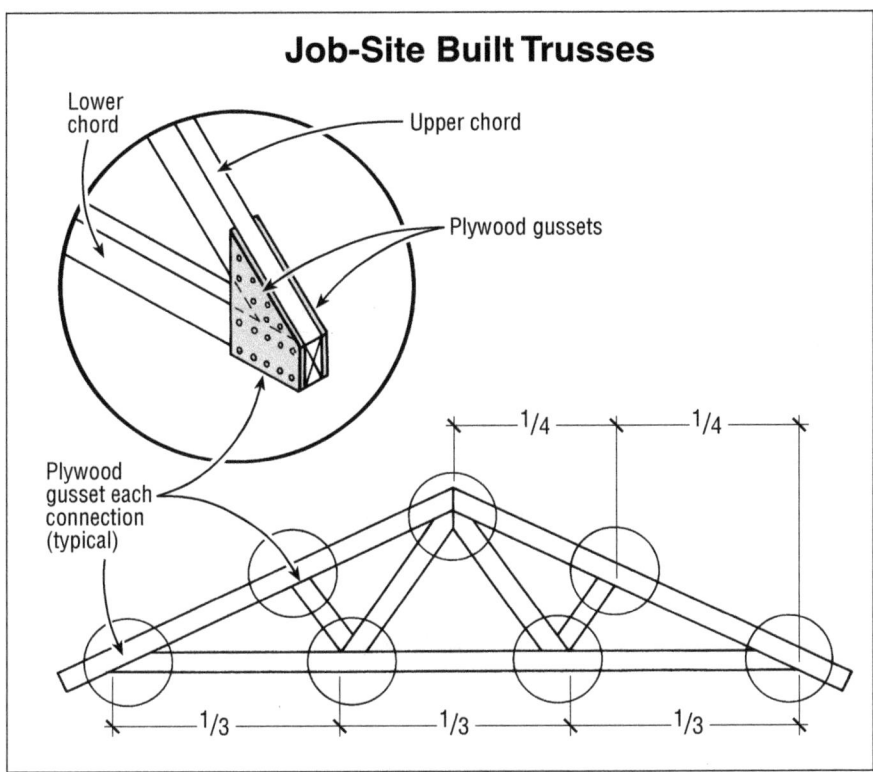

Figure 12-15. Snap a job-built truss in a section view on the subfloor. Nail short 2x4s to create an assembly jig. Divide the joist span into thirds and the rafter span into quarters for a W-truss.

The Dutch Colonial shown in *Figure 12-14* is basically a takeoff from the Gambrel design.

SITE-MADE TRUSSES

Figure 12-15 depicts a typical roof truss you can build on the job using plywood gussets. This is a W-truss. The joist span is divided into thirds and the rafter span into quarters. Unless a portable truss assembly jig is available, snap the truss design on the floor, and make your own jig using blocks nailed to the floor for positioning all the precut pieces until one side of the plywood gussets are installed. *Figure 12-16* shows a simple nail-together truss design.

Figure 12-17 is an example of a nail-in-place truss. The roof is conventionally stacked and then trussed in place. Use this method when a crane is not available to lift prefabricated trusses.

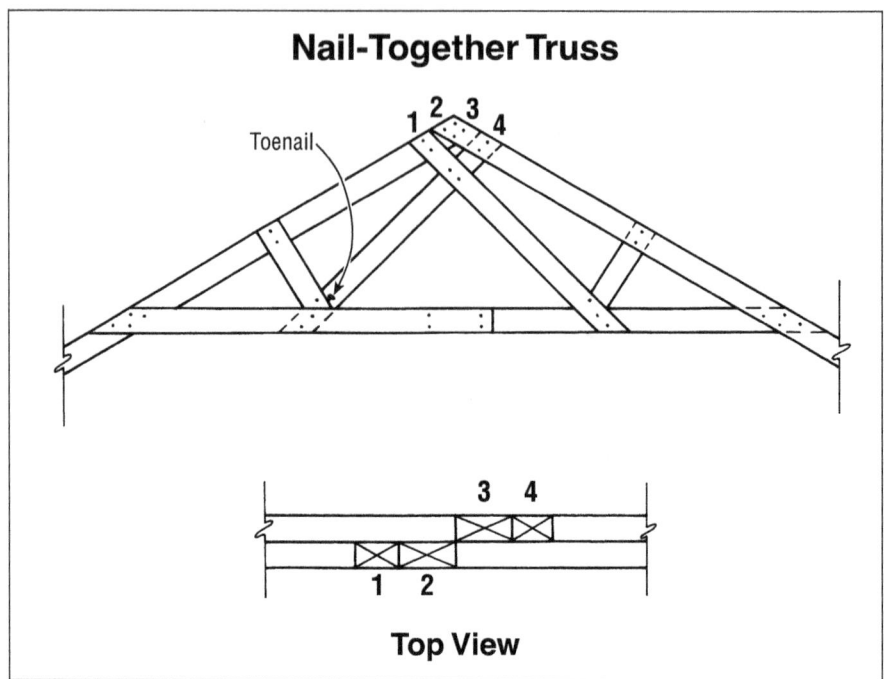

Figure 12-16. An alternative to plywood gussets for the W-truss is the nail-together method.

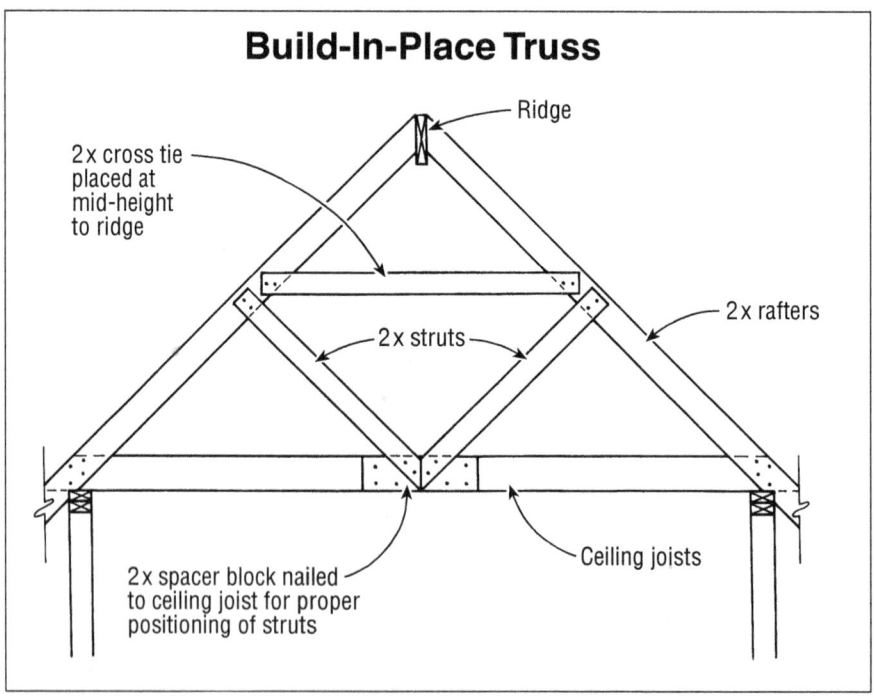

Figure 12-17. When a crane is not available to lift trusses, one option is to conventionally stack a roof and truss it in place.

Chapter 13

Beam Work

MISCELLANEOUS BEAM WORK

Figure 13-1 illustrates a method used to figure beam spacing across a room with or without end-beams against the wall.

Lightweight decorative non-structural ceiling beams can be installed without beam pockets in the wall as shown by ***Figure 13-2.*** Measure the inside span between the walls, and cut the beams 1/4 - 3/8 in. shorter. Nail heavy-duty straps (Simpson Strong-Tie® ST 6215 or similar) to each end centered on the top plates, and install a drywall spacer to the top edge of the beam. Raise the beam to the proper location, and nail the strap into the two top wall plates.

Figure 13-3 illustrates a hidden hanger. By cutting the hanger in above the lower edge of the beam, the bottom flange is hidden in the wood. The sides of the hanger are hidden by pressure blocks installed between the beams.

In ***Figure 13-4***, two different-style post-and-beam corners are illustrated. A miter-cut joint is often used when both sides of the beam are exposed. Two 1/2-in. rebar pins are drilled and driven into the post, and a heavy-duty strap is nailed over the top.

On exposed post-and-beam construction, slightly rout out the middle of the beam end that butts to another beam or forms a miter. This allows a handsaw pass to quickly clean up the joint when assembled since only the exposed edges are touching.

To keep a long drill bit plumb or level when drilling precision holes, stop and check the bit periodically with a short torpedo level. Always mark a through-bolt hole on both sides of the beam, and drill from each side.

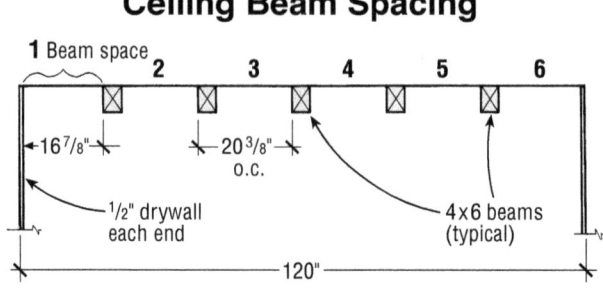

Figure 13-1. To space beams across a room, subtract all the beams and wall-covering thicknesses from the room width to find the actual clear space available, then divide that dimension by the number of spaces desired. The result is the space between beams.

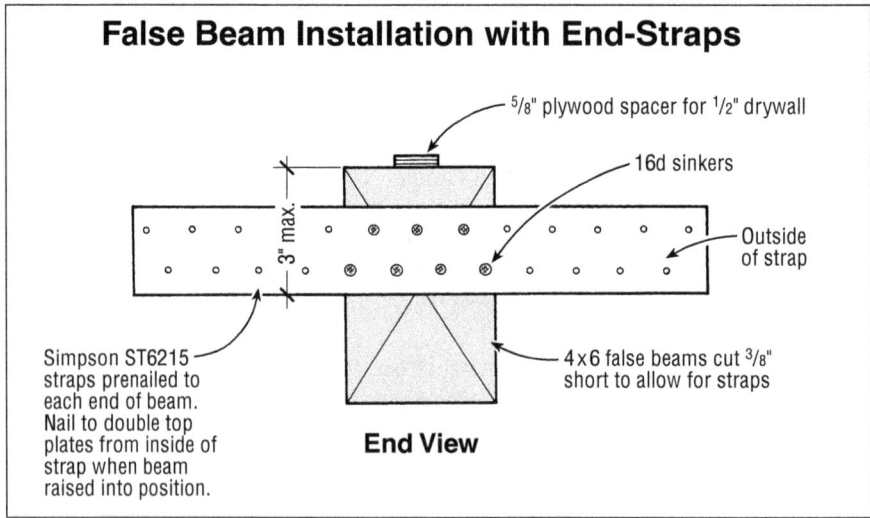

Figure 13-2. Lightweight decorative non-structural ceiling beams can be installed without wall beam pockets by using heavy-duty straps on each end nailed to the top plates.

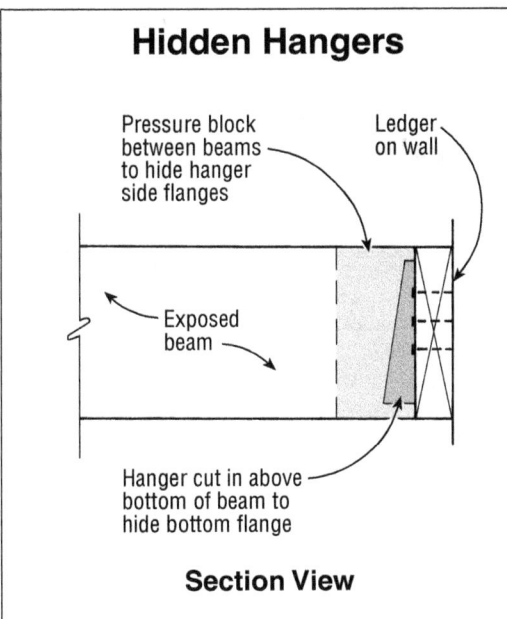

Figure 13-3. To hide a metal hanger on supported ceiling beams, install the hanger in a slice made 1/4 in. above the lower edge of the beam and a pressure block between the beams.

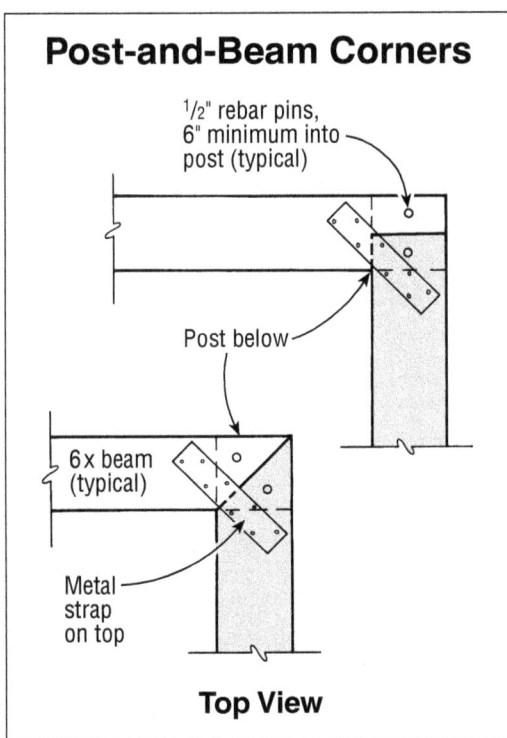

Figure 13-4. Miter or butt joints are the two most common beam corner connections. Use 1/2-in. rebar pins in the post and a strap over the top.

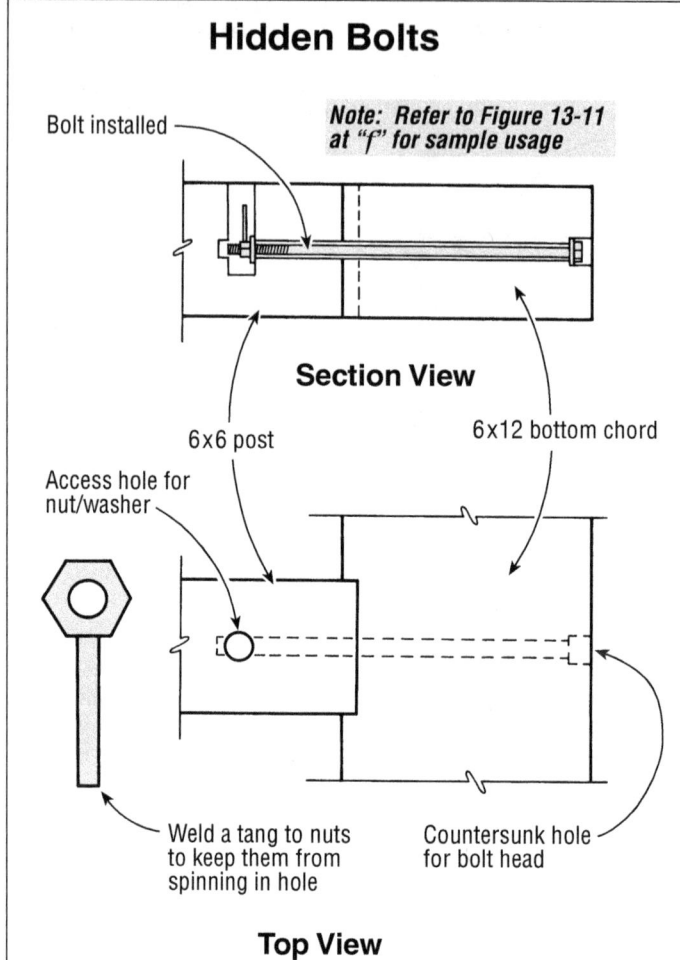

Figure 13-5. Hidden bolts are great for pulling beam intersections together. Size the exposed countersunk holes so they can be plugged later with 1 1/2-in. closet pole dowel.

A hidden bolt is shown in **Figure 13-5**. They are used to pull together beam intersections. By drilling straight down from the top with a large access hole, the nut and washer can be installed on the bolt. Keep the nut from rotating by using a screwdriver or needle-nose pliers, and tighten by turning the bolt. A metal tab welded to the nut is an excellent way to prevent it from spinning. Use a 1 1/2-in. bit for exposed holes so they can be plugged later with a short piece of 1 1/2-in. closet pole dowel.

Figure 13-6 illustrates two different wall beam pockets for structural rafter beams set below the main roof. In method **A**, both top plates have been cut out to receive the full beam. In method **B**, one or both top plates run through the pocket, and the beam is notched to fit under them. Method **B** can be used as long as the structural tapered area shown in Figure 2-22 is not infringed upon. If the beams are non-bearing, use the method

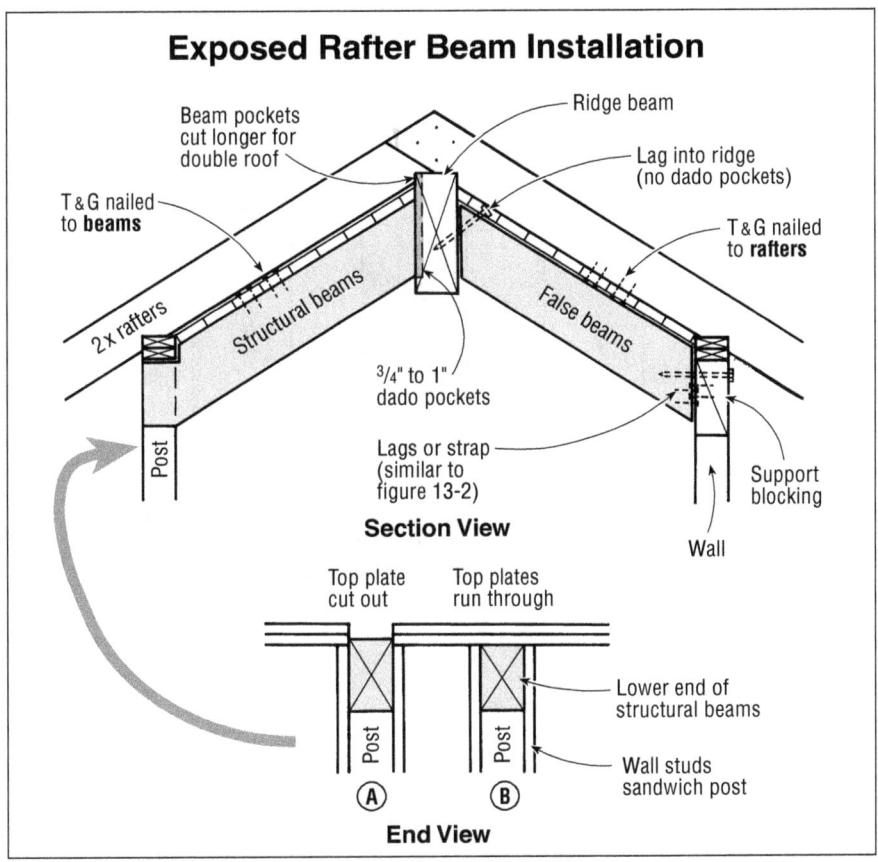

Figure 13-6. Decorative structural rafter beams require routered beam pockets at the ridge and support posts in the wall. Non-bearing beams can be cut to fit between the wall and ridge, and lagged or strapped in place.

from Figure 13-2 or run two lags through the plates from the other side.

Exposed rafter-beam-to-ridge-beam connections should be done using a ³⁄₄- to 1-in.-deep routered pocket at the ridge. Use a plywood jig as a router guide, and dado the pockets before lifting the ridge beam into place. Remember to allow for the router base when making the plywood beam-pocket jig *(Figure 13-7)*. Always run a strap over the ridge between the opposing rafter beams after they are stacked.

If rafter beams are held low to allow for a double roof (Figure 13-6), the ridge height is calculated as shown in Figure 3-13, and the beam pockets on the ridge are cut longer accordingly. Snapping or drawing a section view of the ridge and wall connections will help ensure that the correct pocket heights are found.

The math involved in calculating the height of an exposed ridge beam with rafter beams originating from the top of the exterior walls is explained in the

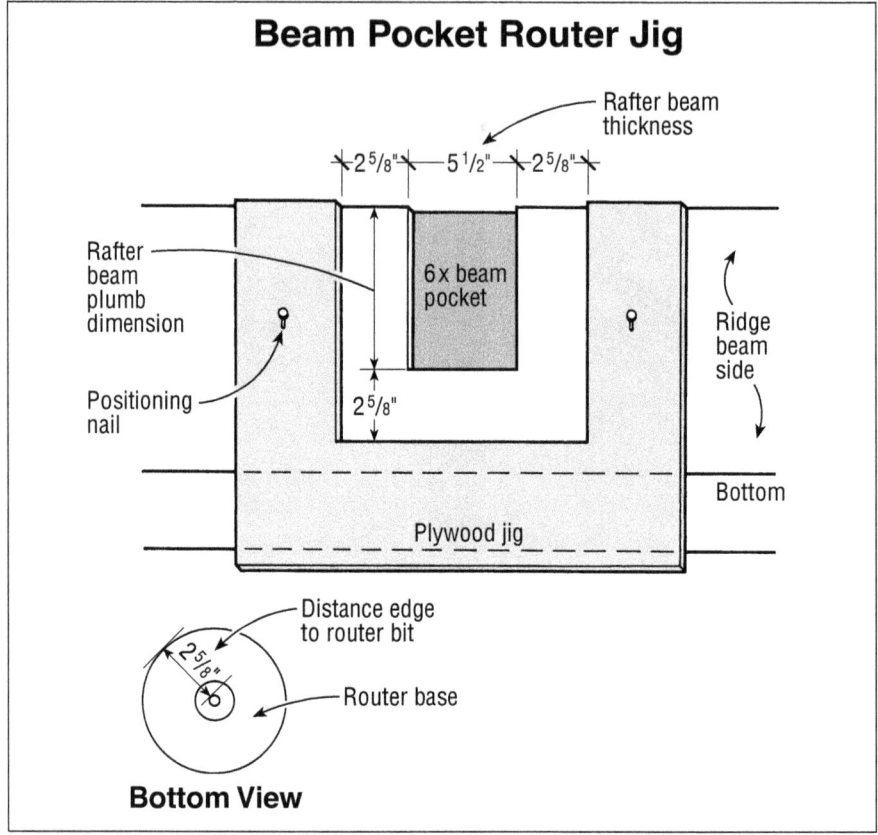

Figure 13-7. Using a plywood jig as a guide, router rafter beam pockets into the ridge while it is still on the ground.

Chapter 6 section "Ridge Height" (page 120) and shown in **Figure 13-8**.

When calculating rafter beam LL, don't forget to add the distance into the router ridge pocket. In Figure 13-8, the run over to the ridge beam from the outside face of wall is 117 1/4 in. and the router pocket is 3/4 in. deep, so the total effective run is 118 in. The LL is found as described in earlier chapters.

Beams can be made to look old or rustic in many ways: use a hand power plane with curved blades to "adze" the beam, feather a chainsaw against the grain, or simply randomly draw-knife the bottom edge corners of an S4S beam *(Photo 13-9)*.

A quick and easy way to install fake corbels under an overhang is shown in **Figure 13-10**. Use a heavy-duty strap attached to the front top edge for nailing up into the rim joist and a strap attached to the back end for nailing into the top plates. A fake wall-extension corbel can be installed with a

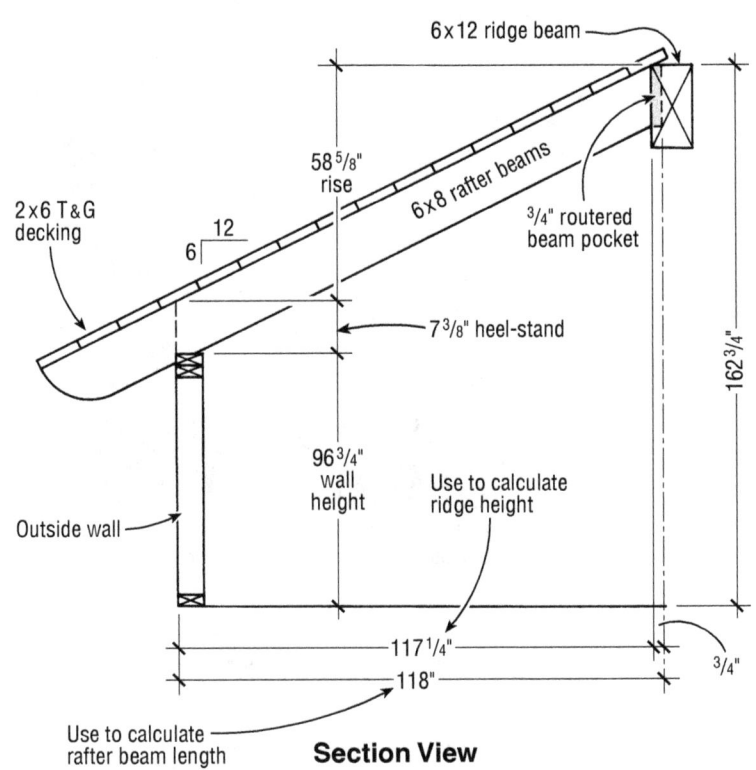

Figure 13-8. Add the rise, heel-stand, and outside wall height to determine total ridge beam height. When calculating rafter beam LL, don't forget to add the distance into the routered ridge pocket to find the effective run.

Photo 13-9. On exposed beam work, a routered pocket makes for the most attractive connection. Both rafter and support beams in this photo have the bottom edges detailed with a draw knife.

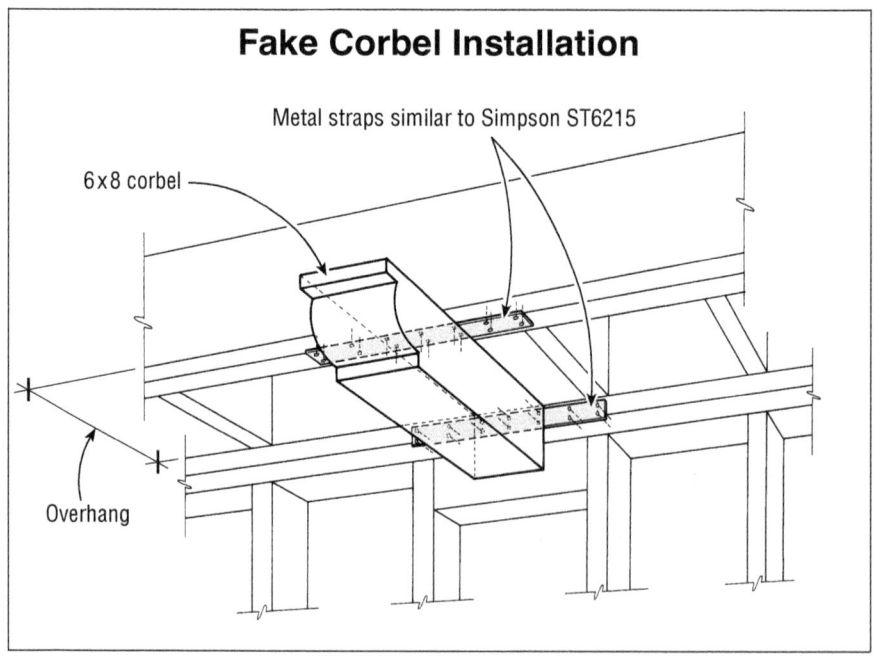

Figure 13-10. A quick and easy way to install corbels under an overhang is to use two heavy-duty straps.

Photo 13-11. This fake corbel was installed using a metal strap on the top run back to the wall plates.

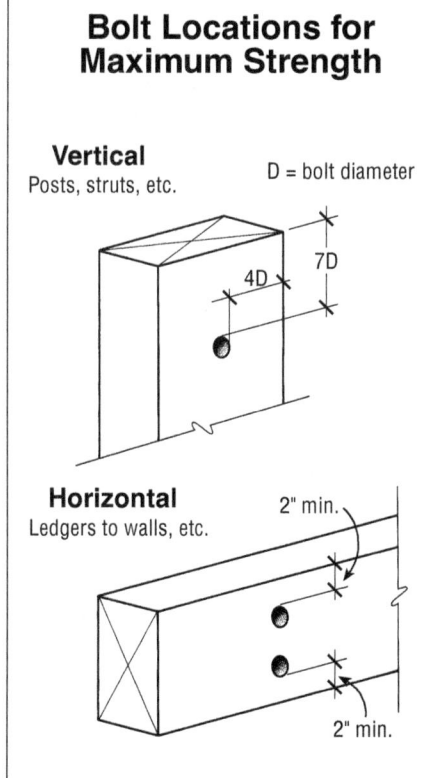

Bolt Locations for Maximum Strength

Vertical
Posts, struts, etc.

D = bolt diameter

4D, 7D

Horizontal
Ledgers to walls, etc.

2" min.

2" min.

strap over the top to the wall plates and a vertical strap nailed to the back end *(Photo 13-11)*. Another option to the back-end strap is to run lags through the wall from the opposite side into the corbel.

Figure 13-12 shows the minimum distances that a bolt should be placed away from an edge to provide maximum strength.

Exposed Trusses

Like tower roofs, exposed trusses are best built on the ground and lifted into place with a crane. Always use free-of-heart-center straight-grain wood to achieve the best results. Start by snapping a full-size truss on

Figure 13-12. Shown are the minimum distances a bolt should be placed away from an edge to provide maximum strength.

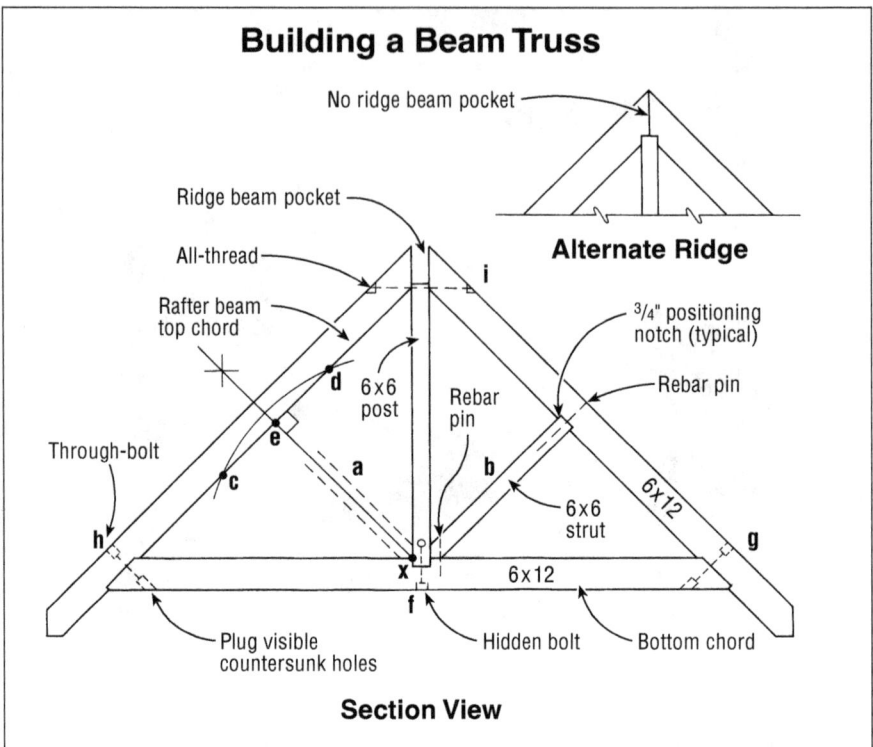

Figure 13-13. Always notch together the various components of an exposed beam truss to restrict any twist. A hidden bolt is placed at **f**. Countersunk through-bolts are used at **g, h,** and **i**. A rebar pin is used at the upper and lower ends of the decorative diagonal struts.

the floor to use as a guide for the various lengths and angles. Always make a practice pattern for special notches. Referring to *Figure 13-13*, notice that the bottom chord, post, and struts have been notched into the adjoining pieces to restrict any twist *(Photo 13-14)*. If possible, run the vertical post up between the two top chords to add rigidity and to keep the rafter beams spread apart to accept the ridge beam (if there is one).

Struts **a** and **b**, which are perpendicular to the top chords, are found by swinging any arc from **x** that intersects the top chord along the bottom edge at two points (**c** and **d**). Next, bisect the distance between the two points, and locate **e**. Snap a line from **e** to **x** to mark the centerline of the strut.

A hidden bolt is placed at **f**, and countersunk through-bolts are used at **g, h,** and **i**. Rebar pins are located on the struts as shown. This method will keep the joints very tight.

Exposed or hidden metal straps can be used instead of the illustrated bolts. Use a Skilsaw® to make a starter groove, and plunge-cut a slot with a chainsaw when installing hidden straps *(Figure 13-15)*.

Photo 13-14. The center post on this exposed beam truss has been notched into the bottom chord to keep it from twisting.

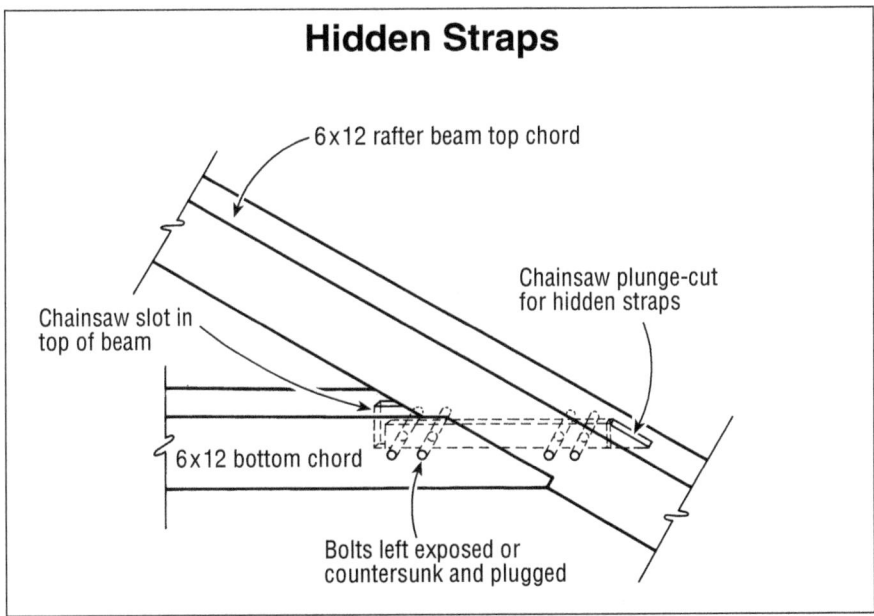

Figure 13-15. Hidden straps can be installed by plunge-cutting a slot in the center of the beam with a chainsaw. Through-bolts run from side to side.

Chapter 14

Stairs

CUT STRINGERS

As with roofs, calculate stairs using LL because it is extremely accurate. To use this method, begin by figuring the total rise from **finished** floor to **finished** floor. It is imperative to take into account the variation in thickness of the flooring material to be used on the lower floor, the top landing and the stairs themselves. With varying materials, it is best to make a story pole to help visualize how much to add or subtract from the bottom of the stringers. Generally, carpet and wood floor are both $3/4$ in. thick, vinyl tile is $1/8$ in. thick, and ceramic tile can vary in thickness from $1/4$ in. when set directly on a slab to $2 1/4$ in. thick when installed with a mortar bed. Divide the total rise by 7. Drop the fractions off the resulting answer to find the number of risers, and use it to divide back into the total rise to get rise per step *(Figure 14-1)*. The number 7 is used as the divider because of the **7-11** stair builder's rule. Always try to keep the rise and run close to those two numbers for the most comfortable stairs. If the riser or tread must vary up or down slightly, pair it with a complementary tread or riser so that together they equal **18** (example: $7 1/4$-in. risers pair with $10 3/4$-in. treads).

Figure the LL for the stringer by applying the Pythagorean theorem. Use total rise and total run (tread width multiplied by number of risers) as the two legs of the right triangle, and solve for the hypotenuse. Mark this total distance **(x-y)** on the stringer. Divide the distance between **x-y** by the number of risers and "step" off as shown. Next, install stair dogs to a framing square at the proper rise and run dimension, and mark the vertical and horizontal cuts using the "stepped" off LL marks as a guide.

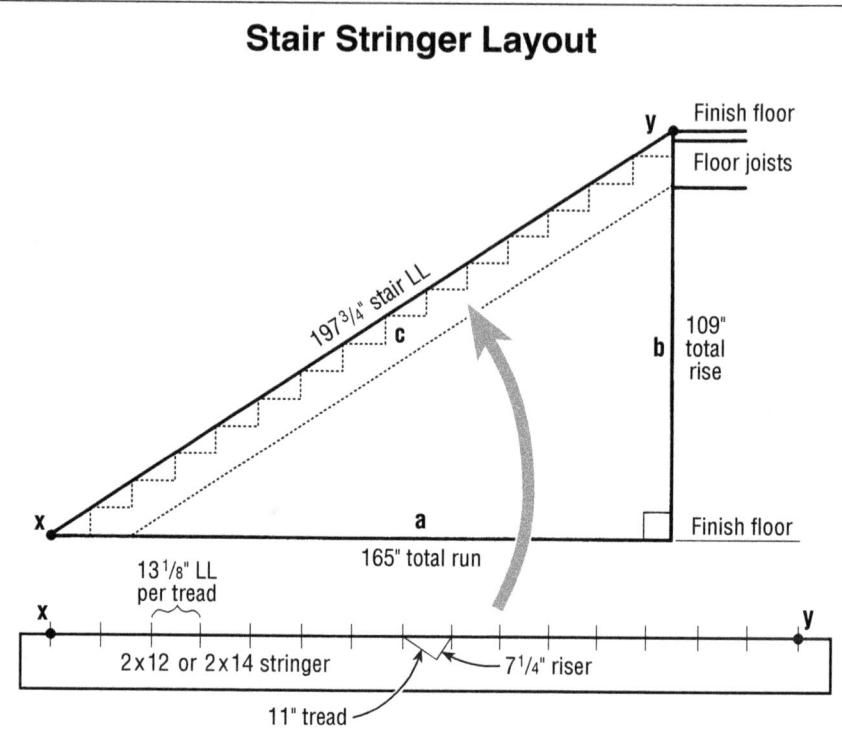

Figure 14-1. Stair stringers can be thought of as roof rafters with notches along the top for steps. Use the total height from finished floor to finished floor as the rise together with the sum of all the tread widths (plus one for the very bottom) as the run, and calculate the total stair stringer LL using the Pythagorean theorem.

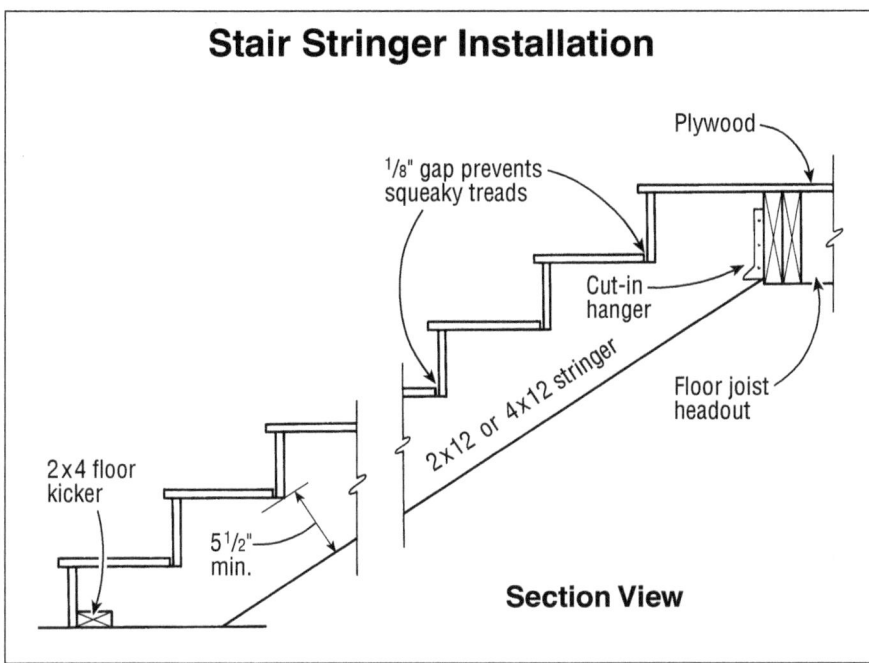

Figure 14-2. For the strongest top connection when building stairs, hold the floor headout at the top of the stairs back one tread width to receive the upper end of the stringer.

When you cut the stringer, don't forget to take the thickness of one tread off the bottom of the first riser and the thickness of one riser off the back of the first tread. For most covered stairs, 3/4-in. plywood works well as both treads and risers, although 1 1/8-in. plywood can be used as the treads for super-duty applications. Use the first stringer as a pattern for the others. The last tread should frame to the same height as the upper floor level for the best stringer-to-floor-joist headout connection *(Figure 14-2)*. With this method, the floor headout for the top landing is held back one tread width from the nose of the first descending riser. Cut a hanger in the top of the stringers for extra strength, and notch the bottom risers at the toe for a 2x4 floor kicker.

To avoid squeaks, cut the treads short to leave a small gap between the tread and riser as shown, or glue/screw the riser to the tread from the backside (construction adhesive and screws are always a big plus when installing treads and risers). Run a temporary strongback or stiffener along an open stringer to keep it straight while installing the plywood treads and risers *(Figure 14-3)*.

Figure 14-4 illustrates built-up stairs. Use this style of construction for short flights of up to four risers and for the corner section of a 90° winder. Rip the stair lumber to the proper rise dimension and box frame as shown. Remember the bottom box will be ripped less the thickness of the tread material. Stack the box sections and toenail them together before applying the treads.

Temporary Stair Stringer Strongback

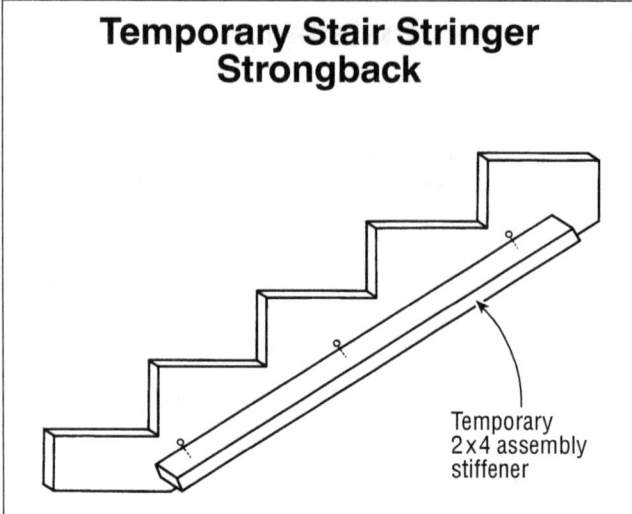

Figure 14-3. Run a temporary strongback or stiffener along an open stringer to keep it straight while installing the plywood treads and risers.

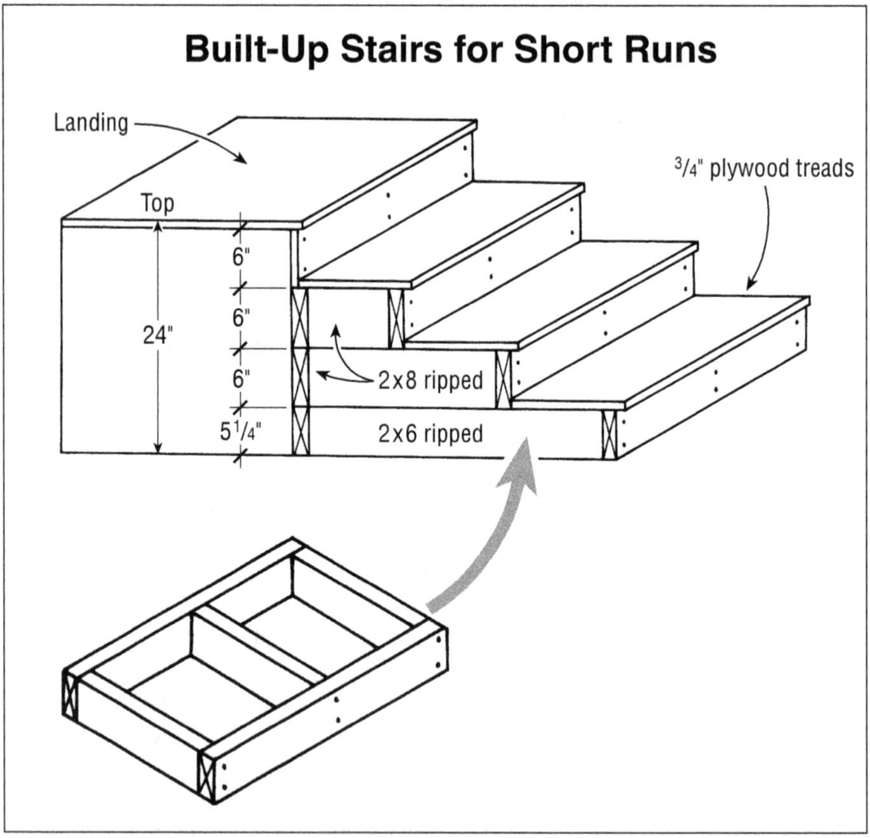

Built-Up Stairs for Short Runs

Figure 14-4. Short flights of stairs can be framed using small floor-like boxes stacked in a pyramid fashion.

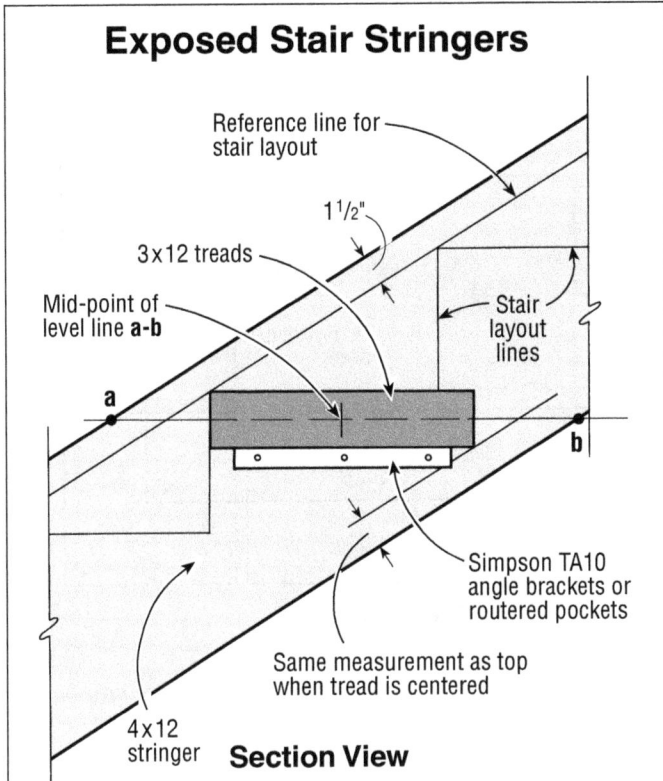

Figure 14-5. Center exposed treads up/down and back/forth on a level line drawn at the pitch of the stairs to find a nosing reference line from which to mark layout.

EXPOSED STRINGERS

Exposed stairs can be built as shown in *Figure 14-5* using stair angles or routered pockets for the treads. Use 4x12 stringers together with 3x12 treads to make attractive, solid stairs. The tread is located on the stringer by bisecting a level line and centering the tread on these marks (up and down and back and forth). Once the distance from the nose of the riser to the edge of the stringer is found, a reference line is marked full-length to use for stair layout.

PYRAMID STAIRS

Three-sided stairs, or pyramid stairs to a landing, are framed like a hip roof. The corner stringers have the same riser, but the tread is cut 1.414 times greater (secant of 45°). Notice in *Figure 14-6* the 45° riser cheek-cuts on the hip stringer: these are often square-cut at the SP of the double 45° cheek-cut. If the stair treads make a bend at an angle other than 90°, a top view can be snapped on the floor to find the tread run and riser cut-angle for the bastard "hip" stringers, or use some of the same trig shown in Figure 8-2.

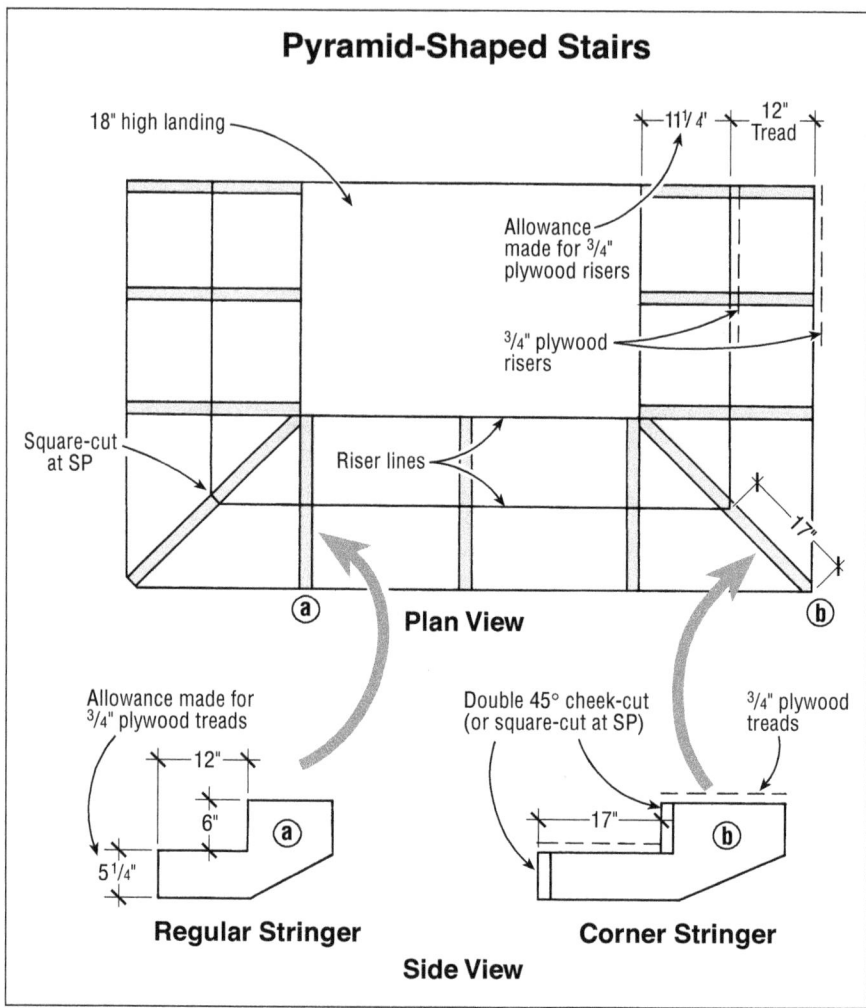

Figure 14-6. Pyramid or three-sided stairs are framed like a hip roof. The corner stringer has the same riser, but the tread is 1.414 times greater (secant of 45°).

90° WINDERS

When building 90° winders, project the inside cornerpoint out diagonally far enough to get a 6-in. minimum tread width along the inside edge to comply with the building code (**A** and **B** of *Figure 14-7*). If possible, adjust the position of point **a** or the number of treads on the winder section to maintain a consistent tread size with the straight runs of stairs at the line of travel (12 in. from the inside edge). Support headers are placed where necessary to terminate and initiate the straight-run stringers. The easiest way to

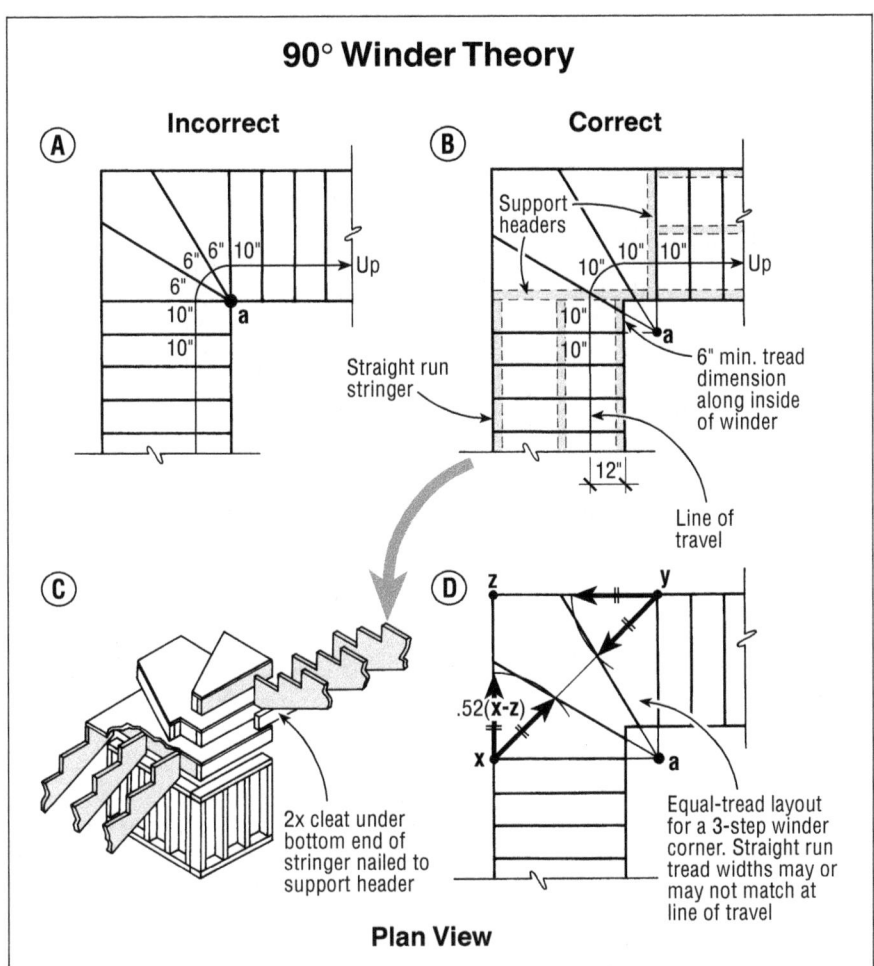

Figure 14-7. For 90° winder stairs, project the inside cornerpoint **a** out diagonally to get a 6-in. minimum tread width along the inside edge. If possible, adjust the number of treads and the position of point **a** to achieve a consistent tread size along a normal travel line measured 12 in. from the inside edge. The .52 ratio shown in View **D** is a quick method to lay out a three-tread winder for equal-size treads at the line of travel.

frame the corner winder section is either to use sandwiched 2x12s/2x4s as risers spanning the stairwell (similar to what is shown in the upcoming section, "Circular Stairs"), or to build a rectangular corner platform at the lowest winder tread height and box-frame in a pyramid fashion the remaining angular treads on top as shown in the exploded view **C** of Figure 14-7.

Larry Haun, author of *Home Building Basics: Carpentry* and *The Very Efficient Carpenter*, uses a simple ratio to quickly lay out equal-width treads at the line of travel for a three-step winder corner as shown in **D** of Figure

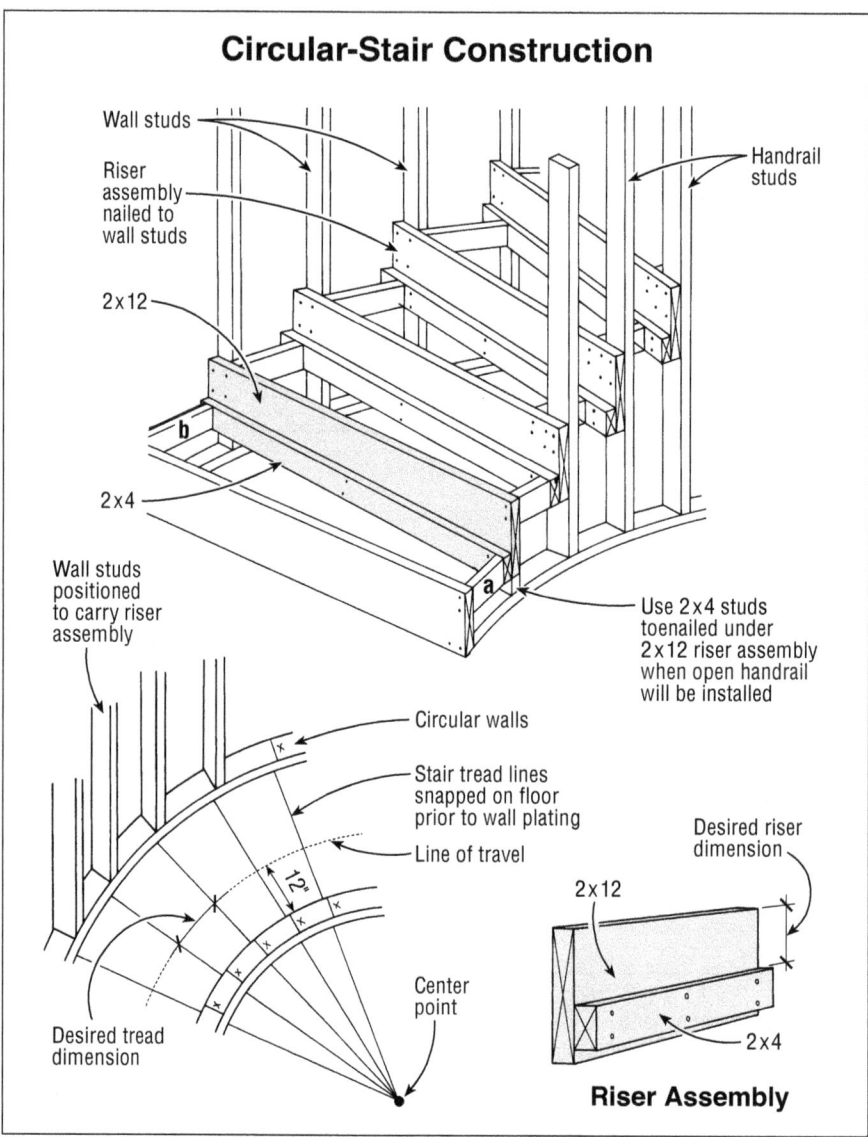

Figure 14-8. Always snap out the circular-stair treads on the floor prior to wall-plating to position the studs where the risers can be attached later. The risers are 2x12s with 2x4 cleats attached at the proper rise to carry the back side of the stair tread.

14-7. Haun multiplies the total set-back distance from the nearest straight-run riser (**x** or **y**) to the 90° outside wall corner at **z** by .52. He then uses the result as a measurement inboard from each end of the diagonal line across the winder section (**x-y**) to locate points through which the riser lines radiate from centerpoint **a**. The .52 ratio only works for three-step winders, but I suppose some of you math-wizard types might be able to calculate the ratios for other winder combinations as well.

Photo 14-9. Circular stairs with an open handrail.

CIRCULAR STAIRS

Figure 14-8 illustrates circular-stair construction with a framed inside handrail. The stairs should always be snapped out prior to wall plating. To do this, lay out the desired line-of-travel tread width 12 in. away from the inside stair circumference. Snap lines through these marks from the center of the circle to locate the inside and outside studs. The risers are built using a 2x12 and a 2x4 sandwiched together as shown. One end of the assembly is nailed to the wall stud at the outside radius, and the other end is nailed to the handrail stud at the inside radius. I find a stair story pole comes in quite handy to mark the proper riser height on the inside and outside studs. Install one handrail stud and one riser at a time working up from the bottom, continually checking everything for plumb/level. Small blocks are placed at **a** and **b** to keep the riser width correct and to add rigidity. Nail and glue 3/4- or 1 1/8-in. plywood treads on top. When finished, the handrail studs are cut to length, and a plywood handrail cap is nailed to the top. The bevel-cut at the top of the handrail studs is found by placing a board spanning from riser to riser up against the inside studs and noting the angle (of course there's always trig). If an open handrail will be installed, cut short 2x4 studs to toenail under the 2x12 riser assembly instead of running them long above ***(Photo 14-9)***.

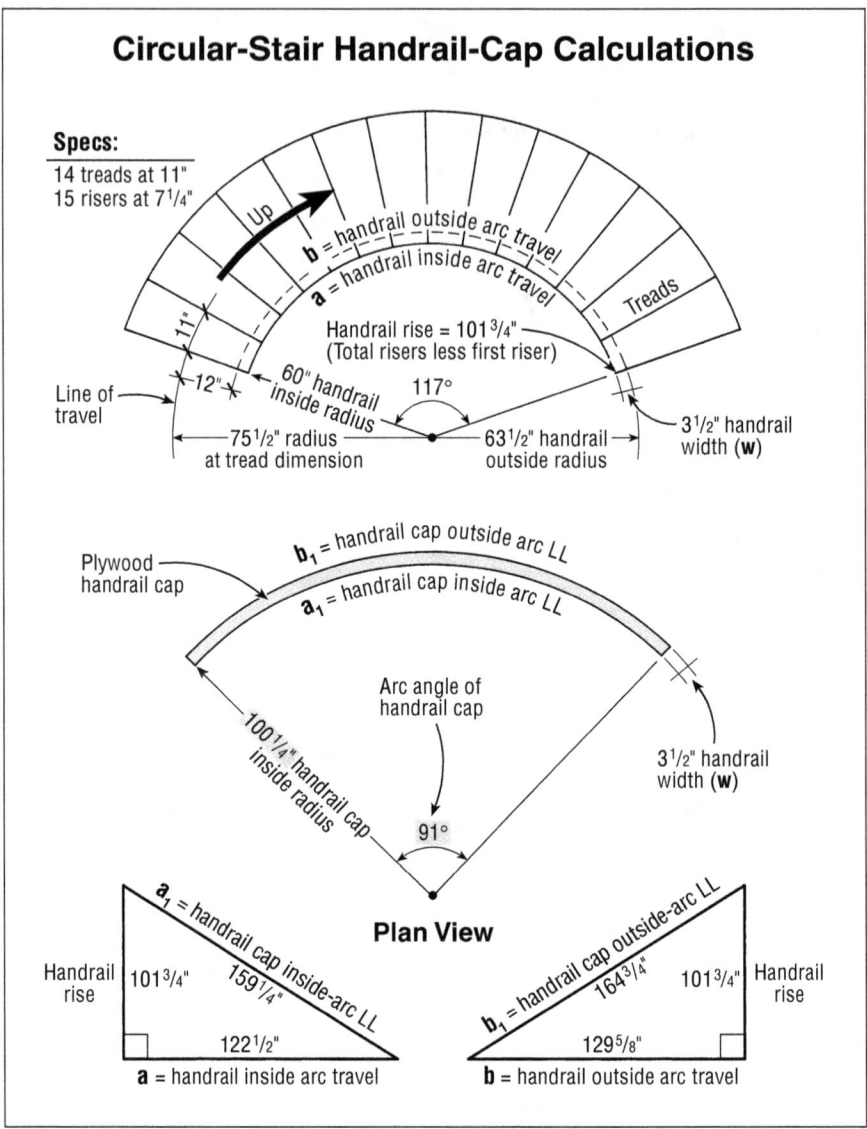

Figure 14-10a. A stairbuilder's formula for calculating the circular-stair handrail cap.

CIRCULAR-STAIR HANDRAIL CAP

Jed Dixon of North Road Stairbuilders uses the following formula for a circular-stair handrail cap. Follow the example in ***Figure 14-10***:

1. Using a protractor on the snapped floor plan (or math as shown) find the arc in degrees through which the circular stairs travel in the horizontal plane.
2. Use this arc in degrees (117°) together with the inside and outside handrail radii (60", 63½") to find the arc lengths **a** and **b**.

278   CHAPTER 14

Method:

a = handrail inside arc travel
b = handrail outside arc travel
a_1 = handrail cap inside arc LL
b_1 = handrail cap outside arc LL
C = circumference
w = handrail width

1. $\dfrac{\text{Number of treads} \times \text{tread width}}{\text{Total } \mathbf{C} \text{ at tread dimension}} = \dfrac{\text{Arc of stair (in degrees)}}{360°}$

2a. $2\pi \text{ (inside handrail radius)} \times \dfrac{\text{Arc of stair (in degrees)}}{360°} = \mathbf{a}$

2b. $2\pi \text{ (outside handrail radius)} \times \dfrac{\text{Arc of stair (in degrees)}}{360°} = \mathbf{b}$

3a. $(\text{Handrail rise})^2 + (\mathbf{a})^2 = (\mathbf{a_1})^2$

3b. $(\text{Handrail rise})^2 + (\mathbf{b})^2 = (\mathbf{b_1})^2$

4. $\dfrac{(\mathbf{b_1} - \mathbf{a_1}) \times 180}{\pi(\mathbf{w})}$ = arc angle of handrail cap

5. $\dfrac{\mathbf{w}}{(\mathbf{b_1} \div \mathbf{a_1}) - 1}$ = inside radius of handrail cap

Example:

1. $\dfrac{154" \{14 \text{ treads} \times 11\}}{474\,1/8" \{\text{total } \mathbf{C} \text{ at } 75\,1/2"\}} = \dfrac{117°}{360°}$

2a. $2\pi(60") \times \dfrac{117°}{360°} = 122\,1/2"$ for **a**

2b. $2\pi(63\,1/2") \times \dfrac{117°}{360°} = 129\,5/8"$ for **b**

3a. $(101\,3/4")^2 + (122\,1/2")^2 = (159\,1/4")^2$ LL for a_1

3b. $(101\,3/4")^2 + (129\,5/8")^2 = (164\,3/4")^2$ LL for b_1

4. $\dfrac{(164\,3/4" - 159\,1/4") \times 180}{\pi(3\,1/2")} = 91°$

5. $\dfrac{3\,1/2"}{(164\,3/4" \div 159\,1/4") - 1} = 100\,1/4"$

Figure 14-10b.

Photo 14-11. A self-supporting circular box-beam stringer.

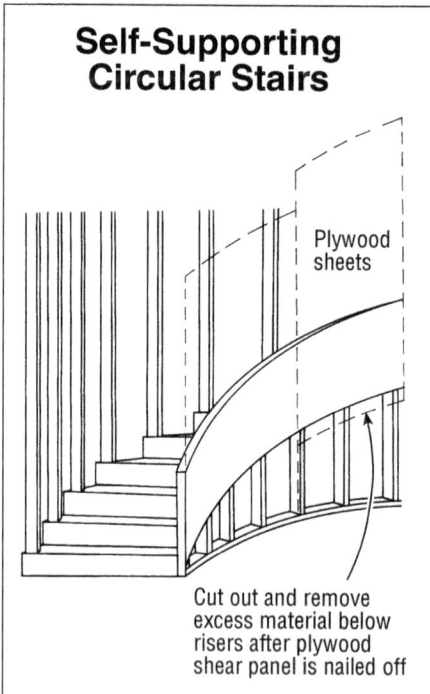

Figure 14-12. To build a self-supporting spiral box-beam stringer/handrail, shear-panel the inside circumference with at least two overlapping layers of plywood from the top of the handrail to the bottom of the risers. After the shear panel has been nailed off, cut and remove everything below the stair treads and risers.

3. Change these arc length measurements into LL dimensions by using a rise/run equation.
4. Substitute these LL dimensions ($159^{1}/4''$, $164^{3}/4''$) into the two formulas to find the inside stair-cap radius and the degrees through which it travels for cutting the plywood handrail cap.

Freestanding circular-stair stringers are generally a job for the professional stair-building shop, but it is possible to build a spiral box-beam-style stringer on-site using several plywood layers that will support some stair runs *(Photo 14-11)*. In this situation, the stairs are framed as shown in Figure 14-8 including a curved plywood handrail cap, except the handrail stud is only tacked to the circular bottom plate since the lower portion will be removed later. The inside curve is then shear-paneled with at least two overlapping layers of plywood from the top of the

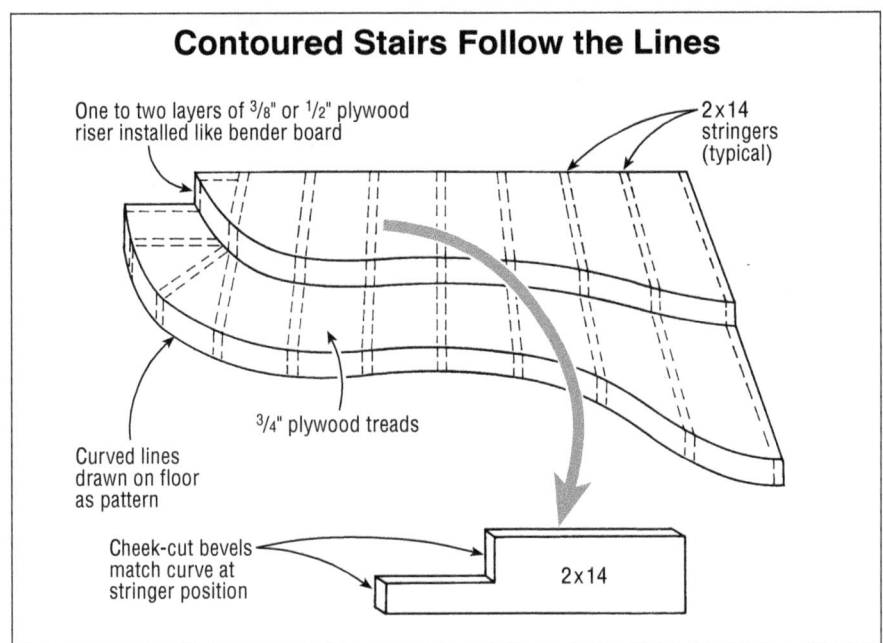

Figure 14-13. Use the curved floor lines as a guide for cutting the riser angles on notched 2x14 stringer joists.

handrail to the bottom of the risers. Run the plywood long in both directions as shown in *Figure 14-12*. Screws can be used instead of nails to help draw the plywood into the curve. Next, trim the excess plywood above the handrail, and use the handrail itself as a guide to mark a line that follows the underside of the treads and risers. Finally, cut and remove everything below this line, and add a curved plywood handrail-style bottom plate to finish off the lower end of the cut handrail studs.

Several folks I know have had success using embedded straight-run LVL stringers intersecting at various angles together with structural cantilever treads and/or risers to form freestanding, large-diameter, partial-turn circular stairs. The support comes from a single short wall at the bottom and the landing at the top. A full-size top view of the circular staircase with the various stringers superimposed is laid out on the floor in actual position. The tread run dimensions and riser face angles are transferred from the floor layout to the LVLs. During assembly, correct stringer location and tread/riser position are set by plumbing up from the floor drawing.

CONTOURED STAIRS

Curved or contoured stairs *(Figure 14-13)* can be built in several ways depending on the circumstance. For some two-step runs, notched 2x14s work well. Other times, each tread must be framed as a complete landing and stacked in a pyramid or wedding cake fashion similar to Figure 14-4. The angled end-cuts for the risers are taken from the curved lines drawn on the floor. Use two layers of $3/8$-in. plywood for the riser and screw them into place if necessary. Space the stringer-joists closer together than normal, or block and shim similar to Figure 2-23 for the best results in forming the curved riser.

Chapter 15

Pick Up

MISCELLANEOUS PICK UP

Backing for towel racks is centered at 52 in. off the floor, while backing for a recessed toilet paper holder is set at 20 in. off the floor. A medicine cabinet is framed at the side of a pullman two stud widths from the back corner in a regular 14 1/2-in. stud bay with wall blocks placed like fire-blocks above 6 ft. and below 4 ft. measured from the floor.

Figure 15-1 illustrates two ways to straighten a bad crown in a stud.

Freestanding handrail walls can be a problem unless held in place by a cabinet. If the floor will be a concrete slab, have 1 1/2-in.-diameter pipes poured in place as shown in *Figure 15-2*, and drill the framing plates to accept the pipe. If the pipe will get in the way during framing, find two pipes sized so that one slides inside the other like a sleeve. Pour the larger one flush with the top of the concrete enabling installation of the smaller pipe when needed. Placing concrete straps (Simpson Strong-Tie® PA28 or similar) during the concrete pour for each side of the wall is another free-standing wall-stiffening method. After the concrete pour, these straps can be bent flat to stay out of the way until needed.

On a wood floor, the studs of a freestanding wall can be cut through the floor and nailed to floor joists or blocks installed between the floor joists *(Figure 15-3)*. Another option is to cut vertical straps through the floor from each side of the wall to blocking installed below.

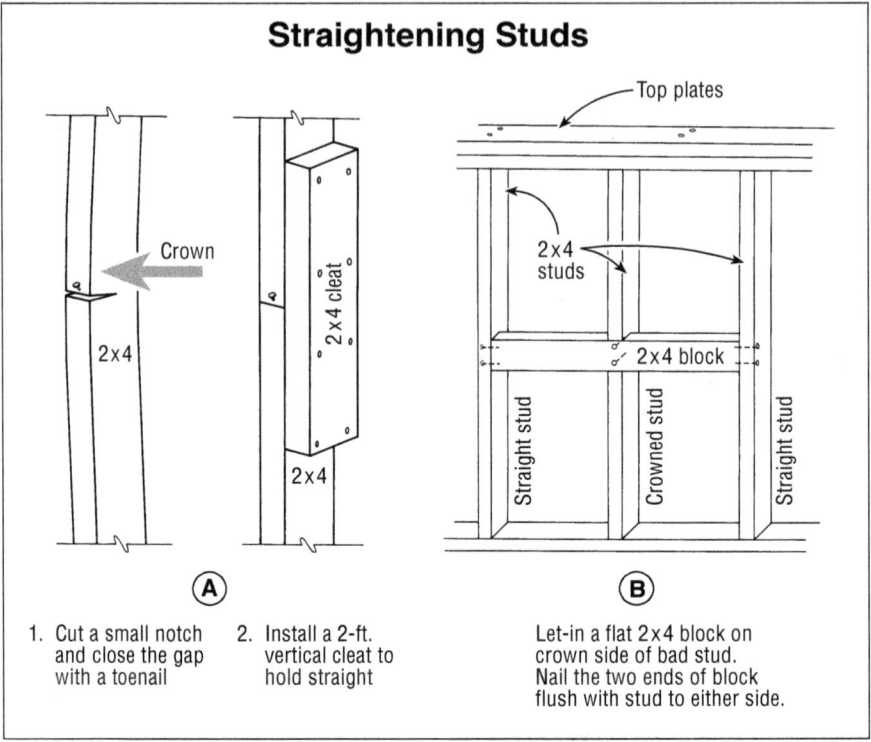

Figure 15-1. Two ways to straighten a bad crown in a stud.

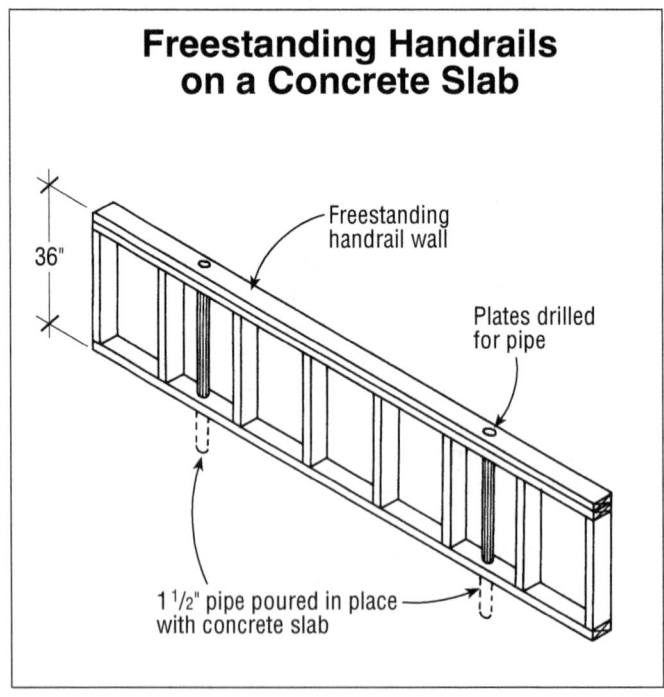

Figure 15-2. Use steel pipes (or a sleeve) positioned in the concrete pour to stiffen up a freestanding handrail on a slab.

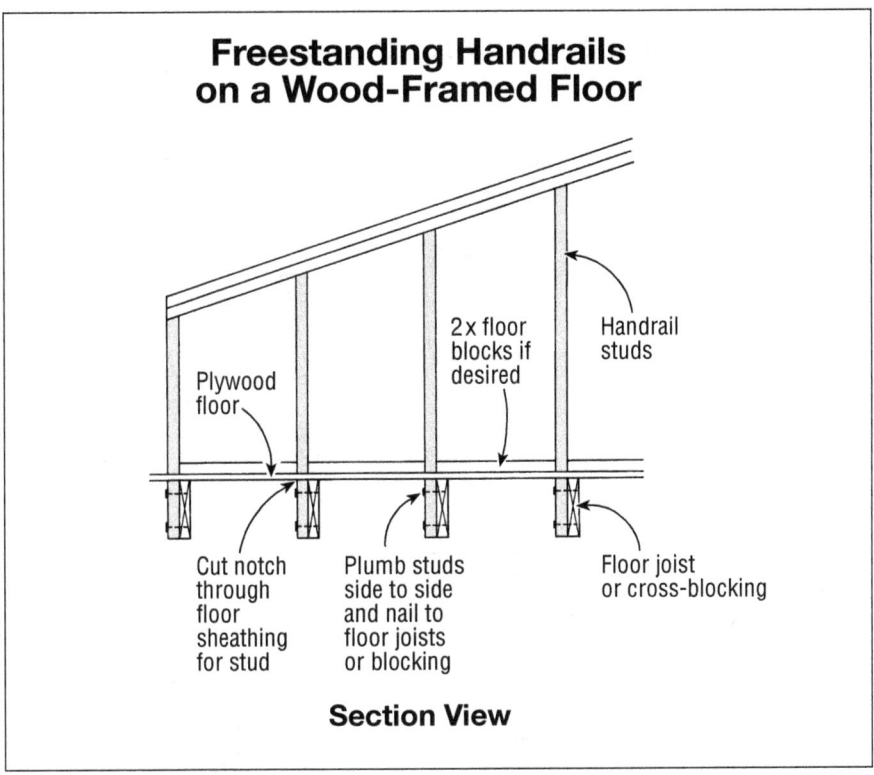

Figure 15-3. To stiffen up a freestanding handrail on a raised floor, cut slots through the floor, and nail the studs to perpendicular floor joists or to blocks run between parallel floor joists.

ARCHES AND CURVES

Concave arches and convex curves are formed using plywood patterns in most cases. For an arched doorway, set the header high and install a small prefabricated arched section underneath during pickup. If a doorway or opening arch radius is not called out on the blueprints but a change in height is noted, snap out the opening on the ground to solve for the curve geometrically (as shown in *Figure 15-4*), or use the formula provided to calculate the radius where **x** is the change in height and **y** is the width of the opening. For barrel-vaulted ceilings or curved soffits, hang 3/4-in. plywood patterns from the ceiling joists every 4 to 8 feet, and nail 2x4s along the edge of the curve *(Figure 15-5)*.

The intersection of two barrel-vaulted ceilings can be quite a challenge, especially if two different widths converge as illustrated in *Figure 15-6*. Think of it as a diamond-hip roof and snap it on the ground. Use one arch to figure the rise at similar points for both the opposite arch and the hip arch by transferring corresponding measurements to the diagonal for the hip and 90° for the other arch. (The formula from Figure 15-4 also works

PICK UP **285**

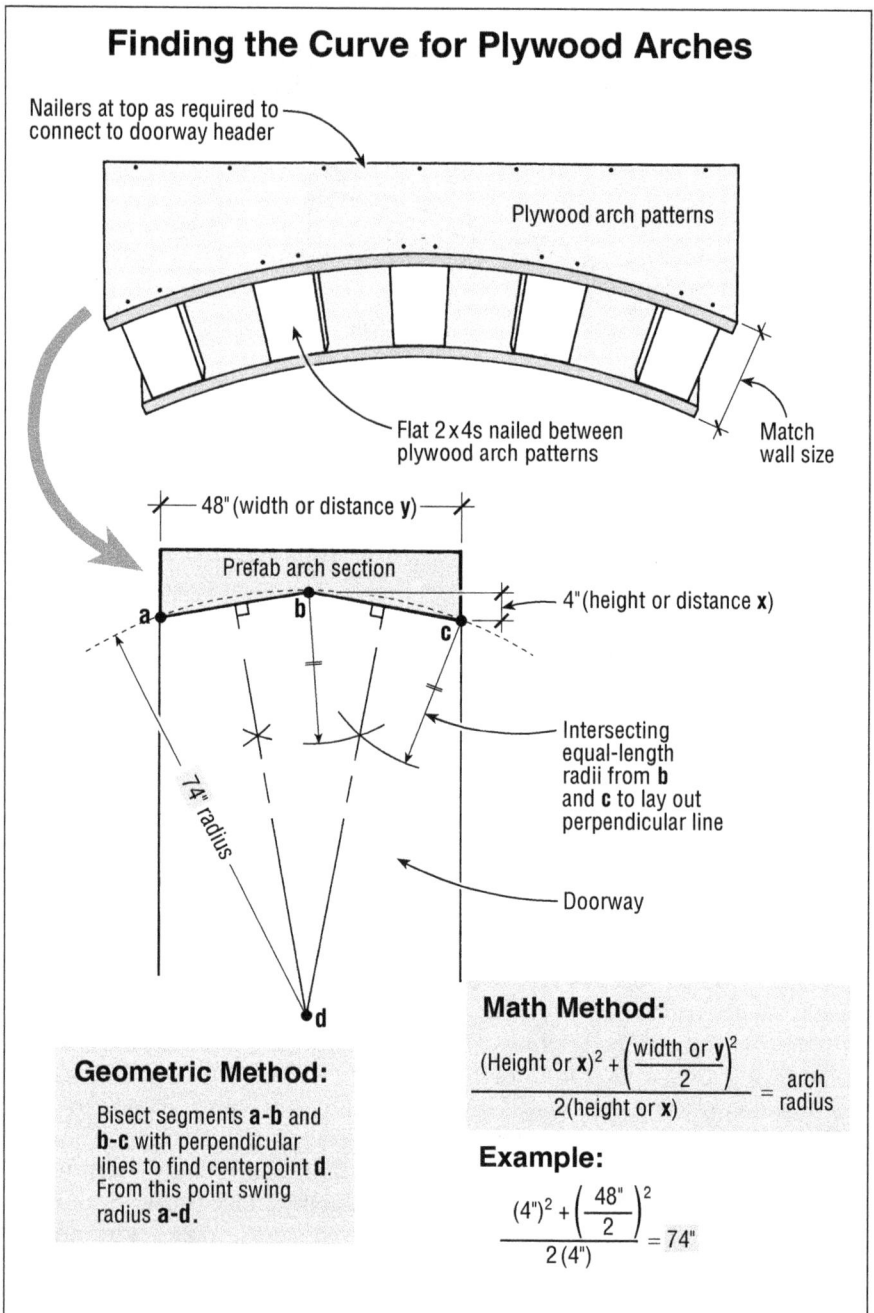

Figure 15-4. If the radius of a doorway or opening arch is not given, it can be solved for geometrically or with a simple math formula.

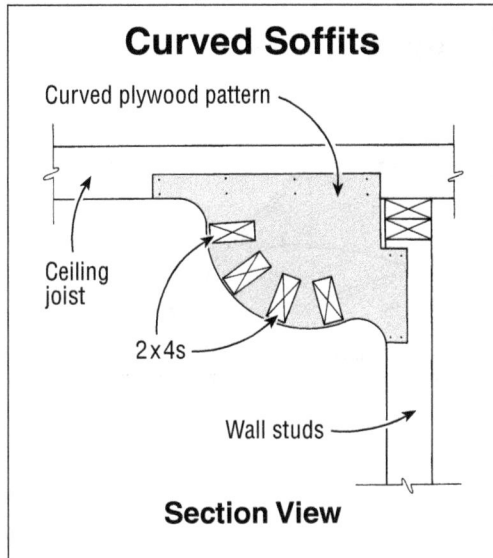

Figure 15-5. For curved ceiling sections, hang 3/4-in. plywood patterns from the ceiling every 8 feet, and nail 2x4s on edge along the perimeter of the curve.

well here if the curve is circular.) With the curves nailed in place, run 2x4 fingers between the regular end curves and the hip curve or install curved ribs from hip to hip. "Jack rafter curves" work well for finishing off a hip-style end to a barrel vault as shown in *Photo 15-7*.

When a required curve is longer than a sheet of plywood, make it larger by sandwiching two overlapping layers together.

CHANDELIER DOMES

A round chandelier dome with an elliptical cross-section or similar is framed like a conical tower roof with many rafters converging to a peak, except a radius cut has been made in the bottom of each of the "rafters" *(Photo 15-8)*. Use 2x12s, 2x14s, or plywood (3/4 or 1 1/8 in.) for the rafters. The number of rafters depends on the circumference of the ceiling opening. As in the Chapter 10 section "Conical Tower Construction" (page 216), divide the circumference by a multiple of eight to get the closest value to the desired on-center spacing. In *Figure 15-9*, sixteen rafters converge at the peak with a 14 1/8-in. -on-center spacing around the 72-in.-diameter circular ceiling opening. Shortening is done as shown in Figure 10-21. When using plywood rafters, cut the first two opposing rafters that butt head to head out of one continuous sheet to make a "king-curve" spanning from side to side. The dome is built working off a plywood circle deck placed in the attic. A square-shaped ceiling-joist opening can be made circular by installing diagonal corner blocks and shimming a plywood rim-band to the shape of the plywood circle above.

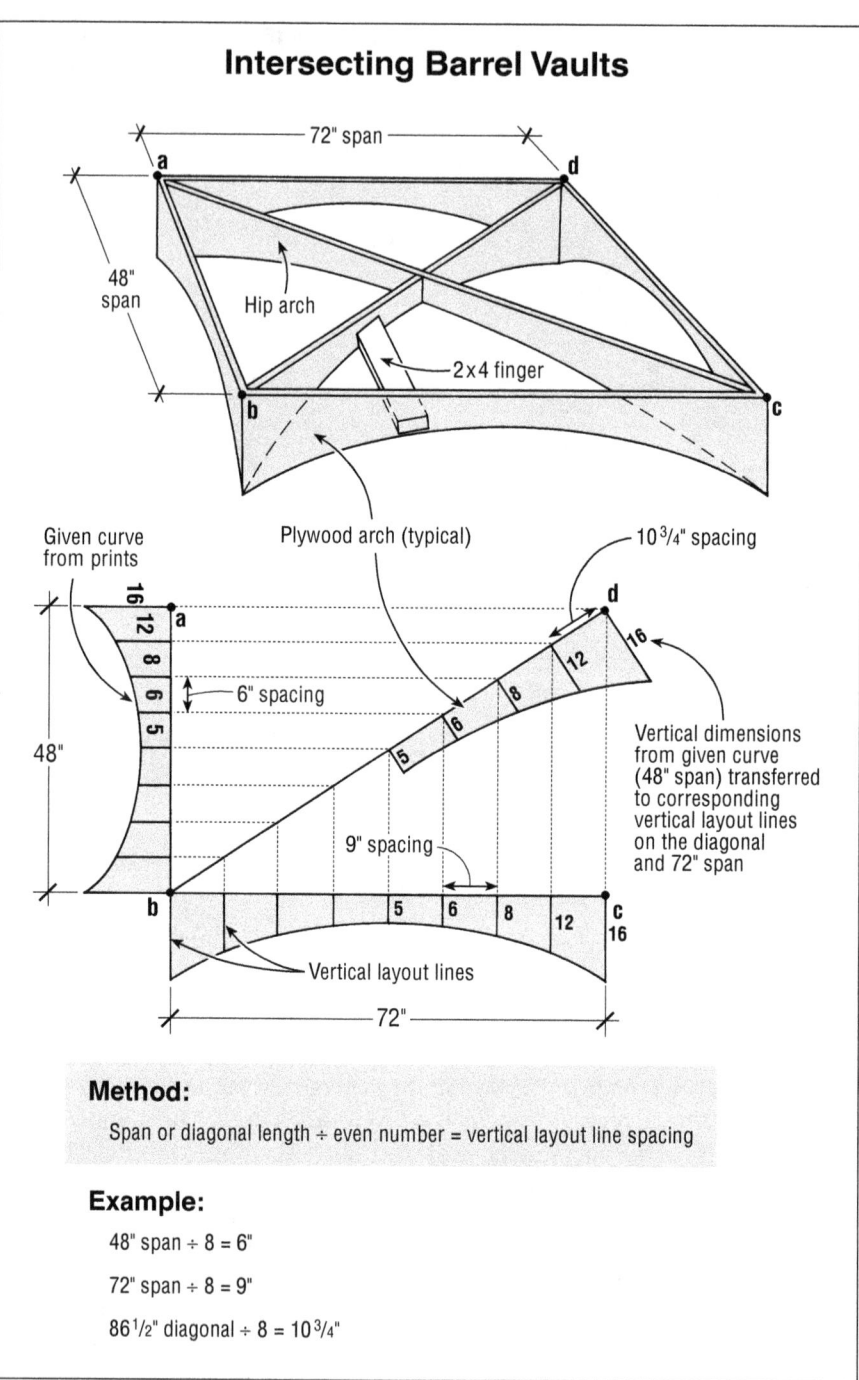

Figure 15-6. Intersecting barrel-vaulted ceilings are snapped on the floor similarly to a diamond-hip roof. Measurements from the 48-in. hallway arch are transferred to the diagonal for the hip arch and 90° for the 72-in. hallway arch; 2x4 fingers or hip-to-hip curved ribs are cut to fit between the various arches.

Photo 15-7. "Jack rafter curves" can be used to finish off the hip-style end to a barrel vault.

Photo 15-8. A large chandelier dome ceiling.

To find the correct elliptical curve for the bottom of the rafters, draw out a full-size cross-section view on the floor *(Figure 15-10)*. Begin with horizontal line **a-c** at the given chandelier's opening diameter (72 in.). Bisect that line with vertical line **d-b**, and measure up from their intersection the given rise (**b** or 24 in.). From point **b**, swing a radius equal to one-half the opening width (**a-d** or 36 in.) so as to intersect the horizontal line **a-c** at two points (**e** and **f**). Connect a string that is the opening width in length (**a-c** or 72 in.) to nails located at **e** and **f**. Place a pencil point inside the string, and — keeping the line taut — draw the ellipse from side to side.

A scale drawing of any unusual shape can be upsized as demonstrated in Figure 15-9

PICK UP **289**

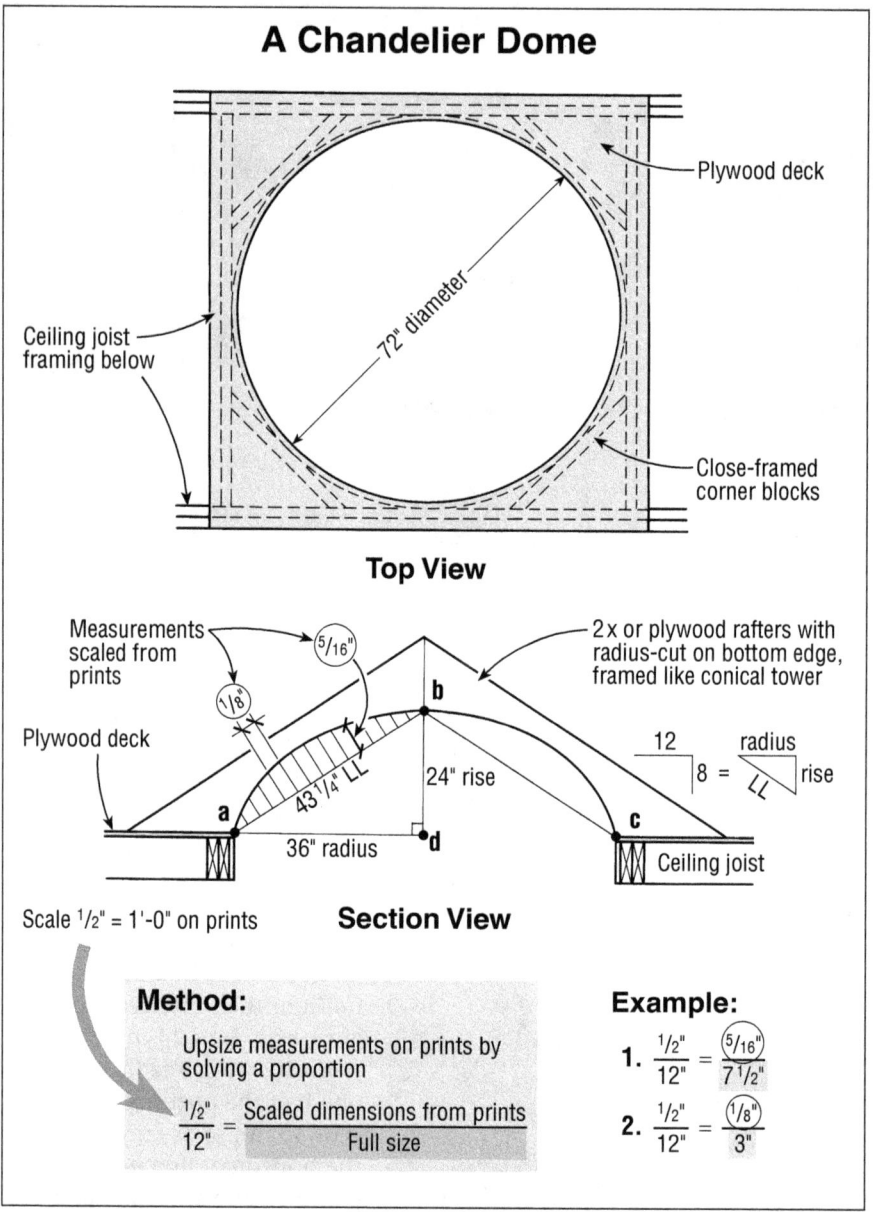

Figure 15-9. Upscale dimensions from a blueprint drawing by measuring up perpendicular from line **a-b** at set distances, and converting to actual size using a proportion.

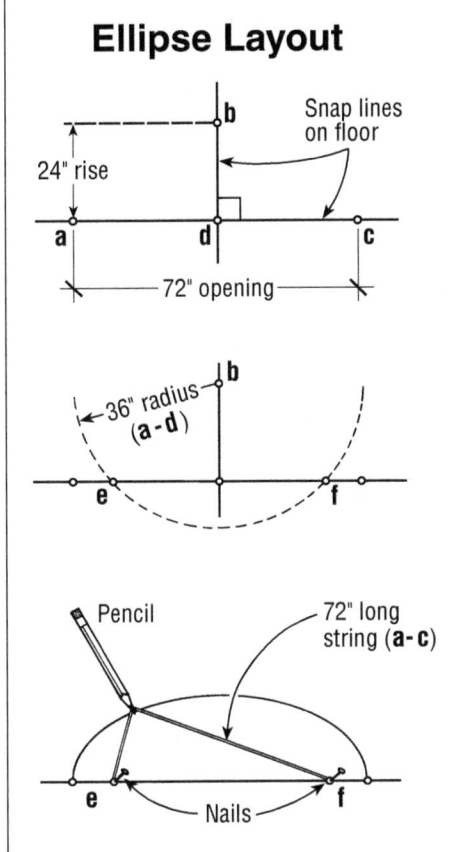

Figure 15-10. To geometrically lay out an ellipse, swing a radius equal to **a-d** to intersect line **a-c** at two points (**e** and **f**). Use a string that is **a-c** in length connected to nails at **e** and **f** as a leash to draw the curve.

by drawing line **a-b**, and measuring up square every so often to find a point on the curve. These measurements are then converted to full size using a proportion and transferred to the side of the rafters to form the desired curve.

SKYLIGHTS

The technique shown in *Figure 15-11* can be used to frame skylight shafts whether they come down straight, widen, or angle in from any direction. In the example, 2x4s are placed between the roof and ceiling headouts and scribed at **x** and **y** to get the cut-lines at each of the four corners. If the cuts at **x** and **y** are beveled due to a sideways offset, place an angle finder (available from several tool manufacturers) on the 2x4 when scribing the cut-lines to find the approximate bevel-cut. After the four corner studs are nailed in place, create an inside drywall corner by nailing 2x4s flat to them as shown. The backing 2x4s can be cut short since there is no need to make them fit tight. Skylights larger than 24 in. by 24 in. will need an intermediate stud or blocking between the corners. On some simple skylight shafts, 3/4-in. plywood can be used as the sides without any 2x4 backing.

COFFER CEILINGS

Figure 15-12 illustrates several coffer ceiling designs. The coffer ceiling can angle in on all four sides or on just two. For a simple style, start by framing a 24-in. ceiling soffit at the desired height around the perimeter of the room. If the perimeter soffit frames to the top of the walls raise the ceiling joists in the middle by nailing them to the rafters like a collar-tie or setting them on short pony walls built in the attic. If possible, position a ceiling joist on each perpendicular side so the coffer ceiling's 2x4 fingers will intersect like a ridge. Otherwise, nail the fingers alongside blocks installed

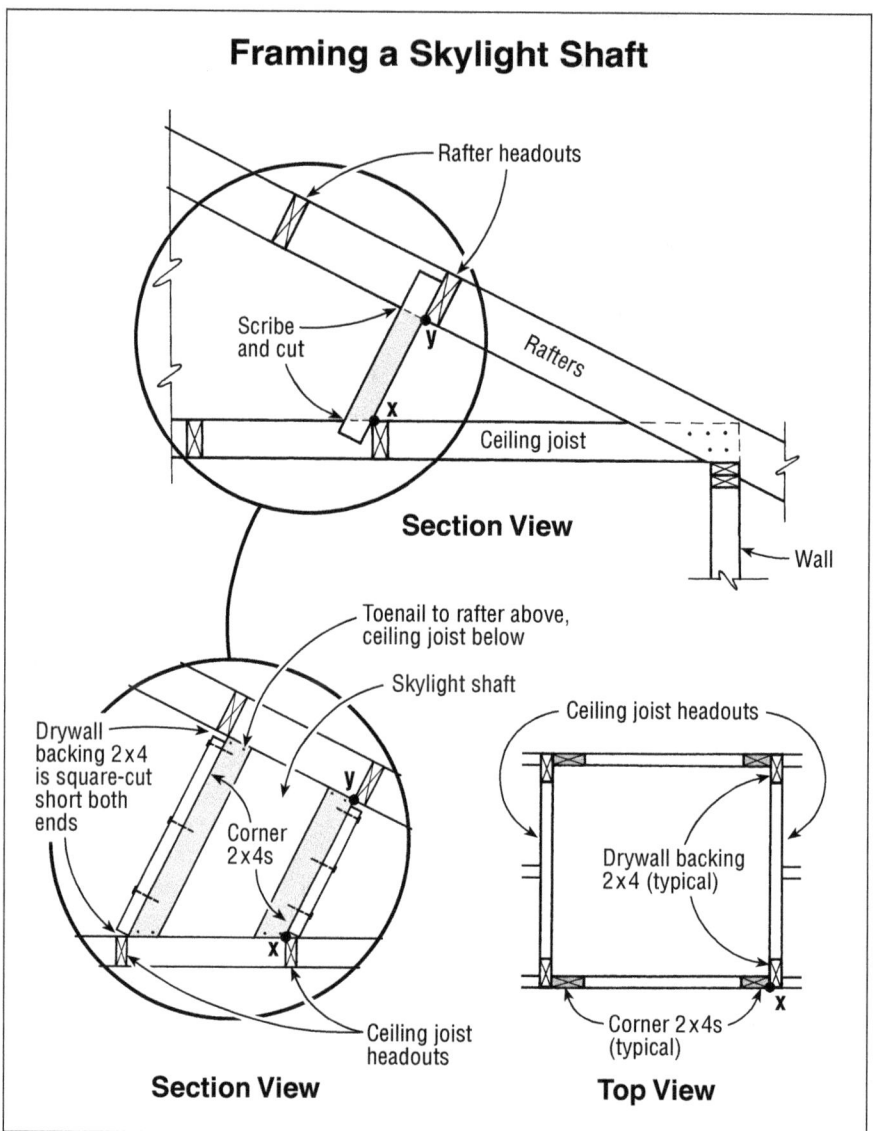

Figure 15-11. In a skylight, corner 2x4s are placed between the roof and ceiling headouts with a backing stud nailed flat to the back side.

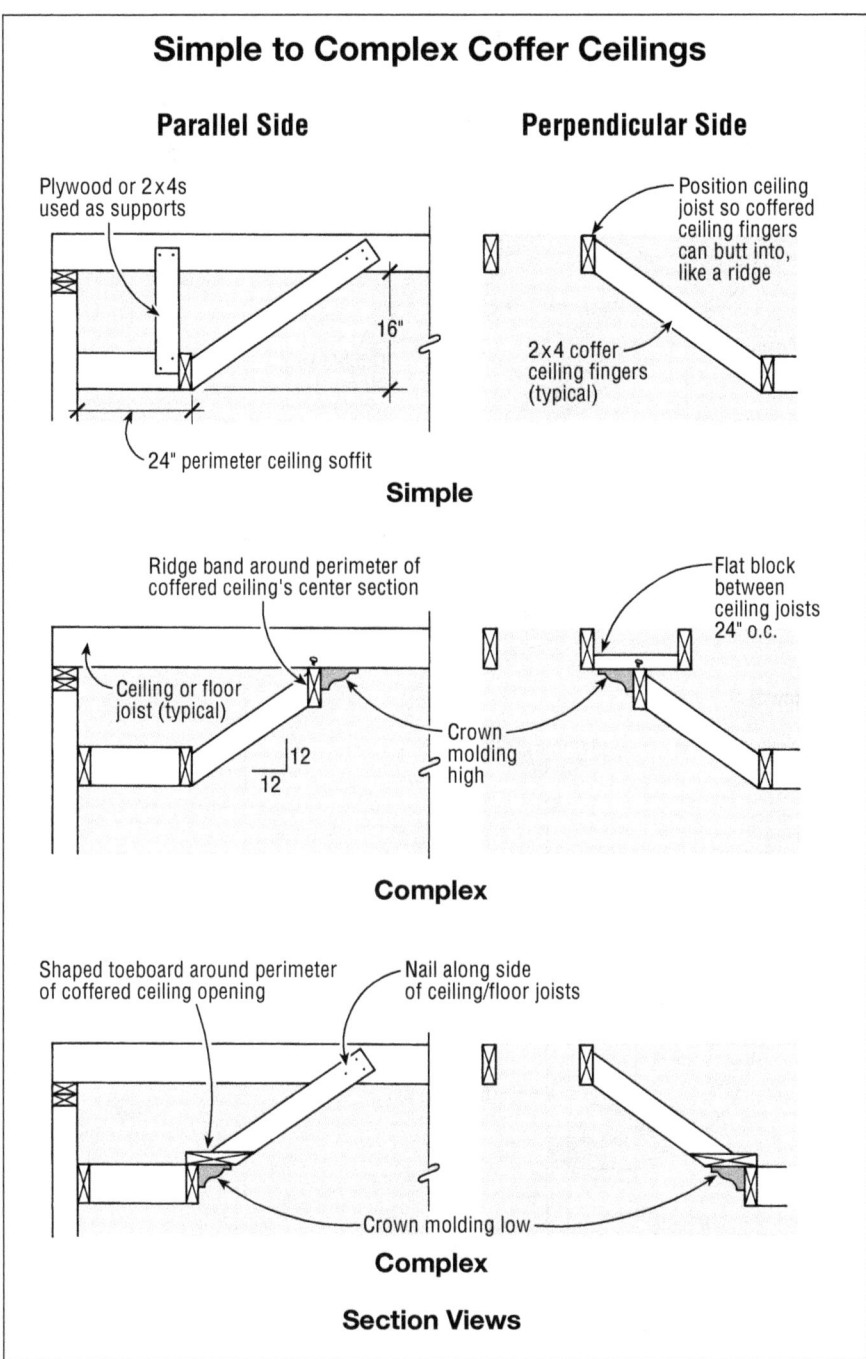

Figure 15-12. On more complex styles of coffer ceilings, a small 90° corner reveal can be framed up high or down low for installation of crown molding.

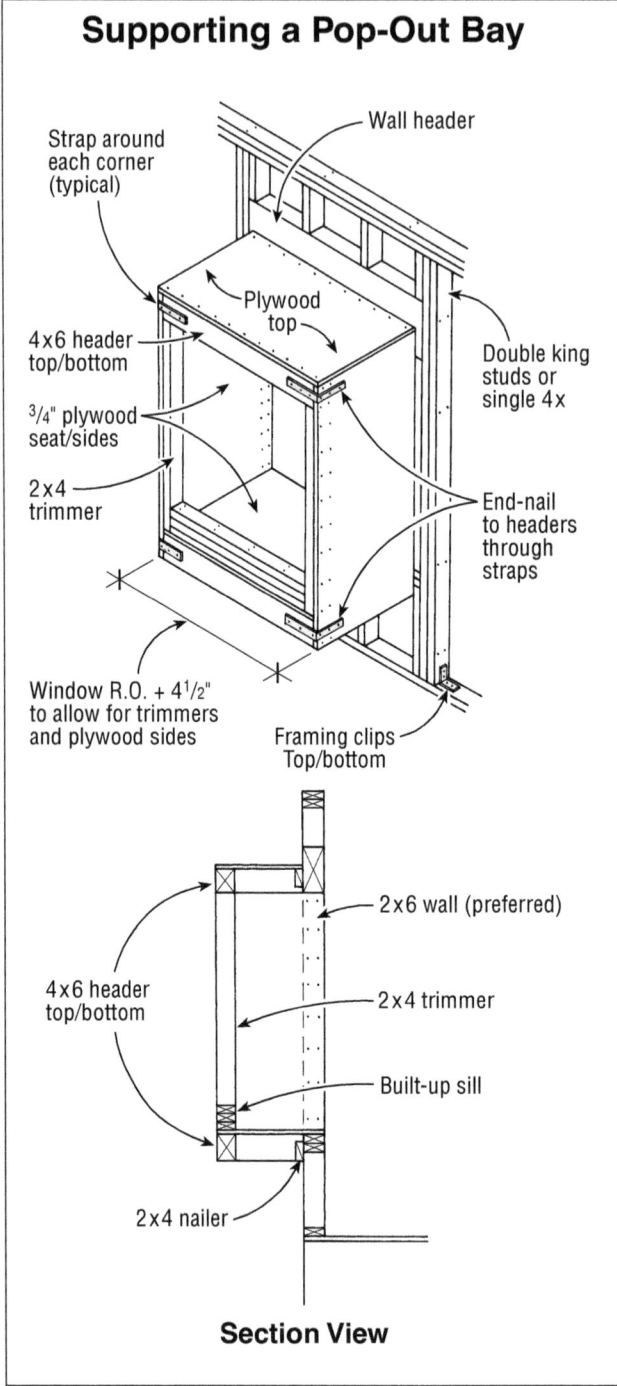

Figure 15-13. The pop-out bay is supported by a piece of 3/4-in. plywood nailed to the trimmer on each side. The king stud should be doubled or be a 4x.

Photo 15-14. A pop-out bay window.

between existing joists. The parallel sides are framed by nailing the 2x4 fingers alongside the joists. Corner fingers are figured and cut similar to a hip rafter. A small 90° corner reveal can be built into the coffer if crown molding will be installed.

POP-OUT BAYS

Figure 15-13 illustrates a fast way to build a pop-out bay window. Make the hole in the outside wall wider than the window rough opening by $4^{1}/2$ in. to allow room for the two exterior pop-out window trimmers and two sheets of $3/4$-in. plywood. The plywood, which is nailed inside the wall opening, extends out the desired amount. The upper and lower pop-out headers are located depending on the desired inside reveal. They should be nailed and strapped as shown in *Photo 15-14*. When insulation is required, widen the side walls outside the plywood.

Appendix A

Reference Charts

Chart 1
Decimal Equivalents

1/8	.125
1/4	.250
3/8	.375
1/2	.500
5/8	.625
3/4	.750
7/8	.875

Chart 2
Rafter Line-Length (LL) Ratios

Roof Pitch/12	COM LL Ratio	H/V LL Ratio
1	1.0035	1.4167
1 1/2	1.0078	1.4197
2	1.0138	1.4240
2 1/2	1.0215	1.4295
3	1.0308	1.4361
3 1/2	1.0417	1.4440
4	1.0541	1.4530
4 1/2	1.0680	1.4631
5	1.0833	1.4743
5 1/2	1.1000	1.4866
6	1.1180	1.5000
6 1/2	1.1373	1.5144
7	1.1577	1.5298
7 1/2	1.1792	1.5462
8	1.2019	1.5635
8 1/2	1.2254	1.5817
9	1.2500	1.6008
9 1/2	1.2754	1.6207
10	1.3017	1.6415
10 1/2	1.3288	1.6630
11	1.3566	1.6853
11 1/2	1.3851	1.7083
12	1.4142	1.7321
14	1.5366	1.8333
16	1.6667	1.9437
18	1.8028	2.0616
24	2.2361	2.4495

$$\text{COM LL ratio} = \frac{\text{hypotenuse}}{\text{adjacent side}}$$

Chart 3
Roof Pitch/Degrees

Roof Pitch/12	Degree Equivalent
1	4$^1/_2$°
1$^1/_2$	7°
2	9$^1/_2$°
2$^1/_2$	11$^3/_4$°
3	14°
3$^1/_2$	16$^1/_4$°
4	18$^1/_2$°
4$^1/_2$	20$^1/_2$°
5	22$^1/_2$°
5$^1/_2$	24$^1/_2$°
6	26$^1/_2$°
6$^1/_2$	28$^1/_2$°
7	30$^1/_4$°
7$^1/_2$	32°
8	33$^3/_4$°
8$^1/_2$	35$^1/_4$°
9	37°
9$^1/_2$	38$^1/_2$°
10	40°
10$^1/_2$	41$^1/_4$°
11	42$^1/_2$°
11$^1/_2$	43$^3/_4$°
12	45°
14	49$^1/_2$°
16	53$^1/_4$°
18	56$^1/_4$°
24	63$^1/_2$°

Chart 4
Roof-Rise (RR) Ratios

Roof Pitch/12	RR Ratio
1	0.0833
1$^1/_2$	0.1250
2	0.1667
2$^1/_2$	0.2083
3	0.2500
3$^1/_2$	0.2917
4	0.3333
4$^1/_2$	0.3750
5	0.4167
5$^1/_2$	0.4583
6	0.5000
6$^1/_2$	0.5417
7	0.5833
7$^1/_2$	0.6250
8	0.6667
8$^1/_2$	0.7083
9	0.7500
9$^1/_2$	0.7917
10	0.8333
10$^1/_2$	0.8750
11	0.9167
11$^1/_2$	0.9583
12	1.0000
14	1.1667
16	1.3333
18	1.5000
24	2.0000

$$\text{RR ratio} = \frac{\text{opposite side}}{\text{adjacent side}}$$

Chart 5

Trigonometric Values

Angle	SIN	COS	TAN	COT	SEC	CSC	
0°	0.0000	1.0000	0.0000	—	1.0000	—	90°
1°	0.0175	0.9998	0.0175	57.2900	1.0002	57.2987	89°
2°	0.0349	0.9994	0.0349	28.6363	1.0006	28.6537	88°
3°	0.0523	0.9986	0.0524	19.0811	1.0014	19.1073	87°
4°	0.0698	0.9976	0.0699	14.3007	1.0024	14.3356	86°
5°	0.0872	0.9962	0.0875	11.4301	1.0038	11.4737	85°
6°	0.1045	0.9945	0.1051	9.5144	1.0055	9.5668	84°
7°	0.1219	0.9925	0.1228	8.1443	1.0075	8.2055	83°
8°	0.1392	0.9903	0.1405	7.1154	1.0098	7.1853	82°
9°	0.1564	0.9877	0.1584	6.3138	1.0125	6.3925	81°
10°	0.1736	0.9848	0.1763	5.6713	1.0154	5.7588	80°
11°	0.1908	0.9816	0.1944	5.1446	1.0187	5.2408	79°
12°	0.2079	0.9781	0.2126	4.7046	1.0223	4.8097	78°
13°	0.2250	0.9744	0.2309	4.3315	1.0263	4.4454	77°
14°	0.2419	0.9703	0.2493	4.0108	1.0306	4.1336	76°
15°	0.2588	0.9659	0.2679	3.7321	1.0353	3.8637	75°
16°	0.2756	0.9613	0.2867	3.4874	1.0403	3.6280	74°
17°	0.2924	0.9563	0.3057	3.2709	1.0457	3.4203	73°
18°	0.3090	0.9511	0.3249	3.0777	1.0515	3.2361	72°
19°	0.3256	0.9455	0.3443	2.9042	1.0576	3.0716	71
20°	0.3420	0.9397	0.3640	2.7475	1.0642	2.9238	70°
21°	0.3584	0.9336	0.3839	2.6051	1.0711	2.7904	69°
22°	0.3746	0.9272	0.4040	2.4751	1.0785	2.6695	68°
23°	0.3907	0.9205	0.4245	2.3559	1.0864	2.5593	67°
24°	0.4067	0.9135	0.4452	2.2460	1.0946	2.4586	66°
25°	0.4226	0.9036	0.4663	2.1445	1.1034	2.3662	65°
26°	0.4384	0.8988	0.4877	2.0503	1.1126	2.2812	64°
27°	0.4540	0.8910	0.5095	1.9626	1.1223	2.2027	63°
28°	0.4695	0.8829	0.5317	1.8807	1.1326	2.1301	62°
29°	0.4848	0.8746	0.5543	1.8040	1.1434	2.0627	61°
	COS	SIN	COT	TAN	CSC	SEC	Angle

Chart 5 (continued)
Trigonometric Values

Angle	SIN	COS	TAN	COT	SEC	CSC	
30°	0.5000	0.8660	0.5774	1.7321	1.1547	2.0000	60°
31°	0.5150	0.8572	0.6009	1.6643	1.1666	1.9416	59°
32°	0.5299	0.8480	0.6249	1.6003	1.1792	1.8871	58°
33°	0.5446	0.8387	0.6494	1.5399	1.1924	1.8361	57°
34°	0.5592	0.8290	0.6745	1.4826	1.2062	1.7883	56°
35°	0.5736	0.8192	0.7002	1.4281	1.2208	1.7434	55°
36°	0.5878	0.8090	0.7265	1.3764	1.2361	1.7013	54°
37°	0.6018	0.7986	0.7536	1.3270	1.2521	1.6616	53°
38°	0.6157	0.7880	0.7813	1.2799	1.2690	1.6243	52°
39°	0.6293	0.7771	0.8098	1.2349	1.2868	1.5890	51°
40°	0.6428	0.7660	0.8391	1.1918	1.3054	1.5557	50°
41°	0.6561	0.7547	0.8693	1.1504	1.3250	1.5243	49°
42°	0.6691	0.7431	0.9004	1.1106	1.3456	1.4945	48°
43°	0.6820	0.7314	0.9325	1.0724	1.3673	1.4663	47°
44°	0.6947	0.7193	0.9657	1.0355	1.3902	1.4396	46°
45°	0.7071	0.7071	1.0000	1.0000	1.4142	1.4142	45°
	COS	SIN	COT	TAN	CSC	SEC	Angle

Secant θ   = hypotenuse/adjacent side   = 13.42/12   = 1.1180 {COM LL ratio}
Tangent θ = opposite side/adjacent side =   6/12   = .5000 {RR ratio}
Cotangent θ = adjacent side/opposite side = 12/6   = 2.0000
Sine θ   = opposite side/hypotenuse   =   6/13.42 = .4472
Cosine θ   = adjacent side/hypotenuse   = 12/13.42 = .8944

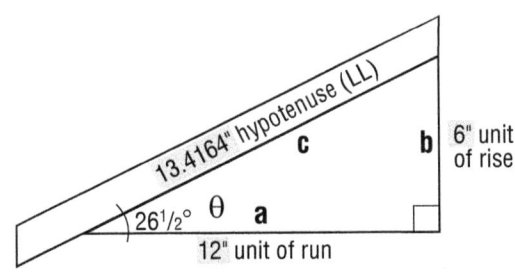

Chart 6

Regular Hip/Valley Backing Angles
(to nearest $1/2°$)

Roof pitch/12	Rip angle (Saw bevel setting)
3	10°
3 1/2	11 1/2°
4	13°
4 1/2	14 1/2°
5	16°
5 1/2	17°
6	18 1/2°
6 1/2	19 1/2°
7	21°
7 1/2	22°
8	23°
8 1/2	24°
9	25°
9 1/2	26°
10	27°
10 1/2	28°
11	28 1/2°
11 1/2	29 1/2°
12	30°
14	32 1/2°
16	34 1/2°
18	36°
24	39°

Chart 7
Side- and Bevel-Cuts on the Hip/Valley Rafter Tail with Square-Hung Fascia

Roof Pitch/12	Side-cut line (framing square setting)	Miter angle (saw bevel setting)
4	$5^{1}/_{16} \times 24$	$42^{1}/_{4}°$
5	6×24	$40^{3}/_{4}°$
6	$6^{13}/_{16} \times 24$	$39^{1}/_{4}°$
7	$7^{3}/_{8} \times 24$	$37^{3}/_{4}°$
8	$7^{13}/_{16} \times 24$	$36°$
9	$8^{1}/_{8} \times 24$	$34^{1}/_{2}°$
10	$8^{3}/_{8} \times 24$	$33°$
12	$8^{1}/_{2} \times 24$	$30°$

Reprinted from The Rafter Book, courtesy of David McIntire

Chart 8

Regular California Valley Sleeper Head/Tail-Cuts

Roof Pitch/12	Head × tail cuts	Perpendicular setback from valley snap-line to bottom corner edge of 2x sleeper
3	$12^{3}/_{8}$ × 12	$4^{3}/_{16}$"
$3^{1}/_{2}$	$12^{1}/_{2}$ × 12	$3^{9}/_{16}$"
4	$12^{5}/_{8}$ × 12	$3^{1}/_{8}$"
$4^{1}/_{2}$	$12^{7}/_{8}$ × 12	$2^{3}/_{4}$"
5	13 × 12	$2^{7}/_{16}$"
$5^{1}/_{2}$	$13^{1}/_{4}$ × 12	$2^{3}/_{16}$"
6	$13^{3}/_{8}$ × 12	2"
$6^{1}/_{2}$	$13^{5}/_{8}$ × 12	$1^{13}/_{16}$"
7	$13^{7}/_{8}$ × 12	$1^{11}/_{16}$"
$7^{1}/_{2}$	$14^{1}/_{8}$ × 12	$1^{9}/_{16}$"
8	$14^{3}/_{8}$ × 12	$1^{7}/_{16}$"
$8^{1}/_{2}$	$14^{3}/_{4}$ × 12	$1^{5}/_{16}$"
9	15 × 12	$1^{1}/_{4}$"
$9^{1}/_{2}$	$15^{1}/_{4}$ × 12	$1^{3}/_{16}$"
10	$15^{5}/_{8}$ × 12	$1^{1}/_{8}$"
$10^{1}/_{2}$	16 × 12	1"
11	$16^{1}/_{4}$ × 12	1"
$11^{1}/_{2}$	$16^{5}/_{8}$ × 12	$^{15}/_{16}$"
12	17 × 12	$^{7}/_{8}$"
14	$18^{3}/_{8}$ × 12	$^{11}/_{16}$"
16	20 × 12	$^{9}/_{16}$"
18	$21^{5}/_{8}$ × 12	$^{1}/_{2}$"
24	$26^{7}/_{8}$ × 12	$^{5}/_{16}$"

Thanks to Brian Cooper for his input in this chart

Appendix B

Applying the Construction Master® Calculator

The included samples can be solved using any of the popular Construction Master® framing-oriented calculators: The Construction Master IV (CM4), Trig Plus III (TP3), or the Construction Master Professional (CMPro). In all examples, the calculator's fractional accuracy has been set to 1/8 inch. While the memory function may differ slightly between models, the [Circ] function can be used to store a linear value on the CM4 model, since it only has one dedicated memory register.

The number of keystrokes required to enter a value can sometimes be reduced by entering it as a decimal rather than a fraction. For example, 1 1/2 inch can be entered as 1.5 [Inch]. To switch into the fractional inch format (or vice versa) press [Inch] a second time.

Pressing [=] twice will repeat the previous operation as shown in Figure 4-10, where it is necessary to subtract a value twice.

The CM4 and TP3 calculators have several new features that help in the unequal-pitch arena. One such feature is additional presses of the [Hip/V] key in Figures 8-13, 8-16, 8-18, 8-19, and 8-22 to display the cheek-cut angles for the irregular hip/valley and jacks.

Figure 3-4 Common Rafters to a Ridge Board

[Off] [On/C]	
6 [Inch] [Pitch]	Enter roof pitch
240 [Inch] [−] 1 [Inch] 1/2 [÷] 2 [Run]	Enter effective run
[Diag]	
Answer: 133 3/8"	Common rafter LL

Figure 3-15 Gable Studs: Production Style

[Off] [On/C]	
6 [Inch] [Pitch]	Enter roof pitch
16 [Inch] [Run]	Enter OC spacing
[Rise]	
Answer: 8"	Gable stud step
1 [Inch] 1/2 [Run]	Enter 2x stud thkness
[Rise]	
Answer: 3/4"	Rise across 2x stud thkness
[Pitch] [Pitch]	
Answer: 26 1/2°	Bevel-cut angle

Figure 4-2 Calculating Hip Rafter Lengths

Off **On/C**	
6 **Inch** **Pitch**	Enter roof pitch
240 **Inch** **−** 1 **Inch** 1/2 **÷** 2 **Run**	Enter effective run
Hip/V	
Answer: 178 7/8"	Hip LL

Figure 4-7 The Longest Hip Jack to Short Point

Off **On/C**	
45 **Pitch**	Enter 45-degree diagonal
1 **Inch** 1/2 **÷** 2 **Run**	Enter board thickness
Diag	
= **Run**	
6 **Inch** **Pitch**	Enter roof pitch
Diag	
Answer: 1 1/8"	LL of 1/2 45° thk 2x
Store in 1st memory	
16 **Inch** **Run**	Enter OC spacing
Diag	
Answer: 17 7/8"	Jack step LL
Store in 2nd memory	
133 **Inch** 3/8	Enter common rafter LL
− Recall 1 1/8" from 1st memory	
− Recall 17 7/8" from 2nd memory	
= Answer: 114 3/8"	Longest hip jack to SP

Figure 4-10 Hip-Valley Jacks for Parallel Situations

Off **On/C**	
6 **Inch** **Pitch**	Enter roof pitch
24 **Inch** **−** 1 **Inch** 1/16 **=** **=** **Run**	Enter building corner jog less 1/2 45° thk of hip and valley
Diag	
Answer: 24 7/16"	Hip-Valley Jack LL

Figure 8-2 Calculating Bastard Hips and Valleys for Dog-leg Roofs

Off **On/C**	
6 **Inch** **Pitch**	Enter roof pitch
119 **Inch** 1/4 **Run**	Enter effective run
Rise	
Answer: 59 5/8"	Roof effective rise
Store in memory	
On/C	
Diag	
Answer: 133 3/8"	Common rafter LL
Run **=** **Run**	
22.5 **Pitch**	Enter 1/2 dog-leg angle
Diag	
Answer: 129 1/8"	Dog-leg hip effective travel
= **Run**	
Recall 59 5/8" rise from memory	
= **Rise**	Re-enter roof effective rise
Diag	
Answer: 142 1/8"	Dog-leg hip LL
Pitch **Pitch**	
Answer: 5 1/2"	Dog-leg hip pitch/12

Figure 8-5 Dog-leg Bastard Hip/Valley Jacks

Off **On/C**	
22.5 **Pitch**	Enter 1/2 dog-leg angle
16 **Inch** **Rise**	Enter OC spacing
Run	
Answer: 38 5/8"	Dog-leg hip jack step run
= **Run**	
6 **Inch** **Pitch**	Enter roof pitch
Diag	
Answer: 43 1/8"	Dog-leg hip jack step LL

Figure 8-7 Dog-leg Bastard Broken Hips

Off **On/C**	Enter roof pitch
6 **Inch** **Pitch**	
336 **Inch** **−** 240 **Inch**	Enter run difference between spans
÷ 2 **Run**	Convert to run
Rise	
Answer: 24"	Difference in ridge height between spans
Store in memory	
On/C	
45 **Pitch**	Enter dog-leg angle
96 **Inch** **Run**	Enter difference between spans
Diag	
Answer: 135 3/4"	Wall length (g - e)
= **Diag**	
22.5 **Pitch**	Enter 1/2 dog-leg angle
Run	
Answer: 125 3/8"	Bastard broken hip travel (b - c)
= **Run**	
Recall 24" rise from memory	
= **Rise**	Re-enter difference in ridge heights between spans
Diag	
Answer: 127 3/4"	Bastard broken hip LL
Pitch **Pitch**	
Answer: 2 1/4"	Bastard broken hip pitch/12

Figure 8-9 Dovetail Hip Calculations

Off **On/C**	
45 **Pitch**	Enter corner-wall angle
36 **Inch** **Run**	Enter wall setback
Diag ÷ 2 =	
Answer: 25 1/2"	Half-corner wall (**a** - **f**)
Rise	
22.5 **Pitch**	Enter 1/2 dovetail-fork angle
Run	
Answer: 61 1/2"	Common rafter run (**e** - **f**)
= **Run**	
6 **Inch** **Pitch**	Enter roof pitch
Diag	
Answer: 68 3/4"	Common rafter (**e** - **f**) LL
Rise	
Answer: 30 3/4"	Rise at transition point "**e**"
Store in memory	
On/C	
Run = **Run**	
22.5 **Pitch**	Enter 1/2 dovetail-fork angle
Diag	
Answer: 66 1/2"	Dovetail-hip theoretical travel
= **Run**	
Recall 30 3/4" rise from memory	
= **Rise**	Re-enter rise at transition point "**e**"
Diag	
Answer: 73 1/4"	Dovetail-hip theoretical LL
Pitch **Pitch**	
Answer: 5 1/2"	Dovetail-hip pitch/12

Figure 8-13 Diamond Hip Calculations

`Off` `On/C`	
6 `Inch` `Pitch`	Enter shallow-side roof pitch
120 `Inch` `Run`	Enter shallow-side theoretical run
`Diag`	
Answer: 134 1/8"	Butting shallow-side common rafter LL
119 `Inch` 1/4 `Run`	Enter shallow-side effective run
`Rise`	
Answer: 59 5/8"	Roof effective rise
`=` `Rise`	
95 `Inch` 1/4 `Run`	Enter steep-side effective run
`Diag`	
Answer: 112 3/8"	Steep-side common rafter LL
`Pitch`	
Answer: 7 1/2"	Steep-side pitch/12
6 `Inch` `Hip/V`	Enter opposing shallow-side roof pitch for irregular hip/valley calculation
Answer: 163 7/8"	Diamond-hip LL
`=` `Diag`	
`Run`	
Answer: 152 5/8"	Diamond-hip effective travel
`Pitch`	
Answer: 4 3/4"	Diamond-hip pitch/12

Figure 8-16 Diamond Hip Jack-Step Length

Off **On/C**	
16 **Inch** **Stor** 5	Enter 16" OC spacing
6 **Inch** **Pitch**	Enter shallow-side roof pitch
119 **Inch** 1/4 **Run**	Enter shallow-side effective run
7.5 **Inch** **Hip/V**	Enter opposing steep-side roof pitch for irregular hip/valley calculation
Jack **Jack**	Press twice
Answer: 22 3/8"	Jack step 6/12 side
Jack	
Answer: 111"	Longest jack 6/12 side: needs shortening for 1/2 51° thk hip
On/C **Conv** **Jack** **Jack**	
Answer: 15 1/8"	Jack step 7.5/12 side
Jack	
Answer: 97 3/8"	Longest jack 7.5/12 side: needs shortening for 1/2 39° thk hip

Figure 8-17 Jack Rafter Head-Cut Layout for Unequal-pitch Hip

Off **On/C**	
6 **Inch** **Rise**	Enter shallow-side pitch as rise
7.5 **Inch** **Run**	Enter steep-side pitch as run
Pitch **Pitch**	
Answer: 39°	Steep-side jack's cheek-cut saw bevel angle (Complement angle 51° is shallow-side jack's cheek-cut saw bevel angle)
3 **Inch** 1/2 **Rise**	Enter jack beam thickness
Run	
Answer: 4 3/8"	Cheek-cut run 6/12 side
= **Run**	
6 **Inch** **Pitch**	Enter corresponding roof pitch
Diag	
Answer: 4 7/8"	Cheek-cut LL 6/12 side

Figure 8-18 The Unequal-Pitch Relationship

Off **On/C**	
6 **Inch** **Rise**	Enter shallow-side roof pitch as rise
10 **Inch** **Run**	Enter steep-side roof pitch as run
Pitch **Pitch**	
Answer: 31°	Steep-side jack's cheek-cut saw bevel angle (Complement angle 59° is shallow-side jack's cheek-cut saw bevel angle)
119 **Inch** 1/4 **Run**	Enter primary span effective run
Store in 1st memory	
On/C	
Rise	
Answer: 71 1/2"	Hip-end steep-side effective run
47 **Inch** 1/4 **Rise**	Enter intersecting span's effective run as rise
Run	
Answer: 78 3/4"	Valley rafter shallow-side effective run
Store in 2nd memory	
On/C	
22 **Inch** 3/4 **Rise**	Enter broken hip steep-side effective run as rise
Run	
Answer: 37 7/8"	Broken-hip shallow-side effective run
= **Run**	
6 **Inch** **Pitch**	Enter shallow-side pitch
10 **Inch** **Hip/V**	Enter opposing steep-side pitch for irregular hip/valley calculation
Answer: 48 1/8"	Broken hip LL
Recall 119 1/4" run from 1st memory	
= **Run**	Re-enter primary span effective run
Hip/V	
Answer: 151 1/4"	Full hip LL
Recall 78 3/4" run from 2nd memory	
= **Run**	Re-enter valley shallow-side effective run
Hip/V	
Answer: 99 7/8"	Valley LL

Figure 8-19 Unequal-Pitch Hip Roof with Equal-Length Overhangs

Off **On/C**	
6 **Inch** **Pitch**	Enter shallow-side roof pitch
12 **Inch** **Run**	Enter OH run
Diag	
Answer: 13 3/8"	Shallow-side birdsmouth LL
239 **Inch** 1/4 **Run**	Enter shallow-side effective run
Diag	
Answer: 267 1/2"	Shallow-side common rafter LL
Rise **=** **Rise**	
Answer: 119 5/8"	Roof effective rise
Store in memory	
On/C	
119 **Inch** 1/4 **Run**	Enter steep-side effective run
Pitch	
Answer: 12	Steep-side pitch/12
Diag	
Answer: 168 7/8"	Steep-side common rafter LL
Pitch **=** **Pitch**	
12 **Inch** **Run**	Enter OH run
Diag	
Answer: 17"	Steep-side birdsmouth LL
Recall 119 5/8" rise from memory	
= **Rise**	Re-enter roof effective rise
Run	
6 **Inch** **Hip/V**	Enter opposing shallow-side pitch for irregular hip/valley calculation
Answer: 292 7/8"	Hip LL
= **Diag**	
Pitch	
Answer: 5 3/8"	Hip-rafter pitch/12
Run	
Answer: 267 3/8"	Hip effective travel

Figure 8-19 *(continued on next page)*

Figure 8-19 (continued)

[Diag] [=] [Diag]	
119 [Inch] 1/4 [Run]	Enter steep-side effective run
[Pitch] [=] [Pitch]	
12 [Inch] [Run]	Enter OH run
[Diag]	
Answer: 29 1/2"	Hip birdsmouth LL
119 [Inch] 1/4 [Rise]	Enter steep-side effective run as rise
239 [Inch] 1/4 [Run]	Enter shallow-side effective run
[Pitch] [Pitch]	
Answer: 26°	Steep-side jack's cheek-cut saw bevel angle (Complement angle 64° is shallow-side jack's cheek-cut saw bevel angle)
12 [Inch] [Rise]	Enter OH run as rise
[Run]	
Answer: 24 1/8"	Hip setback (**x** - **k**)

Figure 8-22 Unequal-Pitch Valley Calculations

[Off] [On/C]	
6 [Inch] [Pitch]	Enter primary span's roof pitch
119 [Inch] 1/4 [Run]	Enter primary span's effective run
[Diag]	
Answer: 133 3/8"	Primary span's common rafter LL
[Rise] [=] [Rise]	
Answer: 59 5/8"	Roof effective rise
95 [Inch] 1/4 [Run]	Enter intersecting span's effective run
[Diag]	
Answer: 112 3/8"	Intersecting span's common rafter LL
[Pitch]	
Answer: 7 1/2"	Intersecting span's roof pitch/12
Store in memory	
[On/C]	
6 [Inch] [Hip/V]	Enter primary span's pitch for irregular hip/valley
Answer: 163 7/8"	Valley LL
[=] [Diag]	
[Run]	
Answer: 152 5/8"	Valley effective travel
[Pitch]	
Answer: 4 3/4"	Valley rafter pitch/12
Recall 7 1/2" pitch from memory	
[=] [Run]	Re-enter intersecting span's roof pitch as run
6 [Inch] [Rise]	Enter primary span's roof pitch as rise
[Pitch] [Pitch]	
Answer: 39°	Intersecting roof's jack cheek-cut saw bevel angle (Complement angle 51° is primary span's jack cheek-cut saw bevel angle)

Figure 10-2 Hexagon Beam Tower Top Connection

Off **On/C**	
60 ÷ 2 **Pitch**	Enter 1/2 angle opposing each hexagon side
120 **Inch** **Diag**	Enter hexagon radius
Store in 1st memory	
On/C	
Run	
Answer: 103 7/8"	Common rafter effective run
Rise	
Answer: 60"	Hexagon half-side (**c - h**)
Run = **Run**	
10 **Inch** **Pitch**	Enter hexagon roof pitch
Diag	
Answer: 135 1/4"	Common rafter theoretical LL
Rise	
Answer: 86 5/8"	Rise at centerpoint "**a**"
= **Rise**	
Recall 120" radius from 1st memory	
= **Run**	Re-enter hexagon radius
Diag	
Answer: 148"	Hexagon hip LL to center-point
Pitch	
Answer: 8 5/8"	Hexagon hip pitch/12
Store in 2nd memory	
On/C	
30 **Pitch**	Re-enter 1/2 angle opposing each side
2 **Inch** 3/4 **Rise**	Enter 1/2 beam thickness as rise
Run	
Answer: 4 3/4"	Effective run of head-cut bevel
= **Run**	
Recall 8 5/8" pitch from 2nd memory	
= **Pitch**	Re-enter hexagon hip pitch

Figure 10-2 *(continued on next page)*

Figure 10-2 (continued)

[Diag]	
Answer: 5 7/8"	LL of head-cut bevel
30 [Pitch]	Re-enter 1/2 angle opposing each side
2 [Inch] 3/4 [Run]	Re-enter 1/2 beam thickness as run
[Rise]	
Answer: 1 5/8"	Effective run of heel-cut bevel
[=] [Run]	
Recall 8 5/8" pitch from 2nd memory	
[=] [Pitch]	Re-enter hexagon hip pitch
[Diag]	
Answer: 2"	LL of heel-cut bevel

Figure 10-4 Octagon Beam Tower Top Connection

[Off] [On/C]	
45 [÷] 2 [Pitch]	Enter 1/2 angle opposing each octagon side
120 [Inch] [Diag]	Enter octagon radius
Store in 1st memory	
[On/C]	
[Run]	
Answer: 110 7/8"	Common rafter theoretical run
[Rise]	
Answer: 45 7/8"	Octagon half-side (**e** - **i**)
[Run] [=] [Run]	
10 [Inch] [Pitch]	Enter octagon roof pitch
[Diag]	
Answer: 144 3/8"	Common rafter theoretical LL
[Rise]	
Answer: 92 3/8"	Rise at centerpoint "**a**"
[=] [Rise]	
Recall 120" radius from 1st memory	

Figure 10-4 *(continued on next page)*

Figure 10-4 (continued)

= **Run**	Re-enter octagon radius
Diag	
Answer: 151 1/2"	Octagon hip LL to center-pont
Pitch	
Answer: 9 1/4"	Octagon hip pitch/12
Store in 2nd memory	
On/C	
22.5 **Pitch**	Re-enter 1/2 angle opposing each side
2 **Inch** 3/4 **Rise**	Enter 1/2 beam thickness
Run	
Answer: 6 5/8"	Effective run of head-cut bevel
= **Run**	
Recall 9 1/4" pitch from 2nd memory	
= **Pitch**	Re-enter octagon hip pitch
Diag	
Answer: 8 3/8"	LL of head-cut bevel
22.5 **Pitch**	Re-enter 1/2 angle opposing each side
2 **Inch** 3/4 **Run**	Re-enter 1/2 beam thickness
Rise	
Answer: 1 1/8"	Effective run of heel-cut bevel
= **Run**	
Recall 9 1/4" pitch from 2nd memory	
= **Pitch**	Re-enter octagon hip pitch
Diag	
Answer: 1 1/2"	LL of heel-cut bevel

Figure 11-1 Bay Roof Hip Calculation-Style A

`Off` `On/C`	
45 `÷` 2 `Pitch`	Enter 1/2 angle opposing each side
60 `Inch` `Run`	Enter bay roof run
`Diag`	
Answer: 65"	Hip theoretical travel
Store in memory	
`On/C`	
6 `Inch` `Pitch`	Enter roof pitch
`Rise`	
Answer: 30"	Rise at centerpoint "**a**"
`Diag`	
Answer: 67 1/8"	Common rafter theoretical LL
`Rise` `=` `Rise`	
Recall 65" travel from memory	
`=` `Run`	Re-enter hip theoretical travel
`Diag`	
Answer: 71 1/2"	Hip theoretical LL
`Pitch`	
Answer: 5 1/2"	Hip pitch/12

Figure 11-1 Bay Roof Hip Calculation-Style B

`Off` `On/C`	
60 `Inch` `Run`	Enter bay roof run
36 `Inch` `Rise`	Enter 1/2 length of front face
`Diag`	
Answer: 70"	Hip theoretical travel
Store in 1st memory	
`On/C`	
`Run` `=` `Run`	
6 `Inch` `Pitch`	Enter front-face roof pitch

Figure 11-1 *(continued on next page)*

Figure 11-1 Style B (continued)

Rise	
Answer: 30"	Rise at centerpoint "u"
Store in 2nd memory	
On/C	
Diag	
Answer: 67 1/8"	Front common rafter theoretical LL
Rise **=** **Rise**	
Recall 70" travel from 1st memory	
= **Run**	Re-enter hip theoretical travel
Diag	
Answer: 76 1/8"	Hip theoretical LL
Pitch	
Answer: 5 1/8"	Hip pitch/12
Run **=** **Diag**	
17 **Inch** **Rise**	Enter 1/2 length of side face
Run	
Answer: 67 7/8"	Side common-rafter theoretical run
Recall 30" rise from 2nd memory	
= **Rise**	Re-enter rise at centerpoint "u"
Diag	
Answer: 74 1/4"	Side common-rafter theoretical LL
Pitch	
Answer: 5 1/4"	Side common-rafter pitch/12

Figure 11-6 Bay Roof to a Wall

`Off` `On/C`	
6 `Inch` `Pitch`	Enter bay roof pitch
34 `Inch` 1/2 `Run`	Enter effective run
`Diag`	
Answer: 38 5/8"	Common rafter LL
`Hip/V`	
Answer: 51 3/4"	Ledger hip LL
`Rise`	
Answer: 17 1/4"	Rise at Ledger ridge
Store in memory	
`On/C`	
`Run` `=` `Run`	
45 `÷` 2 `Pitch`	Enter 1/2 bay departure angle
`Diag`	
Answer: 37 3/8"	Bastard hip effective travel
`=` `Run`	
Recall 17 1/4" rise from memory	
`=` `Rise`	Re-enter rise at ledger
`Diag`	
Answer: 41 1/8"	Bastard hip LL
`Pitch` `Pitch`	
Answer: 5 1/2"	Bastard hip pitch/12

Figure 12-1 Gable Roof Unequal-Height Outside Walls

Off **On/C**	
6 **Inch** **Pitch**	Enter roof pitch
24 **Inch** **Rise**	Enter difference in outside wall height
Run	
Answer: 48	Corresponding run value
Store in memory	
On/C	
Pitch **=** **Pitch**	
24 **Feet** **Conv** **Inch**	Convert given span to inches
− **Run** **−** 1 **Inch** 1/2 **÷** 2 **=** **Run**	Subtract 48" run value and change new span into an effective run (i.e.: subtract 2x ridge and divide the result by 2)
Diag	
Answer: 133 3/8"	LL for short-side common rafters
Run **+**	
Recall 48" run from memory	
= **Run**	Re-enter 48" run value to be added to short-side effective run to create long-side effective run
Diag	
Answer: 187"	LL for long-side common rafters

Figure 12-2 Matching Ridge Heights on Equal-Pitch Roofs

Off **On/C**	
6 **Inch** **Pitch**	Enter roof pitch
192 **Inch** **−** 144 **Inch** **÷** 2 **Run**	Enter run difference between the two spans
Rise	
Answer: 12"	Difference in plate heights

Appendix C

Tool Resources

Big Foot® Tools
Henderson, NY, USA
+1 (702) 565-9954
www.bigfoottools.com
Swing tables, Headcutters, 10" & 14" circular saw conversions

Calculated Industries Inc.
Carson City, NV, USA
+1 (775) 885-4900
www.calculated.com
Construction Master® calculators

General Tools Manufacturing Co., LLC
New York, NY, USA
+1 (212) 431-6100
www.generaltools.com
Clamp-on compass trammel points, angle finders

Johnson Level Tool
Mequon, WI, USA
+1 (262) 242 1161
www.johnsonlevel.com
Metric framing square

Prazi USA
Plymouth, MA, USA
+1 (800) 262-0211
www.praziusa.com
Prazi® Beam Cutters

Simpson Strong-Tie
Dublin, CA, USA
+1 (800) 999-5099
www.strongtie.com
Framing connectors

Stanley Tool Co.
New Britain, CT, USA
+1 (800) 262-2161
www.stanleytools.com
Quick Squares®

Swanson Tool Co.
Frankfort, IL, USA
+1 (815) 469-9453
www.swansontoolco.com
Speed® Squares

Toolhangers Unlimited
Castle Rock, CO, USA
+1 (303) 688-3926
www.toolhangers.com
Saw hangers

Timberwolf Tools
Chicago, IL, USA
+1 (603) 326-6033
www.timberwolftools.com
Timber framing tools, Mafell tools

List of Figures and Photos

Figure 0-1	Rafter parts 1		Figure 2-10	Garage corner ties 37
Figure 0-2	Span, run, and effective run 2		Figure 2-11	Taking out the ups and downs 38
Figure 0-3	Roof-rise ratio and common line-length ratio 3		Figure 2-12	Plumbing up a bay window .38
Figure 0-4	Hip/valley line-length ratio ..4		Figure 2-13	Cutting ceiling joists in the air 39
			Figure 2-14	Stiffening the ceiling 40
Figure 1-1	Square and parallel 7		Figure 2-15	Raising the support beam ...40
Figure 1-2	Reference lines 8		Figure 2-16	Ceiling joists for a hip roof 41
Figure 1-3	Foundation problems 8		Figure 2-17	Quick soffits 42
Figure 1-4	Measurements that work 9		Figure 2-18	Drop ceiling techniques 42
Figure 1-5	Rafter walls run long 10		Figure 2-19	Presetting nails for mid-span blocking 43
Figure 1-6	Plating methods 10		Figure 2-20	Presetting joist hangers with a jig 43
Figure 1-7	Calculating tall wall height 11		Figure 2-21	Toenailing joists in a hanger 44
Figure 1-8	A corner marking tool 12		Figure 2-22	Notching a support beam 45
Photo 1-9	Detailing plates with a corner tool 12		Figure 2-23	Floor joists to a radius 45
Photo 1-10	Marking studs with a layout stick 12		Photo 3-1	Gang-cutting rafters on a set of racks 47
Figure 1-11	Laying out openings 13		Figure 3-2	Racking up rafters for gang-cutting 48
Figure 1-12	Laying out rake wall plates ..14		Figure 3-3	Flushing rafters for drywall ..49
Figure 1-13	A story pole 15		Figure 3-4	Common rafters to a ridge board 50
Figure 1-14	No birdsmouth connection 16		Photo 3-5	A dado-converted Skil® 107 in action 51
Figure 1-15	Production nail pounding ..16		Photo 3-6	Gang-cutting seat-cuts with a swing-table saw 51
Figure 1-16	Nailing end-studs 17		Figure 3-7	Exposed birdsmouths 51
Figure 1-17	Corners and intersections ...18		Figure 3-8	Proper birdsmouth notch depths 52
Figure 1-18	A little free-play 18		Figure 3-9	Finishing ridge-cuts with the sidewinder blade 54
Figure 1-19	Let-in brace angle 19		Photo 3-10	Close-up of the sidewinder blade 55
Figure 1-20	Calculating rake wall SP/LP studs 20		Photo 3-11	Roof cutting demonstration using the Prazi® Beam Cutter 56
Figure 1-21	Rake wall top plates 21			
Figure 1-22	Framing rake walls 22		Photo 3-12	The Big Foot® Headcutter in action 57
Photo 1-23	Cutting off-angle rake wall studs (sequence) 23		Figure 3-13	Common rafters over a ridge beam 58
Figure 1-24	Squaring up a rake wall 24		Figure 3-14	Cutting common rafter laps on the ground 60
Figure 1-25	Rake walls by string 24		Figure 3-15	Gable studs: production style 61
Figure 1-26	Using rafters as a guide for framing rake walls 25			
Photo 1-27	Raising walls by hand 25		Figure 4-1	Hip roof ridge length 64
Figure 1-28	Raising tall walls 26		Figure 4-2	Calculating hip rafter lengths 65
Photo 1-29	Raising walls using wall jacks 27		Figure 4-3	Hip rafter birdsmouth layout 66
Figure 1-30	Raising walls by rope 27		Figure 4-4	Clipping the corner 67
Figure 1-31	Steep-lot underpinning 29		Photo 4-5	Broken hips and other situations 68
Figure 2-1	Tools to get it plumb 31			
Photo 2-2	Plumbing walls with a plumb-bob 32			
Figure 2-3	Plumb and line basics 32			
Figure 2-4	Plumbing tall walls 33			
Figure 2-5	Bracing balloon-framed walls 34			
Figure 2-6	To push or pull a wall 35			
Figure 2-7	Adjusting liner braces 36			
Figure 2-8	More wall racking techniques 36			
Figure 2-9	Rigging axe makes good lever 37			

Figure 4-6	Backing a hip 69
Figure 4-7	The longest hip jack to short point 70
Figure 4-8	Hip jacks: production style ..71
Photo 4-9	Frieze blocks at the hip 72
Figure 4-10	Hip-valley jacks for parallel situations 74
Photo 4-11	Hip-valley jacks 75
Figure 4-12	King hip-valley jacks for diverging situations 76
Figure 4-13	Head-cuts for hip/valley rafters bearing on ridge beams or posts 77
Figure 4-14	Calculating broken hip lengths 78
Figure 4-15	Overlay broken hip 80
Figure 4-16	Snub-nose hip ridge length .82
Figure 4-17	Snub-nose hip-end walls 82
Figure 4-18	Dutch hip 83
Photo 4-19	A hip from an outside 45° corner wall 84
Figure 4-20	Hips from an outside 45° corner wall 85

Figure 5-1	Calculating valley rafter lengths 88
Figure 5-2	Valley rafter birdsmouth layout 88
Figure 5-3	Valley rafter heel-cut 89
Photo 5-4	A backed valley beam in place (a); ripping a backing angle (b) 90
Figure 5-5	Regular valley jack positions 91
Figure 5-6	Regular valley jacks: production style 92
Photo 5-7	A California valley connection 94
Figure 5-8	California valley jacks: production style 96
Figure 5-9	California-cut pattern 98
Figure 5-10	Over/under intersection 99
Photo 5-11	Over/under valley situation 100
Figure 5-12	Offset valley for intersection of different-size rafters ...101
Figure 5-13	Offset valley for intersection of unequal-height walls ..102
Figure 5-14	Offset valley birdsmouth layout 102
Figure 5-15	A supportED valley 103
Photo 5-16	Ridge-to-supporting-valley position 104
Figure 5-17	Centering the ridge 104
Photo 5-18	A supporting hip installation (a); close-up of a hip continuation jack position (b) 105
Figure 5-19	SupportED valley to supportING hip 106
Photo 5-20	Ridge-to-supporting-hip position 106
Figure 5-21	Disappearing valley 107

Photo 6-1	Pre-positioning rafter paks with a crane (a); running lapping rafters (b) 110
Figure 6-2	Garage scaffolding 111
Figure 6-3	Scaffold height 111
Figure 6-4	The sway-stick 112
Figure 6-5	Correct toenailing 113
Figure 6-6	Bracing the ridge 113
Figure 6-7	Hanging precut frieze blocks 114
Figure 6-8	Dovetailing ridge boards together 115
Figure 6-9	Long-run ridge assembly ..116
Figure 6-10	Forces acting on a roof system 117
Figure 6-11	Collar tie lengths 117
Figure 6-12	Roof purlin 118
Figure 6-13	Stacking tailless rafters 118
Figure 6-14	Presetting ridge beams to height 119
Photo 6-15	Hips to a prefabricated steel ridge 120
Figure 6-16	Hip roof stacking basics ...121
Figure 6-17	Hip/valley position at the ridge 123
Figure 6-18	Valley fill position at the valley 123
Figure 6-19	Stacking a chopped-up hip roof 125
Figure 6-20	Positioning a broken hip ..127

Figure 7-1	Common fascia styles 130
Figure 7-2	Fascia lap joints 130
Figure 7-3	Face, miter, and side cuts for square-hung fascia at hip/valley corners 131
Figure 7-4	Outriggers/outlookers 134
Figure 7-5	Flying valleys 135
Figure 7-6	Butted fascia at valley 136
Figure 7-7	One-man fascia hanging ...136
Figure 7-8	Unequal-pitch barge fascia connections 137
Figure 7-9	Unequal-pitch overhangs for rafters with equal heel-stands 138
Figure 7-10	Unequal-pitch overhangs for rafters with unequal heel-stands 139
Figure 7-11	False purlin/ridge beams ..140
Figure 7-12	Valley-cut plywood pattern ..140
Figure 7-13	Roof sheathing techniques ..141
Figure 7-14	Tongue-and-groove roof ready for rigid insulation 142
Photo 7-15	A tongue-and-groove installation tool 142
Figure 7-16	Beam tail setup 143
Figure 7-17	Split-pitch tail kick-up 144
Figure 7-18	Hip/valley beam tails 145
Photo 7-19	Radius beam tails 146
Figure 7-20	Swaled tails around a corner 147

Photo 8-1	A complicated roof from the air 149		Figure 9-4	Shed dormer point of intersection 193
Figure 8-2	Calculating bastard hips and valleys for dog-leg roofs ..150		Figure 9-5	Shed dormer California-cut ..194
Figure 8-3	Dog-leg bastard hip/valley layout 152		Photo 9-6	A standard rafter-style eyebrow dormer 195
Photo 8-4	A dog-leg bastard hip and valley ridge connection ..153		Photo 9-7	California-style eyebrow dormer returns 195
Figure 8-5	Dog-leg bastard hip/valley jacks 153		Figure 9-8	Eyebrow dormer layout ...197
			Figure 9-9	Eyebrow dormer valley position 198
Photo 8-6	A dog-leg bastard valley with square-cut jacks 154		Photo 9-10	Eyebrow rib/bastard valley connection 199
Figure 8-7	Dog-leg bastard broken hips 155		Photo 9-11	Eyebrow rib tail-cut patterns 200
Photo 8-8	Using a standard circular saw to make steep-angled cuts ..156		Photo 9-12	A floor jig for eyebrow rib assembly 200
Figure 8-9	Dovetail hip calculations ..159		Figure 9-13	Eyebrow dormer valley backing 201
Figure 8-10	Dovetail hip rafter layout ..161			
Photo 8-11	A dovetail hip end 162		Photo 9-14	Top view of a stacked rib-style eyebrow dormer 202
Figure 8-12	Hunchback combo rafter for unsupported dovetail hip .163		Photo 9-15	Sheathing a rib-style eyebrow dormer 202
Figure 8-13	Diamond hip calculations ..164			
Figure 8-14	Diamond hip rafter layout ..166			
Photo 8-15	Plan view of an unequal-pitch hip top roof connection ..167		Figure 10-1	Laying out a hexagon tower roof on the floor 205
Figure 8-16	Diamond hip jack-step length 168		Figure 10-2	Hexagon beam tower top connection 207
Figure 8-17	Jack rafter head-cut layout for unequal-pitch hip 169		Figure 10-3	Laying out an octagon tower roof on the floor ..209
Figure 8-18	The unequal-pitch relationship 171		Figure 10-4	Octagon beam tower top connection 210
Figure 8-19	Unequal-pitch hip roof with equal-length overhangs ..174		Figure 10-5	The "Eight-Sided Rule" 211
			Figure 10-6	Easy cut-and-stack octagon top connection 212
Photo 8-20	An unequal-pitch hip roof with equal-length overhangs ..176		Figure 10-7	King-pin octagon beam tower 213
Figure 8-21	Unequal-pitch hip rafter birdsmouth layout 177		Photo 10-8	A king-pin-style octagon tower roof 214
Figure 8-22	Unequal-pitch valley calculations 178		Figure 10-9	Common polygon functions 214
Figure 8-23	Unequal-pitch valley rafter layout 179		Figure 10-10	Twelve-beam tower top connection 215
Figure 8-24	Unequal-pitch valley jack-step 180		Figure 10-11	Finding the center of a circle 216
Photo 8-25	An off-angle California valley 182		Figure 10-12	One big compass 217
Figure 8-26	Off-angle California valley jacks 182		Figure 10-13	Three-sided curve cutting blade 217
Figure 8-27	Backing bastard rafters, part 1 184		Figure 10-14	Conical tower walls go up in sections 218
Figure 8-28	Backing bastard rafters, part 2 185		Figure 10-15	Conical tower window/door openings 219
Photo 8-29	Finding unequal-pitch backing (top and side views) 186		Figure 10-16	Plumb-and-line method for conical tower walls 220
			Photo 10-17	Setting a prefabricated conical tower by crane 220
Figure 8-30	Calculating bastard rafter backing using trigonometry 187		Photo 10-18	Two roof cones ready for fascia 221
			Figure 10-19	Precutting polygon tower roof T&G 222
Figure 9-1	Locating the dormer ridge headout 190		Figure 10-20	Inside polygon-shaped/outside cone-shaped 222
Figure 9-2	Dormer valley calculations .191			
Photo 9-3	A shed dormer from a main ridge 192		Figure 10-21	Conical tower 2x rafter top connection 223

329

Photo 10-22	A 2x rafter conical tower top connection 224	Figure 13-7	Beam pocket router jig 262
Figure 10-23	Cutting plywood sheathing for conical towers 225	Figure 13-8	Revisiting ridge beam heights 263
Photo 10-24	Precut plywood sheathing on a conical roof 226	Photo 13-9	Rafter beam pockets 264
		Figure 13-10	Fake corbel installation 264
Photo 10-25	A beehive-shaped tower roof 227	Photo 13-11	A fake corbel 265
		Figure 13-12	Bolt locations for maximum strength 265
Figure 10-26	California intersection to a conical tower 228	Figure 13-13	Building a beam truss 266
		Photo 13-14	Prefabricated rafter beam truss 267
Figure 11-1	Bay roof hip calculation . . .232	Figure 13-15	Hidden straps 267
Photo 11-2	An equal-sided bay roof . . .234		
Photo 11-3	An unequal-sided bay roof .234	Figure 14-1	Stair stringer layout 270
Figure 11-4	Bay roof hip layout 235	Figure 14-2	Stair stringer installation . . .271
Figure 11-5	Odd-angle bay roofs 236	Figure 14-3	Temporary stair stringer strongback 272
Figure 11-6	Bay roof to a wall 238		
Figure 11-7	Dividing a corner angle . . .239	Figure 14-4	Built-up stairs for short runs 272
Figure 12-1	Gable roof from unequal-height outside walls 242	Figure 14-5	Exposed stair stringers 273
		Figure 14-6	Pyramid-shaped stairs 274
Figure 12-2	Matching ridge heights on equal-pitch roofs 243	Figure 14-7	90° winder theory 275
		Figure 14-8	Circular-stair construction .276
Figure 12-3	Parallel-roof California-cuts (equal pitch) 244	Photo 14-9	Open-handrail circular stairs 277
Figure 12-4	Parallel-roof California-cuts (unequal pitch) 245	Figure 14-10	Circular-stair handrail-cap calculations 278
Figure 12-5	Effective run calculation for unequal-pitch gable 246	Photo 14-11	Circular-stair box-beam stringer 280
Figure 12-6	When different materials meet at the ridge 247	Figure 14-12	Self-supporting circular stairs 280
Figure 12-7	Cantilever eaves 248	Figure 14-13	Contoured stairs follow the lines 281
Figure 12-8	Rake walls at 45° to the roof plane 249		
Figure 12-9	Backing the top of a wall framed at 45° to the roof plane . .250	Figure 15-1	Straightening studs 284
		Figure 15-2	Freestanding handrails on a concrete slab 284
Figure 12-10	California-framed Swiss chalet 251	Figure 15-3	Freestanding handrails on a wood-framed floor . . .285
Figure 12-11	Swiss chalet rafters change pitch 252	Figure 15-4	Finding the curve for plywood arches 286
Figure 12-12	Sloping ridge lines 253		
Figure 12-13	Gambrel roof framing styles .254	Figure 15-5	Curved soffits 287
Figure 12-14	Dutch colonial 254	Figure 15-6	Intersecting barrel vaults . . .288
Figure 12-15	Job-site built trusses 255	Photo 15-7	Barrel-vaulted hallway 289
Figure 12-16	Nail-together truss 256	Photo 15-8	A room-size chandelier dome 289
Figure 12-17	Build-in-place truss 256		
		Figure 15-9	A chandelier dome 290
Figure 13-1	Ceiling beam spacing 258	Figure 15-10	Ellipse layout 291
Figure 13-2	False beam installation with end-straps 258	Figure 15-11	Framing a skylight shaft . . .292
		Figure 15-12	Simple to complex coffer ceilings 293
Figure 13-3	Hidden hangers 259		
Figure 13-4	Post-and-beam corners 259	Figure 15-13	Supporting a pop-out bay . .294
Figure 13-5	Hidden bolts 260	Photo 15-14	A pop-out bay window 295
Figure 13-6	Exposed rafter beam installation 261		

Index

A
Anchor bolts, 10-11
Angled wall, roof layout, 248-251
Arches, prefabricated plywood, 285-286

B
Backing
  bastard hip/valley rafters, 151, 178, 183-188
  bastard hips/valleys using trigonometry, 188
  eyebrow dormer valley, 200-201
  standard hips, 67-68
  standard valleys, 87, 90
Balloon framing
  bracing, 34
  for gambrel roof, 253-254
  plumb and line, 33-34
Barge fascia
  at unequal-pitch gable, 136, 137
  layout, 133-134
Barrel-vault ceilings
  intersection of, 285, 287-288
  plywood patterns for, 285, 287
Bastard hips
  broken, 154-158
  for bay roof, 235-236
  for unequal pitch, 162-166, 170-177
Bastard hips/valleys
  backing rafters, 151, 183-188
  calculating effective run, 170-171
  defined, 149
  dog-leg, 151-154
  fascia for, 132-133
Bathrooms
  backing locations, 283
  drop ceilings, 39, 42
  soffit framing, 39, 42
Bay roofs
  framed to a wall, 237-239
  hip layout, 235-236
  most common styles, 231-237
  odd-angle, 236-237
  with common fascia height, 231
Bay windows
  plumb and line, 34-35, 38
  pop-out, 294-295

Beam tails
  for hips and valleys with no fascia, 144, 145
  for tower roofs, 224
  kick-up at hips/valleys, 144-147
  kick-up type, 143-147
  layout of, 143-147
  radius type, 144, 146
Beams
  allowable bolt locations, 265
  connections in, 257, 259-260, 266-267
  for decorative ceiling, 257-258, 261, 265
  for tower roofs, 205-215
  hidden connectors for, 266-267
  made to look rustic, 262
  notching in floor, ceiling or roof, 44-45
  See also Post and Beam
Beehive tower roof, 226-227
Big Foot® Saw Adapters, 48, 55-56
Birdsmouth
  clipping the corner at hip, 67
  defined, 1
  depth on hip/valley, 67
  for bastard valley, 178
  for bay roof hips, 235-237
  for hip rafter, 65-66
  for hip/valley rafter over ridge beam, 75, 77-79
  for offset valley, 100, 102
  for valley rafter, 87-88, 89
  gang-cutting, 49-51
  proper notch depth, 52, 53
  with unequal-pitch hips, 172-173, 177
Bisecting an angle, 154, 158, 237, 239
Blackline's waterproof chalk, 9
Blueprints, marking up dimensions, 9-10
Bolts
  allowable locations, 265
  drilling beams for, 257
  hidden in beam connections, 260, 266
Box-beam stringer, for circular stairs, 280-281

Broken hips
calculating effective run, 170-171
dog-leg bastard, 154-158
layout of, 78-81
positioning at ridge, 127
stacking, 126-127

C

California corners, in wall framing, 18-19
California-cut
parallel overlapping roofs, 242, 244-246
ridge end, 124
shed dormers, 194
valley jack pattern, 98
California intersection, at tower roof, 227-229
California valleys
attaching broken hip to sleeper, 81
fake valley tail, 134, 135
layout of, 93-98, 122-124
sleeper layout, 94-96
to tower roof, 227-229
used to frame unequal-pitch valley, 181-183
valley jacks, 97-98
Cantilever ratio, for overhangs, 247-248
Cantilevered overhangs, at gable end, 247-248
Ceiling joists
changing direction in hip roof, 39, 41
cutting in air, 35, 39
installing, 35, 39
nailer for kitchen cabinets, 39
stiffening, 39-40
Ceilings
barrel vault, 285, 287-288
coffered, 291, 293, 295
domed, 287, 289-291
Chain saws, for ridge cuts, 56-57
Chalet-style roof, kick up at each end, 251-253
Chandelier domes, 287, 289-291
Cheek-cuts
adjustment at offset ridge, 104, 105
cutting steep angles, 156-157
for bastard hips/valleys, 151
for California valley jacks, 96-98
for hip rafters, 67-68
for polygon rafters, 206-207, 210, 211-213, 215
for unequal-pitch hips, 169
for valley rafters, 88, 91-92
gang cutting on hip jacks, 71-72
setting swing table, 151
Circle, finding center, 216
Circular plates, plywood, for tower walls, 216-217
Circular stairs
handrail layout, 278-280
self-supporting, 280-281
supported, 276-277
Circular walls, for towers, 216-220
Coffer ceilings, 291, 293, 295
Collar ties
length calculation, 116-118
to stiffen rafters, 116-117
when required, 116
COM LL ratio
defined, 4-5
for common rafters, 49
Common rafter line-length ratio, See COM LL ratio
Common rafters
bracing, 112-114
lapping at ridge, 109
LL calculation, 49-50
over ridge beam, 58-60
stacking to a ridge, 109
to ridge board, 49-52
Conical roofs, 219, 221-224
Connectors, See Framing connectors
Construction Master® Calculator, 172, 188, 305-323
Corbels, fake, 262, 264-265
Corner marking tool, 12
Corner ties, in garage, 34-37
Corners, framing, 18-19
Crane
for setting common rafters, 109-110
to lift exposed trusses, 265
to lift eyebrow dormer, 196
to lift tower roof, 215, 219-221, 227
Crowns
place down on racks, 49, 58, 71
straightening in stud, 283-284
Curved floor, framing, 44-45
Curved headers, 218-219
Curved rim joist, from plywood, 44-45
Curved soffits, 285, 287
Curved walls, 216-220

D

Dado saw, for birdsmouth notch cut, 49, 51
Diagonal travel, defined, 2
Diamond hips
  jacks, 167-170
  layout, 162-167
Dimensions, marking up prints, 9-10
Disappearing valley, 107
Dog-leg bastard broken hip, 154-158
Dog-leg hips/valleys, 151-158
Domed ceiling, elliptical layout, 287, 289-291
Doors and windows, layout, 13
Dormers
  eyebrow, 194-203
  gable, 189-192
  hip, 192
  shed, 193-194
  shed, California-cut, 194
Doubler plate, installing, 18-19
Double-shear hangers, 43
Dovetail hips, 158-161
Drop ceilings, framed to ledger, 39, 42
Dutch colonial roofs, 254, 255
Dutch hip, 82-84

E

Eaves, cantilevered at rake, 247-248
Effective run
  defined, 2
  of bay roof to a wall, 237-238
  of common rafters lapping ridge beam, 59
  of common rafters to ridge board, 49
  of hip rafter, 63, 84
  of shed dormer, 193
  of unequal-pitch gables, 246
  of unequal-pitch hips, 170-173
  of unequal-pitch valleys, 177-181
Eight-sided rule
  defined, 211
  for bay roofs, 232, 238
  for dog-leg hip/valley, 150
  for dovetail hips, 160
  for octagon hip pitch, 209
Ellipse, geometrical layout, 289, 291
Elliptical dome ceiling, 287, 289-291
Equal-pitch roof, with unequal-height walls, 241, 242
Exposed beams, *See* Beams
Exposed stringers, 273
Eyebrow dormers
  rib-style, 195-203
  with radiating rafters, 195, 203

F

False beam tails, 143-147
False purlins, 137, 140
Fascia
  barge, 133-134, 136-137
  butted corner at valley, 134, 136
  common height with unequal-pitch valley, 177
  common styles, 129-130
  corner layout for square-hung, 130, 132
  corner layout with unequal-pitch hips, 173-176
  hanging solo, 134, 136
  installing, 129-137
  lap joints in, 130
  layout at bastard hips/valleys and polygons, 132-133
  layout of square-hung, 130-133
  matching height at intersection of unequal-pitches, 136-139
  plumb-hung, 129-130
Fire blocking
  rake walls, 25
  tall walls, 15
  underpinning walls, 28
Floor beams, notching, 44-45
Floor framing
  curved section, 44-45
  techniques 41-45
Floor joists
  blocking for 41, 43
  for curved floor, 44-45
  framing techniques, 41-45
  openings in, 41
Floor squeaks
  due to blocks, 41
  due to hangers, 43-44
Flying valley, 134, 135
Foundation
  checking for square, 7-8
  out of square, 8
Framing connectors
  at beam above joists, 40

at cantilevered overhangs, 247-248
at headers, sills, 17
at soffits, 39, 42
for hanging corbels, 264-265
for hanging false beams, 257-258, 261
hidden in beam trusses, 266-267
See also Simpson Strong Tie®
Frieze blocks, installing, 114

G

Gable dormer, 189-192
Gable roofs
  bracing, 112-114
  equal pitch from unequal walls, 241, 242
  parallel, 242, 244-246
  scaffold for, 109-111
  stacking, 109-116
  unequal pitch, 246-247
Gable studs
  production cutting, 59-61
  step measurement, 60
Gambrel roofs, 253-255
Gang cutting
  birdsmouth notches, 49-51
  gable studs, 59-61
  hip jacks, 71-73
  racks for, 47-49
  ridge-cuts, 49-50, 51, 53-54
  valley jacks, 48-49, 90-93
Garage roof, stacking, 109-115
Garages
  bracing walls, 34, 37
  scaffolding for, 109, 111
Gussets
  for combo rafter at dovetail hip, 160, 163
  for gambrel roof, 253-254
  for site-built trusses, 255-256

H

H/V LL ratio, defined 4-5
Handrail walls, freestanding, 283-285
Handrails, layout for circular stairs, 278-280
Hangers
  cause floor squeaks, 43-44
  double-shear, 43
  hidden for ceiling beams, 257-259
  See also Joist hangers
Head-cuts
  defined, 1

for hip rafters, 67
for hip/valley rafters above ridge beam, 75, 77-79
for jack fill, 48
for unequal hips/valleys, 156-157
gang cutting for valley jacks, 92, 98
Headers
  curved for eyebrow dormer, 195
  for angled wall, 250-251
  for curved walls, 219
  in floor joists, 41
  marking heights, sizes, 13
Headout
  for eyebrow dormers, 198
  locating in gable/hip dormers, 189-191
  locating in shed dormer, 193
Heel-cut
  defined, 1
  layout on commons, 49-50
  See also Birdsmouth
Heel-stand
  defined, 1
  for hip rafter, 66
  See also Birdsmouth
Hexagon tower roof, 205-208
Hidden bolts, in beam connections, 260, 266
Hidden straps, in beam trusses, 266-267
Hillside lots, underpinning, 28-29
Hip dormer, 192
Hip jacks
  for diamond hip, 167-170
  gang cutting, 71-73
  layout, 68-71
Hip rafters
  backing, 67-68
  broken hips, 78, 79-81
  dog-leg, 150, 151-158
  for bay roof, 235-236
  installation, 122
  layout for diamond hips, 166
  layout for regular hips, 63-68
  length calculation, 63, 65
  over ridge beam, 75, 77-79
  position at ridge, 122, 123
  snub-nosed hip, 81-82
  unequal-pitch dovetail, 158-161
Hip roofs
  bastard, 149-188
  broken, 154-158
  diamond, 162-169
  dog-leg bastard, 151-154

dovetail, 158-161
Dutch hip, 82-84
   from 45° corner wall, 84-85
   ridge length calculation, 63-64
   snub-nosed hip, 81-82
   stacking complex, 124-127
   stacking simple, 120-122
   valley at change in wall heights, 98-99
   with unequal pitches, 162
Hip travel, defined, 2
Hip/valley beam tails, 144-147
Hip-valley jacks
   layout for broken hip-to-valley, 73-74, 76
   layout for parallel situations, 73-75
   See also Jack rafters
Hip/valley line-length ratio,
   See H/V LL ratio
Hip/valley rafters
   backing odd-ball, 183-188
   See also Hip rafters; Valley rafters
Hunchback combo rafter, 160, 162

I, J

Insulation, rigid on roof, 142-143
Jack rafters
   for broken hips, 73-74, 76
   for diamond hips, 167-170
   gang cutting, 71-73
   layout for regular hips, 68-71
   layout for unequal-pitch hip, 169-170
   off-angle California, 183
   See also Hip jacks; Hip-valley jacks; Valley jacks
Jack step
   for bastard hips/valleys, 151, 153-154, 180-181
   for broken hip-to-valley, 73-74
   for hip jacks, 68-71, 73
   for unequal-pitch hips, 167-169
   for valley jacks, 90, 93
   See also Step measurements
Joist hangers
   nailing to, 43
   presetting with jig, 43

K

Kick-up beam tails, 143-147
King commons
   for complex hips, 126
   layout and installation, 120-121
King hip-valley jacks, 75-76
King-pin, in octagon beam tower, 211, 213
Kitchens
   drop ceilings, 39, 42
   nailers for cabinets, 39
   soffit framing, 39, 42

L

Laser levels, 33
Layout sticks, 12
Let-in bracing
   for walls, 19
   garage corner ties, 34, 37
Line length
   of broken hips, 78-79
   of commons, 50
   of hip jacks, 68-71
   of hip rafters, 63, 65
   of hip-valley jacks, 73-75
   of valley jacks, 89-91
   of valley rafters, 87-88
Line-length ratio, See LL ratio
LL ratio, defined, 3-5
LL/RR method, defined, 3-5
Lookouts, See Outriggers

M

Makita beam saw, 49, 56, 144
Medicine cabinets, backing for, 283

N

Nailing
   end studs, 18
   production-style presetting, 16-17
Notching, floor, ceiling or roof beams, 44-45

O

Octagon tower roofs
   eight-sided rule, 211
   king-pin method, 211, 213-214
   layout, 208-211, 214
   layout on floor, 209
   pipe method, 211
   simple method, 211, 212
Odd-angle bay roofs, 236-237
Off-angle California jacks, 183
Offset valleys, 100, 102

INDEX   **335**

Openings
 for skylights, 291, 292
 in tower walls, 218-219
 laying out in walls, 13
Outriggers, to hang barge fascia, 133-134
Overhangs
 at rake, 133-134, 247-248
 at unequal-pitch valley, 177-178
 different lengths on bays, 231
 different lengths to match fascia height, 136-138
 equal length with unequal-pitch hips, 172-176
Overlay broken hips, 80-81
Over-under intersections, layout, 98-99

P

Parallel roof, California-cut, 242, 244-246
Pitch, converted to x/12, 151
Plates
 circular for tower walls, 216-217
 for rake walls, 11, 13-14
 scratching, 11-14
Plating
 in gable-roof house, 10-11
 methods, 10-11
 rake walls, 11, 13-14
Plumb and line
 balloon framing, 33-34
 conical tower walls, 219-220
 of bay windows, 34-35, 38
 of tall walls, 33-34
 of tower walls, 219-220
 of walls, 31-33
 techniques, 31-35
Plumb-bob, using, 31-33
Plywood
 arch patterns, 285-286
 circular handrail cap, 277, 280
 for beam pocket router jig, 261-262
 for curved riser, 282
 for curved wall plates, 216-218
 for treads and risers, 271, 277
 kerfed for curved rim joist, 44-45
 plate for tower roof, 219-220
 rafters for domed ceiling, 287
 roof sleeper for eyebrow dormer, 196

 sheathing for tower roof, 224-227
 skylight shafts, 291
 support for pop-out bays, 294
 See also Sheathing
Plywood box beam, curved stringer, 280-281
Plywood gussets, 160, 163, 253-254, 255-256
Pocket doors, header height, 13
Pockets, for ridge beams, 260-262, 264
Polygon roofs, calculations, 211, 214
Pop-out bays, 294-295
Post-and-beam
 connections, 257, 259-260
 corner joints, 257, 259
 trusses, 265-267
 used in tower roofs, 205-215
Prazi® Beam Cutter, 56
Proportions, solving, 158
Purlins
 calculating height, 15
 false, 137, 140
 for gambrel roof, 253-254
 installation, 118-119
 supporting false, 137, 140
 to reduce effective span, 118
Push braces, 34-36

Q, R

Quick Square®, 5, 21, 53, 65, 129
Racking walls, 34-37
Radius beam tail, 144, 146
Radius-cuts, 216
Rafter square, types, 5
Rafter tail, defined, 1
Rafters
 layout of commons, 49-52
 parts of, 1
 tailless, 118, 119
Raising walls, 25-27
Rake walls
 calculating, 19-22
 cantilevers over, 247-248
 cutting studs, 23-24
 fire blocking, 25
 framing, 22-25, 27
 layout, 11, 13-14
 odd angle, 248-251
 scratching plates, 13
 shear paneling, 24-25

sheathing on ground, 24
squaring up, 24, 25
top plates, 21
Reference lines, snapping on floor, 8-9
Ridge
connecting different materials at, 247
for hip roof, 121
height calculation, 120
length in hip roof, 63-64
sloping causes change in roof pitch, 253
Ridge beams
calculating heights, 15, 120, 263
pockets for, 260-262, 264
presetting, 119, 120
supporting false, 137, 140
Ridge boards
bracing, 112-114, 115-116
depth required, 111
dovetailing, 115
installing on long runs, 115-116
Ridge-cuts, gang cutting, 49-50, 51, 53-54
Ridge heights
calculating, 15, 120, 263
for exposed ridge beams, 261-263
for unequal pitch gables, 246
matching from different spans, 241-242, 243
Rigid insulation, roof installation, 142-143
Rim joists, curved, 44-45
Riser height, in stairs, 269
Roof sheathing, *See* Plywood; Sheathing
Roof-rise ratio, *See* RR ratio
RR ratio, defined, 3-5
Run
defined, 2-3
See also Effective run

S

Saw Hanger, 109
Sawblade, modified to cut curves, 217
Scaffold
for gable roof, 109-111
for garage roof, 109, 111
for steep lot underpinning, 29
Scratch
detailing, 11-14
layout of openings, 13

Seat-cuts
defined, 1
making with swing table, 49, 51
See also Birdsmouth
Shear panel
on rake walls, 24-25
pre-snapping nail lines, 34
stud layout, 13
Sheathing
installation, 137, 139-141
for tower roof, 224-227
of eyebrow dormer, 201-202
of hips, 137, 141
pre-snapping nail lines, 34
rake walls on ground, 24
tower roofs, 224-226
unequal-pitch intersection, 170-171
valley-cut, 137, 140
valley-cut pattern, 137, 140
Shed dormers, 193-194
Sidewinder blade
for ridge cuts, 53-54
use of, 53-54, 55-56
Simpson angle bracket, for stairs, 273
Simpson Strong-Tie®
for conical tower, 219
uses, 17, 39, 40, 43
Skilsaw®
converted for dado, 49, 51, 53
for cheek-cuts, 156-157
radius cuts, 216
use in production roof cutting, 54-56
use of, 5, 129
with swing table, 49, 51
Skylights, framing shafts, 291, 292
Slabs
circular plates on, 216
supporting handrail walls, 283-284
Snapping
fast reel chalk box, 9
protecting lines with sealer, 9
wall lines, 7-10
Snub-nosed hip, layout, 81-82
Soffits
curved, 285, 287
framing for kitchens, baths, 39, 42
Speed® Square, 5, 21, 49, 75
Squaring
rake walls, 24, 25
plate lines, 7-8

Squeaks, preventing in floors, 41, 43-44
Stacking
 broken hips, 126-127
 California valley, 122, 123
 complex hips, 124-127
 gable roof, 109-116
 regular valley, 122, 123
 simple hips, 120-122
 tailless rafters, 118, 119
Stairs
 built-up boxes, 271-272, 281-282
 circular, 276-280
 curved, 281-282
 preventing squeaks, 271
 pyramid type, 273-274
 riser/run relationship, 269
 three-sided, 273-274
 winder layout, 274-276
Stair stringers
 installation, 271, 272
 layout, 269-270
Steel connectors, *See* Framing connectors
Steel ridge, prefabricated, 120
Steep building lots, 28-29
Steep-pitch roofs
 fascia for, 129-130
 ridge for, 111
Step measurement
 for bastard jack rafters, 151, 153-154, 180-181
 for broken hip-to-valley, 73-74
 for gable studs, 60
 for hip jack rafters, 68-71, 73
 for unequal-pitch hip jacks, 167-169
 for valley jacks, 90, 93
 See also Jack step
Story pole, to mark cripples, 14-15
Stringers
 box-beam for circular stairs, 280-281
 exposed, 273
Strongback
 for stair stringer, 271-272
 on ceiling joists, 39-40
Studs
 cutting angled, 23-24
 for gable walls, 59-61
 straightening, 283-284
Supported valley
 layout, 100-101, 103-107
 to support dormer, 192
Supporting hip, 105-107

Supporting ridge beam
 rafters butting to, 114
 rafters on top, 114
Supporting valley
 layout, 100-101, 103-107
 to support dormer, 192
Sway braces, 112-114
Sway stick, 110, 112
Swing table
 for birdsmouth seat-cut, 49, 51
 for cheek-cuts, 169-170
Swiss chalet roof, kick-up at each end, 251-253

T

Tailless rafters
 false tails for, 143-144
 layout, 118, 119
Tails, *See* Beam tails
Tall walls
 birdsmouth connection, 14, 16
 calculating height, 11, 14
 fire-blocking, 15
 plumb and line, 33-34
 raising, 25-27
 snub-nose hip-end, 82
Toilet paper holder, backing for, 283
Tools
 author's choices, 57
 Big Foot® Saw Adapters, 56-57
 Big Foot® Headcutter, 56-57
 chalk box, 9
 corner marker, 12
 Groover dado saw, 54-55
 history of in roof cutting, 54-57
 layout stick, 12
 level, 31
 Makita 16" beam saw, 49, 56
 plumb-bob, 33
 Prazi® Beam Cutter, 56
 Quick Square®, 5, 21, 53, 65, 129
 rigging axe, 37
 saw hanger, 109
 Skilsaw®, 5, 107
 Speed® square, 5
 T&G decking clamp, 142-143
 wall jacks, 26-27
 worm-drive saw, 5, 23-24, 53-56, 109
Top plate
 fixing dips and rises, 34, 38

See also Doubler plate; Upper top plate
Towel racks, backing for, 283
Tower ceiling, cutting decking for, 221-222
Tower roof
  beehive shaped, 226-227
  California intersection, 227-229
  conical, 219, 221-224
  layout, 205-229
  polygon calculations, 211, 214
  sheathing, 224-226
Tower walls, 216-220
Tread width
  in stairs, 269
  in winders, 274-276
Trimmers, marking for, 13
Trusses
  built in place, 255-256
  post-and-beam, 265-267
  site built, 255-256
Twelve-sided tower roof, 214, 215

U

Under/over intersections, 98-99
Unequal pitch gables, 246-247
Unequal-pitch hips
  birdsmouth layout, 173, 176-177
  diamond hips, 162-170
  top framing point, 162
  with equal-length overhangs, 172-176
Unequal-pitch relationship, defined, 170-171
Unequal-pitch roofs, top framing point, 162
Unequal-pitch valleys, 177-182
Unequal wall heights, equal pitch roof, 241, 242
Upper top plate, installing, 18-19

V

Valley beam tails
  fake, 134
  layout, 144-146
Valley-cut pattern, 137, 140
Valley fill, gang cutting, 48-49
Valley jacks
  for California valley, 124, 181-183
  for unequal-pitch valleys, 180-181
  gang cutting, 48-49, 90-93, 96-98
  layout for regular valleys, 89-93
  position at valley rafter, 122, 123

Valley rafter
  birdsmouth, 75, 77-79, 87-88, 89
  compared to hip rafter, 87
  layout, 87-88
  LL calculation, 87-88
Valley tails, fake, 134
Valleys
  at change in hip roof wall heights, 98-99
  bastard, 149-188
  California, 93-98, 134-135
  disappearing, 107
  dog-leg bastard, 151-153
  flying type, 134, 135
  layout for gable dormer, 189, 191
  offset, 100, 102
  regular, 87-93
  stacking California-style, 122-124
  stacking regular, 122, 123
  supported/supporting, 100-101, 103-107
  unequal-pitch, 177-182

W

Wall framing
  corners, 18-19
  curved tower, 216-220
  fixing dips and rises, 34, 38
  layout, 10-15
  nailing, 16-17
  plumb and line, 31-35
  pushing or pulling, 34-37
  raising walls, 25-27
  rake walls, 23-25, 27
  tall walls, 11, 14, 25-27, 33-34, 82
  techniques, 15-19
Wall jacks, 26-27
Wall layout, 10-15
Wall plates, adjusting for out-of-square foundation, 8-9
Winders
  box frames for, 271
  layout, 274-276
Window openings, layout, 12-13
Worm-drive saw
  adjustment for cheek-cuts, 151
  cutting angled studs, 23-24
  hanging on rafters or joists, 109
  long cord for, 109
  use of, 5, 129
  with sidewinder blade, 53-54, 55-56
  See also Skilsaw®

Books by Will Holladay

A Roof Cutter's Secrets to Framing the Custom Home

The Complicated Roof – A Cut and Stack Workbook

From the Top Plates Up – A Production Roof Cutter's Journey

The Carpenter Patriot

Stick Framing Roofs

A Roof Cutter's Secrets to Framing the Custom Home – Metric

Videos by Will Holladay

A Roof Cutter's Secrets – live workshop

Roof Framing for the Professional – The Essentials

Roof Framing for the Professional – Advanced Topics

www.ingramcontent.com/pod-product-compliance
Lightning Source LLC
Chambersburg PA
CBHW070402100426
42812CB00005B/1611